The
"Center of the Universe"
The Geopolitics of Iran

A RAND Corporation Research Study

The
"Center of the Universe"

The Geopolitics of Iran

Graham E. Fuller

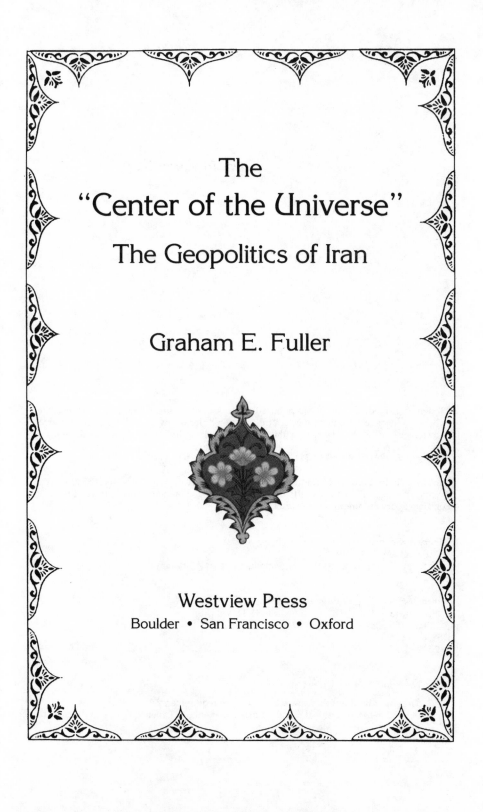

Westview Press
Boulder • San Francisco • Oxford

Published in 1991 in the United States of America by Westview Press, Inc., 5500 Central Avenue, Boulder, Colorado 80301, and in the United Kingdom by Westview Press, 36 Lonsdale Road, Summertown, Oxford OX2 7EW

Library of Congress Cataloging-in-Publication Data
Fuller, Graham E., 1939–
   The "center of the universe" : the geopolitics of Iran / Graham E. Fuller.
      p.   cm.
   Includes bibliographical references and index.
   ISBN 0-8133-1158-6 (HC) — ISBN 0-8133-1159-4 (PB)
   1. Iran—Foreign relations—1979–   . I. Title.
DS318.83.F85   1991
327.55—dc20   91-13011
                                                                                  CIP

Printed and bound in the United States of America

The paper used in this publication meets the requirements
of the American National Standard for Permanence of Paper
for Printed Library Materials Z39.48-1984.

10   9   8   7   6   5   4   3   2   1

This book is dedicated with great love,
appreciation, and deepest thanks
to my parents, Ann and Edmund Fuller,
to whom I owe so much.

Contents

great, unbiased

Preface

I wish to thank The RAND Corporation for generously providing research funds that enabled me to complete this study. I had written only part of the work at the time that I retired from government service in late 1987. I am also grateful to many colleagues at RAND who provided useful criticism of the manuscript: Frank Fukuyama, Nikola Schahgaldian, Paul Henze, and Zalmay Khalilzad. I also owe a considerable debt to many personal friends outside of RAND who generously agreed to review all or parts of the manuscript, especially Sohrab Sobhani, and others whom I cannot acknowledge here. Obviously the failings of the book are my own.

This book is more about the future than the past. It examines the character of Iran's relationships with each of its neighbors in order to identify issues, patterns, and constants within those relationships that are determined both by geopolitics and by the legacy of history. It does not purport to be a history of those relations in any way, except perhaps to familiarize the reader with a rough outline of the way those relations developed. Nor is the book a detailed chronicle of the bilateral relations involved. In the end, I am interested in seeing how aspects of these historical relations may likely reemerge in the future, often under quite different political circumstances and regional dynamics. In short, what is the character of this country we call Iran in its historical experience, and how is that past likely to affect its future?

Because I am interested in future implications of the past conflict patterns in Iran's pursuit of its foreign policy interests, I have not sought to develop new interpretations of established historical events. This study uses secondary sources to provide the basic data of past events. What is new and original in the book is the effort to identify some of these historical continuities and discontinuities and the historical/geopolitical determinants that will probably recur, perhaps in a new guise and under very different regional circumstances. The book sets out to be a guide to potential issues of conflict and geopolitical options that will confront any future Iranian leader as well as other regional leaders and other countries operating in the region. The book also explores a number of potential scenarios for these future conflicts to impart a sense of the range of problems and options involved.

As I note in the body of the book, I am interested in how countries tend to view other countries—almost invariably involving subjective or biased vision. In order to emphasize this point, I have therefore chosen a number of introductory quotations to many chapters, most of which present one or another stereotype—often outrageous—of the country or people involved. These quotations, generally pejorative, are meant to suggest the kinds of stereotypes that figure in the bilateral relations of the countries involved; I am in no way endorsing them as objective or accurate statements about any state or people.

In the end, it is the attitudes of one country toward another that have considerable impact on the "objective" formulation of their foreign policies. They represent the hidden psychological elements of foreign relations that are often ignored in more traditional political science studies. Yet it is these sets of attitudes that are often hardest for foreigners to understand or appreciate because they are not usually part of the public pronouncements of diplomats or the stuff of scholarship. They are nonetheless real for all of that, as outsiders who have resided for long periods in the region know well.

I developed an interest in the cultural and psychological aspects of national behavior during nearly twenty years of life abroad as a Foreign Service officer—mostly in the Middle East—learning languages, reading literature, and attempting to make sense of political patterns of behavior and styles of operation that differ from those in American political culture. These attitudes are more viscerally expressed and often better understood from the literature, fiction, and even films of a country than they are in scholarly studies of politics. My practical concern for the problem came during many years of responsibility for long-range National Estimates at the National Intelligence Council at the CIA—strategic studies aimed at predicting the future course of key world events— where an inordinate amount of time in the 1980s was devoted to revolutionary Iran and its intentions.

This book is intended for those with an interest in the geopolitics of Iran and the Persian Gulf, in Iran's role in broader Middle East politics, and for those who must work with Iran and the region on a practical basis. Although the historical events referred to here are well known to scholars of Iran, I would hope that scholars of the field might also be interested in speculation on the future evolution of politics in the region. Whatever the failings of this book may be, I know of no other book on Iran that attempts to spin out the implications of past events into the future. If my speculations on possible future directions are not congenial to some, I would hope to at least spark some alternative analysis in response from them. But *some* detailed speculation on the range of future political options is imperative for those who work with the area. Indeed, speculation about the nature of future events forces us to examine the past in a different analytical light, seeking to determine where we might expect continuity, and where change.

Lastly, I hope the book will lead to a better understanding of the very unusual country and richly endowed people of Iran—a country and culture for which I have considerable admiration. I seek not to be critical, but to explain. Although the political culture of Iran is complex, it is certainly not "crazy" or "irrational" as was often averred during periods of American confrontation; the basis of Iranian reality must be grasped by all who deal with it. It is unfortunate that Iran and the United States have probably expressed greater visceral anger at each other during the last decade than toward any other countries. If the political culture of Iran can be better understood through this work, I will be gratified.

On a more practical note, I have used the terms "Persia" and "Iran" more or less interchangeably, mostly with the same meaning, although I have tried to employ Persia more in reference to pre-Pahlavi times or as a cultural term. Although Iran was selected by Reza Shah in the 1920s as the new name for the country, it is at least as old a concept as Persia. The term "Persia" more precisely refers to the province of Fars, the cultural heartland of the country. I have also tended to use the term "Russia" in preference to "the Soviet Union" in referring to the future geopolitical relationships between the USSR and the Middle East. As the national republics of the USSR emerge more distinctly, it is *Russia's* relationship with Middle Eastern states that is the central geopolitical fact of the future rather than the defunct concept of the Soviet Union.

The August 1990 invasion of Kuwait by Iraq once again highlights the importance of the Gulf region: Although Iran is not a direct party to the Iraq-Kuwait confrontation, it will figure prominently in the future containment of Iraq and remains strategically the most important country in the Gulf over the long run.

Graham E. Fuller
Thousand Oaks, California

Introduction

The Sovereign, The Pivot of the Universe, The Sultan, His Auspicious Majesty, His Royal Majesty, The King of Kings, the Royal Possessor of Kingdoms, His Majesty the Shadow of Allah, The Khakan.
—*The historical titles of the shah of Iran*[1]

This book is most of all about the future. It seeks to examine Iran's past for clues of future behavior, for threads of interests, continuities of conflict, and certain geopolitical constants that are likely to strongly affect Iran's foreign policy behavior in the decades ahead.

The title of this book, "The Center of the Universe," is a term taken from one of the many historical titles of the shah of Iran, a partial list of which are reproduced above. Expressing neither reticence nor modesty, the shah's title of "Center of the Universe"[2] seems appropriate for an examination of Iran's geopolitical world. Not surprisingly, Iran's view of the world is intensely Irano-centric—with a degree of intensity not always readily grasped by outsiders. To fail to enter into the internal logic of this Irano-centric view is to miss an important facet of Iran's operational behavior. Indeed, this book seeks to examine the concept of Iran as the center of its own universe, its view of itself and of the states that move in the same constellation. During the 1980s Iran indeed dominated international attention in the Persian Gulf as first the Iranian Revolution and then the Iran-Iraq War worked their influences upon the world's political and economic interests. And yet, in the first year of the 1990s in the eyes of much of the world Saddam Husayn of Iraq remarkably supplanted the image of Ayatollah Khomeini as the malevolent force of the Gulf with his seizure of Kuwait. For the moment, too, Iran is *hors de combat*, sidetracked, caught up in the reconstruction of postwar devastation, the aftermath of a severe earthquake in 1989, and the continuing struggles for power unleashed by Khomeini's death. Yet Iran

1

will remain central to the longer range calculus of Gulf politics; this book argues that its long-term importance in the Gulf exceeds that of Iraq, despite current Western preoccupation with Baghdad's military threat. This book dedicates much attention to the Iraq-Iran relationship and its likely dynamic in the future of Gulf politics.

The book is about a great deal more than simply the Iranian world view, however. It is concerned with establishing many of those historical and geopolitical factors, including the inclinations and goals of its neighbors, that have marked Iran's dealings with each of its neighbors over time. The book also seeks to identify shifts in characteristic relations with neighbors, the reasons for such shifts, and the likelihood of either shift or continuity in Iran's foreign policy relations in the future.

Geopolitics is something of an old-fashioned art that classically focuses upon geography as one of the key determinants of state behavior. Traditionally, the location of a state, its neighbors, axes of communication, and physical resources are taken as immutable factors, the basic materials that bound a state's actions. The thrust of this book, however, goes considerably beyond classical geopolitics. If geography determines many key factors in a country's political behavior and delimits its options, so too does its past, its history. Iran's history itself is in part a product of classical geopolitical factors: Neighbors, axes of communication, and invasion routes directly affect the political/military/economic/ethnic experience. And the experience of history works powerfully to mold that elusive characteristic we variously call national culture, political culture, or national character.

In short, this book is written in the belief that nations have unique personalities or cultures, developed over a period of time by the unique melding of many factors that produce a distinctive culture and operating style. The character of the nation has direct impact on the kind of domestic—and foreign—policy that it will conduct. None of the factors identified as part of a nation's personality or character will enable anyone to predict specifically what it will do—any more than the knowledge of aspects of an individual person's personality can tell you specifically what that person will do under varying circumstances. It depends in part upon the circumstances that that personality is called to operate within. But we can all recognize the essential necessity of possessing maximum familiarization with the operating styles and personal char- acteristics of individuals with whom we are going to deal; indeed, we often brief others on how to approach individuals unknown to them. The same goes for nations.

More broadly, this book sets out to do several things:

- To examine some aspects of the style and political culture of the people of Iran as conditioned by historical events, geography, and culture. I seek not only to identify key formative events, but to examine the *perception* of those events in Iran and the region— often as important as the "historical facts" themselves. Myth, image, tradition, and prejudice are powerful determinants in any nation's history—especially when there is a lot of history involved, as is the case with Iran.
- To examine the nature of Iran's historical interactions with each of its neighbors in order to identify the salient issues that have emerged between them, and how they view each other—however far back in time one needs to go to identify root causes and attitudes. Greater emphasis is of course laid on events of this century because their legacy is more immediate.
- To examine how issues between Iran and its neighbors have been dealt with—resolved or not resolved—historically. What were the circumstances under which issues have been put to "permanent" rest in the past? What issues are still dormant? Political surprise usually occurs when a course of events turns a corner; factors long inoperative and ignored suddenly reemerge to become important once again. Can we identify any of those *latent factors*, icebergs in the political sea, in Iran's dealings with its neighbors?
- To identify those factors either in Iran or in neighboring countries capable of transforming political behavior under new circumstances. Under what circumstances might old issues recur as points of contention between Iran and each neighbor?
- To explore the *future prospects* for Iran's relations with each of its neighbors and Iran's behavior in the region. Because unforeseen events—especially coups, wars, and the actions of great powers— often have a decisive impact on regional events, what can we say about possible or conceivable future events in the region—based on historical precedent—that might unleash new or unforeseen conflict? If certain types of major events take place, how might they change the geopolitical calculus?

I recognize that this is a tall order. The number of possible factors are theoretically infinite, making any kind of firm predictions about future interactions almost impossible. However, an examination of the historical record should offer some clues about the possible range of events that might happen in the future.

This book does not presume to spin any single firm scenario about regional events around Iran. The art of forecasting, after all, really consists of identifying alternative courses of events and isolating those factors that help determine which alternative emerges as most likely. This book does seek to identify those key geographical, historical, and cultural issues that might delimit the nature of future interactions. In short, it inquires into the pathology of the region and the kinds of things we need to look out for—even if they never take place. But thoughtful forecasts of events that never quite occur does not imply that such forecasts are "wrong." They simply serve to describe the operating environment, the hidden shoals, the barely visible icebergs that we very much need to be aware of, even if we do not hit them. Indeed, knowledge of the distinct possibility of certain kinds of events will enable us to either prepare for them or better avoid them.

Any book that deals with the future, with possible scenarios for major geopolitical changes and new interstate relations, must inevitably raise scenarios that will be disturbing to some of the states, regimes, or groups in power. In raising these scenarios, my intention in no way is to cast disrespect upon existing ruling institutions in any state. By suggesting the possible shape of future change in the region, I neither intend to advocate such change, nor to wish it to occur, but simply to flag it for the concern of all who live in or deal with the region. Any geopolitical study of the area must be honest in its appraisal of possible—even violent—change if it is to be worth the paper it is printed upon.

*   *   *

As noted above, this book concerns the kinds of attitudes and prejudices that abound in the region and that play hidden counterpoint to public events. My goal is to seek a better understanding of Iran in particular. In seeking to identify salient features of its political culture and operating style, I realize that such cultural observations often say almost as much about the observer as they do about the observed. Indeed, part of the United States' problem in dealing with Iran has been its own inability to grasp the culture and operating style of that country—even under the shah, but especially under the ayatollahs. That I feel a need for a book like this suggests that Americans are often victims of their own political culture and operating styles—styles that are unique in the world. Americans' own prejudices, attitudes, and unusual political history leave them exceptionally ill equipped to intuitively grasp the operating styles of most other states, especially states that are more constrained by ancient historical legacies, memories of the past, and long-term vulnerability to the pressures and ravages of outside states, to war and conquest. Because the United States is so big and its smallest actions possess such clout, Americans feel they can afford to overlook the necessity for sensitivity to the operating styles of others—a luxury no smaller state can afford. This approach has caused problems for U.S. policies over the years. As Howard Wiarda points out in an excellent book on America and the Third World, Americans show

> a fundamental lack of understanding and empathy about the Third World and Third World areas and countries. More specifically, . . . at the root of our foreign policy dilemmas in these areas is a deeply ingrained American ethnocentrism, an inability to understand the Third World on its own terms, an insistence on viewing it through the lenses of our own that such ethnocentrism implies.[3]

This book is more than a plea for understanding; indeed, when Iran seizes American hostages, mere "understanding" will not suffice as an instrument to free them. But without understanding something of what is happening culturally and psychologically within Iran Americans are left even less well equipped to understand how to proceed next.

A topic such as this inevitably involves a considerable degree of personal interpretation and even subjectivity of approach. That is at once the strength and weakness of this study. My search for some understanding of these issues in the Middle East goes back more than thirty years—nearly two-thirds of which were spent living in the region—attempting to explain motivations and styles of political behavior that were not readily apparent, especially to those reared in the American cultural isolation typically generated by the physical vastness of our land.

* * *

In organizational terms the book is broken into specific chapters that deal with each of Iran's neighbors—analysis divided geographically rather than chronologically. Although such analysis by geographical segments may lose some feel for the simultaneity of major events as world history evolves, it does enable the study to focus on the special character of these bilateral relations with all their particular geopolitical features.

* * *

The West has been particularly mesmerized by the phenomenon of the Ayatollah Khomeini. A larger than life figure, he served as symbol for all the deeper anxieties of the West about radical, fanatic Islam. He attained the stature of a greater "hate figure" in the United States than almost any other foreign leader since Hitler—except perhaps Mu'ammar Qadhafi. American judgment about the nature of Iranian behavior—at least at the popular level—has been powerfully colored by this glowering, black-robed figure who characterized America in a medieval vocabulary that conjured up degrees of "Satanicness."

It is therefore easy to be misled into accepting the figure of the ayatollah as Iran personified and to overlook elements of continuity in Iran that exist from the past. It is the thesis of this book that there are strong elements of continuity between Iran's present behavior and that of the past. The wild card, the striking variable today, has been the *intensity of vision* and *violence of means* that Khomeini brought to an Iranian policy that otherwise flows quite naturally out of the Iranian past.

With the sure vision of hindsight, most scholars have now come to view the emergence of the Islamic Republic and clerical rule as a "natural" product of Iranian history. Yet few ever said it was a likely eventuality in the volumes written on Iran before Khomeini. Indeed, even a good understanding of Iran could not have led one to predict the emergence of the clergy at the top of the political pyramid, for it took an extraordinary concatenation of events to bring this particular type of leadership to the fore. But even Khomeini was constrained and impelled by elements of the Iranian past. Although he is now gone, Iran will continue to perceive the world in part through the lenses of this historical experience too, even as Tehran's immediate interests change.

In seeking to examine the geopolitics and historical legacy of Iran, I have tried to avoid writing a history. But this study sifts through history in search of events, clues, repetitions, and trends, seeking to understand the dynamics at work when Iran interacts with the particular character of each neighbor. Because I am looking for broad trends, inevitably I have left a lot out. In the end, efforts to select key historical themes as central to future developments involve some degree of subjective judgment.

I recognize the problems of examining Iran's relations with, say, the Gulf states in isolation from the broader context of other simultaneous and important international events that also powerfully affected Iran's policies toward the Gulf. I try to provide some sense of that broader international environment, but my focus is identification of the range of various policies that Iran has pursued over time. Do they offer any clue to the range of options Iran might consider in the future?

Modern scholars of the foreign policy process are also interested in the interrelationship between a nation's domestic and foreign policies. Quite naturally, internal events considerably influence foreign policy choices. Yet I have not devoted a great deal of attention to this important issue for three reasons.

(1) I am interested in strategic attitudes and decisions rather than tactical ones. Transient domestic input is particularly important when

the details of *short-term* policy formulation are considered, less important when one examines longer range policies, the continuities.

(2) Throughout Iranian history, as nearly all scholars will agree, the figure of the shah has been the primary human determinant of Iranian foreign policy. Various shahs have been more or less aware of domestic forces whose views they must consider—especially among the elite and the clergy—but domestic politics per se have played an almost negligible role in the formulation of Iranian foreign policy until the twentieth century. Indeed, only under the Islamic Republic has one been able to talk of real factions openly contesting foreign policy issues—and even those within a relatively narrow framework.

(3) Even the Islamic Republic acts within the framework of specific realities determined by history and geopolitics, which helps determine its approach to issues.

Whatever the limitations and shortcomings of the study, I hope it will reveal the lay of the historical land and can therefore serve as a road map to alternative routes of Iranian foreign policy options. These alternative routes may not be as readily apparent as we travel down the main roads of current politics. Although Iran may never take the alternative routes, it is important to know that they exist, should unforeseen events suddenly make those alternative routes more attractive. If this book helps illuminate the character, style, and environment of the foreign policy behavior of a very complex country, then it will have fulfilled its purpose.

If readers should disagree with some of the many speculative judgments posed in the book, at the least I hope I will have invited them to then formulate their own—perhaps on issues where they may not previously have thought about formulating a view. In the end this study may raise more questions about Iran's future than it answers—but then, the questions are often more important than the answers anyway.

Notes

1. The titles of the shah, from Sir Percy Sykes, *A History of Persia* (London: Macmillan and Co., Ltd., 1963), First edition 1915, Vol. II, p. 381.

2. "The Center of the Universe" is another popular translation of the Arabic/Persian term "*Qiblat al-'Alam,*" literally "direction of prayer for the world/universe."

3. Howard J. Wiarda, *Ethnocentrism in Foreign Policy: Can We Understand the Third World?* (Washington, D.C.: American Enterprise Institute, Studies on Foreign Policy, 1985), p. 1.

1

The Political and
Social Culture of Iran

You do not know the Persians. . . . You have never had any dealings with them, and therefore you permit yourselves to be lulled into security by their flattering expressions and their winning and amiable manners. But I have lived long with them, and have learned the value of what they say. Their weapons are not such as you have been accustomed to meet in the bold encounter, and the open attack: instead of the sword and spear, theirs are treachery, deceit, falsehood; and when you are least prepared, you find yourselves caught as in a net; ruin and desolation surround when you think that you are seated on a bed of roses. Lying is their great national vice. Do not you remark that they confirm every word by an oath? What is the use of oaths to men who speak the truth? . . .
—*A Kurd disparages Persians in* **Hajji Baba of Ispahan,**[1] 1824

The extraordinary continuity of Iranian history and sophisticated civilization has provided Iran with a multifaceted and tangled national experience and the legacy of a particularly rich and complex national culture. But Persian culture also betrays a profound schizophrenia, born alternatively of an innate sense of superiority stemming from a magnificent imperial past and rich culture, and a nagging sense of inferiority and even insecurity derived from Iran's experience of abject conquest and foreign domination at the hands of Greeks, Arabs, Turks of all kinds, Afghans, Russians, and Western powers. The Persian world is baroque, on the one hand revealing a sense for the extravagant that has produced a magnificent artistic heritage; on the other, it has evolved a subtle, labyrinthine approach to politics that reflects historical insecurities of life under the fickleness and sudden death of absolute monarchy and foreign subjugation.

The experience of domination by powerful British and Russian empires predisposes Iranians to feel that they are never masters of their own fate but rather subject to the wiles of foreign manipulation. Events never have simple explanations but rather reflect the existence of unseen political forces at work behind the scenes manipulating reality. A historically created suspicion and xenophobia is reinforced by the psychological makeup of Shi'a Islam that emphasizes an environment of suffering and injustice as the inevitable price of commitment to the true Faith. A suspicion and arrogance toward the external world is thus coupled with a driving determination for independence and noninvolvement with foreign powers— thereby placing a premium upon exercising the traditional Persian quickness of wit necessary for survival in a world often dominated by harsh external forces that have attempted to dominate Iran.

Western powers often operate from the advantage of superior strategic power in their dealings with smaller countries—a situation that grants the powerful the luxury of operating through the direct and open expression of political intentions. But such powers will find themselves frustrated in encountering an Iranian political style born of relative historical weakness, requiring it to operate through a range of hidden agendas and multilayered purpose. Iran is destined to remain a prickly and difficult power for Western states to deal with, a state intent upon establishing its own hegemony in the region—in a political environment in which Iran perceives itself to have few if any friends. Yet its long civilization and richly endowed national capabilities suggest that Iran could well emerge as one of the most advanced states of the Middle East in years ahead.

Among the various branches of the social sciences, studies of political culture are particularly unfashionable in contemporary U.S. scholarship. It is a fair question to ask whether something called "political culture" or "national character" exists at all; indeed, the very term is sometimes associated with stereotype, and even racism. Although the term "political culture" is perhaps more acceptable than "national character," even this area of inquiry entails elements of disturbingly subjective observation when the observer attempts to translate aspects of social and cultural behavior into political behavior. Indeed, the broader the generalization about a given people or culture, the more subjective it becomes, reflecting at best the observer's own creative and intuitive insights—or, at worst, his own cultural narrowness and even willful prejudices. Such observations by one nation of another are often at least as revealing of the observer as of the observed. But this does not make the observation any less valid in terms of the cultural gap revealed between them.

Such observations can rarely be based on orthodox, quantitative, social science field research—partly because the scope and level of generalization is high and defies scientific measurement. The raw material for such observations comes from a variety of sources including personal experience, a study of the culture, literature, myths, historical record, and observable styles of behavior.

Yet these problems should not deter us from attempting to draw some meaningful and useful conclusions about the national behavior patterns of a given country or nation. We all carry in our own minds models, or "stereotypes," that we apply in our encounters with a great variety of situations, people, institutions, governments, and nationalities. Stereotypes are, of course, dangerous because they draw broad conclusions based on only limited data, knowledge, and experience. But to operate without even *a tentative stereotype* in our minds of what we might encounter in a given cultural situation is to insist that we come to each transaction chastely shielded by a tabula rasa of innocence and ignorance. Empirical research in itself is no guarantee either, for we read much "scientific" analysis that is equally prejudiced or skewed in its conclusions: We know we cannot trust in mere methodology or quantified data to ensure "absolute objectivity." And even genuine experts regularly demonstrate broad disagreement among themselves. In short, we may all witness a select body of "facts," but our differing personal makeups and experiences cause us to attribute arbitrarily different relative weights to these same "facts."

The growth of knowledge about foreign political cultures ideally entails a process of drawing increasingly sophisticated models—or stereotypes—of the reality that we believe we see, buttressed by study and constant sensitivity to new or alternative information by which we continue shaping and moderating our models. To dispense with our working models is an act of naivete. The fact is that sharply different images leap to mind when we talk about dealing with Italians, Germans, Americans, Indians, or Japanese. Even the Foreign Service Institute of the U.S. State Department has acknowledged these sharp ethnic differences, and their importance in operating style, in a fascinating little book entitled only *National Negotiating Styles*—broadly suggestive of something that, even if not called national character, involves distinct and important national characteristics of direct operational significance.[2]

Developing cultures and societies are in one sense easier to describe than those more developed because the traditional culture remains more potent. But in another sense, focusing on traditional culture and its patterns is dangerous because by definition they are in a process of rapid evolution. Although there is a great deal that is very observable about traditional Iranian character and culture, that society has been undergoing a process of extraordinarily rapid change over the past several decades. Contemporary observations about historical political culture will gradually grow less accurate with the passage of time. But the legacy of the traditional operating environment does not change so fast as to lose its validity either.

There will undoubtedly be some who feel I have slipped over into the sin of "Orientalism" in ethnocentrically attempting to typify some aspects of another nation—especially in drawing upon quotations from that ultimate "orientalist," the nineteenth-century British author of the novel *Hajji Baba of Ispahan*, James Morier. Morier's portrait of Iran and its neighbors at the beginning of the nineteenth century—after he had spent a lifetime in the region and its culture—is a classic, recognized as such even by Iranians; it is of course a masterpiece of deliberate hyperbole and stereotype, yet still immensely revealing. *Hajji Baba* is more literature than anthropology, but a reading of it is a valuable experience for contemporary Westerners steeped in antiseptic political science theory that often only poorly transmits a direct feel for mind-sets radically different from our own. Indeed, one could argue that the American mind-set is the least representative of all of the rest of the world, and therefore all the more culture-bound and insensitive in its often disastrous dealing with other peoples. The only good news is that Americans may be at least beginning to recognize this problem in themselves.

Much of this book is concerned with views and attitudes of Iranians and their neighbors toward each other. Most of the lead-in quotations to chapters are not selected to reveal immutable truth about the character of these countries so much as to indicate the historically generated power and tenacity of stereotype among those peoples—stereotypes about which we should not be ignorant. These quotations are meant to reveal important existing operational attitudes rather than describe reality. Yet it is often this "reality" of historically stereotyped attitudes in the region that helps inform the actions of regional players—at least as much as an "objective" assessment of reality.

At this stage in world history, and especially of U.S. social development, we are often uncomfortable with anything that tends to characterize national behavior. The twentieth century has seen appalling examples of racism and bigotry at work—evils as old as time, but more systematically and frighteningly implemented as systematic policy under the power of the modern state apparatus. In the United States in particular, with its uniquely multiracial society, people do not wish to be seen as insensitive to the feelings of others. Indeed, some of this newfound sensitivity has gone so far that Americans often prefer to ignore *all* national or ethnic differences in the hopes that they thereby express a new kind of sensitivity toward others. This too is unrealistic and condemns us to close our eyes to rich differences in ethnic makeup. Simply because an interest in, and awareness of, ethnicity can be abused does not mean that we should be incapable of celebrating it in a positive sense or of considering it in dealings with other countries. Even the United States,

for all its multiracial character, is itself still sharply—and often negatively—characterized by foreign observers who believe they witness
special characteristics in American political and social culture, and even
national character, that are profoundly problematical.

It is in that spirit, then, that I offer some thoughts about Iran—a
country for whose culture I have profound admiration. In the final
analysis, the question remains before us: What useful generalizations
can we make about Iran, its people, geopolitics, history, and national
experience, that might facilitate our understanding of that country and
make dealing with it less of a surprise?

*   *   *

Americans probably understand Iran as a national culture considerably
less well than they do most other countries with whom they have been
locked in conflict or crisis. A primary reason is that Americans have
not had a great deal to do with Iran historically until the emergence
of a rapid, close collaboration at the political, military, and commercial
levels starting in the 1960s. The last shah was best known to the
American public simply as a "friend," presiding over an "island of
stability," to use the words of President Jimmy Carter. Our perceptions
were then jarred by the apparent suddenness of the fall of the shah
and the visceral deluge of anti-American impulses that emanated from
the Khomeini revolution—embodied in a series of dramatic events: the
hostage crisis, the Iranian "cultural revolution," Lebanese Shi'ite suicide
missions supported by Iran against U.S. Marines, and the broader image
of Islam inflamed. The characterization of the United States as "the
Great Satan" was perhaps the ultimate shock for an American nation
inclined to think of itself—often naively—as driven by essentially
altruistic and idealistic impulses in the conduct of its foreign policy. In
recent history perhaps only China has seemed as "unfathomable" as a
political culture, similarly driven by a surge of powerful anti-Americanism
during the Chinese Cultural Revolution in the 1970s. And China had
less reason to feel culturally threatened than Iran did.

What, then, are some of those qualities of Iran and its people that
have consistently impressed those who have lived and worked there,
read their literature, studied their culture, and dealt with Iranians in a
variety of circumstances? This chapter now turns to an examination of
many of those qualities. The major themes of the culture emerge from
diverse sources: from Iran's historical experience, the character of its
creative culture, its tradition of statecraft, the nature of its social interactions, the role of the individual and the family under highly authoritarian
rule, and the experience of Iran with the West.

Extravagance of Spirit

One look at a Persian rug and many of the qualities of the Persian mind spring out. This is a culture given to extravagance—in nearly all its features. Intertwining arabesques, crowded floral motifs, lush prose, sensuous and evocative verse—all suggest the floweriness inherent in the Persian mode of expression. This quality has produced superb artistic creations in the field of poetry, painting, music, design, metalworking, plastic arts, prose literature, cuisine, architecture, and decoration. Even Persia's religious poetry subtly weaves in almost sensual concepts of "God the Beloved," a figure for whom his followers experience deep yearning and longing in the metaphors of love. Persian prose style traditionally embraces extreme richness of metaphor, complexity of simile and allegory in its expression. The spoken language establishes complex hierarchies of courtesy in elaborate and subtle forms of address pervading daily usage, all designed to express relative positions of authority, rank, deference, and even degrees of obsequiousness. Neither Turkish nor Arabic regularly employ equivalent turns of phrase to such an extent in their common daily speech. A distinguished modern Iranian writer captures, for example, the praise lavished upon a religious leader some decades ago by his followers upon his arrival:

> An unusual murmur rose. Everyone was praying in some way for Mawlana's life and soul and honor. "All of us in this part of the bazaar, young and old, are dedicated to you," they were saying. "Our lives and property belong to you. May the Lord make our children your alms and sacrifice! May the Lord not shorten or diminish your shadow over the heads of us, the poorest of the poor! God himself sent you to end oppression and injustice done to defenseless creatures. You're our protector, the crown on our heads. The reward for this deed of yours today will be greater than for a thousand fasts and prayers and pilgrimages. May the Lord take years from the lives of us and our wives and children and the rest of our household and add them to yours. The Prophet himself would kiss your face if he were here today, for you upheld his honor before the other prophet.[3]

Persians highly appreciate such richness and hyperbole. Even under the intellectual austerity of Khomeini, Iran still reverted to its cultural roots to express its latest anti-Western rhetoric in vivid terms of "Great and Lesser Satans"; U.S. imperialism is strikingly characterized as "world-devouring global arrogance." The last shah was perhaps more circumscribed in the use of these kinds of terms, although he too had scant regard for Western democracy. These concepts are central to the Persian vocabulary and infuse the Persian world vision.

This extravagance of style has historically extended itself into foreign policy as well, in a Persian tendency to overreach itself—to allow ambition, rhetoric, and extravagant goals to outrun capabilities and means, frequently leading to national disaster.[4] These characteristics were abundantly present in the many of the Safavids and in the few ambitious Qajar rulers from the nineteenth century to World War I. The last shah exhibited a similar penchant in his exorbitant quest for a more formidable military force than Iran had seen for centuries. Yet the shah reflected Persia's burning frustration at its long-term impotence against foreign forces—forces that have dominated Persia's very existence for over two hundred years and in previous eras as well.

Iran's conduct of the Iran-Iraq War exhibited similar tendencies to skirt dangerously near the point of irrevocable confrontation with the United States, in part bolstered by Tehran's belief in its power to impose pain unacceptable to the other party. This conviction has been coupled with a supreme confidence in the righteousness of its cause. Iran will thus see itself as the natural hegemon of the region, the ultimate arbiter of regional security arrangements—even if this status is beyond its power. Despite extravagance of rhetoric and claim, however, the Islamic Republic has shown growing ability to realistically measure its capabilities and to reach a more sober assessment of risk—a quality less characteristic of Iran in previous periods. Extravagance is tempered by an increasingly informed awareness of the reality of forces around it.

The qualities of Persian extravagance extend even to areas of religious doctrine. Iran has long attracted the visionary, the apocalyptic. "Medieval Iran was a Mecca of malcontents, rebels, hermits, prophets and mystics."[5] Shi'ism is a doctrine that embodies much of this same extravagance, an apocalyptic vision of human life in which passion, suffering, and oppression are fundamental themes that impress themselves upon the Shi'ite psyche. Thus, the ritual annual passion play of the martyrdom of the Imam Husayn at Qarbala in A.D. 680 becomes political allegory for suffering in the search for God's justice on earth. Justice as an abstraction becomes a religious goal in itself—justice against the oppressors. This Shi'ite vision of life and politics is far more emotional, more apocalyptic, more Manichean in its distinct realms of Good and Evil, more martyr-oriented, than is orthodox Sunni Islam. Extravagance as a Persian gift—richly informing the arts and culture of Iran as well as its daily life—is one of those qualities difficult to isolate out in analysis of foreign policy. Yet it is suggestive of a political style that is inclined toward bold and vivid interpretations of international events. International conflict becomes imbued with the moral qualities of Good and Evil rather than the attributes of an amoral, pragmatic struggle for power.

This extravagance has regularly led to a willingness to take romantically inspired risk. The Shi'ite element in politics suggests acceptance of suffering and adversity in pursuit of a just cause as a natural and an inevitable part of the evolving plan of God—rather than something externally imposed that must be quickly eliminated or alleviated. Khomeini mentioned repeatedly throughout the war that God may not intend for Iran to prevail in important upcoming battles, or even in the war. Indeed, failure itself can be a further sign that one's own side is imbued with righteousness; victory is not the measure of justness nor justice; the sufferings of failure are to be proudly borne rather than shunned.

An extravagance of rhetoric, then, must be understood as a reflection of the passion, zeal, and visceral drive of the Persian polity asserting its superiority in a world where suffering is just as likely an outcome of conflict as is victory. All nations feel passion and commitment in the course of national conflict, but the Persians may likely require a clearer indication of defeat and failure before they alter course. If mere defeat were the criterion of failure, alteration of policy course might be easier. But when acceptance of the role of suffering and martyrdom is added, defeat becomes a more ambiguous signal because it carries elements of religious virtue and even moral fulfillment in its own right.

Extravagance and elaborate courtesy fulfill important functions within society as well. A description of the kind of interpersonal behavior that has developed in the historical uncertainties of Lebanese politics also has direct bearing on the Persian situation:

> Indeed, exaggerated hospitality, which often assumed ritualized and ceremonial dimensions, coexisted with free-floating hostility. A lavish display of hospitality—perceived broadly here to include forms of coexistence, accommodation, guarded contact, and political pacts and covenants—was more a strategy for warding off hostility than a genuine and selfless demonstration of kindness and affection. The process of so-called "mutual lies" through which contentious groups recognized and managed their differences, had almost become the hallmark of Lebanese politics. By keeping relationships undefined and deliberately ambiguous, all such strategies sheltered groups from the pain of the harsher realities.[6]

As this description of modern Lebanese society would indicate, some of these qualities are not unique to Iran but may have parallels here and there in other Middle Eastern or Third World societies as well. Yet, they are strong features of Iranian society, requiring recognition by the foreign student of Iran. And the overall agglomeration of Iranian characteristics does amount to a particularly Iranian profile.

Continuity as an Ancient Culture

Iranians are imbued with the powerful sense of pride that Iran is one of the most ancient cultures of the world, dating back well before Cyrus the Great, founder of the Achaemenid Empire in the sixth century B.C.—the first "world empire" known to history—that spanned great portions of the then-known world, from India to Greece, Central Asia to Egypt. Other great Persian dynasties with major world sway succeeded it: the Parthians, the Sassanian Empire, the Arab/Persian Abbasid Caliphate, and the Safavid dynasty.

As proud bearers of such an ancient culture, many Iranians nurture deep feelings of superiority toward their neighbors that border on cultural arrogance. This syndrome is also recognizable in other states that can demonstrate unbroken cultural and political continuity directly back to ancient and great civilizations, such as India and China.

A sense of continuous nationhood is a heady quality in the Middle East where most other nationalities have come only recently to any sense of nation as nation-state. The Egyptians are probably the only other major exception in the region—another people that feels self-confident in its sense of ancient, continuous, local, finite, historical identity. Most Middle Eastern countries have stepped upon the stage of history, as nations, only in the twentieth century; their new, narrow national entities sit less comfortably.

Arabs, for example, have a deep sense of pride in their own history, but the concept of who is an Arab has been subject to immense changes of viewpoint over the centuries. Originally the term "Arab" was strictly limited to a beduin out of the Arabian peninsula. Islam carried the nascent Arab/Islamic culture and Arabic language out of the peninsula to a variety of other peoples, many of whom were Semitic in stock, but who definitely were not considered "Arabs" in the seventh century when Islam burst upon the world: the Egyptians, the Syrians, the Iraqis, the Algerians, and so on. Persians have been Persians in Persia for as long as recorded history. And they have the state institutions to show for it.

The very distinctiveness of the Persian race and culture is defined by the non-Persians that bound Iran on all sides. Today only in western Afghanistan and in Soviet Tajikistan is there any culture that is fundamentally comparable to Iran in ethnic and cultural terms, and even there most of the people are not Shi'ite—creating a major cultural gulf between them and Iran.

Persians have long emphasized the dichotomy between "Iran" and "Turan"—the latter referring to the sea of Turanian (i.e., Turkic) peoples of the steppe, who have surrounded the Persians for much of history. The terms "Iran" and "Turan" are almost Manichean in their suggestion of basic divisions between Light and Dark, Good and Evil, culture and barbarism. Persians have felt surrounded by enemies with no natural friend or ethnic ally anywhere. The adoption of the totally distinctive creed of heterodox Shi'ism as the official religion in the sixteenth century powerfully reinforced this latent paranoia, setting Iran religiously at odds with most of the Muslim world—even today.

Despite a clear sense of ethnic identity, the Persian political system does not repose securely, for Iran is in many ways a mosaic of disunity, of historically imposed differences that render difficult the creation of national unity. Well over 40 percent of Iran's population is non-Persian, often quite distinct ethnically and linguistically. Azerbaijanis, Kurds, Turkomans, Baluch, Arabs, various Turkic tribes, Armenians, and other groups provide raw material subject to centrifugal forces that can threaten to sunder the country. The sheer weight and longevity of Persian culture impels Iran's many minorities to feel proud and part of cultural "Iran" when threatened by outside forces, yet neither they nor the Persian ethnic community consider them to be fully Iranian. Such weaknesses born of division have been observed by foreign powers and have often served as an inviting opening wedge for foreign interference. Iranians themselves are vividly aware of the manipulative handles that such distinctions provide to the outside world, rendering ethnicity a sensitive topic—involving an unspoken but subtle undercurrent of suspicion about the loyalty of given ethnic or regional groups. These religious, ethnic, linguistic, and cultural differences have yet to be definitively subsumed into a general sense of Iranian nationalism. Although major progress has been made in the modern period, a truly united Iranian nation has yet to be forged—a source of anxiety to any Iranian authority. Yet Persians' confidence in their roots is far from supreme; Persian historical experience has tainted even the sense of cultural superiority.

Cultural and Ethnic Arrogance

Every Persian knows that there has been a Persia for nearly three millennia. The historical personality is deeply rooted. Persians have no doubt that Persia is a superior culture—far superior tq the Arabs whom Persians historically perceived as crass beduin of the desert, "eaters of lizards," lazy and unversed in the ways of civilization. And Turks, despite their impressive military capacity, are perceived as sluggards, slow-wits, incapable of subtlety and refinement. Iranians are convinced that their wit is nimbler than that of any of their neighbors or foes. In short, Iran maintains some sense of innate arrogance toward the surrounding world and a supreme confidence in its cultural superiority.

And yet perhaps the confidence is not quite so supreme. For history has jarred these deep reserves of superiority repeatedly, ultimately infusing the collective personality with a nagging sense of insecurity. Despite Iran's long existence as a people and a nation, it has been subjected to an array of foreign conquerors that has shaken the sense of national unity and of stewardship of their own national destiny. Successive conquests of Iran started over two thousand years ago with Alexander the Great, followed by the humiliating Arab conquest of Iran under early Islam, the Mongol hordes of Genghis Khan and Tamerlane, the powerful armies of the Seljuk Turks, the humiliating Afghan invasion, and finally capped by British and Russian domination and even occupation of Iran. These conquerors and many other invaders have seized control of Iran for long periods of time, inflicting severe psychic scars on the Iranian nation. An Iranian holy man in Isfahan recounts his views:

> I saw countless kinds of people with all varieties of different languages and customs and habits and rites and religions who came in one gate and went out another and how often not a single creature had been left alive nor any structure left unrazed. Arabs and non-Arabs, Turks, and Tajiks and Turcomans, Mongols and Afghans, strangers and kinsmen, all came parading through and vanished like phantoms in a dream. The city's history and geography mixed inextricably like fact and metaphor and left my helpless eyes incapable of distinguishing history from legend and truth from falsehood. . . . Our city passed from hand to hand like a polo ball and its people suffered agonies and burned in flames. Then as they recovered, the Mongols' unspeakable and conscienceless violence and injustice descended on them and their possessions, like a heavenly fire of wrath and rage.[7]

Although many of these conquerors ultimately made their own lasting contribution to the overall mosaic of Iranian culture, and have even been absorbed into it, the experience has nonetheless been traumatic. Few nations possessing such a distinctive long-term cultural entity have witnessed as many devastating conquests as has Iran—except perhaps China.

Iranian culture is thus left deeply schizophrenic: An ingrained sense of cultural superiority is constantly eroded by feelings of insecurity and inferiority in the Persian state's historic inability to order its own destiny. Periods of glorious empire and Persian cultural domination of broad regions alternate with periods of helplessness before powerful foreign forces—an accelerating negative trend as Persian history moved into the twentieth century. Of all the glorious dynasties of Persia, indeed only two have been truly Persian in origin: the Samanids and the Zands. Persians seem to have more discomfort in reconciling these contradictions than many other peoples of the Middle East—and it complicates their vision. Paranoia threatens to insinuate itself into the qualities of a national trait.

When faced with foreign superiority in the modern age, especially in the technical realm, many Persians feel that to admit ignorance is to lose face—in a society where face is the paramount vehicle of one's self-esteem and where external appearance is all.[8] To admit ignorance can become a process of humiliation, tending to evoke a response in Persians of bravado and boastfulness.[9]

The Culture of Conquest by Foreigners

To suffer conquest obviously engenders strong negative consequences and reactions among those subdued. Chief among the reactions is a sense of loss of control over one's own destiny. Historically, of course, nearly all men have been nakedly vulnerable at some point to the whims of fortune and the caprices of arbitrary rule. When a foreign enemy culture and foreign military order impose themselves upon a people, however, massive dislocations and reorientation of the local political culture and its hierarchy of influence result—an experience utterly beyond the ken of American culture, except perhaps in the American South after the Civil War.

A former ruling elite must suddenly come to terms with new masters— whose goals, preferences, methods, and style are uncertain. Personal success, wealth, security, and public accomplishment in life can only come through correct reading of the foreign master. One must learn to meet the foreign ruler's needs—all the while manipulating the political and social situation to one's own ends if one is to survive. Fortunes and lives can be made and lost in a twinkling, depending on one's skill in accommodation and manipulation. Success in the end is determined by the foreign master. Indeed, one quickly becomes deeply dependent upon the foreign presence; it informs one's most basic calculations.

Iranians are therefore perceived to be acutely sensitive to the role of the foreigner in their culture and politics. This constant eye to the foreign power breeds, on the one hand, a cynicism about the nature of power. On the other, it can evoke an obsequiousness based on anger and contempt for the dominant ruling presence, coupled with recognition that the will of such foreign power cannot be crossed except at great personal risk. *Cherchez l'etranger*—identify the foreigner who lies at the heart of political events.

Foreign intervention may even be welcomed by one faction or another if it can disrupt an otherwise untoward course of events for a given group of individuals. A high premium is placed on jockeying for advantageous position with the foreign powers-that-be. Indeed the foreigner becomes an integral part of the political system, the ultimate recourse when one finds the rules of the local political game are not working to one's advantage. The *deus ex machina* does exist—he is the foreigner.

If the ravages of the great conquerors were not enough to inflict a sense of insecurity and vulnerability on the Iranian psyche, the subtler snares of nineteenth-century European imperialism brought it to a sharper head. The rivalries of two great imperial systems, the British and the Russian, managed to dominate, emasculate, and finally render utterly impotent the entire state structure of Iran at the turn of twentieth century. The British in particular were imagined to be lurking behind nearly every event in the region, masterfully dominating the daily reality. The less clear the foreign hand, the more convincing the case for its existence and ability to work in unseen ways. In Iran to this day the British are still popularly paid the ultimate tribute of mastery of Machiavelli's craft: They are believed to lie at the very epicenter of the international spider web of intrigue—the most clever and cunningly manipulative force of them all. The United States may be distinguished by Khomeini as the Number One Satan, but Washington has yet to attain quite the same level of cunning in the Iranian mind as have the British—"perfidious Albion."

And yet it is not all fantasy. Iranian suspicions and paranoia are richly fulfilled in the annals of the imperialist's role in the country—not only in dominating Iranian life but also as the ultimate king-maker and king-breaker of Iran's Peacock Throne. The British and Russian role in the rise and fall of many of the enfeebled nineteenth-century Persian shahs was central—as it was in the fate of Persia's first experiments in parliamentary government at the turn of the century, where both sides cynically manipulated the Parliament's attempt to gain rudimentary control over the imperial state.

The fate of Reza Shah Pahlavi (1925–1941), a towering figure in modern Persian history, the founder of the modern Pahlavi dynasty, says it all. The first modern Iranian leader to reestablish central control over the state and to build a sense of national power and independence throughout the country, he found himself peremptorily dethroned by combined British and Russian forces when he refused to break diplomatic ties to Nazi Germany following the invasion of the Soviet Union by Hitler in 1941.

The pattern was only confirmed when his son Mohammed Reza Pahlavi, the last shah, was restored to his throne—with the covert intervention of the United States and Great Britain in 1953—after fleeing the country under the pressures of the nationalist-populist movement of Prime Minister Mossadegh. The shah subsequently seemed to feel that if he could handle the two superpowers correctly, then his reign was secure; he attributed minimal importance to internal forces. Indeed, the shah went to his grave with the conviction that in the end it was the United States that had deliberately pulled the plug on his regime by encouraging the rise of fundamentalist forces.

> On one occasion in the early fall [1978], the Shah had turned on [U.S. Ambassador] Sullivan, recited almost every incident of unrest, and declared that it was all so sophisticated that it must be the result of foreign intrigue against him. The KGB were not capable of coordinating such protests, he said, so it must be the work of British intelligence and the CIA. Well, he said to Sullivan, he knew that the British had never liked him. But why had the CIA turned against him? Had he done something wrong? Or had Washington and Moscow reached some grand design in which Iran was divided between them as part of a plan for world condominium?[10]

Many Iranians still believe Khomeini was the creation of the United States—allegedly to punish the shah because he had become too independent-minded on oil-pricing policy. Yet others believe that Khomeini was actually petulantly installed by a Great Britain deeply angry at the United States for having displaced it in the political order of the Middle East.

The Environment of Conspiracy

The awareness of the existence of hostile forces and their manipulative power, coupled with a sense of frustration about one's own inability to deal with the threat, has created a strong belief in the existence of conspiracy. Rarely are events to be taken at face value, for to assume them as such is (a) to indicate ignorance of the superior forces around oneself or one's nation and (b) to demonstrate the stupidity, naivete, or insensitivity not to perceive the hidden motives of others. This social and political conspiracy-mindedness is not, of course, unique to Iran but is widespread in the Middle East as a whole and in almost any cultures where weakness and suffering at the hands of powerful exterior forces encourage similar attitudes. Nonetheless, the art would seem to be raised to a higher level in Iranian culture than in most other countries.

Untoward events, therefore, do not simply happen, nor do events happen in isolation. It is imperative to recognize the existence of powerful external forces that dominate or control events; it is essential to bring some analytic order to a chain of events to demonstrate the deeper meaning, the plan, or even the plot that exist behind them. Many Iranians will regularly choose the most complex explanation of political events as the most likely, particularly in gauging the intention of foreign powers. The specific interpretation may vary with the particular ideological outlook of the observer. But the greater the foreign power, the more incomprehensible and naive it would seem to assume that a particular series of developments might be unrelated. Even when one assures such an Iranian that one is personally aware of the role of, for example, American ignorance, lack of attention, inconsistency, bureaucratic oversight, or lack of interest as key factors lying behind a given series of actions (or inactions) of the U.S. government, an Iranian will assume the speaker is either naive or himself dissembling: It is impossible that the mighty U.S. government would be capable of error, oversight, or uncoordinated action. (The accidental and tragic shooting down of the Iranian airbus in the Persian Gulf by the U.S.S. *Vincennes* in the final months of the Iran-Iraq War in 1988 was believed by virtually all Iranians, in Iran and in exile, to have been a deliberate act; this interpretation ironically led to a hastening of Iran's decision to end the war based on the belief that the United States would stop at nothing to bring defeat to Iran. Any other interpretation was almost inconceivable—and worse—naive.) And the CIA itself is attributed with a ubiquity, omniscience, and omnipotence that is virtually superhuman. This attitude has led to a vastly exaggerated reflection of the role of U.S. (and even more, British) intelligence in helping bring the shah back to his throne in 1953 (where the political and social circumstances were ripe to do so) and in the CIA's limited relationship with SAVAK in the shah's later reign. Legal, cultural, or operational limits to the CIA's power are not recognized; the CIA's apparent failure to observe the deterioration in Iran and "to save the shah" in the end can only be evidence, therefore, of a deeper unspoken U.S. political agenda—all the more worrying because the immediate goals of that agenda are not fully evident.

A penchant for the conspiratorial mentality is thus a central feature of Iran's political outlook, particularly in international politics. As we have noted above, historical patterns of victimization at the hands of outsiders is a key source of this mentality, suggesting that it is not all paranoia.[11] Such a mentality is unlikely to change radically until Iranian society as a whole—and other societies around it as well—develop a greater sense of openness and awareness of the workings of other states to enable them more readily to rule out conspiracy as a central feature

competence are not at issue: One simply does not give another Persian sensitive and potentially manipulable information about oneself. It is hardly surprising that the shah specifically did *not* seek medical treatment from the United States but rather from the French when he developed cancer; to have revealed his condition to the United States would have exposed him to complete vulnerability from an (always) impermanent ally.

Such behavior translated into diplomatic practice is exasperating to U.S. officials who may be ignorant of the mentality and culture behind the Iranian negotiating style—a style in which dissimulation, deception, delay, indirection, the partially empowered emissary, the mixed personal and official agenda of the intermediary, and the use of foreign contacts to gain marginal personal advantage in domestic politics all hopelessly complicate the picture.

Social Mobility and Living by One's Wits

In striking distinction to the absolute power of the shah over the centuries has been the remarkable relative social mobility that characterizes Iranian society. Most Iranians instinctively sense no ceiling to the potential fulfillment of their ambitions. Indeed, social class and origin have never played a critical role in the ability of individuals to rise and attain the summit of power. Iranian history is replete with examples of those of humble origin who have made it to the top. But if social origin is no hindrance, then neither are virtue and talent prerequisites either. The system gave prizes to those who lived successfully by their wits. The rogue, the adventurer—all could aspire to greatness. The very arbitrary quality of central power enabled power and position to be suddenly thrust upon the skilled actor, providing Iranian society with a crude kind of egalitarian counterpoint to the absolutism of imperial rule.[19] Reza Shah came from an exceedingly humble background and even today the Islamic Republic has elevated figures of extremely varied background to positions of great power.

An ability to live by one's wits suggests also elements of opportunism. If the order of things is regularly imposed by the outside forces, and one is subject to an arbitrary system heightening the fickleness of life, it follows that opportunity must be seized when it appears—creating a sense of almost amoral opportunism. In much of the contemporary West, personal morality has only recently come to be generally reinforced by a basic belief that the social order is inherently acceptable—made so through the workings of just laws and impartial bureaucracy; the citizen has come to believe he should be able to rely on the social, political, and administrative order to obtain relative justice. The public practice of personal morality thus serves to perpetuate and protect that rule of law. But when, as earlier in the West and in much of the world today, the order is seen as unjust and manipulated by foreign or other opportunistic forces, then the exercise of personal morality in that system is foolish, pointless, and naive. One must seize one's advantage where it lies in a system that grants no quarter. The process of bargaining is not meant to arrive at a just price, but to test relative wit and strength.

Bargaining from a Position of Weakness

The diplomacy of the weak and the vulnerable must therefore be far more resourceful and skillful than that of the powerful. The powerful, after all, can rely to a great extent on sheer power alone, while the weak must develop compensatory skills. Many Third World diplomats in dealing with the West are usually far more resourceful and flexible in finding diplomatic arrangements, face-saving compromises, and avoidance of direct showdowns than are large Western powers. (Indeed, terrorism itself is a weapon of the weak, used to compensate for the superior firepower and power projection capabilities of Western powers. The practitioners of terror must take care not to allow terrorism to fray relations to the point where it is firepower that resolves the issue.) In these areas of subtle diplomacy, the Westerner, secure in his relative strength, may be outclassed.

The Personal Relationship

Because the Iranian political and social systems decree that one deal with personalities and not with institutions, the personal relationship to this day transcends any formal or institutionalized relationship.[20] Institutions are meaningless in the absence of the personality who gives it life and character and defines its power. One can have no confidence in an impersonal institution, whereas an individual is real, responsive to interchange, and answerable. Negotiation or bargaining is conducted on the basis of personalities—with all the built-in mechanisms of indirect or oblique communication designed to save the faces of all parties and to avoid a flat, demeaning negative. The use of the intermediary thus becomes a highly developed art, enabling unofficial parties to shadowbox with each other without confrontation, to feel out positions before any formal proposals are made, to avoid the definitive no.

During periods of supreme weakness in the face of British and Russian domination of Iran at the end of the nineteenth century, Iran developed a series of devices designed to stave off confrontation that are still valuable today. Despite the centralization of power, government still consisted of various ministers and working groups who developed the skill of delay in negotiations into a fine art, attributing to the complexity of committee responsibility what was really deliberate indecision. While observing the proprieties of formal negotiations, complex back channels of discussion would be underway, all designed to avoid formal conflict or to stave off definitive or conclusive answers that could not satisfy the receiving party.[21] The real substance of interchange took place entirely outside the formal discussions. "This procedure was successful in a society in which time was of little consequence and where mental agility and imagination were highly prized."[22] An observer of the shah in 1967 perceived similar qualities:

> Without a doubt, the Shah leads most of his countrymen in the art of Persian politics . . . refusing to crystallize issues to the point where definite choices are made, thus disappointing or offending someone; never allowing any individual to become too powerful or too popular; never being so publicly identified with events that it is impossible to shift the blame onto others; and cultivating an ambiguity in political life that softens critics by pretending to espouse their hopes while reassuring vested interests by rarely carrying out promised reforms.[23]

For all of these reasons, Iran still prizes the use of the intermediary, whose status derives from his own personality and personal contacts and not from formal position. And such an individual—because he is an individual and in search of opportunities—invariably will have his own private agenda apart from his quasi-official one. Such private agendas prove deeply distressing to U.S. policymakers who seek straightforward responses free of any side interests. Although such phenomena are not unknown within the American political system as well, within the Persian scheme of things there is no individual in any role who is not also pursuing some private agenda as well, either for himself, his family, his political circle of intimates, or all of the above. (In a classic encounter, a British Foreign Service officer noted that while he was kidnapped, beaten, and held hostage by Iranian security officials for a day in 1987, one of his guards, assigned to keep him tied up, asked in the course of conversation for help in getting a visa for the U.K.)[24] Personal relationships thus need not depend on the character of the formalized relationship.

Persians are thus unlikely to be satisfied with the formality of a relationship, the official character of the contact, or the external trappings of an office. It is important to sense the personality, the style of the interlocutor. One tries to make these relationships as "irregular," as unofficial and personalized as possible, because then one can sense what one is really dealing with. The Westerner who wants to "get on with it" and approach issues formally, procedurally, and frontally will be deeply frustrated by the oblique approach of his interlocutor. And however empowered that Westerner is in negotiations, his Persian counterpart will likely seek to authenticate that representative through contacts with other officials or seek contacts outside normal channels for passing messages and assessing the true character of bargaining positions. Iranian officials would never entrust important relations to mere formal channels or public channels; those channels may actually conceal the real exchange.

These qualities are not unique to Persians and are probably recognizable—at least in part—as comparable to features in many other societies where institutions are only weakly developed. These qualities are acutely developed among Iranians however. At the risk of erroneously ascribing these characteristics as products of specific historical developments (*post hoc, ergo propter hoc*), it is inconceivable that the specific character of Persian history has *not* been a major formative element in producing these characteristics.

Submerged Cultural and Political Characteristics

A risk in any analysis of political culture is to take the present as the norm or the absolute, and to directly extend it forward as a reliable prognosis of the future. Such a "straight-line" analysis of Iran done before the fall of the shah would have unquestionably slighted the Shi'ite clergy as the key element of Iranian society. Indeed, had historical events moved slightly differently, it is entirely possible that the clergy might never have come to power at all. The clerics nonetheless would still have remained a fundamental component, a vital undercurrent of politics, whose existence the unwary political actor could ignore only at great peril. What, then, are some of those other characteristics of Iranian culture that in fact happen to be submerged now as a result of clerical rule? What are those factors that could easily emerge again in a postclergy reign?

An interesting counterpoint to Iran's xenophobia lies in its historical ability to *absorb* foreign invading cultures and incorporate them in the new social order. "Iran is easy to swallow but hard to digest," as the saying goes. Such onslaughts as the Greeks of Alexander of Macedon, the Arab conquest, the Mongol invasion, the Turkish invasions, and indeed the assault of the West in the nineteenth and twentieth centuries— all have been integrated in one sense or another into the Iranian political and social cultures, producing a remarkably sophisticated culture. Engagingly, Iranians suggest that it was "they who conquered Islam" by the powerful political and cultural Persian imprint placed upon their

Arab conquerors in the course of the Perso-Arab Abbasid Caliphate and the flowering of medieval Islam in Persian Central Asia. "Defeat makes us invincible," as a Persian once remarked. Only China has demonstrated comparable absorptive capability in swallowing and sinicizing whole series of external conquerors.

Might this absorptive capacity in the end emerge strongly in a postclerical culture? Once Iran has vented its moral spleen on the West and the United States, is it possible that it might prove exceptionally adept at adopting major elements of Western life and comfortably making them its own? The immensely intelligent, persevering, and gifted Iranian character could well excel at arriving at some new synthesis of Western and Islamic life not readily suggested by the absolutist vision of the current Islamic cultural revolution.

Indeed, the Islamic Republic has also come in judgment of much of what has come before it. It eschews the fawning obsequiousness of the imperial court and prefers a greater bluntness and directness in dealing with the world and in setting forth its intentions. The Iranian public, well aware of the honeyed words of the imperial court system of favorites, admired the seeming incorruptibility of the Ayatollah Khomeini. While no one, least of all Iranians themselves, expect the character of Persian social intercourse to change overnight, the modernizing process under the Islamic Republic may be gradually moving toward producing a newer generation of Iranian in which directness, and even certain kinds of democratic values, are more highly esteemed than before. The passing of a 2,500-year-old monarchy may help facilitate this long process.

In yet a different variation, Iran could have some success in consolidating its position as a "moral center of Islam" in the Muslim world. It is remarkable to consider that neither Reza Shah nor Mohammed Reza Shah were interested in exploiting the religious character of Shi'ism to foreign policy ends in the region. The most obvious reason, of course, was that any "Shi'ite policy" would only have strengthened the hand of the shah's clerical opponents. But this is still an astonishing omission of opportunity on the part of a state that expressed clear ambitions to expand its authority in the Gulf. No successor regime to the Islamic Republic is likely to pass up the use of this instrument.

Playing the role of "moral center of Islam" would obviously be aimed at serving Iran's own state needs, but it could provide a longer range ideology or source of authority to its foreign policy if it could claim a unique moral authority in crafting some kind of new Islamic character in regional politics. Iran finds itself a direct rival to Saudi Arabia in this respect, however, which, by virtue of Saudi custodianship of the Holy Places of Mecca and Medina, lays claim to the certain moral authority in speaking for Islam worldwide.

The Shahname *Versus* 'Ali

But Iran is not all Islam either. The Shahname on the one hand and the Prophet Muhammad's son-in-law, the Imam 'Ali, on the other encapsulate the deeper civil war that lies within the Iranian consciousness. One face of Iranian culture is the secular/nationalist epic *The Shahname*, The Book of Kings, the literary classic of Iranian culture codifying the glorious Iranian kingly tradition—both in mythical and in historical periods; this epic pointedly leaves off its chronicle of the Iranian experience with the conquest of Iran by Muslim Arabs—the second face of Iranian culture. But it was not mainstream (Sunni) Islam that ultimately came to dominate: The Imam 'Ali—through whom the Shi'a trace the divine line of ascent from the Prophet Muhammad and the foundation of Shi'ite faith—personally symbolizes the Shi'ite Islam that conquered Iran. Iran cannot yet decide whether it is more Iranian or Muslim. The Pahlavis made special efforts to regularly invoke the glories of pre-Islamic Iran, particularly the last shah who lavishly celebrated at Persepolis the 2,500th anniversary of Iranian monarchy. This glorification of the pre-Islamic tradition is absolute anathema to the clergy who view it as a period of *jahiliyya*, or ignorance of the word of God. Despite the categoric pronouncements of the clergy today, Iran has far from sorted out this issue of its dual pre-Islamic and Islamic legacies.[25] Most Persians will probably never give up the glories of pre-Islamic Iran, for it is what distinguishes them absolutely from their neighbors, even more than does (Persianized) Islam in its Shi'ite form.

Future Iranian leaders will need to cope with this dichotomy. Perhaps the reemergence of some degree of the nationalist, pre-Islamic legacy will serve to moderate Iran's more zealous Shi'ite side—in emphasizing a tradition that is unique to Iran.

Nimbleness and Mobility

In the end, the qualities of wit and cunning, while common to a number of societies, are important features in the makeup of Iranian culture and behavior to a special degree. This importance suggests a political culture that is capable of surprise, mobility, and sudden change, where the personality is still much more important than institutions or formal declaratory policy. Indeed, the formality and ponderousness of monarchy perhaps lent a greater rigidity to policy and style to Pahlavi Iran than is true under the more freewheeling, free-for-all, and collegial style of the clergy. I would speculate that the greater the degree of popular participation in Iranian politics, the more freely these "national characteristics" will emerge. Brief periods of parliamentary government lend credence to this theory, as partially free elections have brought a variety of actors to the parliamentary scene who express their feelings on a broad variety of issues, shorn of diplomatic nicety or the calculated language of a government statement.

In a dangerous world where one must be forever vigilant to survive against forces of Evil, or the forces of a great power in the vicinity, a premium is placed on being able to outwit the enemy. Even where the Islamic Republic is willing to conduct relations with most of its Middle Eastern neighbors on a relatively flat playing field, the same does not go for the great powers. In engaging the great powers, no holds are barred. One moves with extreme caution, but one must never show weakness. It is imperative to belittle the enemy, to gain small moral or psychological victories over him as part of the process of defending one's own honor. Indeed, the very state-to-state relationships with large powers almost seem to become personalized in Iranian eyes.

The policymaker will surely encounter the characteristics described above in dealing with Iranians of varying levels of sophistication. Iran will remain an extremely prickly state for the West to deal with, constantly concerned that its independence, freedom, and honor is about to be compromised. Any Iranian government will view foreigners—especially Americans, British, Russians—with the greatest suspicion. True alliances are unlikely; alliances will always be highly tactical in nature and enveloped in the suspicion that partnership today may be readily transformed into betrayal or exploitation tomorrow.

In the end one American diplomatic observer reduced Iranian behavior to "a highly complex, subtly nuanced system which governs personal as well as public behavior, but underlying it all is a strong sense of self-preservation and a bias toward anarchy."[26] The strong central leadership is essential to keeping the intensely individualistic character of Iranian society from flying apart under centrifugal stress. Unless a strong central ruler can suppress these characteristics of Iranian society from influencing too openly its foreign relations, Iran's foreign conduct will continue to reflect the complex national qualities and characteristics described above. And nobody is better at the Persian game than the Persians.

Notes

1. James Morier, *The Adventures of Hajji Baba of Ispahan* (New York: Modern Library, 1954), p. 141.

2. Hans Binnendijk, ed., *National Negotiating Styles* (Washington, D.C.: Foreign Service Institute, Center for the Study of Foreign Affairs, 1987).

3. Sayyed Mohammad Ali Jamalzadeh, *Isfahan Is Half the World*, trans. W. L. Heston (Princeton: Princeton University Press, 1983), p. 147. Originally written in Persian in 1956.

4. Rouhollah K. Ramazani, *The Foreign Policy of Iran, 1500–1941* (Charlottesville: University Press of Virginia, 1966), pp. 32, 50.

5. Ryszard Kapuscinski, *The Shah of Shahs* (New York: Harcourt, Brace and Jovanovich, 1982).

6. Samir Khalaf, "Ideologies of Enmity in Lebanon," *Middle East Insight* Summer 1988, p. 11.

7. Jamalzadeh, *op. cit.*, pp. 204–205.

8. The Persian term for face, or prestige, is *abru*, literally "water of the face"; to humiliate or dishonor someone is referred to as "spilling the water (or "covering") of someone's face"—*abru-ye kasira rikhtan*.

9. Jack C. Miklos, *The Iranian Revolution and Modernization* (Washington, D.C.: National Defense University, National Security Essay Series 83-2, 1983), p. 56. This small book contains interesting and succinct personal observations into Persian national character as experienced by an American diplomat with long experience in Iran.

10. See William Shawcross, *The Shah's Last Ride: The Fate of an Ally* (New York: Simon and Schuster, 1988), p. 29.

11. As Henry Kissinger was alleged to have remarked after an initial few months as Secretary of State: "This job has done wonders for my paranoia; at last I have real enemies!"

12. Joseph M. Upton, *The History of Modern Iran* (Cambridge, Mass.: Harvard Middle East Monograph, 1960), p. 27.

13. Reza M. Behnam, *Cultural Foundations of Iranian Politics* (Salt Lake City: Utah University Press, 1986), p. 103.

14. Miklos, *op. cit.*, p. 59, quoting the shah.

15. William O. Beeman, *Language, Status, and Power in Iran*, as quoted and paraphrased in Khosrow Shakeri, *The Soviet Union and Iranian Communism, Part I*, "The Historical Background, the Socio-political, the Socio-economic, and the Social Psyche," p. 87, a manuscript in progress. Dr. Shakeri's work, including his perceptive analysis of Iranian political culture, is a work of great value and fascinating insight. William Beeman's own book is an extraordinary venture into the Persian language and Persian social conduct as a means of formulating rank and status in Iranian society; an indispensable work on Iranian character and social behavior.

16. Richard N. Frye, quoted in Behnam, *op. cit.*, p. 97.

17. Upton, *op. cit.*, p. 3.

18. Miklos, *op. cit.*, p. 58.

19. This, and a wealth of other fascinating and important insights and analyses of Iranian political behavior, is contained in Khosrow Shakeri's *Victims of Faith: Iranian Communists and the Soviet Union, 1905–1985*, forthcoming.

20. Despite what we have said about a kind of egalitarianism of opportunity stemming from the fickleness of absolute authority and the chance for unexpected advancement through luck and cleverness, this is not to describe a system in

which talent offers any kind of a guarantee of advancement. On the contrary, "position and status in Iranian society were not achieved, but were generally ascribed through personal ties to family and friends; this personal network played a major role in determining one's place in the sociopolitical system." See Behnam, *op. cit.*, p. 102.

21. Upton, *op. cit.*, pp. 29–30.

22. *Ibid.*, p. 30.

23. George B. Baldwin, "The Foreign-educated Iranian," *Middle East Journal* (17/3), quoted in Beeman, *op. cit.*, p. 24. It would, however, be a mistake to assume that these qualities are uniquely Iranian; astute Western politicians will recognize many devices here that are part of any skilled politician's repertoire. The point is that in Iran they are raised to a higher level of art form.

24. See John Simpson, *Inside Iran* (New York: St. Martin's Press, 1988), p. 177.

25. The persistent celebration of the key Iranian holiday *Now-Ruz*, or New Year, is a distinctly pre-Islamic phenomenon, for example, but the Islamic Republic has not been able to root it out.

26. Miklos, *op. cit.*, p. 60.

2

Iran and Iraq:
The Battleground of Cultures

The splendid golden dome [in Qarbala, Iraq] with beautiful minarets was soon matched by a blue dome which looked out of place among mudbrick huts. . . . The caravan was greeted by a strange motley crowd. Ragged Arabs; men with dull faces, wearing fezes; turbaned men with shrewd faces, shaved heads, henna colored beards and nails, telling their beads, walking around in sandals, loose cotton pants and long tunics. Persian, Turkish and guttural Arabic spoken from the depth of the throat and entrails deafened the ear. The Arab women had dirty tattooed faces and inflamed eyes, and wore rings in their noses. A mother had forced half her black breast into the mouth of the dirty baby in her arms. . . . In front of the coffee house an Arab was picking his nose and rubbing the dirt out from between his toes. His face was covered with flies and lice crawled all over his head.
> —Sadegh Hedayat, "Seeking Absolution," an Iranian traveler's
> unflattering description of his pilgrimage to Iraq, 1932[1]

We start our examination of Iran's relationship with the surrounding world with a look at Iraq, the country with which Iran has so recently been locked in long and bloody conflict. Geopolitics have placed Iraq at the front line between the world of the Persian and the world of the Arab. Despite major influences of each culture upon the other in historical times, ethnic and cultural feelings of hostility still run deep, heightened by modern nationalism. As both Iran and Iraq overthrew their respective monarchies and became revolutionary states within twenty years of each other, the infusion of ideology into the process each time has exacerbated the rivalry yet further.

The seeds of permanent conflict today lie most particularly in border disputes of over 100-years standing—where mutual antipathies seem to deny permanent resolution; in the existence of a Shi'ite majority in Iraq, which has centuries-old organic ties with Iran, serving as a permanent source of friction between Baghdad and Tehran; and in the Kurdish minority in both countries which serves as levers

34

of subversion for each state against the other—but in which Iran enjoys the advantage.

Ancient and enduring rivalry between these two cultural regions will be perpetuated in dispute over Gulf leadership/security issues and oil politics. In principle, issues of common concern and a common search for stability could help unite the policies of Iran and Iraq in the region, but friction and conflict are more likely to dominate the character of bilateral relations. Both Iran and Iraq could be headed for greater internal instability as a result of internal minorities. For Iraq, any move by the Shi'ite majority there toward greater political voice or democratic participation in the future raises the spectacle of a majority Shi'ite government— a first in the Arab world with major implications for the region.

After its defeat in the Iran-Iraq War, Iran seemed destined to a long period of subordination to a resurgent Iraq. The Gulf War changed all that, however. Iraq's destruction hastened by at least five years Iran's return to a position of natural dominance in the Gulf and as the natural counterbalance to any Iraqi bid for hegemony.

The Cultural Conflict

Iraq as the Cultural Frontier

The borderlands between Semitic and Persian cultures, the longest and most consistent clash point over the millennia for Iran, lie today between Iran and Iraq. This confrontation point of cultures has grown in intensity as both countries have moved toward increasingly nationalist forms of political expression.

Yet, the turf over which this cultural conflict takes place is not well delineated. We are not talking about mere border problems, endemic in any case to many Middle Eastern states. The peoples of these two cultures have inevitably been cast into intimate relationships together in the past—sometimes in the form of dominance of one over the other, sometimes as a condominium—with each deeply influenced by the other. Such cultural intertwining often exacerbates and complicates the cultural conflict, as it does today. At the popular level, most Persians have long nourished a strong antipathy toward Iraqi Arabs—the above literary passage suggesting something of the visceral and racially oriented attitudes of Persians toward Arabs in general.

Mesopotamia—"The Land Between the Rivers"

The great cultures of Mesopotamia—present-day Iraq—impressed themselves upon Iran from the earliest times when Iranians lived next door to the great empires of Babylonia and Assyria. Later, as the renowned Persian conqueror Cyrus the Great and his successors in the mid-sixth century B.C. established the first "universal empire" of the world—the vast Achaemenid Empire reaching from Greece to India at one point— the land that is now Iraq fell under Persian domination. But Mesopotamia in turn lent to the Achaemenids institutions and even cultural trappings that helped "universalize" the nature of Persian Achaemenid rule—a dialectical interaction that Iranians are uncomfortable to acknowledge.

One thousand years later, in the wake of the politically and psychologically shattering Arab/Islamic conquest of the great Persian Sassanian dynasty, Arab and Persian once again found themselves linked in a new symbiosis. On this occasion a conquered Iran eventually impressed itself so heavily upon the newly emerging Islamo-Arab culture that many Iranians boast that in the end it was Iranian culture that "conquered" the Perso-Arab Abbasid Caliphate. Indeed, the Abbasid Caliphate—the preeminent caliphate of all Islamic history in its long-term formative impact—established its capital in Baghdad, all the while drawing many of its chief cultural and administrative features from the institutions of the previous Persian Sassanian Empire.

This period, coupled with the later medieval heyday of Islamic culture in Persian-dominated Central Asia, represents some of the high points of world Islamic culture, founded upon this fusion of Iranian and Arab culture. Poetry, arts, music, philosophy, historiography, and administrative institutions—central to the basic legacy of Islamic civilization—owe their origins to this cultural fusion.

But cultural fusion in the past is not a formula for cordiality between the two states in the age of nationalism. The language of the Iran-Iraq War, particularly from the Iraqi side, constantly invoked the symbolism of seventh-century Arab-Persian military confrontation—the battle of Qadisiyah in 636—in which Arab Islam first breached the gates of the Persian world. Iraq still uses this symbolism to characterize the contemporary struggle, speaking of a "modern Qadisiyah." The cultural clash will not easily fade, especially when it is further fueled by other frictions, discussed below.

The Religious Conflict

If the cultural borders between what was Persian and what was Arab had ever been at all distinct, Islam thus blurred them. On the one hand, Islam provided a shared religious ideology for nearly a thousand years that had not existed between them before. On the other hand, the picture grew more complex as these same marchlands of Mesopotamia early on in Islamic history became the cradle of the newly emergent heterodox

sect of Shi'ite Islam. We easily overlook the fact, with our close identification of the Iranian state with Shi'ism, that Iran did not formally
become a Shi'ite state until as late as the early sixteenth century when
the faith was officially adopted by the zealous new Safavid dynasty of
Iran. To be sure, Shi'ism early on had found adherents in the lands of
Persia—as one of the many heterodox faiths that regularly flourished
there—but it was not the official faith, much less the majority faith,
until Shah Isma'il imposed it upon the people in 1500.

With this momentous formal embrace of Shi'ism, Iran in effect closed
itself off from much of the rest of the Islamic world. Indeed, the very
choice of Shi'ism as the national faith was partly conceived as an
ideological force to distinguish it from its Ottoman Turkish rival. Safavid
Iran proceeded to engage in territorial and religious wars with the
Ottoman Empire for the next hundred years or so, bolstering its own
distinct religious identity that would place it in conflict with most of
its Sunni neighbors, including most of what is now Sunni-dominated
Iraq. Intellectually as well, Iran's Shi'ite faith served to close off fertile
Persian minds to intellectual trends in the broader Sunni Muslim world
and to develop ideological rigidities of outlook that did not serve the
state well.

Historical Issues of Conflict Between
Iraq and Iran

Apart from the historic cultural tensions of the borderland area, a
number of more concrete major issues have recurred in the relations
between the two states in the modern period as a legacy of geopolitics.

Iraq and the Shi'ite Connection

Even though the Iranian identity has become inextricably linked with
Shi'ism, history has nonetheless determined that the very centerpieces
of Persian Shi'ite faith—the two most holy cities of Shi'ite culture, Najaf
and Qarbala—were fated to remain on Iraqi soil. Pilgrimage to these
holy cities and shrines—which in emotional terms for a Shi'ite is more
important than pilgrimage to Mecca—plays a central role in the expression
of Shi'ite faith. But Iranian pilgrimage to the Shi'ite shrines of Iraq
remains hostage to this day to the political climate between the two
states.

If history dealt the holy Shi'ite shrines to Iraq, Iraqi political life has
also been immeasurably complicated through the existence of a Shi'ite
majority in Iraq itself. Although this large Shi'ite grouping—some 60
percent of the Iraqi population—is primarily Arab, its feelings toward

Shi'ite Iran are both intimate and ambivalent. Although Arabs rarely share much love for Persians, the second-class status of the Shi'ites in Iraq in modern times has further encouraged them to orient their religious, intellectual, and even much of their political life toward Iran.

Indeed, the several holy Shi'ite cities of Iraq have produced a flowering of Shi'ite culture and thought that is central to Shi'ism as a whole. It was the Shi'ites who brought an otherwise backwater Iraqi province of the Ottoman Empire into prominence and distinction during the last three hundred years. Shi'ite clerics in Iraq were intimately connected with Iranian politics and were accepted as possessing important theological and political clout in Iranian affairs by the shahs themselves.[2] Indeed, many of the clerics were themselves Persian, or of Persian origin, and Persian blood continues to be common among the Iraqi Shi'a community. The Shi'ite culture of Iran simply cannot be cordoned off from the Shi'ite culture of Iraq. It is no accident that Ayatollah Khomeini himself moved to Najaf in Iraq in 1965 soon after his expulsion by the shah. Residence there was the next best thing to full political participation in Iranian politics from inside Iran—which is why the shah ultimately persuaded Saddam Husayn to expel Khomeini from Iraq as well.

The major stature of Iraqi Shi'a in Iraqi intellectual life naturally led them into a prominent role in the Iraqi nationalist struggle for independence, following the emergence of Iraq as a new state after World War I. Iraqi Shi'a were adamant in their opposition to the establishment of a British mandate over Iraq in the early 1920s and led a revolt against it. Shi'ite opposition to the British, led by the Shi'ite clergy, was far more outspoken than the Sunni opposition, which was more inclined to reach a modus vivendi with the British. Iran itself also denied Iraq political recognition as an independent country for nearly nine years following the establishment of Iraqi statehood, until the special privileges for foreigners in Iraq were abolished. The British viewed the Shi'a in Iraq as politically obstreperous, and, indeed, the Shi'a refused to participate in elections for a number of years, believing that Iraq under British mandate was a captive country. The British were periodically forced to exile many Shi'ite religious figures, some of whom were of Persian origin.[3]

Only after Iraq achieved independence in 1932 did the Shi'a begin to participate more fully in internal Iraqi politics, but they had already set a pattern for their future political isolation, stemming from their earlier nonparticipation. To be sure, many Shi'a were rural, tribal, and uneducated, as was the bulk of the Iraqi population. But an educated, politically sophisticated leadership of the Shi'ite community continued to play important activist roles in Iraqi politics, believing that their majority status should bestow upon them a greater national leadership role. Indeed, the Shi'a made distinct progress under the Iraqi monarchy (1921–1958) in improving their national position and even their degree of participation in politics, but the trend was not to continue.[4] With the series of revolutionary regimes in Baghdad starting in 1958, the Shi'a soon came to face a more *general exclusion* from Iraqi politics, thus heightening the major Shi'a-Sunni tensions that exist to this day. (Many of the Shi'a youth turned against the Ba'th party by joining the Communist Party of Iraq, but many others moved in the direction of Islamic fundamentalism.)[5]

Intellectual ferment among the Shi'a community burgeoned under the adversity of revolutionary, Sunni-dominated governments after 1958. Feeling a need to rise to the challenge of secular revolutionary ideology of the Ba'th party and the attractions of the Iraqi Communist party to young Shi'a, the clergy broke several decades of political silence to articulate its own alternative religious/ideological vision, most notably through the writings of Shi'ite leader Muhammad Baqr al-Sadr. Al-Sadr's writings place him clearly in the mainstream of modern Shi'ite thinking, directly linked with the Shi'ite intellectual trends underway in Iran as well—demonstrating the continuing importance of the Iraqi Shi'a in the broader Shi'ite intellectual world. Although the Shi'ite call aimed at attracting both Sunnis and Shi'a through a more universalistic message of Islam, in the end the Shi'a movement in Iraq was still perceived by most Iraqi Sunnis as essentially Shi'a in character and thus never drew significant support outside the Shi'a community—a problem nearly all Shi'ite activists have encountered everywhere, as we shall see.[6]

The Iran-Iraq War was a period of even more severe testing for the Iraqi Shi'a. The critical question mark was how they would respond when torn between conflicting loyalties to the Iraqi state and Arabness on the one hand, and religious and cultural ties to Iran on the other. Historically in the Middle East, religious ties have generally proven at least as potent as a binding social/political force as have ethnic ties. In any case, the Iraqi state under Ba'th party control did not wait to find out. Leading elements of the Shi'ite community were brutally intimidated by arrests, expulsions, and executions, including the execution in April 1980 of the leading Shi'ite leader himself, Muhammad Baqr al-Sadr, and members of his family. Harsh and peremptory actions by Iraqi security forces left little doubt of the punishment that the state would mete out to any upon whom the shadow of possible disloyalty might fall. Tens, perhaps hundreds, of thousands of Iraqi Shi'a were either expelled or fled from the country,[7] many of them Iraqis of either Persian origin or assimilated. At the same time—employing a little carrot along with a heavy dose of stick—Iraqi President Saddam Husayn undertook to improve the quality of life and share of the national budget for the major Iraqi Shi'ite cities, including the Holy Shrine cities. In addition, a number of Shi'ites acceptable to the Ba'th party were brought into the Ba'th government—but never in such a way as to challenge Ba'thi principles or Sunni dominance of the state.

The Iran-Iraq War provided some indicators about the character of the Iraqi Shi'a, who make up the majority of the enlisted men in the army; the Shi'ite community did, in the end, maintain basic public loyalty to the Iraqi regime, whatever their private feelings may have been. The penalties for treasonous activity during the war of course left no room for ambiguity. Shi'ite opposition had all but ceased after 1981. But the Ba'th regime will have to recognize that it was the Shi'a foot soldiers of Iraq—the majority of the enlisted ranks—who gave their blood for Saddam Husayn's regime, fighting against their Persian co-religionists. They are owed a considerable debt for their sacrifice to a regime they basically find unpalatable.

But will the Iraqi regime recognize the necessity of making major political concessions to the Shi'ite community by allowing it more of the major voice the Shi'a believe they deserve in Iraqi affairs? That community will always offer openings to Iran to serve as a vehicle of influence in Iraqi politics. It cannot be otherwise; the two are too organically linked. This connection is the genuine dilemma for the Iraqi state, especially as long as it is dominated by a tiny, narrow, harshly authoritarian Sunni political elite.

The struggle is far from over. If and when Iraqi Shi'ites start to press again for a more prominent political role, Iran will not stay aloof. The several hundred thousand Iraqi Shi'ite activists still resident in Iran from the start of the war will be significant instruments in the future Shi'ite movement in Iraq.[8] Many of them are organized into the "Supreme Assembly of the Iraqi Revolution in Iraq" (SAIRI), which remained poised in the wings during the Iran-Iraq War to take over in Iraq in the event of an Iranian victory. These elements provide a sure recipe for continuing mutual interference in each other's affairs and future political conflict between the two countries.

Following the defeat of Baghdad in the 1991 Gulf War, Saddam Husayn was mortally wounded politically; domestic and international pressures led inevitably to his fall. Domestic Iraqi demand for even broader change in regime is also growing. Iraq has distinguished itself over the past twenty years as the harshest and most rigid political system in the Arab world—even toward the Sunni population. Those qualities were exacerbated by the long war with Iran. No liberalization will emerge without at least the fall of Saddam Husayn and his coterie and requires thoroughgoing perestroika within the Ba'th party itself. Should liberalization occur, the legitimate participation of the Shi'a community in Iraqi politics will be high on the list of priorities. But will greater voice in Iraqi politics in the end help bind the Shi'ite political identity to the Sunni-dominated Iraqi regime? Can this community help improve and normalize relations with Iran, or will they become a pawn in the struggle for regional dominance between the two states? The best guess is that politics in Iraq have not yet evolved to the point where the Iraqi Shi'a will be "trusted" to be loyal and to where Iran will not view them as a natural fifth column to be manipulated. Stirrings among the Iraqi Shi'a will in any case be one of the major inevitable events in postwar Iraq and a central issue in the relations between the two countries.

Several factors will influence the Iraqi Shi'a's role as a potential fifth column. First, the adoption of representative democracy in Iraq would go a long way toward settling Shi'ite grievances. Although the Ba'th has claimed that its ideology of nonsectarian nationalism will meet the Shi'a's demand for equality of opportunity, the Ba'th has never represented a genuinely democratic force. True equality for the Shi'a can only emerge through democracy. Yet genuine democracy poses the Sunni elite with a harsh dilemma, for the electoral power of the Shi'a majority will be considerable. Indeed, open elections will enable the Shi'a to dominate the Iraqi political scene, very possibly introducing considerable Iranian influence into Iraqi politics. Democracy over the longer run is likely to play a highly *destabilizing role* in Iraqi politics until the two religious communities attain some new, freely arrived at modus vivendi, far removed from the brutal authoritarianism of the past.

If Saddam Husayn and the Ba'th party are dealt a setback or destroyed as a result of the U.S.-led war against Iraq's seizure of Kuwait, the prospects for Iraqi instability and Shi'ite political influence there will automatically increase. The actions of a Shi'ite majority in Iraq will have untold consequences on the Iraqi political system and will probably usher in a period of intense Sunni-Shi'a struggle for power that has largely been suppressed under harsh authoritarian Ba'thi rule. The Shi'ite majority in Iraq will surely attempt to dominate Iraqi state policies. The potential impact of these developments cannot be underestimated.

Conversely, the religious role of the Holy Cities of Najaf and Qarbala may diminish or change character. Najaf, once the undisputed center of learning for the Shi'ite world, has declined somewhat due to its extreme isolation from Iran over the past decade of war. Similarly, many of its most-distinguished Persian clergy have been expelled. The importance of the Iranian religious city of Qom has correspondingly risen over the past decade, and it now rivals Najaf in many respects. Lastly, there is not full accord among Iraqi Shi'a with Khomeini's vision of the Iranian Republic, especially on the question of the direct rule of the clergy (*Velayat-e-Faqih*)—just as there is far from universal support for this concept even among the Iranian clergy themselves.[9] Theological differences may thus grow between the two sides. But in the end, the organic linkage of the two communities remains. How it evolves will depend most directly upon the policies of the Iraqi regime itself.

Iran must be extremely circumspect in counting on the Iraqi Shi'a to actually tilt policy in favor of Iran at some time in the future. Although cultural and religious ties will always remain important, the Iraqi Shi'a are Arab as well as Shi'a and will not wish to be taken for granted by leaders in Tehran. In the end this Shi'a connection will probably prove more destabilizing than constructive between Iran and Iraq. The Shi'a community is destined to play a key role in the interplay of relations between the two great rivals of the upper Persian Gulf, as the classic Arab-Persian conflict continues to play itself out into its third millennium.

The Arab Minority in Iranian Khuzestan

If Iraq is vulnerable to its suppressed Shi'a majority, Iran's own ethnic vulnerability was also directly tested through Iraqi attempts to suborn the Arab population of the Iranian province of Khuzestan during the Iraqi invasion at the outset of the war. Khuzestan (often referred to by Arabs as "Arabistan") contains both a high percentage of ethnic Arabs as well as most of Iran's key oil installations—all in the vicinity of the Iraqi border opposite the Shatt al-'Arab waterway. Although separatist Arab nationalist sentiment has long been present in Khuzestan, and has been manipulated first by the British and later by the Iraqis as a pressure point against Tehran, the Arab population of Khuzestan in recent times has been sharply diminishing in proportion to an influx of Persian population, the latter playing an ever-larger role in the region as it develops.[10] Despite some Iranian doubts about the loyalty of the Arab population, the Iranian Arabs of Khuzestan were quiescent during the Iraqi invasion in the early days of the Iran-Iraq War. It would appear that this Arab minority element will probably no longer be a significant instrument in the relations between the two countries. In a sense this is heartening, for it suggests that at least some historical problems of ethnic enclaves do continue to move toward de facto resolution with the assimilation of the minority population in question. Most larger minority conflicts in the region are not moving in that direction, however.

Border Issues

Border problems furnish a permanent geopolitical backdrop to the relations between the two countries. These border disputes predate the modern Iran-Iraq struggle, going back at least to contention between

Iran and the Ottoman overlords who ruled Iraq for several hundred years. But border disputes basically *reflect* the broader geopolitical tensions between two power centers rather than create them. The chief border problem involves particularly important strategic interests for Iraq: dispute over the Shatt al-'Arab waterway.

Iraq's overwhelming geostrategic vulnerability is its largely landlocked character, with only some fifteen kilometers of access to the Persian Gulf. The Shatt al-'Arab river—the Arabic name significantly revealing its borderland character, "the Arab shoreline"—is the confluence and delta of the Tigris and Euphrates rivers down to the Gulf. It constitutes Iraq's sole lifeline of navigation between the Gulf and Iraq's interior. It also represents the border between the two countries for at least the first sixty kilometers up from the Gulf. Iraq sees its strategic lifeline as permanently vulnerable, hostage to good relations with Iran. Indeed, the Iran-Iraq War vividly fulfilled geopolitical speculation about Iraqi dependence upon this waterway, for it was militarily denied to Iraq as an outlet promptly at the beginning of the war. The desire to rectify this vulnerability played a decisive role in Saddam's calculations to annex Kuwait in 1990.

The complex history of the dispute dates back at least to Ottoman-Persian negotiations of 1639 and has periodically served as grist for dispute and negotiations right down to the outbreak of the Iran-Iraq War. Although long treaties set forth in immense detail aspects of mutual rights and obligations in sharing this strategic waterway, the heart of the issue is whether Iraq's heavy dependence on the waterway in fact justifies its insistence that the whole river—rather than a division at the *thalweg*, or central channel—should lie under Iraqi control.

In times of "normal" friction between the two states, minor strategic advantage might be derived from Iraq's sole possession of the waterway: Iraqi goodwill would be required for Iran to transit the Shatt. Such in fact has been the case during some periods of the dispute in the past. In the event of real war or military confrontation, however, *legal rights* to portions of the river make little difference—as the Iran-Iraq War has demonstrated. Even if Iran were to accept Iraqi legal control of the Shatt, Tehran is entirely capable of closing down at any time Iraqi access to the Shatt by military force. Indeed, once the shooting war ended, Iraq's first postwar demand to Iran in negotiations was full possession of the river. Yet Saddam in the fall of 1990 proved astonishingly willing to give up all his "gains" of the Iran-Iraq War—including demands for full control of the Shatt—in his effort to neutralize Iran as a potential anti-Iraqi force during the Kuwaiti confrontation. Apparently concerned that Iran could exploit Iraqi preoccupation in Kuwait to regain those small areas of Iranian territory held by Iraq at the end of the war,

Saddam gave them all up in return for a peace settlement. Saddam apparently also calculated that his new "acquisition" of Kuwait would more than make up for any ceding of demands to all of the Shatt.

The question of the Shatt—possession, access, control, and usage—has now been "settled" and resettled for over 140 years of contested negotiations and will probably be a bone of contention between Iran and Iraq long into the future. Each side will strive to gain maximum legal rights so as best to serve its interests and establish legal grounds for action if violations and further disputes occur. But Iraq has already reached the bitter conclusion that it can no longer permit its security to remain hostage to its previously limited access to the sea. Iraq's use of the Shatt will always remain at the mercy of Iran when military conflict arises. Indeed, Iraq threatened in the 1988 negotiations to actually reroute the Shatt away from the border so as to keep it entirely within Iraqi territory. The cost of such a venture is unknown and it would surely constitute a *casus belli* for Iran. Iran may claim that free access to the Shatt is critical to its own important cities of Khorramshahr and Abadan, but Iran does at least enjoy numerous other ports all along the Gulf that provide strategic alternatives in the event the Shatt is closed due to hostilities. This is just one feature of the immense geostrategic advantages that Iran enjoys over Iraq and that makes Iran's role the central one in Gulf politics in the future.

A critical question of the 1990 Kuwaiti crisis was whether Iraq would gain increased access to the Gulf at the expense of Kuwaiti territory in any resolution of the conflict. Saddam's overreaching ambition lost him the chance to achieve border adjustments that would have affected Iraq's Gulf access and reduced the strategic importance of the Shatt. Iran, furthermore, will always strongly oppose any such a gain by Iraq because it would permanently strengthen Iraq's geopolitical position in the Gulf.

Both countries are in fact seeking to limit strategic dependence upon the Shatt by establishing further sets of alternative pipelines and routes to diminish exposure of their respective cities and facilities. The Shatt's strategic importance in the calculations of each may therefore diminish for the first time in several centuries.

The Kurdish Issue

The Kurds are one of the last major ethnic groups in the Middle East who have not yet successfully established a serious, sustained, united political movement able to command international attention in the way the Palestinian movement has. A key factor inhibiting international attention to the Kurdish struggle is the massively destabilizing character of the problem. Any "resolution" of the Kurdish problem that called

for the creation of a Kurdish state would be catastrophic to the territory
and interests of at least two states—Turkey and Iraq—and a serious
blow to the territorial integrity of Iran.

- For Iraq, a Kurdish state would include the greater part of Iraq's
  oil fields.
- For Turkey, a Kurdish state would involve the loss of nearly all of
  southeastern Turkey.
- For Iran, the territorial loss would be relatively slightly less than
  for Turkey or Iraq, mainly representing economically marginal,
  though sizeable, territory in northwest Iran. Kurdish separatism
  would open up, however, other ethnic separatist issues in Iran.

The Kurdish issue need not automatically constitute an irresolvable
bilateral problem between Iran and Iraq. The Kurds represent a primarily
domestic problem to the government of each state as each struggles
with demands for Kurdish autonomous rights. But in periods of tension
between the two countries, the Kurds represent an instant lever of
influence capable of creating chaos within the borders of the other. The
"Kurdish card," however, lies more in Iranian hands than in Iraqi. By
virtue of population size and the location of the Kurdish population in
the key oil-producing zones of Iraq, Iranian manipulation of the Iraqi
Kurds is vastly more costly to Iraq than the converse: Iraqi manipulation
of Iranian Kurds.

The shah very successfully exploited the Iraqi Kurds in his struggle
against Iraq between 1972 and 1975, inflicting losses of 16,000 Iraqi
soldiers and creating some 60,000 civilian casualties. Once Iranian support
was withdrawn, however, the Iraqis were able to achieve the surrender
of most of the Kurdish rebels within two weeks, even if they could not
put the problem to rest.[11] Indeed, the causes of the rebellion were in
no way resolved by Iraqi military victory—on the contrary, resentment
ran deeper than ever and the Kurds simply awaited another day and
another external benefactor to help them pursue their cause. The shah's
precedent was not too mean for the ayatollah to turn to: Tehran strongly
supported Kurdish resistance inside Iraq during the Iran-Iraq War, enabling
the Iraqi Kurds to make immense territorial gains against Baghdad and
serving as a constant thorn in the side of the Iraqi army operations in
the border areas.

The Kurdish issue not surprisingly emerged again after Saddam
Husayn's defeat in the Gulf War, with uprisings occurring spontaneously
all over Iraqi Kurdistan. Iran reportedly assisted the Kurds as well as
a simultaneous Shi'ite uprising in southern Iraq that was crushed in
March 1991. The establishment of "temporary" enclaves in northern

Iraq by U.S. and international forces to protect the Kurds provides powerful impetus for the development of Kurdish autonomy in the future. Kurdish-Shi'a cooperation against Baghdad—ineffectual to date—will likewise remain a potentially effective instrument to oppose continued Ba'thi rule.

The "Kurdish card" will always be present for Iran to employ against Iraq as long as hostile relations exist between the two. Iran will probably seek to maintain some level of active ties to the Kurdish resistance in Iraq in order to keep its Persian Gulf rival preoccupied. Only in the event of genuine reconciliation between Baghdad and Tehran would the Iranians likely withdraw all support from the Iraqi Kurds—until the next round of conflict between Iran and Iraq.

The Kurdish issue in the meantime is growing more complicated. The late twentieth century, with its growth of education and communications, has ironically fostered more, not less, nationalism, religiosity, localism, and particularism. The Kurds would be a remarkable exception if their movement does not grow in intensity in the coming decades. For the first time, Kurds from all three countries—Iraq, Iran, and Turkey—are now traveling abroad in greater numbers than ever before for education. Tens of thousands are employed in many different European countries such as Germany, Austria, Denmark, and Sweden. They are encountering each other in the free environments of Europe and the United States in ways not possible in their home states. They now have opportunity to discuss their common cause and their particular grievances in each of their countries of origin. Kurds are now producing books, propaganda, research on Kurdish national questions, and are beginning the process of raising an overall Kurdish national consciousness that cuts between states. Kurdish workers, forbidden education in their own language in Turkey, can now educate their children in Kurdish in Swedish schools.

This nationalist dynamic is likely to be on the upswing. Nationalist grievances and aspirations will be whetted by European and American interest in human rights—in which Iran, Iraq, or Turkey are not likely to come out very well. Turkey in particular will suffer here because of its application to the European Economic Community (EEC) and its membership in NATO. EEC ties provide further opportunity for human rights charges to be leveled against Turkey, particularly in the United States where Armenian and Greek communities, already hostile to Turkey, will be quick once again to exploit this issue against Turkey in Congress.

Will Iran continue to exploit the Kurdish issue against Iraq in light of the potential risks to Iran itself from its own Kurdish population? Iran can actually manipulate the Kurdish issue with probably only limited cost to its own Kurdish problem. Of the three countries, Iran is most easily able to handle the Kurdish issue and even to move toward some kind of reasonable autonomy solution that will elude the other two states. This is another permanent Iranian geopolitical advantage over Iraq.

The Political Environment of Conflict

The relationship between Iran and Iraq differs considerably with the *type* of regime in power in each state. More deeply rooted areas of friction can be overlooked, finessed, or even "solved" when the two states seek to avoid confrontation and focus on their respective internal agenda. Yet these same issues can spearhead major conflict or even provide a *casus belli* if one of the states suddenly perceives an interest in engaging in sharpened rivalry or challenge to the other. In the modern period, that is, since Iraq became an independent and sovereign state, we can identify at least three strikingly distinct phases that produced a very different dynamic in the bilateral relationship: monarchy in both countries (1920s–1958); radical Iraq versus conservative Iran (1958–1978); radicals in power in both Iraq and Iran (1978–present).

Monarchy in Both States

With monarchy at the helm in both states, relations between the two were probably at an optimal level. Both Reza Shah and King Faysal of Iraq in the 1930s believed in the value of good neighbor relations in order to get on with domestic issues. Conflict in no way involved challenge to the other's legitimacy or existence, but rather dealt with more concrete border issues. Ideology was almost nonexistent; therefore in this period most issues were susceptible to relatively peaceful resolution. National antipathies toward one another were not absent, they were simply not exploited.

The generally harmonious bilateral relations of this era were reflected in the reaching of several settlements: settlement after three years of constant negotiation of border differences in 1937; the signing of the important multilateral Sa'dabad Pact (8 July 1937) among Iran, Turkey, Iraq, and Afghanistan providing for mutual security guarantees and mutual support in stamping out subversion from any foreign quarter.

An interesting feature of this period is that Iraq did *not* feel its Arab ties were incompatible with good ties with Iran. Arab nationalism had not yet attained its forceful, radical character that placed it on a collision course with Iranian ambitions in the decade after World War II.

In the post–World War II period, Iran's relations with Iraq maintained the same even keel, with both countries joining in the five-power Baghdad Pact for mutual and regional defense in 1955. On this occasion, however, Iraqi nationalist sentiment was deeply concerned that the pact had overtones hostile to Arab nationalism. Iraq's decision was strongly opposed by Egypt and other Arab states, but the Iraqi monarchist government of that time prevailed and objections were overcome.

In the period of joint monarchy, therefore, Iran's relations with Iraq were relatively harmonious. This situation reflected both states' desire for internal development, cooperation against regional threats, and an overall philosophical approach that did not seek confrontation. Conservative elites sought to protect both their positions and the stability of the social order. A pro-Western "old guard" was in power in Iraq that fitted comfortably with the world outlook of Reza Shah and Mohammed Reza Shah at the time. Public economic aspirations were still unwhetted by rising expectations. Monarchy tended to mask undercurrents of nationalist antipathy between the two countries. But all this was to change with the revolution in Iraq which sharply altered the tone of regional politics.

The Fall of the Iraqi Monarchy

A coup in Iraq in 1958 overthrew the monarchy and changed overnight Iraq's orientation. The new policies were anti-Western and far more in harmony with the broad Arab nationalist sentiments sweeping the Arab world. Iraq's interests swung away from its Levantine orientation and turned sharply toward the Gulf region, bringing Arab nationalist ideology to a Gulf state for the first time. Iran was quick to spot the challenge—which arose quickly with Iraqi territorial claims over Kuwait in 1961. With the ascension of the Pan-Arab socialist Ba'th party to power in Baghdad briefly in 1963—and then permanently in 1968—Iran was faced with a new power in the Gulf capable of challenging Iran's own ambitions.

But the shock of the Iraqi revolution was only the beginning. The unexpected announcement in 1968 of Britain's intentions to withdraw forces from the Gulf formed the single greatest catalyst to increased rivalry between Iran and Iraq to assume the British mantle of power. Hegemony in the Gulf had been the exclusive preserve of foreign powers—mainly European—for several centuries. Now the Gulf was up for grabs among the regional forces, with the United States uncertain about where its own role lay. Iran was determined to assert its "historic rights" and stabilizing mission in the Gulf while Baghdad trumpeted its calling to support nationalist revolution and to preserve the "Arabness of the Gulf." Rising tides of nationalism on the Arab side lent greater fervor to the issue. The ingredients of a longer term, modern, nationalist-ideological clash were now injected into the geostrategic rivalry.

Among the ingredients of this clash between Tehran and Baghdad were oil rivalries and the stability of the small Arab shaykhdoms. Iraq perceived Iran as possessing expansionist ambitions in the Gulf and serving as an anti-Arab nationalist, generally pro-Western force in regional politics, all the while maintaining ties with Israel. Iraq and Egypt spoke of liberating the Arab population of Iranian Khuzestan. And the shah was engaged in devoting vast portions of the national income to arming Iran with state-of-the-art Western weaponry. In short, sharp ideological differences, combined with increasingly ambitious military capabilities on both sides, significantly raised the level of confrontation between Baghdad and Tehran. The growth of nationalist sentiment in the region and the greater role of mass movements in Arab politics unquestionably also sharpened the Baghdad-Tehran confrontation.

Despite nearly two decades of conflict between revolutionary Baghdad and monarchical Iran, relations did tend to improve on the tactical level after the 1975 Algiers agreement settled outstanding issues between them, especially on the Shatt al-'Arab and the Kurdish issue. Iraq in particular had to recognize that it needed to settle with the shah, end the debilitating Kurdish conflict that the shah had supported, and bring some stability to the internal Iraqi scene. Both states sought to avoid further overt bilateral conflict and there was some consultation on security issues in the Gulf. But the relationship was basically uneasy. Although neither side sought actual war with the other, the ingredients for conflict were growing with the ambitions of the two states. Iraq's regional clout was expanding and it was playing an increasingly larger part in oil politics as its new reserves began to thrust it potentially out ahead of Iran as a producer. By 1978 Iraq was bidding for leadership of the Arab world by leading the campaign that expelled Sadat's Egypt (and close ally of the shah) from the Arab world for what was termed the Camp David sellout of the Arab cause. If bilateral issues between Iran and Iraq had been temporarily laid to rest, serious geopolitical rivalry for dominance in the Gulf was still inherent in the relationship. And Iraq remained one of the key torchbearers of radical ideology in the Arab world.

But tensions were to rise still higher, for Tehran in 1979 was to undergo its own revolution that injected powerful new doses of Shi'ism, Iranian nationalism, and genuine mass movement into the struggle. Populist ideologies and mass movements by their very existence seem to be invariable progenitors of heightened conflict in the region.

The Iranian Revolution

In 1979 Iran was seized with not one but two extraordinary events in the history of the modern Middle East: a genuine popular revolution, toppling 2,500 years of Persian monarchy, and the establishment of the region's first Islamic Republic, headed by clerics. Both events unleashed forces in Iran which were to have major impact on the region, and most immediately upon Iraq. For yet one more Middle Eastern state had crossed the divide from monarchy to revolutionary ideological populism, accompanied by all the wrenching challenges to neighbors and dislocations to the Middle East state system that this phenomenon has regularly invoked. (Similar systemic upheavals took place after coups—not revolutions—that led to the fall of monarchy in Egypt to Nasser in 1952, the fall King Idriss to Qadhafi in Libya in 1969, and the fall of the Iraqi monarchy to Qasim in 1958.)

Renewed confrontation between Iran and Iraq did not instantly come with the fall of the shah. Indeed, Iran's early nationalist government of Bazargan started off with positive public statements about new bilateral relations. And Iraq, at the outset of the revolution, was delighted with Iran's withdrawal from the Central Treaty Organization (CENTO), the breaking of Iran's ties with Israel, and its move toward nonalignment. However, the seeds of ideological collision had now been laid even if it had not yet flowered. The real collision loomed with the actual accession of the radical clergy into power.[12] Khomeini's powerful personal and ideological crusade against Ba'thist Iraq was a key ingredient leading to the outbreak of war.

But the conflict far transcended Khomeini's personal views. We have noted above the unstable character of Iran-Iraq relations before the fall of the shah and the centrality of the Iraqi Shi'a to the clergy. In the end almost any new revolutionary regime in Iran would have probably hastened the grand showdown between the two Gulf superpowers over the struggle for hegemony in the region—especially with so many newly emergent small Gulf shaykhdoms as objects of rivalry for control. (These issues will be discussed in greater depth in the next chapters.) Common views between Baghdad and Tehran toward important questions like CENTO, Israel, and nonalignment were simply irrelevant in the context of national rivalry. Indeed, both states became rivals for the same banner of radical regional leadership. This situation strongly suggests that radical national states contiguous to each other are not likely to be long united by common ideological purpose. Radical states in the Middle East have generally demonstrated more competition among them than unity of purpose. (Conflict between revolutionary Egypt and Libya, revolutionary Egypt and Syria, revolutionary Egypt and Iraq, revolutionary Syria and Iraq, revolutionary Libya and Algeria, and so on, are examples of this phenomenon.) Thus, in the absence of any overwhelming common enemy between Iran and Iraq, the historical relations between these two states, bolstered by internal revolutionary regimes, were bound to produce some kind of heightened rivalry, inevitably leading to showdown.

Rivalry Down the Gulf

In sum, Iran's relationship with Iraq is more fraught with conflict than any other of Iran's bilateral relations. It remains the oldest cultural enmity in Iranian history and is reciprocated in Iraq's eyes. As the two most powerful states in the Gulf, both will seek to impose their stamp on the evolving character of Gulf politics, despite Iraq's defeat in the war against the United States. Gulf politics will surely be turbulent in the decades ahead as other monarchies eventually give way to republican or revolutionary governments in the various shaykhdoms. Irredentist challenges and claims are foreordained as new Gulf governments seek greater power and influence in regions with uncertain borders and a shaky sense of national unity and national entity. Economic problems will increase frustrations of downtrodden groups—particularly Shi'a elements—in these states.

Iran and Iraq cannot look with impunity upon these political struggles to come in the Gulf. Iran *under any regime* cannot remain indifferent to opportunities to extend at least moral support, if not more, to Shi'ite communities seeking to strengthen their communal position or even to come to power. It is striking that the shah felt so constrained by hostility to his own Shi'ite clergy that he could never bring himself to invoke the Shi'ite cause in his own quest for dominance in the Gulf; but the genie is now out of the bottle. No successor Iranian regime of whatever political stripe is likely to want to deprive itself of this ready-made pretext to assert Iranian interests in the Gulf—especially to refrain from exploiting the already existing fifth column.

In a similar vein, Iraq will be equally determined to prevent Iran from exploiting regional Shi'ite populations to Iranian ends, especially when Iranian success would only encourage Iraq's own Shi'ite majority to claim greater voice within Iraq. Even if Iraq adopts a far more benign policy toward the conservative Gulf states than it did in the 1960s and 1970s—when "export of the revolution" Ba'thi-style was the dominant fear in the entire Arabian Peninsula—Iraq cannot afford to watch Iran seek advantage in any Gulf turmoil. At the least Iraq will be interested in establishing some kind of local political/subversive capabilities if for no other reason than to be able to preempt pro-Iranian revolutionary activity in the name of the Ba'th or some other Arab/Sunni cause.

Oil

Oil policy will be a significant source of friction between Iran and Iraq in the future. Both states require major financial resources for reconstruction. Both will obviously have an interest in OPEC policies that maximize oil revenues. But how they will be maximized will remain the bone of contention. Iran has long protested Iraq's claim to a right to the same share of market production as Iran has, pointing out Iraq's much smaller population that suggests relatively lesser need. It was precisely over Iraq's demand that Kuwait restrain its oil production in the summer of 1990—in order to raise the price of oil—that Iraq's attack eventually took place.

Even the combined action of Iran and Iraq to restrain pumping is not sufficient in itself to help maintain prices in any case—especially if Saudi Arabia does not support the policy. The outlook thus suggests that every-man-for-himself will again be the rule after the shock effects of the Kuwaiti crisis wear off. In the next decade, as OPEC regains its old clout on the world oil market with the diminution of non-OPEC oil supply, perhaps some cooperation here might be possible. Iran has the longer record—going back to the shah's central role—of trying to keep production down.

But even if there is some agreement on tactics, the two states will probably contest the leadership of Gulf oil policy, in which the Saudis must be a key factor. One critical question is, which of the two states requires revenues faster for its own internal and foreign policy goals? Probably Iraq, with a heavy Iran-Iraq War debt, needs to rebuild its economy after the crippling U.S.-Iraqi war, and needs to keep its sullen population bought off. Baghdad's attack against Kuwait vividly demonstrated that impatience—particularly as Baghdad has shown determination to continue a long-term military build-up. Conversely, bread and butter issues are increasingly critical to the future of the Islamic Republic as clerical charisma wears ever thinner and domestic unrest grows under the dismal economic conditions Iran now faces. But Iraq remains a much more "turn-key" economy than does Iran, suggesting that it will require a higher order of income, or repression, to keep public dissatisfaction down.

Potential Common Interests

A number of potential common interests exist between Baghdad and Tehran should tactical circumstances ever persuade the two states to pursue mutual interests instead of a more natural rivalry. These issues include the Kurdish question, potential threats or pressures from the Soviet Union, other foreign intervention in the Gulf, and cooperation against Israel. A Shi'ite regime in power in Baghdad might also find some greater commonality of regional interests with Tehran.

The Kurdish Question

Although each state—but especially Iran—can exploit the Kurdish issue to the detriment of the other, they might both feel sufficiently threatened by the prospects of a future Kurdish state to unite forces against the eventuality. Urgings and pressure from Turkey to oppose movements toward Kurdish autonomy could hasten such a policy of cooperation. In the long run, however, cooperation is not terribly likely: Iran has much less to lose than Iraq from Kurdish problems and it is the more likely of the two to wish to retain this "card" for use against Iraq.

Threat from Russia

Concern over Soviet intentions and activities toward the Northern Tier states in the past helped bring monarchist Iraq together with monarchist Iran into two regional defense pacts. Soviet subversion and support for strong local Communist parties in Iran and Iraq particularly hastened these agreements. Ba'thi Iraq has been historically concerned about the Iraqi Communist party and the Soviet role in the region, despite its own treaty of friendship with Moscow. Russian support in the future for either a comprehensive Kurdish state or for indigenous Communist parties—both very unlikely since the advent of the Gorbachev era—could bring about greater cooperation between the two. The order of magnitude of the Russian threat would have to be quite considerable, however, to serve as a meaningful longer term unifying factor.

Cooperation Against External Intervention in the Gulf

The exclusion of non-Gulf powers from the Gulf has long been Iranian policy, under both the shah as well as Khomeini. Iraq, too, ever since the fall of the monarchy, has viewed nearly all external intervention in the Gulf essentially as an "anti-Arab" act. It took the specter of Iranian military victory in the Iran-Iraq War to bring about sharp change in Iraq's policy—impelling Baghdad to welcome outside help—American and European. Once the Iran-Iraq War was over, Iraq immediately reverted to its earlier policies of hostility to outside powers in the Gulf, especially as Iran itself sharply reduced its military posture in the Gulf and began moves toward moderation. Only a persistent, severe long-term ideological and military threat from Iran could ever temper Iraq's objection to foreign forces in the Gulf. Such an Iranian threat could only be significant in the event of a dramatic weakening of Iraq's military power (resulting from the joint foreign attack against Iraq beginning in January 1991) or a threat of internal chaos and collapse inside Iraq which conceivably could tempt Iran to once again seek to impose a Shi'ite regime in Baghdad.

Interestingly, several months before the Iraqi invasion of Kuwait, Saddam Husayn—shrewdly playing to Iran's anti-Western ideological impulses—suggested that perhaps both Iraq and Iran had been victims of Western conspiracies to keep the war going and to bleed both states. Once faced with the reality of the entire world arrayed against Iraq's invasion of Kuwait, Saddam astonishingly felt the urgent need to bring Iran over to his side, producing his ill-considered peace treaty with Iran that gave up Iraq's war gains in return for a peace treaty. Under these circumstances, Saddam again sought to appeal to Iran's strong historic hostility to the presence of foreign troops in the Gulf, especially U.S., by suggesting that both states should make common cause against the U.S. military build-up in Saudi Arabia. Iran's government correctly understood that the Iraqi seizure of Kuwait posed a long-term geopolitical threat to Iran's interests that far surpassed the danger of the U.S. presence, but Iran's radical elements seemed to waver in this assessment of the relative threats. In the end it does not look like even the U.S. presence in the Gulf will bring Iran and Iraq into common cause on this issue—at least as long as Iraq threatened to permanently annex Kuwait. With the liberation of Kuwait, however, a postwar Baghdad government and Tehran could well jointly press for removal of the U.S. presence in Saudi Arabia and for joint condemnation of Saudi willingness to summon the "imperialists" at all to the proximity of the Holy Places.

Cooperation Against Israel

The last years of the Iran-Iraq War provided room for speculation that Iran might seek some face-saving ideological grounds to end the conflict without having attained its goals; Khomeini could have claimed he had ended the war in order to focus on the Arab-Israeli conflict. That rationale was strengthened by the outbreak of the Palestinian uprising on the West Bank (the Intifada), suggesting there was room for pursuit of joint "Islamic goals" in Palestine. Indeed, the Saudis goaded Iran about why it sought to "direct arrows at our hearts instead of helping us to liberate Jerusalem and the Arab Islamic territories in Palestine."[13] Iran in principle could turn its ideological zeal against Israel even now, seeking to strengthen Tehran's position in the Arab and

Muslim world, and calling the bluff of such allegedly "anti-Zionist" states as Saudi Arabia who are long on talk and short on action. This kind of appeal would also have been embarrassing to Iraq during the Iran-Iraq War when the Iraqi position on the Arab-Israeli situation was muted and "moderate." Should a renewed Iraqi radicalism emerge even after Saddam Husayn, joint Iran-Iraq action against Israel is still not inconceivable.

Iraq might be loath, however, to cooperate with Iran on the Arab-Israeli issue out of concern that it would only serve to strengthen Iran's own position in the region as a direct rival to Iraq's own ambitions for leadership of the Arab cause. Baghdad furthermore would not want its own pursuit of the "Arab cause" diluted by Iran's insistence upon converting it into an overall Islamic cause. Iraq's bitter rival Syria has long cornered the hard-line rejectionist approach to Israel as well, thereby requiring either Syria to drop this position or a radical reorientation of Syrian-Iraqi relations before Iran-Iraq cooperation against Israel might be possible.

Nonetheless, some ideological combination of Iran and Iraq in an anti-Israel cause over the longer run should not be categorically ruled out, especially if the Palestinian problem should become more deeply exacerbated. Iraq's own ideological drift in the direction of radicalism, restlessly pursuing a quest for the dominant leadership role in the region, increases the possibility of cooperation. Particularly if a future Syrian regime should come to terms with Israel, the way will then be open for Iraq to seize the role of leftist leadership in the Arab world.

Iran's reaction to this Iraqi bid will most likely be determined by the character of the Iraqi threat to Iran's own security and interests in the region. If Iraqi aggressiveness is directed toward the establishment of direct hegemony over the smaller states in the immediate region, then Iran would be the direct loser in any Iraqi gains. Iran could well cooperate with Iraq to destabilize the Saudi regime, however, if Iraq otherwise did not seem to be threatening either Iran or the smaller Gulf states. If Iraq is directing its attentions primarily further afield, to Israel, Iran-Iraq cooperation becomes more likely. In short, ideological cooperation between the two states will primarily be tempered by Iran's calculation of the character of its overall, permanent, rivalry with Iraq.

Wild Cards

A number of unforeseeable wild cards exist that could change the character of relations between the two states.

Implications of Shi'ite or Islamic Revolution in Iraq

Iraq successfully intimidated the Iraqi Shi'a during the Iran-Iraq War and crushed a Shi'ite uprising after the war with the United States; Shi'ite animosity against Baghdad therefore runs deep, and the issue is far from resolved. In the event of a Shi'ite takeover of power in Iraq— or even of fundamentalist Sunni elements—it is reasonable to assume some significant shift in Iran-Iraq relations. Both states might then work for the further extension of either Islamic revolution, or at least Shi'ite rights, elsewhere in the Arab world—certainly in the Gulf.

The critical geopolitical question will still remain: could Iran-Iraq rivalries, and Arab-Persian rivalries, be subordinated for long enough periods of time to create real cooperation between Shi'ite Iran and a Shi'ite Iraq? Although relations would notably improve, the force of the same old traditional geopolitical rivalry at work is not likely to preserve even this relationship over the longer run. Nonetheless, significant change in Iraq's future, involving a dominant role for the Iraqi Shi'a, is more than a possibility—it is a probability. The impact on Iran-Iraq ties would be considerable. This is not to say that the ties would automatically work toward sweeping Islamic revolution in the Middle East. The chances are good that an Iraqi Shi'ite regime would rapidly come to resent inevitable heavyhandedness from Iran if Tehran sought to play a "big-brother" role in directing Iraqi policies. But the power equation would be definitively changed.

Moderation and Democratization in Both States

In theory both states can evolve toward greater moderation and possibly greater democratic character. Under these circumstances both states could reach a somewhat more comfortable modus vivendi in which each state would be interested in the preservation of stability—not to say the status quo—in the Gulf. Policies reminiscent of the monarchist period of both states could emerge in which each state has major interests other than challenging its neighbor. Joint management of future political and social upheavals in the Gulf shaykhdoms could then become possible. Although such a situation of cooperation may emerge over the longer term, the present era of religious and nationalist fervor does not suggest that this stage is on the horizon.

In the end, Iraq is likely always to remain firmly committed to some kind of leadership role in the Arab world, a role which places it in conflict with Iran, especially in a struggle over the "Arabness" or "Persianness" of the Gulf. Despite a brief effort by some clerics at the outset of the Iranian Revolution to end Gulf conflict by renaming it "the Islamic Gulf," the idea never took. Persian nationalism was still there. Islam is very unlikely to successfully paper over geopolitical and ethnic incompatibility. The battle for the Gulf is only beginning.

Notes

1. Sadegh Hedayat, "Seeking Absolution," from *Modern Persian Short Stories*, ed. Minoo Southgate (Washington, D.C.: Three Continents Press, 1980), p. 5.

2. Elie Kedourie, "The Iraqi Shiis and Their Fate," in *Shiism, Resistance, and Revolution*, ed. Martin Kramer, (Boulder, Colo.: Westview Press, 1987), p. 136.

3. Majid Khadduri, *The Gulf War* (New York: Oxford University Press, 1988), pp. 21–25.

4. See Chibli Mallat, "Iraq," in *The Politics of Islamic Revivalism*, ed. Shireen T. Hunter (Bloomington: Indiana University Press, 1988), pp. 71–72.

5. See Khadduri, *op. cit.*, p. 109.

6. See Chibli Mallat, *op. cit.*, for a good discussion of this intellectual movement in Iraq, pp. 74–76.

7. Khadduri, *op. cit.*, p. 115, quoting Iranian sources, reports that 40,000 were expelled. Mallat, *op. cit.*, p. 79, states that the figures are more reliably somewhere between 200,000 to 350,000. The figure is of some importance because it suggests the magnitude of political oppositional force still resident in Iran that will have impact upon the future of Iraqi politics and which can serve as bearers of Iranian influence in Iraq in the future.

8. The Shi'ite community remains basically politically divided three ways, however: those more radical and activist forces now in exile in Iran, a more quietistic group of 'ulama under the leadership of Ayatollah Abu'l Qasem Kho'i, and those 'ulama who have sought accommodation with the Ba'th. See Mallat, *op. cit.*, p. 79.

9. Khadduri, *op. cit.*, p. 116.

10. Richard W. Cottam, *Nationalism in Iran* (Pittsburgh: University of Pittsburgh Press, 1979), p. 117.

11. Christine Helms, *Iraq: Eastern Flank of the Arab World* (Washington, D.C.: Brookings Institution, 1984), pp. 148–149. Although the rebellion crumbled rapidly after the cessation of the shah's support, this is not to suggest that Iran created the rebellion on its own; Tehran simply provided the weapons to enable the Kurds to express their own national ambitions.

12. R. K. Ramazani, *Revolutionary Iran* (Baltimore: Johns Hopkins Press, 1986), p. 58.

13. See "Saudi Asks Iran to Rejoin Fight Against Israel," *Washington Post*, 28 December 1987.

3

Iran and the Gulf, Part I:
The Mists of History

No better illustration can be found of the influence of physical conditions on character than the invincible repugnance to the sea which the Persians, who are cut off from it by mountain barriers, have always shown, a repugnance which is as strong today as when Hafiz gave up his voyage to India. . . .
—*Sir Percy Sykes, 1915*[1]

As dearly as the Persians wish to assert a historical claim to hegemony in the Gulf, the mists of history afford little gratifying evidence to support any claimant. Although there is no question whatsoever that the term "Persian Gulf" is the ancient, time-honored, and accepted name for that body of water, names nonetheless grant no special privilege. Iran has not been by nature a sea power at any juncture in its history—indeed, has scarcely controlled its own Gulf coast until the twentieth century—but the past fleeting Iranian presence there has served to convince the collective Persian historical memory that the Gulf itself is indeed Persian in character. The national memory is far more important and deeply rooted than any reality or legal brief ever could be. Thus recognized international usage of the historic term "Persian Gulf" seems to be taken by Iran as international affirmation not only of a name, but of an implicit right to dominance—a right in fact possessed by none.

European domination of the Gulf from the fifteenth century onward, culminating in solid British control from the beginning of the eighteenth century, arrested the natural evolution of a local Gulf struggle for power, thereby opening up a long-delayed scramble among regional claimants with the precipitous British departure from the Gulf in 1971. Indeed, it is impossible to speak of Iran as a true power in the Gulf until the reign of the last Pahlavi shah, when, for the first time, Iran began to acquire the wherewithal to place national power and military strength at the service of national myth.

58

The discovery of oil in Iran in 1908 opened a fateful new age; the critical need for Western access to the oil resources of the Gulf removed the sovereign right of the local states to dispose of their oil wealth as they wished. This nearly unique de facto limitation of regional sovereignty will remain a permanent source of friction—especially with Iran and the other large oil-producing states.

*   *   *

We have examined the character of the deeply rooted conflict between Iran and Iraq, both across their respective borders and in their ambitions for influence down the Gulf. The next few chapters look more closely at the Persian experience in the Gulf itself and at the likely character of Iran's future involvement. Indeed, Iran's dealings with the Arab world as a whole will be profoundly shaped by Iran's specific relationship to the Gulf Arab states. The Gulf, furthermore, will be the cockpit in which conflicting Iranian, Iraqi, and Saudi aspirations are to be played out in the decades ahead. This first of three chapters on the Gulf assesses the nature of Iranian claims to a dominant role in the Gulf and the ambiguities that history provides.

A Rose by Any Other Name . . .

The name "Persian Gulf" describes the problem. The earliest application of the word "Persian" to the body of water was by the ancient Greeks. The term in Persian *Khalij-e-Fars,* literally "The Gulf of Fars (Province)," probably first emerged into history in the tenth century with the Arab historian Mas'udi, in recognition of the proximity to the Gulf of the Persian province of Fars. Portuguese usage of the term in the sixteenth century helped solidify the term in the West. But the name contains the seeds of the issue: Whose Gulf is this strategic body of water? For Iran, with its acute sense of historical roots stretching back to the first millennium B.C., the term is fraught with pride, suggestive of a historical Persian aegis over the waterway. In fact, names aside, the Gulf, as an international body of water, "belongs" to no one.

But the Arabs in the modern period have taken exception to the use of the term "Persian Gulf" in international usage, similarly believing that the name somehow carried the seeds of legal claim. Thus the standard term now in contemporary Arabic usage—and often in their English—is "the Arab Gulf," (*al-Khalij al-'Arabi*). Diplomats and scholars often ease their problem simply by dropping all proprietary adjectives and noncommittally referring to it as "the Gulf." Indeed, in the early days of the Islamic Republic in Iran, Ayatollah Sadegh Khalkhali proposed that the spirit of the new regime would be best expressed by renaming the Gulf "the Islamic Gulf." Whatever the merit of the suggestion, the idea did not take. Even the ayatollahs were unwilling to seemingly abandon their national birthright. In any case, international usage clearly sanctions the term "Persian Gulf," but the use of the term in itself should in no way legitimize either Persian or Arab aspirations to dominance over the body of water.

A Gulf, or a Persian Lake?

Persians are deeply convinced that the Gulf has been a Persian lake ever since Cyrus the Great and the first Persian world empire. It is an article of faith deeply etched into the Iranian psyche, engendering deeply emotional responses toward the "rightful dominance" of Iran over most of the Gulf. Persian culture runs rich and deep in mythology and cosmogony—the comprehensive cultural vision of how the world began and the Persian place in it. A sense of the Persian Gulf, as an integral part of the realm of Persian culture and civilization, is an ineradicable part of the Iranian world view. Yet the term "gulf" in English—entirely inadvertently—ironically also suggests some additional sense of Persian estrangement from what lies across it.

The cloudy mists of ancient history tend to obscure for us just what the presence of Iranian culture and influence in the Gulf may have been. For we are not talking here of Persian control of land on the Arab side of the Gulf. To the Persian it is a question of *cultural* dominance and the weight of Persian presence in the Gulf area as a whole. From 500 B.C. until the nineteenth century Persia has in fact tended to be the dominant state and culture in the Gulf region, but only in the sense that there were rarely any countervailing major political and cultural forces on the narrow, lightly populated coastal strip on the *Arab* side of the Gulf. Persian cultural self-confidence—and arrogance toward its Arab neighbors in the Gulf—has reinforced this belief that the Gulf littoral could produce no rival of equally weighty cultural presence. Yet some of the facts are inconvenient to the belief.

- In actuality most observers have agreed that the Persians have never really been seafarers. Sir Percy Sykes in his *History of Persia* spoke of the Persians' "invincible repugnance to the sea";[2] Sir Charles Belgrave stated that "Persians as a race have a strong disinclination for the sea, although the tribes on the coast are seafaring people, but they, in many cases, are the descendants of Arabs who crossed the Gulf and settled on the Persian coast."[3] Another eminent British student of the Gulf, J. B. Kelly, noted that "the sea has never been the Persians' natural element."[4]

- The Persians have almost never possessed a navy until very recent times. They have thus rarely if ever been able to exert sea power in the Gulf. The great oriental tales of navigation in and around the Gulf have usually involved seafaring *Arabs*, rather than Persians. A contemporary scholar of Iran noted that Arabic is "common all along the Persian Gulf."[5]
- Geographically the Gulf coast of Iran is cut off from the high Iranian plains by steep mountains, rendering the high Persian plains almost inaccessible from the Gulf coast except from a few areas.
- It is interesting to note that even in modern Persian fiction the peoples and life of the Gulf coast of Iran have been presented as something of a novelty, living in a different climate and culture— a regional curio requiring better understanding by Iranians as modern Iran focuses more heavily on developing its position on the Gulf.[6]

Thus even the Gulf coast of Iran itself has not been an integral part of the *classical* Persian cultural domain; it has rather been a backwater inhabited by non-Iranian peoples, usually independent traders, seafarers, and fishermen of primarily Arab or, at most, mixed blood, who had little direct participation with the classic Persian civilization of the high plateau.

Indeed, much of the Persian belief in the continuity of Persian dominance of the coast may rest psychologically on the fact that Iran is the sole Gulf state to possess one entire side of the Gulf coast. Firm Persian government control even of the whole length of its *own* Gulf coastline is only a modern phenomenon, however—punctuated by brief periods of vigorous Persian activity in the Gulf itself:

- Darius the Great in the sixth century B.C. expressed interest in a sea route to India from the Gulf.
- Skirmishes occurred between Arabs and Persians in the early fourth century A.D. when Bahraini Arabs raided the Persian coast.
- The Sassanians briefly seized Bahrain shortly after it became Islamicized in the seventh century, up until the fall of the Sassanians to Arab Islamic armies in 641.[7]

Indeed, much of Iran's historical frustration probably stems from the contrast between possessing the dominant state power in the overall region for long periods—compared to a weaker, less-developed Arabian peninsula—and Iran's historic impotence in actually being able to exert some control over Gulf events before the mid-twentieth century.

Iran, in effect, has only in modern times emerged to play the major role it has often aspired to in the Gulf. In the past Persia was oriented toward threats far more from its north (Mongols, Russians), east (Turkic peoples, Afghans), and west (Iraq and Turkey), rather than from the Gulf south. Historically therefore, the south, the Gulf, was not a meaningful or practicable field of concern because: no threats to Persia emerged from the Gulf and the sea (until the arrival of European fleets); Iran had no capability to meaningfully engage in Gulf politics, which by definition required projection of sea power; and European powers, especially Britain, prevented it from any exercise of such power. In short, Iran was not truly a Gulf power until the last shah.

Europe Enters the Gulf

Iran really only reemerges on the political scene—following centuries of foreign domination under the Mongols and the Seljuk Turks—to establish the Safavid state in 1499. This first Shi'ite state to control Iran was infused with religious and nationalist zeal to recreate the glories of past Persian rule—and perhaps to extend its power into the Gulf. But new forces were now on hand to rival Persia for control of the Gulf: The great European age of exploration had begun, variously propelling the Portuguese, the Dutch, and the British into significant roles in the Gulf.

The Portuguese enjoyed free reign in the Gulf for nearly a century. They even established a foothold on the Persian islands of Hormuz and Qeshm until Shah Abbas reached agreement with the British to help expel them, leading to the destruction of the Portuguese fleet in 1622. Thus ended the Portuguese era, the memory of which is still invoked by a scattering of crumbling Portuguese fortresses around the Gulf.

The Dutch made significant mark upon the region for a period of nearly 100 years as the next chief rival to the British. They too gained control of various Persian port cities, including Bandar Abbas, until they were permanently dislodged by one of the great Persian rulers, Shah Nadir the Great, in 1727. With the departure of the Dutch, the British now assumed the position of dominant power of the Gulf. This authority was to be exercised unbroken until the strategic watershed of 1971 when the British withdrew their security commitments to the Gulf. During most of this period the Persians were largely bystanders to Gulf events, with neither central government control nor adequate instruments of war with which to assert state interests.

Iran's Moment of Glory—and a Precedent Is Set

One notable and important exception to Persian impotence and neglect of the Gulf came with the brilliant blaze of glory of Nadir Shah. Nadir assumed power at a time when Persia had been overrun and virtually dominated by both Ottoman Turkey and Russia. Even more devastating was invasion by the Sunni army of resurgent Afghanistan, which seized the Iranian capital of Isfahan, destroyed Safavid rule, and moved down to the Gulf coast. Nadir, in a stunning turn-around of Persian fortune, managed to expel the Afghans and all other foreign invaders by 1727. He then dedicated himself to establishing a real Iranian presence in the Gulf.

In a period of intense activism and imperial ambition, Nadir Shah extended Persian control of the coast from Basra to the Makran coast of present day Pakistan. He recaptured Bahrain, and took part of Oman in 1737. Nadir chose Bushehr (Bushire) as the command point for newly resurgent Persian sea power. He acquired some twenty to thirty ships, largely manned by Portuguese and Indian sailors, and planned to develop a shipyard. But these plans and ambitions were to perish, along with Nadir, who died at the hand of an assassin in 1747.[8]

Nadir's reliance upon foreign sailors suggests just how novel Iranian exercise of sea power was in that era. But Nadir's exploits rank high in the Iranian historical memory and to their overall claims to a presence in the Gulf. Indeed, Nadir's venture merits special attention because there was to be no real recurrence of meaningful Iranian sea power until the twentieth century. In the meantime, the Gulf under British protection assumed a series of names reflecting its evolving character.

"The Pirate Coast"

Among the colorful titles attributed to the Gulf is that of the "Pirate Coast." Although the British first brought this term into usage in the eighteenth century, the profession of piracy had long been exercised in Gulf waters. Geographically the coast is well suited to piracy with its heavily indented coastline, shoals, and coral reefs. As a major trade artery of Mesopotamian cultures with India, China, and Africa, the Gulf has generally been a source of rich booty. Classical writers starting in the eighth century B.C. refer to the dangers of Gulf navigation due to ravaging pirates.

Indeed, the only force to rival the British in the Gulf during the late eighteenth century was the extensive "international force" of pirate operations along the "Pirate Coast." At one point the combined force of pirate fleets was able to marshall some 60 large ships and 800 smaller craft operating with some 19,000 seamen to prey on Gulf commerce.[9] It was to end this scourge that the British finally established in 1820 a General Treaty of Peace, which aimed at freeing the Gulf from piracy and regulated relations among the small shaykhdoms of the coast. The then "new" name for the Gulf, "The Trucial Coast," further reflects the lack of any clear-cut national identity attached to the Gulf in British eyes.

Apart from its swashbuckling sense of romance, the phenomenon of piracy in the Gulf suggests something more about the character of the Gulf historically. Only rarely until the modern era has any *single power* been able to police the Gulf sufficiently well so as to eliminate the scourge of piracy. That, too, suggests the absence of any kind of continuous authority over the area. Only with the century-long Portuguese era in the Gulf—ending roughly in 1662—did piracy first begin to be suppressed. After Portuguese decline, pirating privateers reigned supreme and unfettered again until the scourge became so great—brazen attacks on the British East India Company shipping and even British man o' wars— that the British finally put an end to it in a vigorous naval campaign during 1820.

Piracy was not simply an economic venture, however. Pirate allies were important to local powers as a means of exercising political influence in the Gulf as well; otherwise few regional forces could command sufficient naval resources on their own to exert major political/military influence upon their neighbors. In the most flagrant and fearsome combination of them all, the radical fundamentalist Wahhabi forces of Saudi Arabia at the turn of the nineteenth century briefly reached a working arrangement with the Qawasim pirates (of what is today's United Arab Emirates) to terrorize and conquer most of the Gulf coast. The fanatically puritan doctrine of the Wahhabis served to strengthen the pirates and confer upon them the legitimacy of a "religious mission" while the Wahhabis themselves were able to use the pirates as an instrument of power projection. The several millennia of piracy provide further indication that there had been no "natural hegemon" of the Gulf, despite persistent Iranian belief that it was Iran.

"The Trucial Coast"

Yet another name for the Gulf helps fill out the portrait of the character of Gulf politics in recent centuries. Prior to the imposition of a Pax Britannica in 1820, which enabled a "Trucial Coast" to be declared, Gulf politics consisted of a wild kaleidoscope of shifting alliances in which port cities and strategic Gulf choke points regularly changed hands. Three major locations seemed critical to the Gulf balance of power: the city (and island) of Hormuz just off the Persian coast in the Hormuz straits; Muscat, on the Arabian Sea coast of today's Oman; and Bahrain. Any quest for solid control of the Gulf required the sympathetic disposition of these cities.

What Is Arab and What Is Persian?

The historical record is confused even more by the uncertain ethnic character of many Gulf elements:

- The Gulf coast of *Persia* was widely inhabited by *Arab* clans who had migrated over from the Arab side and who held sway in the various Iranian cities and ports. Travelers report, for example, at the corrupted quality of Persian spoken in Bushire in the early nineteenth century.[10]
- These local Arab rulers sometimes intermarried with Iranians and were in a process of Persianization of sorts. They maintained tenuous relations with the Persian governors of the inland provinces, sometimes paying various degrees of tribute, depending on the circumstances.
- The Persian government, especially by the nineteenth century, was rarely if ever in a position to exert its will over these coastal rulers.
- The coastal rulers had historically dealt on a quasi-independent basis with the European naval powers in the Gulf, often seeking the Europeans' aid to extend the rulers' authority to other points in the Gulf, or gaining the support of other local powers to do the same.
- Concepts of regional control were very flexible, with kaleidoscopic shifts in the dominance of one local power over another along the coastal region.

Iran, the one continuous great state in the region, has had only minimal control and tenuous relationships with the various rulers of the Gulf. These relationships have been continuous enough, however, to give Iran a sense that the coastal areas once lay under Persian rule or authority. Indeed, places such as Bahrain or Oman have in fact been under authority based on *Iranian soil* in the past. But often those very authorities based in Iran were themselves largely or wholly Arabs on the coast, who maintained vassal or other relationship with Iranian authorities inland. The Iranian authorities in the capital were themselves rarely ever in a position to impose their own will on these coastal rulers; they were, therefore, just as glad to delegate the authority to de facto rulers along the Persian coast.

The ethnic argument for historical dominance of the Gulf is equally complex: Such is the force of Persian culture that many of these populations living on the Persian coast—though Arab in blood—gradually absorbed the Persian language, customs, Shi'ite religion, and cuisine. Are they any the less "Persian" if they are assimilated into greater Iranian culture, which has a long history of absorbing vast numbers of external peoples, both conquerors and conquered? Lastly, there has long been a major settlement of Persians on the Arab side of the Gulf, playing major roles in the commerce of Kuwait, Bahrain, Dubai, and elsewhere. While all these issues easily lend themselves to powerful ethnic emotions and sensitivities on both sides, they are not susceptible to any clear-cut resolution.

The Impact of the British

The presence of the British in the Persian Gulf was of singular importance because it effectively eliminated the opportunity for any regional powers or states to dominate the Gulf. Indeed, British supremacy in the Gulf inhibited the "normal" regional evolution and struggle that might have led to the emergence of a major regional Gulf power. Any regional exercise in power projection—especially across the Gulf— required resources not at the command of any of the potential players.

Apart from British influence in the Gulf, Iran itself became increasingly incapable of exercising influence in the Gulf due to the debility and weaknesses of both the late Safavid and the Qajar dynasties. One final effort came in 1865 when Nasreddin Shah attempted to establish a navy and sought British help to do so. The British vetoed the idea out of concern for what Iran's intentions might be.[11]

Iran would thus have to wait until the establishment of Pahlavi power under Reza Shah in the 1920s before making any serious effort at all toward creation of power in the Gulf. This continuing impotence of Iran in the face of long-term British hegemony was deeply resented by the Iranians and undoubtedly contributed to Iran's intense commitment to establishing meaningful Iranian power in the Gulf today.

As British influence increased, its presence became ever more galling to Iran—particularly because British dominance over Iranian internal affairs showed parallel growth. As if to rub in Iran's impotence in the Gulf, by 1892 the Iranian coastal town of Bushire (Bushehr) became the very headquarters for the British political resident who exercised Britain's sway over the Gulf. Not surprisingly, the British viewed Iran as a totally unconstructive force in the Gulf, attempting to hinder British authority at every turn—including British efforts to eliminate piracy, slave-traders, the establishment of navigational aids, communications facilities, and so on. "Whatever improvements were introduced to the Gulf . . . were invariably interpreted by the court of Tehran as affronts to its dignity, and used as pretexts for renewed bombast about Persia's sacred and immutable rights."[12] In short, whatever the administrative "benefits" Britannica brought to the Gulf, they were scarcely welcomed by Iran. Britain and Iran had now become starkly unequal rivals for Gulf power— at a time when no other force in the Gulf perceived the British as a strategic adversary. Here, too, we see that Iran already had a sense of being challenged in the Gulf in a way that no other regional state could.

Oil—and Its Massive Geopolitical Consequences

In 1908 another fateful strategic milestone is set: the discovery of oil in Iran. The existence of oil helped consolidate Britain's position of major influence over Iran and its determination to remain in the Gulf. And by now the concept of "security of Gulf oil supply" was permanently entering the lexicon of Western security vocabulary, permanently establishing the de facto right of the industrialized West to intervene in the Gulf balance of power—down to today. (Few other regions of the world are so designated as absolutely critical to the great powers: Even the "lifeline" of the Suez canal turned out to be much less than that when the unthinkable happened in the 1967 Arab-Israeli war and it was shut down for years. The Panama Canal also has also been regarded as so strategic in character that the country of Panama may not be permitted the sovereign right to close it.)

But the importance of Gulf oil in terms of the Western economies transcends both these waterways; its geopolitical importance is simply nonnegotiable—thereby becoming a nonnegotiable infringement of Gulf state sovereignty—a fact of which Iran is well aware. This places the geopolitics of the Gulf in a special category—"artificial" in the sense that local powers will not ever be allowed to exercise full local sovereignty if it should affect oil supply–and as long as this commodity retains its crucial character in the industrialized economies.

First Stirrings of Egyptian Interest
in the Gulf

One other regional state made its presence felt briefly in the Gulf in the nineteenth century, perhaps as a small harbinger of twentieth-century interest: Egypt. Although Egypt in the first half of the nineteenth century was nominally under Ottoman control, independent power was emerging in the person of the Ottoman governor Muhammad Ali, who was later to assert the total independence of Egypt. At the height of the Wahhabi fundamentalist threat to the Holy Places in Mecca in 1810, when their puritan zeal led them to desecrate the very tomb of the Prophet, the Ottoman sultan asked Egypt to send forces to crush the Wahhabi movement. (Wahhabi power in the Gulf will be discussed at greater length in Chapter 6.) In a long campaign, the Egyptians not only destroyed Wahhabi power for several decades, but themselves reached the Gulf coast and briefly exercised Egyptian power from the Arabian Peninsula.

While Egypt was not able to maintain control of the peninsula beyond 1841, the exercise presaged intense Egyptian interest in the "Arabness" of the Gulf—in opposition to Persian influence—under Nasser in the 1960s. Indeed Egypt in early 1988 also demonstrated interest in the defense of the Arab Gulf against Iran, and committed itself to supplying forty to sixty combat pilots to the Iraqi Air Force and allowed a large number of the Egyptian work force in Iraq to be drafted into the Iraqi army, resulting in the ultimate capture of some ten thousand Egyptians by Iran.[13]

These Egyptian interludes, while not of great strategic significance, provide interesting insight into the depth of the broader Arab interest in the Gulf—carrying distinct anti-Persian overtones. Emerging Pan-Arab interest in the Gulf was to change totally the character of Iran's own strategic interests there.

We have thus witnessed the confusing picture presented by the question of "whose Gulf" it is in geostrategic terms of power. As J. B. Kelly noted with characteristic sarcasm: "Like their Safavid predecessors, the Qajar shahs held as an article of faith that wherever in the world a Persian foot had trod became from that moment onwards irrevocably Persian, however long the place in question may have lain under foreign domination."[14] In the next chapter we shall see how the Pahlavi dynasty began to turn the reach of the Iranian geostrategic dream into some kind of reality—in a Gulf game increasingly complicated by the emergence of many new players with differing agendas.

Notes

1. Sir Percy Sykes, *A History of Persia*, Vol. II (London: MacMillan and Co., Ltd., 1963), p. 271.
2. *Ibid.*

3. Sir Charles Belgrave, *The Pirate Coast* (London: G. Bell and Sons, Ltd., 1966), p. 16.

4. J. B. Kelly, *Arabia, the Gulf and the West* (New York: Basic Books, 1980), p. 313.

5. Richard W. Cottam, *Nationalism in Iran* (Pittsburgh: University of Pittsburgh Press, 1979), p. 31.

6. See, for example, stories such as "The Warm South" by Shahpur Qarib, "Agha Julu" by Nasir Taqva'i, and "Of Weariness" by Ahmad Mahmud, all contained in *Modern Persian Short Stories*, edited and translated by Minoo Southgate (Washington, D.C.: Three Continents Press, 1980).

7. Most of the data in these paragraphs is taken from Rouhollah K. Ramazani's *The Persian Gulf: Iran's Role* (Charlottesville: University of Virginia Press, 1972), p. 9.

8. *Ibid.*, p. 13.

9. Kelly, *op. cit.*, p. 287.

10. Belgrave, *op. cit.*, p. 118.

11. Ramazani, *op. cit.*, p. 18.

12. Kelly, *op. cit.*, p. 311.

13. See Nader Entessar, "Egypt and the Persian Gulf," *Conflict*, Vol. 9, 1989, pp. 120–121.

14. Kelly, *op. cit.*, p. 311.

4

Iran and the Gulf, Part II: Iran and the New Arab Challenge

The Arabs are actually newcomers to the role of rival or threat to Iran in the Gulf. Previous threats to Iran in the Gulf had come primarily from the European presence: Portuguese, Dutch, and British. The Arab radical challenge, beginning in the late 1950s, opened a new phase of geopolitics. In the shah's perception, some kind of alliance with the United States was a welcome assist if Iran was to confront the Arab radical challenge, maintain Iranian hegemony in the region, and secure itself from Soviet pressures.

The shah's policy of alignment with the West was an aberration from a more traditional (and current) Iranian hostility to outside powers and reflects both the shah's desire for support in attaining his regional ambitions as well as his perceived need for external assistance in bolstering his domestic position. These concerns for security led him in the end to curtail Iranian territorial ambitions in the Gulf in the 1970s in the interests of establishing some kind of working relationship with the newly emergent independent Gulf shaykhdoms. All of these shaykhdoms still offer room for future Iranian political involvement, if not intervention, as each state faces its own internal crises and strives to preserve monarchical rule.

This second chapter on the Gulf analyzes two precedent-setting phases of Iran's modern involvement in the Gulf. This period represents the first time that Iran had both the freedom and the wherewithal to significantly influence Gulf political events—while facing a challenge to the shah from radical Arab ideologies; for the first time newly emergent, small, independent states appeared on the Gulf political scene no longer under British protection and were forced to reach their own modus vivendi with Iran. The third chapter on Iran in the Gulf will examine a range of potential scenarios involving Iranian Gulf policy in the future.

Arab Meets Persian Again

Our contemporary vantage point makes us vividly aware of the contemporary clash of Arab versus Persian power. Yet, until the 1950s, despite cultural frictions, there had not really been any new *Arab* state challenge to the Persian state for nearly a thousand years—ever since the Arab conquest of Iran in 641. For Persians, the Arabs are thus relative newcomers in terms of exercising major power in the Gulf regional power game.

More "normal" Arab-Persian confrontation in the eighteenth and nineteenth centuries was further delayed by the presence of British power as umpire in the Gulf. Iran itself was also too weak to challenge much of anybody in the Gulf at that time. In effect, the evolution of a regional power struggle was put on hold by the British presence.

Indeed, despite the sudden, remarkable reemergence of Iran under Reza Shah in the 1920s—as an independent, sovereign, unified, and centralized state for the first time in centuries—Iran even then still had no confrontation with those Arab states that were in the process of gaining their own independence after World War I. Even independent Iraq, now a monarchy in the 1920s, enjoyed relatively comfortable relations with Iran both before and immediately after World War II. "Diplomatic relations" in this period, of course, were confined largely to the province of the two monarchs.

The 1950s, however, brought drastic new Arab realities to the Middle East—directly affecting Iran. The Arab world had wakened to the vigorous and powerful doctrine of Arab nationalism under the leadership of Egypt's Gamal Abdul Nasser. Although Arab nationalist sentiments had been brewing in most Arab countries at least since World War I, the new doctrine was now forcibly expressed by the state in *Pan-Arab* terms, buttressed by three potent new ideological elements: sharply focused anti-Western, "antiimperialist," revolutionary ideology; a growing wave of Third World consciousness and solidarity, giving greater voice to the masses in expressing emotions, frustrations, and nationalist aspirations; the active interest of the USSR in supporting and arming these movements against Western interests.

The Old Gulf Looks East . . .

It is hard to remember that, in any *political* sense, the small Arab coastal states of the Gulf had almost never been part of the mainstream

Arab Near East. They lived on a body of water in which the great cultural power—half the Gulf—was Iran. And the Gulf looked out into the Arabian Sea and the coasts of India. Trade and cultural patterns have been oriented to the East rather than the West since the second millennium B.C. Indeed, British control of the Gulf was administered out of the Colonial Office in India, not from the Arab world. The Gulf was generally cut off by the vastness of the Nafud desert from Arab politics to the west: the Levant, Egypt, and the Mediterranean. The Gulf looked east and north not only in terms of its several millennia of trading patterns but also in employment of mercenaries, usually ethnic Arabs, from the Persian coast and praetorian guards from Baluchistan on the borders of the subcontinent; merchants from the subcontinent played major mercantile roles in the local markets.

... While the New Gulf Turns to the Arab West

Yet Egypt's new nationalist ruler, Colonel Nasser, was proposing in the 1950s a new *Arab* political orientation for the Gulf region. Indeed, Nasser's revolutionary role in the Arab world did not simply involve politics. For the smaller Gulf states it ushered in a revolution in self-identity.

Iran was directly challenged by these developments in at least four respects.

- First, millennia-old antipathies of the Arabs against Persians reasserted themselves in a new, *political* form. Arab nationalism excluded Persians by definition.
- Second, the new Arab nationalism was distinctly opposed to the "old order"; the institution of monarchy was viewed as a reactionary anachronism, thwarting the "will of the people." The shah was one of many targets.
- Third, the shah not only enjoyed cordial terms with the West and the United States but also was seen by Arab nationalists as an instrument of the West. He was perceived to owe his throne to the intervention of British and U.S. intelligence after being threatened by the populist movement of Mossadegh in the early 1950s. As the shah saw his own security interests converging more closely with the West, Arab nationalists saw him serving to foil the central Arab nationalist goal of "keeping the Gulf Arab"—and nonaligned. (Significantly, Iranian nationalists, especially those around the old Mossadegh movement in the 1950s, indeed shared the feeling that the shah was serving Western interests; they had some sympathies for Nasser's anti-Western and antiimperialist rhetoric—although they

did not agree with Nasser's geopolitical goals for the Arab world against Iran.)[1]
- Finally, and very importantly, Iran remained on good terms with the state of Israel despite the shah's generalized support for Palestinian rights.

Iran thus found itself the object of vilification from the newer revolutionary Arab states led by Egypt. Nasser's support was extended automatically to virtually any force in the Arab world that aspired to nationalist revolution or anti-Western goals. The threat was not idle; Nasser's influence shook several regimes to the very core: In Lebanon, Jordan, Saudi Arabia, Iraq, Kuwait, Yemen, and elsewhere the force of Arab nationalism was deeply destabilizing in terms of the old regimes. The Gulf was a natural target of Egyptian propaganda and subversive activity—especially given the vulnerable nature of its weak and monarchy-studded traditionalist states up and down the coast.

Opposition to Iranian influence was a key element of Nasser's policies. If Iran was "threatening to Persianize the Gulf" and lay claim to Bahrain, then the Arabs delivered their riposte through vigorous claims to Iran's oil-rich border province of Khuzestan (with its significant ethnic Arab population)—sharply heightening Iran's security concerns.[2]

The overthrow of the Iraqi monarchy in 1958 was a major turning point: Tehran was now confronted with the emergence of an aggressive new nationalist regime in Iraq, supported by the increasing role of the USSR as the primary patron and arms source for radical Arab nationalist ambitions. Such a confluence of events drew the shah more deeply into a grander security design with the United States. Both Iran and Arab states allied to Moscow were acting upon self-fulfilling prophesies in their suspicions of one another, writing a harsh new chapter in the ancient Persian-Arab rivalry, but this time partially enlisting the superpowers into the equation and strengthening the security dilemma for both Arabs and Persians.

Antishah opposition in Iran tended to discount both the Soviet and the radical Arab threat to Iran, viewing the shah's policies as purely responsive to U.S. policy needs and a reflection of Iranian imperial ambition, using the external threat to meddle in the region.[3] While there doubtless was a confluence of interest between the United States and Iran in opposing radical Arab and Soviet forces in the region—which the shah also bent to his own domestic ends—the forces of radicalism in the 1950s and 1960s were very real. In the context of the Cold War and Soviet policy toward the Third World, the United States found the strategic implications of such radicalism deeply disturbing, even when such radical movements often stemmed from primarily domestic roots. If Iranian nationalist forces had been in power in that period instead of the shah, the chances are that Iran would *not* have cooperated closely with the United States on strategic matters, but would still have eventually seen a challenge to Iranian power and influence from both the USSR and the radical Arabs. But a nonaligned Iran would have posed less of a challenge to Arab radicalism as well. And the absence of the superpowers and the Cold War would indeed probably have served to lessen the intensity of the regional confrontation.

The magnitude of the radical Arab/Soviet challenge—at least in the shah's eyes—is mainly responsible therefore for what we might view as a *grand aberration* in Iran's geopolitical orientation. As most of the material of this book demonstrates, Iran has rarely had close ties with Western states—despite a willingness to play off British, French, Germans, Russians, and Americans. It has almost consistently been a victim of Western power. Nor has Iran ever felt a need to align itself with the West until the last shah. In this light, the Khomeini revolution restores Iran to a more natural posture of "neither East nor West" in the region. But the revolutionary challenge of Iran's revolution to virtually all its neighbors proceeded to rob Iran of the fruits of that nonalignment, perpetuating to some degree its regional isolation.

Britain Throws the Gulf Up for Grabs

The British announcement in 1968 that it was planning to abandon its 150-year-old security role in the Gulf came as a cataclysmic revelation to the regional powers of the Gulf—already deeply enmeshed in growing tensions and rivalries. Britain was abandoning its role as policeman of the Gulf and, in effect, throwing the Gulf up for grabs. The decision could not have come at a worse time from the point of view of regional stability.

Apart from the swirl of nationalisms, revolutions, oil discoveries, and the emergence of fragile new Gulf political entities into the hurly-burly of Arab politics, the Cold War was also beginning to recruit players onto its respective teams. The region increasingly came under pressure to align with either "progressive" or "reactionary" groupings. Although economic cost clearly played a role in the British decision to pull out, the "anti-Empire" ideology of the British Labour party also weighed in heavily. How long Britain could have in fact maintained a basically colonial presence in the region even under a Conservative government, however, is open to question.

The Door of Opportunity Opens for Iran

Britain's withdrawal was a signal event in the history of Iran's role in the Gulf. Iran's sole potential military challenger was pulling out, opening the door to the fulfillment of ancient Iranian ambitions to serve as guardian and hegemon of the Gulf.

The shah's aspirations were further reinforced by the United States. Washington clearly could not simply assume the British role itself and required regional allies to help maintain Gulf security. Saudi Arabia and Iran were to emerge as the "Twin Pillars" of a new regional security regime. Of the two, Iran obviously was the more powerful, the more willing, and the more ambitious.

Yet another watershed for Iran was its creation of a significant navy—the first Gulf state to develop genuine naval power. Iran's new naval power radically altered the character of Iranian power in the region and lent teeth to what had largely been Iranian bluster about Iranian interests in years past. "Three destroyers, four frigates, four corvettes, twenty patrol boasts, a dozen or so hovercraft, and an assortment of mine-sweepers, landing craft and support ships . . . a naval air wing of three squadrons of aircraft and two dozen or more helicopters . . ."[4]—all went to make up a formidable new naval capability that may have lacked in training and experience but that placed Iran at least a decade ahead of any of its regional competitors and gave it a pronounced vision for possibilities of power projection well outside the Gulf.

Britain's departure also required that the security status of the many small shaykhdoms of the Gulf be resolved as they moved toward independence. The British were anxious to work out a security arrangement that would unite these ministates into a broader confederation that might help them survive the perils of inter-Arab politics. Nor were these perils imaginary. A series of clandestine subversive radical nationalist and leftist organizations were at work in the Gulf, including the Popular Front for the Liberation of the Arab Gulf, the Front for the Liberation of South Yemen, the Dhofar Liberation Front, the Bahrain Liberation Front, and others whose goals were to overturn the insecure rulers in favor of ideological regimes in the mold of revolutionary Egypt, Iraq, or the People's Democratic Republic of Yemen.

Iran's own claims and special interests in the disposition of these states placed the shah foursquare in the middle of these plans. But of all the Gulf states, it was Bahrain that enjoyed the distinction of being number one on Iran's list of unfulfilled territorial aspirations.

The Bahrain Controversy

Bahrain, more than any other place in the Gulf, perfectly encapsulates the dilemma of Iranian involvement in Gulf Arab affairs. Intricate legal documentation exists to bolster the respective parties' territorial claims; what is most important for us to note is the basis for the perceptions of each side. Iran's claim to Bahrain was one of the major vehicles for expression of Iran's ambitions in the Gulf and appropriately dates back at least to the seventh century A.D. when the Sassanian monarch dispatched Persian troops to the island and controlled it until the fall of Iran to Arab Islamic armies later in the century. Not surprisingly, Persian historical memory attributes an overall Persian presence in the Gulf back to virtually 600 B.C.—such is the reality of quasi-myth.

Volumes of diplomatic correspondence, claims, and counterclaims surround the Bahrain issue. In the post–World War II period Iran twice reasserted its claim to the island and declared it a fourteenth province of Iran, citing numerous periods in history when Iran controlled Bahrain. Britain acknowledges Iranian control of Bahrain only for a period from 1753 to 1783—with Britain itself establishing a protectorate over the island starting in 1820. But by the 1970s the Gulf also presented a radically different picture. New threats abounded. Iran's concern for the island had evolved from an essentially *territorial and nationalistic* claim to one based more on geopolitics and strategic/security issues.[5] For Tehran it became at least as important to *deny* the Gulf to territorial and ideological enemies as it was to gain control itself. This recognition was to pave the way for an amicable settlement of the dispute.

Iran remained ever suspicious of British motives down to the end of the British pull out, based on nearly a century of British manipulation of Iran. British efforts to unite all the Gulf shaykhdoms in one large confederation were opposed by Iran, out of a belief that they would become vehicles for indirect continuation of British control of the Gulf.

Whatever suspicions still lurked in Iranian minds about the motivations of other Gulf players, the shah recognized that he would have to come to terms with the new states of the Gulf and could not afford to alienate them. As noted above, the shah's interests now focused especially on strategic and security issues rather than on purely territorial issues. The preservation of conservative monarchical regimes was infinitely preferable to the prospects of local revolution supported by Nasser (gone from the scene by 1970), by revolutionary Ba'thist Iraq, or by the new Communist state in South Yemen. Indeed, the numerous revolutionary groups in the Gulf supported by radical Arab states represented genuine security threats to these fragile new state structures; radical subversive capabilities were blocked primarily by the long-term maintenance of skilled British Special Branch officers in charge of internal security in each of the new states.

The shah thus decided to acquiesce to the independence of Bahrain on the face-saving condition that a UN referendum be held that would enable the citizens of Bahrain to express their preference between independence or unification with Iran. Bahrain overwhelmingly chose independence.

Iran also supported Bahrain and Qatar's preference for separate independence as opposed to federation in the newly emerging United Arab Emirates (UAE). From the Iranian perspective, if there was to be a UAE, better a smaller UAE, more malleable and susceptible to Iranian influence in the Gulf, than a larger state would be. Thus, by the time of British withdrawal in 1971, Iran had accommodated itself to the emergence of an independent Bahrain, Qatar, and a UAE.

Iran and the UAE: Playground for Rivalry

The UAE, by its very nature, will probably present the greatest future opportunity over the longer run for regional and external players to upset the status quo. Bound together out of a patchwork quilt of some five shaykhdoms and ruling families, the UAE to date has nonetheless been the most successful experiment in Arab unity anywhere in the Arab world. It has proven hardier, and continued to move in the direction of functional federalism faster, than most observers would have wagered. The Iran-Iraq War, potentially deeply disruptive to fragile political entities in the Gulf, actually served to steel these entities and strengthen security ties under the buffeting of major conflict.

Although Bahrain had been the preeminent Iranian territorial claim, the shah also contested the UAE's historical entrepot, the city-state of Dubai, as well as several strategic and oil-bearing small islands belonging to the UAE.

Despite Iran's ultimate dropping of these claims and acquiescence to the creation of the UAE, the shah clearly favored a limited UAE that excluded Bahrain and Qatar and was not above playing hard and fast partisan politics within the *internal* structure of the federation. A policy of differentiation among the various shaykhdoms of the UAE can afford Iran considerable influence within the UAE for some time to come.

Dubai, the Special Ties That Bind

Dubai is one of the few traditionally established ports along the entire Arab coast of the Gulf and historical entrepot for trade to Iran. Its dhows ply the Gulf waters daily in legal and illegal trade between the two coasts. Not surprisingly, a sizeable Iranian community of traders has grown up in Dubai over several centuries, serving to keep the Iranian presence across the Gulf a living reality on the Arab side. Dubai also has oil fields that extend out into areas claimed by Iran, giving Tehran special hold on Dubai's goodwill. The ruler of Dubai had also been close to the shah, symbolizing the symbiotic relationship between these two states. And Dubai is chief rival to Abu Dhabi for preeminence within the UAE structure.[6]

The shah regularly played on Abu Dhabi-Dubai rivalries by encouraging Dubai toward expression of its own natural inclination to loosen the federal structure within the UAE framework. At Iran's urging, Dubai, in a very destabilizing act, virtually withheld support from its own sister shaykhdom Ras al-Khaima in a territorial dispute with an external state, Oman.

In sum, Iran's politicking within the UAE was hardly perceived as an overall stabilizing factor by most in the Gulf, despite the shah's talk of regional security and the status quo. In the case of the shah's support for Oman in its dispute with Ras al-Khaima over the critical area on the tip of the Strait of Hormuz, the shah was actually supporting *change* in the status quo—thereby establishing a truly destabilizing precedent in the crazy-quilt character of UAE member states' borders.

For all its remarkable success, the UAE will remain the state potentially most vulnerable to sudden change and internal struggle of any in the Gulf, due to its federal character, its lack of distinct "personality" as a definable historical entity, and the chances for violent change of regime in any of its constituent states. There will likely always be some Gulf player that might find such a change in its own interests and support it, opening the way to struggle among Saudi Arabia, Iran, Iraq, and Oman. The Iran-Dubai connection could be particularly important, although as a noncontiguous state, Iran cannot make realistic *territorial claim* to Dubai. Another UAE member state, Fujaira, would probably see greater virtue in association with Oman than with the UAE. Iran, or any other external state, would thus be in a position to support some kind of separatism in the UAE. When the old monarchical order is challenged by coup or disorder in any one of the constituent states in the future, the entire structure will be challenged. The larger states will not likely remain aloof from the struggle. The UAE, more than any other Gulf state, faces at least the possibility of dissolution, partition, or territorial loss to its neighbors. The future evolution of the UAE is certain to play a signal role in future Gulf conflict.

Oman

Oman, looming directly across the straits from Iran, lies closer to the huge Iranian land mass than any other Gulf state except Kuwait. Logic might suggest that Oman therefore fears Iran's power and influence to a high degree. In fact, it does not. Oman probably has the best ties with Iran of any state in the Gulf as a whole. The analytic problem is to decide why relations have been relatively good in this century and how characteristic this close association is likely to be in the future.

As we noted in an earlier chapter, Iran and Oman have had much to do with each other historically. Persian mercenary forces landed in Oman and occupied Muscat for about eight years in the eighteenth century. Muscat, in turn, was for long periods of time the de facto ruler of the Persian port city of Hormuz—leasing it from Persian monarchs who were unable or unwilling to exercise close control over this inaccessible coastal area far from the center of Persian politics.

In more recent times, however, far from coveting Oman, the last shah saw monarchical Oman as a bastion against radical Arab nationalism. The Omanis were profoundly impressed with the fact that Iran was the only regional state to send major military support to aid them in the 1970s in combating the Marxist uprising in Oman's Dhofar province—an insurgency supported directly by the People's Democratic Republic of Yemen and Iraq and supported indirectly by the USSR—and China for a period. Iran's expeditionary brigade, possibly a decisive military factor toward the end of the conflict, demonstrated even more clearly Iran's direct concern for Oman's security against radical forces in the peninsula. Saudi Arabia, strikingly, did almost nothing—even though the threat was of considerable importance to Riyadh as well; Riyadh was miffed at the precedent of Iranian troops on the peninsula and did not enjoy smooth relations with Oman in any case.

Omani relations with Iran during the 1970s were universally good and both countries undertook to share the duties of patrolling the narrow Strait of Hormuz. Not surprisingly, Oman's interest in Gulf security focused primarily on freedom of navigation through the strait. But Oman also participated in discussions of other regional security plans and proposed one of its own, involving the provision of strong technical and economic support from the wealthy oil-consuming nations that consume Gulf oil.[7]

Surprisingly, the Islamic revolution in Iran did not transform Iranian relations with Oman as one might expect. To be sure, the new revolutionary regime in Tehran found the same fault with the Omanis as did the Arab radicals: Oman's close security ties with both Britain and the United States.

- The British are deeply involved in the Omani defense establishment with large numbers of senior British officers seconded to the Army in various advisory capacities.
- In 1975 the United States gained access to air facilities at the British-controlled base at Masirah Island. Oman indeed was interested in working with the United States in playing a role in broader Western

security planning against potential Soviet inroads into the area—
while benefiting directly from all the military and commercial
assistance that this would involve.
• Security ties with the United States mushroomed with the establishment of the U.S. Rapid Deployment Force, soon to become U.S.
CENTCOM, granting the United States new access and storage
rights in Oman.

Needless to say, these Omani policies were anathema to Tehran's vision
of "neither East nor West"—as was Oman's almost unique maintenance
within the Arab world of diplomatic ties with Egypt after Camp David.
Indeed, these Omani military ties to Western states presented an initial
complication to Oman's membership in the nascent Gulf Cooperation
Council (GCC)—but not enough to disqualify it.

The outbreak of the Iran-Iraq war probably played an important role
in diverting potential Iranian pressure on Oman's unusually exposed
position due to ties to the United States and the United Kingdom. Oman,
deeply suspicious of historic Iraqi intentions and subversive actions in
the Gulf, did not move to assist Iraq as did Kuwait and Saudi Arabia.
Oman stayed more nonaligned than any other Gulf state. Oman's shared
hostility toward Iraq is likely to perpetuate good ties between Iran and
Oman until significant political change emerges in Oman.

Other factors also played a role in facilitating Oman's good relations
with revolutionary Iran. Oman's relatively small Shi'ite population—
some 10 percent—has been quiescent, although closely watched. The
Shi'a are mostly of Hyderabadi origin—from the Indian subcontinent—
and thus not automatically close to either Iranian or Arab Shi'a. Oman
has furthermore possessed a uniquely open Islamic religious environment,
much due to the majority percentage of *Ibadhi* Muslims. This relatively
small Islamic sect is unusually tolerant of other Islamic and non-Muslim
religions, helping preserve considerable religious tranquility in Oman.
In short, Oman has not provided fertile religious ground for exploitation
by Iran.

With the end of the Iran-Iraq War, however, Oman presents one of
the most significant targets for revolution in the Gulf. It poses an entirely
different problem than the UAE. The UAE lacks political identity and
solidity as a historically coherent and distinctive state. Oman, on the
contrary, is highly distinctive, "a real place" with solid sense of its own
deep historical and special ethnic identity. Although the present sultan
has made major steps toward bringing the country out of its former
isolation and backwardness, political tensions are nonetheless very real.
The regime is strongly authoritarian. The military is still dominated by
British officers, and despite serious attempts to "Omanize" the country,

the process has not proceeded far enough or deeply enough to prevent strong nationalist resentments from building up. The U.S. presence grew during the Iran-Iraq War. Apart from the large number of British in high and sensitive places in the government, much of the working level of the economy and administration is largely in the hands of other foreigners—Indians, Pakistanis, Baluch, and others—who will ultimately also become an ever greater source for nationalist resentment. An antiforeign backlash could arguably emerge that will spark disorders or even a coup in the future. Oman provides the most extreme example of a Gulf state that has "entered the Arab world" only within this decade. Mainstream Arab world politics were little known and were well outside of Omani political life until the last decade. Oman for long did not pay the usual lip service to the Palestinian issue. Increasing numbers of Jordanians, Palestinians, and Egyptians are finding places in Oman's educational and media sectors and are assisting in raising the general level of "Arab consciousness" in Oman. The consequences of this trend upon the population, coupled with resentment of the massive foreign role in Oman, bodes for possible dramatic military change in this Gulf state almost more than in any other. And the ruling Sultan Qabus has no heir.

Under these circumstances, Oman's relations with Iran in the future present something of a question mark. A good case can be made that Oman's closeness to Iran has stemmed primarily from Oman's "non-Arab" policies for several decades as well as an antipathy to radical Arab forces. If revolutionary change should occur in Oman—more likely of a strong *nationalist* rather than religious orientation—would Oman alter its traditional close ties with Iran? Iran's major goal in Oman—under almost any foreseeable Iranian regime—will be to secure the elimination of the foreign military presence in Oman at such a strategic choke point in the Gulf. Any move by a future Omani regime to expel the strong foreign—and particularly Western—presence would meet with strong support from Iran.

However, a nationalist movement would also lay much greater emphasis on Oman's *Arab* character and demonstrate greater solidarity with other Arab states. As we will see in later chapters, however, Oman will not likely feel a strong sense of solidarity with the rest of the peninsula, despite an increased sense of Arabness. These developments will leave Tehran ambivalent toward Oman, but Iran will likely consistently en-courage Oman's traditionally independent view of Arab and peninsula affairs.

Oman under nationalist leadership would almost surely express vastly less concern for threats to the country from the Soviet Union—highly unlikely under its reformed policies anyway. Although Oman is now concerned with radical external threats to the region, its particular long-standing anti-Soviet stance primarily reflects the major military and economic benefits it derives from a close security relationship with the United States. A nationalist regime will be less interested in offering the United States military facilities in Oman.

On balance, if a postmonarchy Oman diminishes its foreign military ties, it will be moving in a direction approved by Tehran. Immediate control of the Strait of Hormuz will remain a powerful mutual interest of both states. But even here their interests differ somewhat. Iran is potentially threatened along all its coastline from foreign warships that enter the Gulf. Oman is not so directly threatened once a ship passes through the Straits. Oman is more likely to accede to Iran's security concerns about passage—but will also remain vulnerable to pressure from Saudi Arabia or Iraq if ships entering are perceived as threatening to those states.

Oman's most likely long-term enemy will be Saudi Arabia. Oman has a long memory of suffering attack from the Saudi Wahhabi fundamentalist movement, which swept across the Arabian Peninsula twice in two centuries and posed serious threat to Oman and the lower Gulf states. Omanis are convinced that the Saudis do not wish them well and that the Wahhabi character of the Saudi state still nurtures unfulfilled expansionist instincts—a kind of "Wahhabi manifest destiny." (This issue will be discussed at greater length in Chapter 6 on Saudi Arabia.)

The implications of a more hostile Omani-Saudi relationship—possibly now, but even more likely later if a nationalist regime should come to power in Muscat or Riyadh—are considerable. If Iran and Saudi Arabia are on a longer term collision course in the Gulf, then Oman most likely would find itself an ally of Iran on an anti-Saudi basis.

Who Is Keeping What Secure from Whom?

The prolific historian of Iranian foreign affairs R. K. Ramazani spoke of a "Pax Iranica" in the Gulf during the 1970s.[8] This decade is indeed important in demonstrating major facets of Iran's behavior under a conservative rather than revolutionary regime. But I have trouble with the term "Pax Iranica" for the 1970s because it implies that Iran was the instrumental force in keeping—or imposing—the peace. Iran contributed significantly to the peace mainly by largely refraining from hostilities itself and reaching agreement with most of its neighbors on festering border and territorial issues. It did not, however, actually serve to *enforce* that peace, except for its significant role in helping put down the Communist-supported Dhofar rebellion in Oman. This first decade (the 1970s) of unrestricted Iranian power in the Gulf, therefore, provides only modest guidelines in helping us to predict post–Iran-Iraq War Iranian behavior patterns in the Gulf—except in terms of the reach, and growing capability, of Iranian national ambitions as expressed by the shah.

Iran did participate, to be sure, along with other Gulf states in deliberations on security problems and strongly advocated a regional approach to security. But the problem of "Gulf security" was infinitely compounded by the difficulty in defining the very problem: In the Gulf, who is keeping what secure from whom? That dilemma still exists down to today. Several alternatives views of this problem exist:

1. *Radical Arab states* in the 1960s and 1970s sought to keep the Gulf secure from Western influence, "Western imperialism," and from Iranian power—the "West's proxy" in the Gulf.
2. *Monarchical Iran* sought to keep the Gulf secure from radical Arab and Soviet influence.
3. *Smaller Gulf states* sought security from Iran, Iraq, and even Saudi Arabia, as well as from other radical nationalist Arab states in the Middle East. Today, none of them will want the Gulf "left to the Gulf powers."
4. As of today the *Islamic Republic* of Iran seeks to keep the Gulf secure from the two superpowers (the Greater and Lesser Satans), from general Western influence in the Gulf states, from Iraq, and from Saudi Arabia, that is, from virtually everyone.
5. *Iraq* seeks to keep the Gulf secure today from Iranian, Israeli, European, and especially U.S. influence. It could only seek external support in the event that its war with the United States weakens it for the next decade against any resurgent Iranian power.
6. The *West* has been interested, first, in protecting all of the Gulf from Soviet influence, and, since 1979, from Islamic fundamentalism and Iranian expansionism, and, since 1990, from Iraqi expansionism as well.

Common security policies will therefore be extremely difficult to attain given each party's special agenda. Almost no common denominator exists. Even the goal of keeping major external powers out of the Gulf is only an interest of the three largest Gulf states—and not all of the time. Iran's aggressive ideological intentions and prowess on the battlefield in the Iran-Iraq War temporarily altered even Iraq's preference for a "Gulf for the Gulfis." The smaller states will regularly welcome outside powers when they can provide protection from concrete and specific threats from hegemonic Gulf powers.

In sum, Iran could adopt a more aggressive or radical policy toward the smaller Gulf states if it should come to feel that one or another of these states is up for grabs, or has become an instrument of policy for either Iraq or Saudi Arabia. Iran could then become interested in some kind of *preemptive political action* in those states. Iran under these conditions will seek to develop in advance some political clout in the Gulf states, perhaps even cell structures, simply as preparation for preemptive action if and when one of those states starts to falter politically or fall under the political influence of an enemy.

Notes

1. Richard W. Cottam, *Nationalism in Iran* (Pittsburgh: University of Pittsburgh Press, 1979), p. 116. See also Nader Entessar, "Egypt and the Persian Gulf," *Conflict*, Vol. 9, 1989, p. 112.

2. Rouhollah K. Ramazani, *The Persian Gulf: Iran's Role* (Charlottesville: University Press of Virginia, 1966), p. 41.

3. Cottam, *op. cit.*, p. 335.

4. J. B. Kelly, *Arabia and the Gulf and the West* (New York: Basic Books, 1980), p. 313.

5. Ramazani, *op. cit.*, p. 46.

6. John Duke Anthony, "The Persian Gulf in Regional and International Politics," in *The Security of the Persian Gulf*, ed. Hossein Amirsadeghi (New York: St. Martin's Press, 1981), p. 190.

7. Ramazani, *op. cit.*, p. 122.

8. R. K. Ramazani, *Revolutionary Iran, Challenge and Response in the Middle East* (Baltimore: Johns Hopkins University Press, 1986), p. 115.

5

Iran and the Gulf, Part III: Living with a Republican Iran

Khomeini and the shah, although they employed quite different tactics, both provide examples of Iranian foreign policy continuity in their determination to maintain Iran's hegemony in the Gulf. Indeed, Khomeini's introduction of Islam as a major factor in the politics of the Gulf and Iran's use of the Shi'a communities of the Gulf in one sense have provided more effective entree for Iran into Gulf politics than the shah's own stated determination to defend the Gulf status quo.

Iran will, nonetheless, need to determine whether to pursue the narrower goal of support for Shi'a community rights in the Gulf or a broader, more universal Islamic agenda. It cannot do both successfully. An Islamic foreign policy need not in any case automatically employ terror and subversion.

Iran will be determined to keep all foreign powers out of the Gulf; only some vastly greater external threat to Iran—such as the United States or the Soviet Union—would be capable of altering this basic Iranian antipathy toward Western ties. Iraq alone has not yet constituted that kind of threat. Although some cooperation between Iran and Iraq against the monarchical status quo is conceivable, it will most likely be discouraged by the desire of both radical Baghdad and radical Tehran not to cede undue opportunities for influence to the other in the region. Otherwise, the smaller Gulf shaykhdoms will be the raw stuff of future power struggles within the Gulf. Iran will in any case prefer to deal with a weak and divided Gulf Cooperation Council. The basic dilemma of Gulf security planning for all interested parties remains: Who is securing what against whom in the Gulf?

This chapter examines the changes that the Islamic Republic of Iran has introduced into Gulf politics, the new use of Islam by Iran as a policy instrument, and a look at Iranian policy options in the Gulf in the future. Iranian policies and options in the Gulf naturally depend on more than Iran itself: Events and policies in the other states of the region will markedly determine Iran's actions as well.

This chapter, therefore, examines a few of the possible scenarios and changes that can be anticipated in future Gulf politics.

Iran Joins the Revolutionary Camp

The cataclysm of the Iranian Revolution not only revolutionized Iran itself but also turned upside down the entire structure of Gulf politics and alliances—catching the world by surprise at the same time. Iran had stood as a symbol of the status quo in the Gulf ever since World War I—with the exception of contesting the British formula for the region upon British withdrawal. This stance reflected not only the conservatism of a monarchy, but the desire not to allow radical forces any inroads that could be exploited against Iran. Tehran even swallowed its historical contempt for Saudi Arabia and attempted to work meaningfully with Riyadh on security issues following the British pullout. With Khomeini's accession to power in Tehran, however, a new order was in the making. In a stunning ideological flanking maneuver, Iran now bypassed revolutionary Iraq and any latent Arab nationalist movements in the Gulf, laying down a "superideology"—as equally threatening both to revolutionary Iraq as it was to the traditional Gulf Arab monarchies. No longer would the old radical agenda of Arab nationalism, social justice, and antiimperialism suffice to protect radical Middle Eastern regimes from being ideologically flanked. *Islamic* legitimacy, as defined by the radical Shi'ite vision of the ayatollah, now became the only valid litmus test of legitimacy acceptable to Iran—a test in which Baghdad as readily as Saudi Arabia was found wanting.

Revolution had once again changed the geostrategic game in the Gulf. Iran, the weightiest player in the game, had just shifted out of the conservative column into the radical. For Tehran the status quo was now the enemy. The emergence of this "superrevolutionary" force now threatened all states, forcing them—ultimately even radical Iraq—to adopt a defensive position. This Gulf Arab front, eventually uniting against Iran, was an extraordinary precedent, almost unknown in modern times—suggesting that only a virulently dangerous Iran is capable of galvanizing the disparate forces of the Gulf entirely against it. It also suggests that Iran ideally will be prudent in the future in order to avoid creating such a united front against it.

Changing the Rules of Self-Preservation

For the Gulf states the Iranian *bouleversement* changed many of the time honored rules of the self-preservation game. These small shaykhdoms had historically evolved their own set of defensive principles based on the maxim that "when elephants fight, the grass always loses." Many of these principles are typical of almost any small state facing the realities of the great regional states around them—whose mere whims can wreak havoc:

- Avoid international controversy whenever possible. Avoid taking sides. Maintain neutrality on all issues for as long as possible so as not to offend either side. Offer to mediate on issues of conflict so as to seize the highroad and legitimate a position of neutrality. Vote with the great regional powers on issues that matter strongly to them but do not matter strongly to you.
- When pressure from a great state is overwhelming, employ "preemptive capitulation" so as to avoid direct conflict. Where possible, play off that power against another. Employ "checkbook diplomacy" whenever necessary to buy off potential bullies and challengers.
- Bring your wealth to bear to create social programs that will buy off any potential internal opposition.
- *In extremis* turn to whatever great power—regional or external—that can save you from imminent danger.

For most Gulf states—especially Kuwait, sandwiched as it is between three potentially predatory powers—defensive strategy involves periodic review of what might be called a "rotating enemies list." The immediate threatening state of the moment is dealt with in part by accommodation, in part by leaning toward the other states—but always in the full knowledge that tomorrow the enemy may change: If not Iraq, then Syria; if not Syria, then Iran; if not Iran, then Egypt; if not Egypt, then Saudi Arabia—the list of potential threats is long and cyclical, shifting with the times.

The Legitimacy Trap

The subtlest snare of all for the small Gulf states is the "legitimacy trap"—a phenomenon Iran exploited fully against Gulf states seeking external aid to shield themselves from the hot breath of Islamic revolution. If Gulf regimes felt threatened internally from their own people—fearful of the emotions that Iran might unleash especially among their Shi'ite subjects—was this not prima facie evidence of their weakness and nonlegitimacy in Islamic terms? Iran accused those states interested in Western security ties of purveying "American-style Islam" within their own societies, of selling out to alien and imperialist forces to protect themselves from the righteous wrath of real Islam. And by taking such a posture, Iran itself was of course establishing its own Islamic legitimacy as arbiter of the Islamic legitimacy of others.

Receipt of Western security support and protection could therefore very well mean a kiss of death to the legitimacy of these regimes—much as the establishment of security ties or provision of military bases to the British or the United States in the 1950s and 1960s dangerously exposed many Arab states to assault from radical Arab nationalism. This legitimacy trap is a permanent feature of Middle Eastern politics: Alliances between Muslim countries—especially monarchies—and the West can be very costly to both parties in the end. They usually are only a last resort.

Enter a New Corporate Player—
the Gulf Cooperation Council

The outbreak of the Iran-Iraq War created precisely the very dilemma traditionally feared by the Gulf states: A critical strategic choice was about to be forced upon them. Their initial reaction, however, was shrewd, positive, and constructive: the formation of the Gulf Cooperation Council (GCC) involving all the small states of the Gulf, plus Saudi Arabia.

The establishment of the GCC as a broader organization in May 1981 flowed out of the logic of events in the Gulf during the 1970s. The Gulf states had demonstrated increasing interest in strengthening their overall economic and security relations. And the Gulf states were concerned with *all* possible threats to their security—which included the Soviet threat after the invasion of Afghanistan and even a potential threat from the United States itself, which had engaged in a great deal of public saber rattling stemming from the days of the first oil embargo in 1973 when Washington openly discussed invasion or "food embargoes" against some of the oil states.[1] Thus the idea of some regional cooperative and defensive grouping was hardly new. A number of self-serving plans had been proposed separately by the shah, Iraq, and the Saudis during the preceding decade. The adroitness of the Gulf states came in seizing advantage of the war to exclude the two elephants, Iran and Iraq, both of whom could be viewed as constituting the problem as much as they were the solution.

Saudi Arabia was the architect of the GCC plan and took pains to conceal its real goals from Iran and Iraq until the plan was in place. Indeed, the war was Saudi Arabia's chance to take the lead in Gulf affairs as its two rivals became locked in mutually exhausting combat.[2]

The formation of this new entity—initially conceived more in economic terms but rapidly taking on defense aspects—tossed yet one more new factor into the complex equation of Gulf defense politics.

Iran and Iraq both objected strongly to the formation of the GCC: Iran perceived the council as directed against it. Iraq saw the council as a Gulf effort to slip out from Baghdad's own preferred Arab-state security system in the Gulf—which was Baghdad's counter to the shah's own long-time goal of a *comprehensive* Gulf security arrangement, headed by himself.[3] And the GCC member states themselves were divided on how neutral the GCC should actually be in the conflict.

With the birth of the GCC, Iran would be less able to profit from the fractured and disparate quality of Gulf states, or to intimidate them quite as easily. Nor could Iraq. As the conflict drew on, however, and the prospects of Iraqi collapse in the face of militant Islam increased, the GCC states began to recognize that some measure of assistance to Iraq was required. The Iraqis also made a number of not-so-veiled threats and statements suggesting that failure to support Iraq could have untoward consequences.

Iran's Strategic Dilemma—Mishandled

Indeed, over the course of the war Iran gradually managed to push most of the GCC states toward unambiguous support for Iraq—a position they would have preferred not to adopt except *in extremis.* Kuwait and Bahrain were the most immediately threatened, followed by Saudi Arabia. Oman and the UAE were less directly threatened and more cautious in their anti-Iranian posture. Geopolitics seems to have played a determining role here: The further removed the state was from the war front, the greater the degree of neutrality.

But if Iran's goal was to secure GCC neutrality in the war context, it failed miserably. Iran's dilemma lay in trying to square several conflicting goals in the Gulf simultaneously: (1) to ensure Gulf state neutrality in the conflict—lessening or eliminating Gulf state support for Iraq; (2) to establish Iranian political and military hegemony over the Gulf as a whole; (3) to win over long-term Gulf state acquiescence to Iranian domination of the Gulf; (4) to challenge the legitimacy of the Gulf state rulers and to seek their replacement over the longer term by the creation of new Islamic republics; (5) to maintain an open confrontation with the United States in the region and eliminate Gulf state security ties with the United States.

If Iran had played its diplomacy right it could probably have attained a significant degree of Gulf state neutrality in the war, but not by launching ideological attacks and subversive efforts against the Gulf states at the same time. Given the long-range ideological nature of Iran's goals, the Gulf states could not afford that kind of an Iranian victory.

Inherent ambivalence is therefore built into the relationship between Iran and the GCC as well. On the one hand, Iran prefers that its Gulf rivals be as weak as possible—to enhance Iranian ability to influence or determine their policies. On the other hand, the creation of an entity to defend the Gulf by its own resources was a step toward a long-time Iranian goal: eliminating the need for foreign defensive intervention. Iran, after all, had just recently come into its own as dominant force in the Gulf with the British withdrawal.

Iran's policies toward the GCC remained ineffective throughout the war. Real GCC neutrality could have been a boon to Iran in the war, but Iran's tactics—military attacks against Kuwait, the use of terrorism and subversion against Kuwait, Bahrain, and Saudi Arabia, anti-Saudi political rioting in Mecca, and attacks against shipping—all pushed the GCC states into a scarcely concealed support for Iraq, and beyond. Yet GCC rhetoric consistently indicated a desire to maintain diplomatic ties with Iran—except for Saudi Arabia, which was ultimately driven to the brink in the spring of 1988 to break relations. All had consistently sought to mediate the conflict. The real desire of the smaller member states historically is, of course, to remain outside of conflict and to serve as peacemakers.

Iran's treatment of the GCC states in the future involves complex equations of interest. First, if Iran's primary policy goal is to keep the Gulf free of foreign intervention, then presumably it will wish to reduce those kinds of threats it once posed that serve to bring the United States, the Europeans, or the Soviet Union into a regional military security role. Iran would seek to use the GCC's natural inclinations toward neutrality and accommodation to its own ends in isolating Iraq. If, however, Iran is determined to export the Islamic revolution and create Islamic republics up and down the Gulf, then it will clearly only play into the hands of Iraq, which would itself assume the role of GCC protector and "guardian of Arabness" in the Gulf, however much the GCC itself distrusted this Iraqi role.

Iran's own goals would seem best served by the first policy—one of accommodation with the GCC and reduction of threat to it. It would appear that Iran is in fact moving in this direction. But Iran's calculations are complicated by at least two other factors:

1. Iran's revolutionary imperative has so far impelled it in the direction of strong ideological stance—in which assaults against traditional rulers take high precedence in the fulfillment of revolutionary goals.

When does a revolution abandon more unrealistic and counterproductive ideological goals in favor of more pragmatic ones? How does it affect the purity of the revolution and the raison d'etre of the regime? This debate will probably continue in Iran for a long time.

2. Saudi membership in the GCC greatly complicates the equation: Saudi Arabia is both a potential threat to GCC members themselves and is itself a true long-term rival to Iran—unlike other GCC members who will always seek accommodation out of weakness. Iran may well seek to detach Saudi Arabia from the GCC over the longer run, or seek to dilute Saudi influence in the GCC by seeking membership itself. Under present circumstances Saudi Arabia is extremely unlikely to acquiesce to Iranian inclusion.

Lastly, the GCC does not represent a completely monolithic organization in any case. Each state has its own interests and differing perspectives on Iran. As a general rule, relations with Iran improve the further down the Gulf one gets—partly perhaps as the local Shi'ite population diminishes as well. Kuwait has the worst relations with Iran among the smaller shaykhdoms, Oman the best. Iran will almost certainly prefer to deal bilaterally with most member states of the GCC rather than with the GCC as representative of those states.

The GCC possesses some additional value to Iran in that it will invariably take a more moderate position toward Iran than its most anti-Iranian member. This will mildly circumscribe or dilute the policies of those less well disposed toward Tehran.

Iran's Islamic Challenge to the Gulf

Since the end of the war with Iraq, Iran has downplayed talk of Islamic revolution throughout the Gulf. Yet the spread of the Islamic revolution is inherent in its ideology and cannot be easily abandoned. Iran will still seek to fulfill its own ideological aspirations, to create potential new Islamic allies in the region, to weaken its enemies and rivals, and eliminate the Western and especially U.S. presence there. In the past Iran has employed the following instruments of persuasion and intimidation:

- Open preaching of its revolutionary principles;
- Ideological, financial, diplomatic, psychological, and logistical support to Islamic elements in the surrounding countries, including training in subversion and terror;

- Direct challenge to the ideological legitimacy of the present rulers
  of the Gulf, especially those strongly supporting Iraq;
- Appeals to all Islamic fundamentalist elements including Sunnis to
  support Islamic revolution and the create a new Islamic order
- Use of Shi'a minorities (Shi'a *majorities* in Bahrain and Iraq) for
  subversive purposes and to stir up social revolution. Iran appeals
  to them as the "downtrodden" and "oppressed of the earth"
  (*mostaz'afin*)—invoking the full vocabulary of Shi'ite martyrdom and
  suffering.

In the end, a decade after the revolution, Tehran's foreign policies in
the Gulf have not been particularly successful. To be sure, Khomeini's
message has been effective enough to cast dismay and fear into the
ruling elites of nearly all the Gulf countries. In the early years of the
revolution he was actually able to stir up demonstrations, riots, and
disorders as well as stimulate a number of terrorist acts—especially
against Kuwait. But in the end the Gulf countries have shown that they
are not yet in a prerevolutionary situation ripe for Iranian exploitation.
    Several factors account for this lack of success so far, including: ethnic
dislike of Persians on the part of most Sunni Arabs in the Gulf;
unwillingness or failure of Gulf Sunni communities to raise the social,
political, and economic levels of the Shi'a communities—which they
view as taking place at Sunni expense; sharp differences among Shi'ite
and Sunni fundamentalists on tactics and strategy; markedly different
social and economic circumstances in the Gulf states than obtained in
Iran under the shah: The shaykhdoms possess far more egalitarian
societies, different and more traditional social structures, and are usually
well-cushioned economically with liberal social welfare programs; lack
of any demonstrable evidence that the Islamic Republic has yet discovered
a more successful political alternative that can alleviate the pressing
economic and social needs of the region.
    The emergence of fundamentalist Islamic forces in the Gulf was not
in any case the product of the Iranian Revolution. Indeed, an Islamic
resurgence—both Sunni and Shi'ite—was clearly evident among Gulf
Arabs throughout the 1970s, as in many other Arab countries. The causes
were numerous, but nearly all observers agree on several common
sources:

- The secular leftist ideology of Arab nationalism was perceived as
  largely bankrupt following the crushing defeat of the Arabs in the
  1967 Six-Day War and the death of Nasser in 1970.
- Interest in the potential political power of Islam was emerging—a
  return to the native religious heritage in an effort to find new

solutions. (Indeed, it did not escape Arab attention that the Israeli state itself powerfully combined the forces of its own religious heritage with those of military power, technology, and self-confidence.)

- The rise of Arab oil wealth and petrodiplomacy contributed to Arab ability to spread Islamic doctrine, especially on the part of Saudi Arabia.
- Massive new oil revenues had a general dislocating effect upon more traditional social and economic systems, including the creation of newly wealthy classes. (Thus both wealth *and* poverty can serve to stimulate greater Islamic radicalism.)

The Iranian Revolution was the catalyst that propelled the issue of Islamic politics to the center of world political thinking. But it is important to recognize that the revolution has two separate effects, which should not be confused in assessing its impact upon the Islamic world as a whole.

The face of the Islamic revolution in Iran has not been an attractive one to the rest of the world—Shiite, Sunni, and non-Muslim. Few Muslims would wish to emulate the *practice* of Islamic Republican government as exercised in Tehran, with its withering austerities, ideological rigidities, long, wasting support for a war, its harsh punishments and executions, and overall hardships. Iran is still far from being an attractive model for how to run a state or apply Islam. Only as Iran moderates and registers success in its domestic policies might its approach strike resonance elsewhere in the Gulf. All Sunnis and even some Shi'a believe that Khomeini's arrogation of all power to himself as the Ruling Jurisprudent (*Vali-e-Faqih*) is heretical. Shi'a are most despised as a sect by those Sunnis who live near them—in the often intolerant atmosphere of Middle East society. Shi'a by definition are thus hardly a source for emulation to most Sunnis. And most Arabs just don't like Persians.

But the demonstration effect of the revolution has been profound. Even to those who have not the slightest wish to pack their bags for Tehran were impressed with the power of the revolution: The ayatollah must have done something right to be able to topple the shah with all his might and U.S. support and to humble and expel the United States in the process. By dint of his very success, the ayatollah has become an inescapable model of ideology and revolution for all who would bring Islamic government to their own countries. And just as most Communists in the world were not deterred from their ideology by witnessing the ugly reality of Communist practice in the Soviet Union and China, so most proponents of Islamic government believe there is nothing inevitable about the character and practice of Islamic governance that foreordains them to emulate Iran.

The demonstration effect of the revolution was considerable in the first years in the Gulf following the revolution—producing unrest and riots among the Shi'ite populations in Kuwait, Bahrain, and Saudi Arabia. Islam had been reintroduced into the political process. The movement initially took political form.

- Personal representatives of Khomeini with close ties to Bahrain and Kuwait sought to stir their populations to mass political action to introduce Islamic practice into society. Old grievances of the Shi'ite communities surfaced as Iranian propaganda began to flood the area, highlighting the second class status of Shi'a.
- An Islamic Liberation Front was established in Bahrain with direct ties to Tehran. The resulting Shi'ite rioting and disorders unnerved local security forces.
- Kuwait and Bahrain were compelled to expel some of the leading Shi'ite religious leaders involved in the political activity and agitation.

By 1980, however, the generally political character of the initial Gulf Shi'ite disorders was evolving into newer tactics emphasizing terror and sabotage—again closely linked with Tehran. The escalation of violence reflected the outbreak of the Iran-Iraq War, the role of Kuwait as a supply line to Iraq, and the increasingly tough measures imposed by the Gulf states to quell Shi'ite disorder. Kuwait was struck by a number of bloody terrorist and sabotage incidents over the next few years, including industrial and diplomatic targets (attacks on the U.S. and French Embassies.) In late 1981 an elaborate coup plot was uncovered in Bahrain designed to topple the monarchy and replace it with an Islamic Republic. The Bahraini authorities believed evidence of deep Iranian involvement in the plot to be overwhelming.

What was worse, the deep concern of the security authorities up and down the Gulf about the loyalty of their own Shi'a citizens contained elements of a dangerous self-fulfilling prophesy. As Shi'a were removed from sensitive positions in government and businesses, as they came under increased scrutiny and suspicion, they were in fact further alienated from their own societies. This suspicion cast upon Shi'ite loyalty will continue to be among the main causes of Shi'ite disaffection in the future. The war may have ended, but the issues that gave initial rise to Shi'ite dissatisfaction have not, and discontent will probably grow. And it is Shi'ite Iran rather than Shi'ite-oppressing radical Iraq that will have the greatest influence over the Gulf Shi'a population.

The Sunni population of the Gulf reacted rather differently. Historically they have had little sympathy with Shi'ite aspirations. The strongly Iranian flavor to the Islamic movement sharply limited its appeal to Sunnis—even to those interested in Islamic government. After all, in the Gulf the problem involved a lot more than just abstractions about forms of government. Islamic revolution implied the overturning of the entire social order. On the much more personal level, it meant the elevation of a formerly downtrodden social caste (Shi'a) into power over the heads of the Sunnis, that is, one's own neighbors coming to power. For this reason, Sunni groups advocating a greater role for Islam in government relegated their activities almost exclusively to the area of overt political activity: publicity, formation of Islamic societies, and emphasis on education. There was almost no discernible cooperation between Sunni and Shi'ite Islamic activists. This has been a critical blow to Khomeini's aspirations for a universal Islamic appeal.[4]

The Shi'ite clergy in Bahrain, for example, have generally tended toward quietistic interpretation of Islam that does not lend itself to political activism. But they have had to compete with modernizing and reformist trends within the Shi'ite community. And although Shi'ites in Bahrain and Kuwait have represented something of a disenfranchised class, this has not automatically spelled economic deprivation. A reasonably strong middle class had developed that was probably less open to revolution than in other Shi'ite communities. Although the resentments of social grievance are real and continuing, and the appeal of Islamic values has unquestionably grown in the region, it has not so far added up to a truly revolutionary environment. In short, the conditions that created revolution in Iran were not duplicated in the Gulf in either the 1970s or 1980s.

If Khomeini's impact was initially sharp and mesmerizing, in the end the force of the Shi'ite movement in the Gulf seemed heavily dependent upon Iranian personalities and support, both in propaganda and logistics. The movement did not seem to draw strongly enough upon native resources to maintain itself as a powerful revolutionary movement. Although all Shi'ite Arabs feel special ties to Iran as the sole Shi'ite state in the world—and now the center of Islamic revolution—they are not without some sense of ambivalence toward the old Arab-Persian dichotomy. Iran and the Shi'ite revolutionaries were not able to overcome this dichotomy and translate it into effective political power.

How Universal Is Khomeini's Revolution?

Khomeini's name is inextricably linked with Iran and Shi'ism. But one of the revolutionary features of his message is that it *transcends*

Shi'ism as a faith and lays claim to a universality that embraces all of Islam. Indeed, most modern radical Islamic thinkers reject meaningful differences between Sunni and Shi'ite practice, considering them irrelevant relics of historical accident that have no bearing on the contemporary problems of the modern Muslim—problems of law, faith, morality, just and legitimate government, and society.

Whatever the impact of the Khomeini revolution, the failure over the last decade of Sunni and Shi'ite Islamic activists to cooperate in any significant way in the Gulf has been a major setback for Iran. Social pressures in the Gulf are not diminishing with time, however, but rather increasing—now exacerbated further by the dislocations of the Iraqi invasion of Kuwait and the Iraqi challenge to the contemporary "corrupt" social order of the Gulf. The pace of change in the Gulf has likely been accelerated, offering renewed opportunities for Iran to exploit developing social and political tensions in the Gulf.

Interestingly enough, the appeal of Khomeini's message tends to grow in inverse proportion to its distance from the Gulf and from Shi'ite populations. In those areas where Shi'ite populations are large, the ayatollah's call is a clear vehicle for Shi'ite aspirations to new position and power—and hence profoundly distasteful to the Sunni population. In distant areas such as Malaysia and Egypt, where Shi'ites are virtually nonexistent, the abstract message can be appreciated without the social baggage of minority demands and sectarian upheaval implicit in the Shi'ite politics of the Gulf and Lebanon. (Indeed, in Malaysia some Sunni radicals have styled themselves "Shi'a" purely to connote their zeal, not their theology.)

The Shi'a: New Card in the Iranian Deck?

It is astonishing to recognize that a leading scholar of Iranian foreign policy wrote a book about Iranian policy in the Persian Gulf, published in 1972, in which the word "Shi'ite" does not even appear in the index.[5] Such a remarkable omission suggests that a reputable scholar felt the existence of Shi'ite communities in the Gulf under the Pahlavi dynasty was not a relevant factor in Pahlavi foreign policy. And indeed he was right, it was not—primarily due to the shah's anticlerical policies.

The Iranian Revolution brought about a sea change in the Iranian policy view of the Gulf Shi'ite communities—not so much in Iranian goals in the Gulf, but in choice of Iranian policy instruments. Manipulation of these communities, with whom the Iranian clergy had long maintained significant ties, has provided Iran with a major new playing card in Gulf politics. This approach has become one of the important innovations of the Islamic Republic to Iranian foreign policy thinking.

But will this line persist into the future? How would a successor regime to the clergy play the Gulf Shi'ite issue? I find it inconceivable that any successor regime, whether Communist, nationalist, or secular, would entirely forgo use of this Shi'ite instrument of influence in Gulf and Arab politics. Any Iranian successor regime will, of course, have to consider the political trade-offs involved because manipulation of the Shi'ite communities will obviously taint relations with the rulers of those countries in other respects.

A Moderate Islamic Republic?

How might Iran's Islamic Republic adopt a more moderate position toward the Gulf states? In effect Iran will have to give up universal Islamic revolution for a policy of "Islam in one country"—to paraphrase Stalin's expression in the 1920s about abandoning the goal of world communism for communism in the Soviet Union alone—until circumstances were more propitious. Indeed the parallels go further: If the relentless imposition of revolutionary ideology starts damaging the broader national interests of the revolutionary state, choices must ultimately be made. Fomentation of revolution in the Gulf is not, at this point, a real option for Iran by which to strengthen its hand in the Gulf. The ambivalence in Iranian Gulf policy goals must be resolved.

The decision to pursue an ideological foreign policy will not, in the end, be decided strictly on its own merits. As other ideological states such as the Soviet Union have demonstrated, ideology is also the *vehicle* for factional struggle. A hard-line faction pushes its ideological line abroad as part of a power struggle against moderate factions. Ideological struggle is thus partially driven by factional struggle—even when the real issue at hand is not always ideology per se.

A deideologized Iran will basically seek to retain the small Gulf states as allies, or instruments, in Gulf politics. Iran would be able to play a reasonable defensive role in the region only if its own policies are seen as more moderate than some other regional threat. At present the only alternative regional threat is Iraq. A highly aggressive Iraq serves to bring Iran and the other Gulf states together to face the common foe. Iraq's traditional ideological and subversive strength is now augmented with formidable, experienced military clout and a ruthlessness and brazenness vividly proven by its invasion of Kuwait. Under any circumstances, Iraq cannot use its military force to invade Gulf states—other than Kuwait—without directly attacking Saudi Arabia as the access point, abruptly changing the strategic balance in the region. Iraqi actions will thus be a key determinant in Iran's relationship with the small states. The major destruction wrought upon Saddam's military power does not change this long-range reality.

What kind of Islamic policies are likely in the newly sober postwar Iran? The clergy almost surely will not be willing or able to abandon the Islamic character of its foreign and domestic policies. But an Islamic foreign policy need not be implemented with the full virulence of the past. Several possible "Islamic features" are likely to persist in Iran Gulf policy.

1. Continued close contact with the Gulf Shi'a. These contacts will be for intelligence and organizational purposes but will probably avoid terrorism or violence under normal circumstances.
2. Continued preaching of the Islamic message, urging states to adopt Islamic values, Islamic government, and a truly nonaligned foreign policy, including the cessation of all security ties with the United States.
3. Efforts to create or perpetuate international Islamic bodies sympathetic to Iran's own political views—and as rival organizations to Saudi-dominated Islamic groups.
4. A willingness to take advantage of political turmoil in the Gulf. As noted in the previous chapter, several of the Gulf states are likely to face some kind of internal upheaval from one point of view or another in the future. Iran will be poised to support Shi'ite political action in these countries if the opportunity arises— including in Iraq. But Iran will find it useful to avoid explicit clarions for revolution until the situation is ripe indeed.
5. An effort to weaken Saudi ties with the smaller GCC states.
6. A return to some kind of comprehensive regional security scheme, especially one designed to include Iran and to counter any hint of an *Arab* security plan for the Gulf.

The Legitimacy Trap Revisited

The Iraqi invasion of Kuwait in August 1990 resuscitated once again the same dilemma for states that had just survived the Iranian ideological onslaught: In terms almost completely reminiscent of the Ayatollah Khomeini, Saddam Husayn, too, blasted the willingness of the Gulf states to turn to the United States for security support, especially Saudi Arabia, which welcomed several hundred thousand U.S. troops and vast military equipment. Although Saddam Husayn has no credibility as a democrat, and himself was the recipient of excessive Western financial and military support during the Iran-Iraq War, he nonetheless has successfully raised the issue of the legitimacy of the Gulf state leadership and their stewardship of "Arab" oil. These charges find resonance within the Arab world where there is both envy for the wealth of the Gulf Arabs and anger at the limited benefits the poorer Arab states receive from the oil-rich shaykhdoms. The policies, and indeed very legitimacy of the Gulf state governments—now under assault not from Shi'ite Persians but from a Sunni Arab ruler—are more seriously threatened than ever before.

However the Kuwaiti crisis is resolved, it will have permanently affected the longetivity of the Gulf state rulers. The Kuwaiti royal family can never return to the status quo ante; a greater degree of democracy will inevitably be sought by the population as Kuwait is put back together again. These steps toward greater political participation in Kuwait will find immediate resonance further down the Gulf where those shaykhdoms, too, will be increasingly compelled to accept greater public participation in the governmental process.

The genie of democracy, first unleashed by the Iranian challenge to the legitimacy of the Gulf rulers, has now been reinforced by the Iraqi challenge and probably cannot be successfully contained. While democracy is the only avenue to eventual reform and longer term stability in the Middle East, over the shorter term it will prove quite destabilizing as new political forces emerge and the old ones are challenged. Increased political and social turmoil in the Gulf will be the inevitable result. Iran will have strong interest in exploiting these trends to its own benefit—both to strengthen its own position and to deny influence to Iraq and Saudi Arabia.

Could Iran Seek External Assistance?

It is difficult to imagine the circumstances that would impel Iran to turn to outside powers for security assistance in the Gulf. A major external security threat would most likely have to emanate from either the United States or the Soviet Union to cause Iran to turn to the other power to attempt to deter the threat.

The long reform process and the internal chaos in the Soviet Union strongly suggest that Moscow is unlikely to pose a major security threat to the Gulf in the foreseeable future. (Soviet threats to Iranian territory are discussed in Chapter 9.) A Soviet threat to the Gulf today would most likely emerge not over ideological orientation but from conflict over oil access or from an attempt by one state to gain monopoly over Gulf energy resources. The Soviet Union very likely will also come to play some kind of role as regional peacekeeper in the event of local

Gulf conflict threatening oil supplies. Iran, however, will generally resent such a role by any external power—indeed, the U.S. role in the Iran-Iraq War was directed specifically against Iran—and Iran even opposed U.S. military intervention directed against Iraq in 1990 and 1991. Iran will not turn to another external power unless the order of threat to Iran is exceptionally high.

The growth of a major Soviet military presence in the Gulf, especially if it included a permanent naval presence or the establishment of bases there, would draw distinctly negative Iranian reaction. Only if Soviet behavior were highly threatening, however, would Iran turn to the United States to help offset aggressive Soviet influence. In short, Iran will strongly oppose any significant Soviet military presence in the Gulf if it enhances Soviet ability to influence the course of Gulf politics or to intervene in local Gulf conflict.

Throughout the 1980s, the United States was consistently perceived by Iran as the greater threat of the two superpowers. If the USSR does not pose a threat to Iran's own interests in the Gulf, Iran will continue to oppose U.S. presence and exercise of power in the region—and oppose any states that support that U.S. presence. Although the old East-West rivalry is largely a thing of the past, Iran will unquestionably find Moscow's newfound commitment to multilateral internationalism far less threatening to Iran's own interests than the U.S. tendency toward unilateralism.

Iran will seek to eliminate U.S. power from the Gulf area as quickly as possible and will devote its own policy energies to speeding the U.S. withdrawal of ships, naval facilities, and air defense arrangements. It will actively seek to persuade other Gulf states that have supported a U.S. presence (Kuwait, Bahrain, Saudi Arabia, and Oman) that the need for it has passed. Indeed, Iran in 1990 had already begun urging Oman to recognize that a renewal in 1990 of Oman's military agreement with the United States was no longer necessary.

A New Regional Security Order?

The Iraqi invasion of Kuwait has raised ever more urgently the question of a long-term regional security arrangement. Although the United States has been both willing and able to perform the role of security guarantor on an ad hoc basis, the United States is not perceived as a neutral force in the region: On the contrary, the United States is heavily laden with the baggage of the many decades of Cold War interventionism, often tarred with "imperialism," and is perceived as the chief ally and supporter of Israel. Over the longer run, therefore, the United States is not the ideal state to spearhead a continuing process of security intervention. Even those states that seek the U.S. security umbrella pay some price in terms of their own legitimacy and independent standing in the region. A new post–Cold War era in which we now have—for almost the first time—a functioning United Nations, presents new opportunities for regional and multilateral security arrangements less burdened with the symbolism—positive and negative—of the United States. New arrangements must inevitably emerge in the Gulf that go beyond mere ad hoc groupings of nations to meet a given security threat, but which are more systematically designed to deal with regional aggression and that include all states of the Gulf. Iran may itself have a strong interest in such an arrangement if it can help obviate U.S. (or Soviet) unilateral interventionism, and Iran conceivably could take the lead in augmenting or supplanting the GCC itself.

Any regional security organization that includes Iran, Iraq, or Saudi Arabia contains the dilemma of "appointing the foxes to help guard the chicken coop." Those three states are potentially as much of the problem as they are of the solution. Yet regional security is unthinkable in any terms that exclude them as well. It may be that a regional security arrangement will come to be linked or associated with a larger UN Security Council arrangement that can bolster regional forces and help prevent their larger members from subverting the regional arrangements. Other states that could augment the organization and provide greater regional balance are Pakistan and Turkey. No such organization is on the horizon right now, but its logic is compelling and surely will represent the focus of regional state security thinking in the 1990s.

Iran, the Preeminent Power of the Gulf

These hypothetical scenarios indicate some of the major operational factors at work in the determination of Iranian national interests. At the heart of these speculations lies one central thesis: that Iran is fundamentally the preeminent power of the Gulf. The defeat of Iraq in the Gulf War only hastens its return to preeminence. Its major interest is the preservation of unrivaled power in the region. In this way Iran will behave much like India, Indonesia, or other regional great powers: It will oppose any outside power that tends to dilute the exercise of local power, however revolutionary or moderate its policies may be at any point. The passion Iran attaches to the development of power in the Gulf is partly rooted in Iran's frustration in trying to assert the control that history, myth, and ambition tell them is their own birthright. No other state in the Gulf can begin to lay similar claim in terms of historical continuity of interest. The very stymieing of these ambitions by Great Britain, and later the United States, only serves to intensify the frustration. Even today there is no sea power in the Gulf able to challenge Iranian sea power, except possibly Saudi Arabia. That country, too, has no tradition of exercising power at sea; its limited manpower and experience probably will limit its future role to a largely defensive one. But the unique character of the Saudi challenge will be the subject of the next chapter.

Notes

1. R. K. Ramazani, *Revolutionary Iran, Challenge and Response in the Middle East* (Baltimore: Johns Hopkins University Press, 1986), pp. 119–125.

2. Nadav Safran, *Saudi Arabia, The Ceaseless Quest for Security* (Cambridge, Mass.: Belknap Press of Harvard University, 1985), pp. 372–374.

3. *Ibid.*, p. 373.

4. For much of the content of this discussion I am particularly indebted to Joseph Kostiner's excellent chapter "Kuwait and Bahrain" in *The Politics of Islamic Revivalism*, ed. Shireen T. Hunter (Bloomington: CSIS and Indiana University Press, 1988); and Marvin Zonis and Daniel Brumberg, *Khomeini, the Islamic Republic of Iran, and the Arab World* (Cambridge, Mass.: Harvard Middle East Papers, Harvard Center for Middle Eastern Studies, 1987).

5. I refer to Rouhollah K. Ramazani's *The Persian Gulf: Iran's Role* (Charlottesville: University Press of Virginia, 1972). Nor is this comment specifically meant to criticize a scholar who has spent a lifetime in the field of Iranian foreign policy. The fact is that it was possible to write a book about Iran in the Gulf in the 1970s without singling out for special attention the role of the local Shi'ite communities as a major part of Iran's foreign policy calculus— except where those Shi'a were themselves of Iranian origin.

6

Iran and Saudi Arabia:
The Clash of the Fundamentalists

The pilgrimage has produced a vast corpus of bigoted lore about Shiite pilgrims and Sunni hosts. . . . At the root of the Sunni lore is the belief that Shiites feel themselves compelled to pollute the holy premises.

In 1943, an Iranian pilgrim was summarily beheaded for allegedly defiling the Great Mosque with excrement which he supposedly carried into the mosque in his pilgrims's garment. Ibn Saud remarked to some Americans that "this was the kind of offense which might be expected of an Iranian." The verdict in the local coffee houses held that "the Iranians always act that way. . . ." [1]

—Saudi popular views of Iranians

In their short history the Saudis have engaged in great bloodshed compared with any similar movements such as theirs. They have compiled a record of great massacres in Mecca itself, [as well as] in Medina. . . . The Saudi rulers have demonstrated in their slogans . . . that they would commit any kind of crime.

The revenge for [the spilling of Iranians'] sacred blood [in Mecca rioting] will be to divest the control of the holy shrines and holy mosques from the contaminated existence of the Wahhabis, these hooligans, these malignant people. The true revenge is to remove the colossal and precious wealth belonging to the Islamic world which lies under the soil of the Arabian Peninsula . . . from the control of criminals, the agents of colonialism. . . .

—Hojatolislam Ali Akbar Rafsanjani
on the killing of rioting Iranian pilgrims in Mecca, 1987

Saudi Arabia, guardian of the Islamic Holy Places and a Sunni state par excellence, stands as the chief ideological rival to Shi'ite Iran. Iran's readoption of religious ideology as its main motivating characteristic places it on a collision course with the conservative state of Saudi Arabia—whose leadership has always used its own religious credentials as a foundation for both legitimacy and foreign policy. Cultural views of each state toward the other have never been flattering.

103

Although Saudi Arabia is clearly still a stable and responsible state on the international scene, monarchies nonetheless do not possess an auspicious future in the Middle East. The leadership of the kingdom still views with great concern the spread of democratic doctrine in the region and is working anachronistically to discourage these trends throughout the region, all the while supporting Sunni fundamentalist Islamic forces as a counterweight to Iran. Saudi Arabia's willingness to host a massive U.S. military presence in the kingdom in 1990 to oppose the Iraqi invasion of Kuwait will hasten the erosion of that autocracy.

Revolutionary change in Saudi Arabia—whenever it comes—may transform the character of Gulf politics more radically than either the Iraqi or Iranian revolutions did and will very likely unleash destabilizing reconsideration of the borders of the Saudi kingdom with the Gulf shaykhdoms that historically have been under strong Saudi influence. Such reordering of relations will immediately draw Iran and Iraq into a three-way fray that will have unforeseen consequences for the Gulf.

This chapter completes our examination of all the complex geopolitical interrelationships within the Gulf as a whole. Saudi Arabia is the third leg of the great Iranian-Iraqi-Saudi triad that will help determine the broad character of Gulf politics in the future.

Early Fundamentalist Movements

Radical expansionist Islam did not first come to the Gulf with the Ayatollah Khomeini. It came out of the Arabian peninsula—repeatedly— as early as the first Arab beduin tribesmen pouring out of Mecca and Medina in the seventh century, conquering most of the Middle East in only a few decades of brilliant blitzkrieg. It burst upon the scene again nearly two hundred years ago with the appearance of the powerful fundamentalist Wahhabi movement, nurtured in the central vastness of the Arabian desert.

The Gulf is now witnessing a confrontation between two quite powerful and disparate Islamic forces facing each other from across the Gulf. One is Persian and Shi'ite, the other is Arab and Sunni. Both are contending for the heart of the Gulf and the role of long-term hegemon there. Yet the nature of these contending forces are psychologically quite different.

The fervor of Iran's revolutionary vision remained high for nearly a decade, whetted by the strife of war; only since the Gulf cease-fire in 1988 has its zeal seemed to slacken. Saudi Arabia, conversely, has long since matured out of the radical, driving phase of the Wahhabi movement that twice in two centuries spread its power throughout most of the Arabian peninsula. Over the past several decades Riyadh has in fact assumed a defensive posture against the forces of radicalism which have—so far unsuccessfully—assailed it from both the Arab nationalist movement of the 1950s and 1960s and from the radical Islam of Iran of the 1980s.

The revolutionary and expansionist force of Arabia is now in a quiescent phase. But both Iran and Saudi Arabia instinctively recognize that they are engaged in the kind of traditional struggle by which Islamic politics have been fought ever since the Prophet: not in ethnic, national or class terms, but in religious terms—challenging the very legitimacy of each other's rule. Not very far beneath the surface also lie basic issues of territorial control and old-fashioned Arab-versus-Persian sentiment. Indeed, Saudi Arabia has generally excelled at accommodating itself in one way or another to radical forces in the Arab world over the past several decades. The radicals have challenged it both for its form of government—monarchy—and its conservative policies, which have included generally close terms with the West. Such accommodationist policies were intended to deflect Gamal Abdul Nasser's radical Arab nationalist drive for influence over the Arab world. Yet it is radical Iran that has now cast the struggle in terms of *religious illegitimacy* of Saudi rule. It is not surprising, therefore, that one of the key battlegrounds of this struggle is not in the air or on the sea, but on the Pilgrim's Way around the Holy Places in Mecca.

Hajj Wars

Khomeini repeatedly avowed that the Hajj—the pilgrimage to Mecca that all Muslims are urged to fulfill once in their lifetimes—is a supremely *political* occasion. For the writ of Islam is not limited to the private relationship between man and God; it extends also to the character of the state and the obligation of the ruler to fulfill his historic obligation to extend the force of Islamic Law into the life of his people. Thus, asserted Khomeini, it is the obligation of the Iranian pilgrim—indeed, all pilgrims—to demonstrate against those forces that oppress Islam, and against the unlawful and irreligious character of the Saudi regime itself. For Khomeini, such political expression at the Holy Sites had far greater religious import than the mere fulfillment of the Hajj by the individual pilgrim.

The main feature of Islamic politics is that political movements of protest, interstate rivalry, territorial wars, and other elements of politics are nearly always expressed in religious and doctrinal forms. Challenging the religious legitimacy of one's opponents is the basic act of confrontation. And the Saudi ruling family has reacted more viscerally and sharply to Khomeini's challenge to its religious legitimacy than it ever has to Iranian acts of military aggression or sabotage. Following the Iranian-inspired riots in Mecca during the 1987 Hajj, in which hundreds of Iranian rioters were killed, Iran unleashed its harshest-ever barrage of invective against the ruling family's Islamic legitimacy, demanding that the custodianship of the Holy Places be removed from Saudi hands. This Iranian challenge struck a highly sensitive Saudi nerve, sparking for the first time a break in relations. Even more significantly, Saudi King Fahd formally moved to drop the non-Islamic, secular title of king (*malik*) and to reassert as his primary, formal title the role of "Custodian of the Holy Places." This title conferred far greater legitimacy on his position as Sunni ruler than the title of king would have ever done. By such things is the current conflict between Saudi Arabia and Iran measured.

The Emergence of a Saudi Gulf Role

The Arabian peninsula has rarely served in history as a center of power for exercising hegemony over the Gulf. To be sure, the early Islamic conquests out of the Arabian Peninsula extended the faith around the entire Gulf and eventually into Iran and further east. But there has been no *state* in the Arabian peninsula remotely capable of consistently rivaling Iran until after World War II. The fundamentalist and expansionist Wahhabi movement in the early nineteenth and again in the early twentieth centuries brought Saudi power to the edge of the Gulf and temporarily established sway over some of the local Gulf rulers, but it did not think in terms of Gulf hegemony—including the waterway as a whole—which was basically the domain of Great Britain.

The Character of Saudi Diplomacy

Saudi policies present a markedly different kind of challenge to Iran than do the policies of the more active and aggressive Iraq. First, Saudi Arabia is the largest state on the Arab side of the Gulf—automatically conferring upon it a role of major rival. Since maturing as a state following the accession of the remarkable King 'Abd-al-'Aziz al-Sa'ud after World War I, Saudi Arabia has increasingly followed a conservative and cautious foreign policy of nonconfrontation and accommodation in inter-Arab and regional politics. It successfully withstood the challenge of revolutionary Egypt in the 1950s and 1960s, and of revolutionary Iraq in the 1960s and 1970s. It has managed to maintain its Arab credentials successfully enough to stave off any serious revolutionary challenge, while using its "checkbook diplomacy" to blunt other potential challengers such as Syria and the early radicalism of the Palestine Liberation Organization.

Now shorn of the elan of the early Saudi state, Saudi policy over the last four decades has basically become defensive in character. Similar to the policies of other, smaller Gulf states, Saudi Arabia has studiously avoided involvement in regional conflict wherever possible. Conflicts anywhere in the Arab world create divisions, force all parties to take sides, and result in making inevitable—and potentially dangerous— enemies. To avoid involvement in potentially risky conflict, Riyadh has sought to play the mediator in regional conflicts enabling it to maintain decent relations with both parties to conflict, gain legitimacy for its act of noninvolvement, and gain possible credit for the peacemaking role.

The Saudis have often opted for shorter term tactical accommodation even when it has come at the expense of longer term strategic cost, most particularly in its consistent efforts to mollify radical Syria. Riyadh has always sought to maintain good ties wherever possible with radical states in the region that pose potential threats. This means adoption of the more radical positions on Arab "motherhood" issues such as Palestine and the PLO; here Saudi Arabia has not moved against the Arab consensus and often has only moved when the main radical opponents— particularly Syria—acquiesce.

Riyadh will have recourse to force against more powerful neighbors only *in extremis* and in self-defense and when other options are exhausted. It will even less willingly invoke U.S. defensive support unless the nature of the challenge is so great as to outweigh the "delegitimizing" character of reliance upon foreign—and especially U.S.—strength. (With Iraq's invasion of Kuwait in August 1990 the security threat to Riyadh became so imminent as to outweigh Riyadh's reservations and to accept the U.S. security embrace—regardless of cost.) Military conflict—regardless of one's own strength—is to be avoided for two reasons. First, it requires strengthening the armed forces, which could potentially turn against the regime itself. Secondly, any defeat, however small, is to be feared because of the negative impact it has upon the image of the ruling family. Saudi policy moves slowly and does not get out in front of any issue. Temporize and let issues resolve themselves where possible has been the Saudi formula.

The legitimizing value of ownership of the Holy Places is constantly emphasized. Even radical states on occasion find value in burnishing their own Arab/Islamic credentials through association with the Islamic character of the Saudi state—as well as the Saudis' occasionally useful ties with the United States.

This set of instinctive policy guidelines—never articulated or even acknowledged in any way—have served the Saudi state in good stead over the last half century. But they also tend to preclude a major leadership role for the country, for taking a leadership role by definition places the state at the forefront of struggle, creates enemies, and involves risks. It is in fact Saudi Arabia's size and financial power that have not permitted it to remain totally aloof from regional strife.

The Saudis have moved much less circumspectly when dealing with other smaller and less challenging states. Riyadh exercises powerful influence over many of the smaller Gulf states as the regional "super-power" of the peninsula—and now through the GCC. Riyadh has not hesitated to use shows of force or actual military engagement in brief conflict with neighbors such as North and South Yemen, Oman, and several shaykhdoms within the United Arab Emirates. But even Marxist South Yemen in its heyday has periodically caused the Saudis to exercise restraint in its dealing with it, out of Saudi fear of the power of Aden's ideological challenge—if not of its military strength.

These characteristics reflect a cautious, conservative state that has successfully used its oil wealth and accommodationist policies to stave off the influence of time and to keep at bay the social and political change evolving elsewhere in the Middle East. It has also consistently played an important and responsible role in Arab politics over several decades of regional turmoil. Serious long-term internal opposition has not developed yet within the kingdom due to the astuteness of its rulers and its socially oriented use of wealth. Demand for greater participation in the political and governing process has so far been successfully sidetracked through policies of social welfare—wealthsharing, government jobs, and the vigilance of capable internal security services that shrivel any incentive to rock the political boat.

Historical Saudi-Iranian Relations

Iran and Saudi Arabia have little history of long-term mutual hostilities; the two states rarely encountered each other until the modern era. Iran has generally held Arabs in contempt as "uncivilized" and "lizard eaters"—a prejudice that extends back at least as far as the Arab conquest of Iran when largely beduin Arab armies from the Arabian peninsula were the spearhead of the invasion. The term "Arab" strongly implies "beduin" in common Persian parlance.

We noted in earlier chapters on the Gulf the aggressive role Saudi Wahhabi forces played along the Gulf coast for a number of years in both the early nineteenth and early twentieth centuries when Wahhabi power temporarily threatened small Gulf rulers. Iran, like other Arab powers, was well aware of the zealous, puritanical, and fundamentalist character of Wahhabi Islam—and Persians were even more aware of its strong anti-Shi'ite character from its raids into the Shi'ite Holy Places of southern Iraq when in 1802 Wahhabis desecrated the holy Shi'ite shrine of Qarbala. But it was the modern Arab challenge to Iran of Egypt's Nasser starting in the 1950s that directed Iran's attention to Saudi Arabia as a significant player in the Arab equation. For Nasser also threatened the Saudis, and concern for the spread of Arab radicalism in the Gulf became of mutual concern to both Riyadh and Tehran. The 1958 overthrow of the monarchy in Iraq brought the threat of radical Arab nationalism to the doorstep of both the shah and the Saudis.

While sharing this common concern, there was little love lost between the two states. It is impossible to view Iran's relations with Saudi Arabia independently of the overall "cold war" between Iran and the Arabs. Saudi Arabia was a member of the Arab League, which, under strong Egyptian influence, had launched an aggressive diplomatic and propaganda assault against "Iranian imperialism" in the Gulf. Britain was seen by the Arabs as permissive toward Iranian ambitions in the not-yet-independent small shaykhdoms of the Gulf still under British control. Iran was equally angered at what it perceived to be a concerted campaign against Iranian historical interests in the Gulf, an overall Arab design to expel Iranian nationals from the area and even to claim for the Arabs Iran's oil-rich province of Khuzestan.

The prospects for British withdrawal from its security role in the Gulf brought the shah to recognize the necessity of accommodation with Saudi Arabia and the Gulf states. Iran could ill afford to allow these states to fall into radical hands—comprised of Egypt (sharply moderating after Nasser's death in 1970), Syria, Iraq, and the People's Democratic Republic of Yemen (PDRY), which was strongly supportive of subversive and revolutionary movements in the Gulf and the peninsula. Iran had equal ambitions for influence in the shaykhdoms and maintained some actual territorial claims against them. In a process of improving ties and settling bilateral problems, Iran reached a series of agreements in the early 1970s with the regional states to normalize territorial and other disputes. In October 1968, Iran specifically achieved a compromise solution with Saudi Arabia over the continental shelf and an agreement to share a major off-shore oil field. The Saudis were also pleased at Iran's willingness to abandon its claims to Bahrain and at Iranian acquiescence to the establishment of the United Arab Emirates comprised of the former Trucial Coast shaykhdoms.

However, the shah was also reportedly skeptical of Saudi Arabia's attempt to use Islamic solidarity to establish regional security.[2] Yet the shah seemingly was wrong in minimizing the role of religious ideology—indeed, Islamic solidarity represented the only ideological card that Saudi

Arabia could play to enhance its power in the region. And in the hands of Ayatollah Khomeini, of course, the Islamic call has turned out to be singularly destabilizing to regional security. The shah was probably additionally annoyed with Riyadh's use of the religious card because the Saudis were already nascent rivals for influence in the newly evolving post-British Gulf. Once again, the shah's distaste for the power of the Shi'ite clergy in Iran helped deflect him from playing any religious gambit in the Gulf power stakes or from fomenting trouble among the Shi'a community along Saudi Arabia's Gulf coast.

Fundamental Saudi distrust of Iran was further demonstrated in their ambivalence toward Iran's dispatch of Iranian troops to Oman in the 1970s to put down the Marxist—and anti-Saudi—PDRY-supported rebellion in Dhofar province. It was the first extension of Iranian military force onto the mainland of the Arabian peninsula in nearly 250 years, but it was of much symbolic importance given Iran's vision of its own role in the Gulf in the future. Saudi Arabia, strangely, provided virtually no aid itself to Oman to help put down this serious guerrilla movement that was ideologically hostile to Saudi Arabia as well and whose victory would have had major untoward consequences for Saudi Arabia itself.

The Future Saudi-Iranian Struggle

The Gulf states have proven remarkably stable. They have maintained order and groped their way toward some greater sense of cooperation and meaningful unity over the past decade, and have worked to stabilize the region as a whole. More important, they have withstood the severe buffeting of the Iran-Iraq War, a conflict that reasonable observers might have predicted to be disastrously destabilizing for many of these fledgling states. Kuwait was defeated not by the revolutionary doctrines of Ba'thist Baghdad, but by the armed force of a massive Iraqi invasion. The Gulf rulers have used their oil incomes sufficiently wisely heretofore to stave off major political unrest internally and to weaken the appeal in the public mind of any potential rival claimant to power. In geopolitical terms they have pursued policies broadly supportive of Western interests in the region as well—for which the West, if not the native populations—are grateful.

Yet, as we have previously noted, the Iraqi invasion of Kuwait unleashed forces that have challenged the legitimacy of the Gulf rulers, the permanence of their borders, and their stewardship of "Arab" oil wealth. These challenges carry weight, not because they were so hypocritically levelled by Saddam Husayn, but because there is a modicum of truth to the charges. The Gulf states have yet to face the challenges of modernization and democratization that will in all likelihood transform them, their governments, their philosophies, and possibly their borders. These challenges are far sharper now that the Cold War is over and the concept of democracy is gaining credence in the world. The Middle East itself is ripe, indeed long overdue, for major social and political changes that will meet the aspirations of the local populations for a greater voice in their destinies. The Gulf states thus face a period of severe testing in the decade ahead. If it is not the likely move of Kuwait toward democratization that will affect them, they will be even more threatened by the prospect of fundamental change in Saudi Arabia. For it has been the large regional states, undergoing their own revolutionary changes, that have exerted the greatest impact on Gulf stability in the past: the 1958 collapse of the Iraqi monarchy and the fall of the shah in 1979. Any further collapse of the old order on the Arabian peninsula will alter the kaleidoscope of political relationships once again. To state that the old order will ultimately disappear is not to suggest that these regimes are currently unstable or tottering, but simply that monarchies as a system of government have a dim future. Radical change—coups or revolution—will introduce at least two types of major systemic change to the region:

1. Shaky shaykhdoms immediately become objects of Gulf power rivalry for influence and whet irredentist appetites. The collapse of any one of them will stimulate conflict among the Gulf powers in the new political fluidity that disorder brings.
2. Revolutionary change in Saudi Arabia will have vastly greater consequences, almost certainly transforming the state from a conservative status quo power into a much more aggressive and possibly expansionist force in the Gulf—thereby creating a new geostrategic challenge to both Iran and Iraq. There has not been an overthrow of a monarchy in the Arab world that has not brought sharp radicalism in its wake.

The Small Gulf States as Objects of Spoil

The collapse of monarchy in any of the Gulf states immediately poses challenge to the stability of its neighbors in the new environment. The Iraqi invasion of Kuwait will probably lead to the restoration of a new Kuwaiti government that will embrace far greater political participation from the population than before, sending the "specter of democracy" down the Gulf. The demonstration effect of coups and revolution in the Middle East is considerable. The borders among many of these Gulf states have never been well-defined, nor are they in most cases natural borders resulting from clear ethnic or geographic dividing lines. The United Arab Emirates, in particular, are a crazy patchwork quilt of contrived borders that defy modern statecraft and administrative common sense. They represent a Balkanized series of compromises, reflecting the role of tribal politics and the personalities of their traditional rulers attempting to reach mutual accommodation. The solder that holds them together has yet to face the hot blast of revolutionary or ideological fire from an immediate *land* neighbor that could melt existing arrangements overnight in the name of some aggressive new cause or social movement—either from the right or left.

In fact, however, the UAE came through the Iran-Iraq War fairly handily, keeping its lines of communication with Iran quite deliberately open. The war may yet have served as a valuable testing ground and experience for small Gulf state unity. The crucial internal challenges nonetheless still lie ahead.

Nearly every single Gulf state has a list of unresolved territorial and border questions that await resolution or have only recently been resolved. Characteristically, such historical claims are not always "permanently" resolved even when agreement is reached between specific rulers under specific historical conditions. This was precisely the pattern we have witnessed in Iraq's seizure of Kuwait, justified on the basis of old claims alternately abandoned and restored by various Iraqi governments. "Resolved claims" can always be reopened as political weapons of successor regimes; rejection of a previous territorial "sell-out" becomes the rallying cry of the new order. These Gulf territorial disputes, both resolved and unresolved, will unquestionably become grist for the ambitions of new rulers in one or another Gulf state—particularly if they are the bearers of a new ideological message or a new political order.[3]

Saudi Arabia as a Revolutionary Power

The third and most likely regional state that could pose potentially serious challenge to the small Gulf states would be Saudi Arabia. But such a scenario would require a profoundly altered Saudi Arabia, one that had undergone virulent nationalistic or radical Islamic revolution—one bent upon active projection of its power and its ideology throughout the Gulf. Such a possible change does not appear likely in the near future. But when radical change does come about, it is most likely to reflect the growing discontent of an increasingly educated and Westernized middle class that demands a greater voice in the conduct of Saudi statecraft.

Historically, the collapse of authoritarian regimes usually involves violence. Recent change in the USSR and in Eastern Europe, however, now raises the prospect of evolutionary change in a state like Saudi Arabia—the emergence of a new order of middle-class leadership gradually tolerated by the ruling family. This is the ideal, even if not the probable outcome; neither the present leadership of the kingdom nor the known princes in the chain of succession are likely to readily accept any sharp change in the traditional order because they themselves all represent an older generation.

The challenge to the Saudi royal family has grown sharply with the Iraqi invasion of Kuwait and Saudi willingness to accommodate a major U.S. troop presence for an indefinite period. Saudi Arabia's acceptance of U.S. troops further strains the traditional Saudi style of behavior based on aloofness, some distance to the United States, and Saudi "neutrality" in Arab conflict. The kingdom has been exposed to the searing eyes of the foreign press, and world attention has come to focus on the autocratic character of Saudi rule. Saudi dissidents now see greater opportunity to demand a greater voice for the middle class in the decisionmaking process of the state. If the Saudi regime is not careful, it may end up embracing the U.S. military presence—as much to guarantee the royal family's longevity and control as to protect against external enemies. The kingdom cannot long afford the U.S. presence before the legitimacy of the ruling family itself starts to drip away slowly into the sands. Close dependence on the United States to meet future long-term Saudi security needs will also weaken the kingdom's stature in the Arab world in the aftermath of the punishing U.S. war against Iraq.

Violent change might occur in the event of some foreign policy debacle in which the Saudi royal family was perceived as insufficiently responsive to a foreign challenge to an Arab cause. Severe violence or war on the West Bank or Jordan could serve as one such catalyst—especially if the United States were seen to be strongly partisan to Israel—although the royal family historically has been quick to articulate popular feelings of domestic outrage on such occasions anyway. The long-term fallout of the Saudi-supported U.S. assault against Iraq in 1991 may also prove damaging to the royal family's legitimacy.

A new united Yemen now possesses as large a population as Saudi Arabia and has penetrated much of Saudi society and its commercial circles. Saudi-Yemeni tensions are certain to grow in the future, immensely exacerbated by Saudi expulsion of over a million Yemenis from the kingdom because of San'a's support for Saddam. Both Yemen and Saudi Arabia nourish irredentist views against each other. Lastly, Iran will almost certainly dedicate major continuing efforts to delegitimizing the

Saudi ruling family, especially because of the central role of the kingdom as host to the U.S. military presence in the Gulf.

If and when such a new radical Saudi state came into existence it would be formidable:

- It possesses the greatest oil reserves in the world and a high capacity to affect international oil policy.
- It is already capably armed by the West.
- It maintains custodianship over the powerful ideological and emotional instrument of the Holy Places—bestowing a unique kind of Islamic legitimacy to the state.
- The Saudi state shares land borders with eight other states—in which nearly every border is far from permanently determined—giving ample room for Saudi irredentism to play a role if the state wished. It has several important sea borders as well with Iran, Egypt, Sudan, and Ethiopia where conflict could take place.
- The Saudi population, especially in the central Najd, has long enjoyed a reputation for traditional xenophobia that could forcefully shape the character of a successor state.
- History marks the country as the breeding ground of powerful and zealous expansionist tribal forces over the past two hundred years. Saudi Arabia's only major weakness lies in its small population base and oil-dependent economy on which to build great regional power.

Such a turnabout in Saudi Arabia would be profound—almost surely involving the overthrow of the royal family. A new regime would start by eliminating even the name Saudi Arabia—dropping the name of the ruling Al-Sa'ud family from the title. While such a new regime conceivably could be secular, leftist, and nationalist in character, the custodianship of the Holy Places almost demands that any future Saudi regime utilize its religious credentials as a key element of its foreign policy. In any case, the new Arabian state would markedly reshape the constellation of forces in the Gulf, challenging the two other major Gulf powers that in their day themselves underwent radical and expansionist revolutionary regimes: Iraq and Iran. How might Iran act under those circumstances? Instant radical ally? More likely instant radical rival, unless somehow the two states were firmly allied against some other mutual threat in the region. Even then, regional geopolitics suggests these two countries would not long be allies. Revolutionary Islamic Iran would probably not long welcome the advent of a new revolutionary power in Saudi Arabia— even if it were Islamic. Regardless of how religiously based such a new Saudi regime might be, it is still the center of *Sunni* Islam. This fact almost guarantees that the new Saudi state would move swiftly into conflict with the heart of revolutionary Shi'ite Islam. However "universal" each state may feel its message to be, great power politics would almost certainly quickly destroy pretense of common cause. The spoils of the conflict would inevitably be the smaller Gulf states—now even more at the mercy of a newly resurgent Arabian revolutionary power. This is the one circumstance under which Iran more conceivably could then adopt the position of guarantor of the status quo and protector of the established Gulf order. Iran would nevertheless be hard put to block Saudi military action against Saudi Arabia's immediate land neighbors. Iraq, too, might adopt a position of support for the status quo rather than permit massive Saudi expansion of Gulf oil holdings and the explicit challenge to Iraqi power in the Gulf. Indeed, both Iran and Iraq might have common interests in limiting the growth of new Saudi expansive power.

Change in Gulf-Saudi Relations

As we noted in an earlier chapter, several states next to Saudi Arabia face uncertain futures that could affect Iran's interests in the Gulf.

Bahrain

Bahrain is already on the way to becoming a dependency of Saudi Arabia now that a physical link between the two exists—a causeway from the Saudi mainland to Bahrain that immensely facilitates the entry of Saudi troops into Bahrain in the event of disorders. The Saudis would be particularly disinclined to countenance disorders by the Shi'a majority there, especially because of the possible spillover effect into Saudi Arabia's own Shi'ite areas in the Eastern Province of the country.

Instability and Shi'a-Sunni clashes are likely to increase as Bahrain's oil runs out around 1996 and the economy begins to suffer.[4] The Shi'a population will be hardest hit and labor disorders will become far more likely. At that point, Saudi economic aid to Bahrain will make the island particularly subject to Saudi influence. That influence—especially the sterner aspects of Wahhabi culture in what is a relatively tolerant Bahraini society—will not be welcomed by the population at large, especially by the Shi'a who historically fear Wahhabism.

Under such circumstances, Saudi Arabia will be cast into the potentially volatile role of defender of the status quo and opposed by forces seeking change. The Sunni minority population on Bahrain will feel highly ambivalent—torn between dislike of a Wahhabi-asserted right of eminent domain on the one hand and an aversion to the rise of local Shi'a power on the other. Iran almost certainly would react strongly against such a situation and directly oppose the extension of Saudi power.

The UAE

The UAE will undergo a period of turmoil as social change hits the individual shaykhdoms. The UAE has no history as a country and very little to bind it together. Saudi Arabia could possibly find itself absorbing parts of the UAE if internal politics or internal political change should render it unviable as a state. It would contest much of this territory with Oman. (See Chapter 5 for a more detailed discussion.)

Qatar

Qatar is almost an appendage of Saudi Arabia already. If disorders were to develop in the country, the Saudi military would move quickly and Riyadh would be tempted to annex it as an additional province of Saudi Arabia. Given historical ties between Qatar and Saudi Arabia, it is unlikely that any other state would be in a position to effectively block Saudi absorption of Qatar.

Oman

Oman has a powerful sense of its own nationhood and could never accept being absorbed by a greater Saudi Arabia. Border problems exist between the two countries that have not been settled. Nonsettlement of these issues reflects deeper animosities and frictions between the two countries that are almost surely likely to emerge in the future when Oman's monarchy comes to an end and nationalist elements take over. (See Chapter 5.)

Kuwait

With the expulsion of Iraqi forces and the restoration of Kuwaiti sovereignty, the pressures have sharply intensified for greater political pluralism in Kuwait. Resistance by the ruling Al-Sabah family to genuine change augurs poorly for peaceful evolution toward greater democracy. U.S. policy may also be reticent to push for such reform before the new Kuwaiti order hardens once again.

A democratic Kuwait will nonetheless attract Saudi ire, and a revolutionary Saudi Arabia is likely to threaten Kuwait's future independence, if not its territorial integrity. Both Iraq and Iran are in a position to deny Kuwait to a radical Saudi Arabia should it be threatened, although such "altruism" by either Baghdad or Tehran in the future will be viewed with deep suspicion by Kuwait.

Kuwait will always remain vulnerable to the great powers of the region. It remains susceptible to instability given its mixed religious population and history of periodic quasi-democratic government, which has given the population a taste for much greater political freedom. Resentments within Kuwait will run high against the expatriate Palestinian population that largely sided with Iraq during the invasion. A radical Saudi government would be well placed to stimulate further radical trends in the country, if the country has itself not already been radicalized as a result of the Gulf War, opposition to the ruling family, and close dependence on the United States for security. Kuwait can only look to a larger international order to protect it since its immensely strategic exposure to all three great states of the Gulf limits its choices sharply. It may well be doomed to be the cockpit of the Persian Gulf.

Conclusion

Saudi Arabia thus has yet to emerge as a full-fledged rival to Iran among the "great powers of the Gulf." Under its present form of government it is unlikely to depart from its current defensive approach to foreign policy—and hence is unlikely to undergo significant internal change without marked change in the regime itself. It remains to be seen how much the experience of the Iraqi invasion of Kuwait will affect the internal Saudi order and push it in the direction of reform and pluralism. While nearly all states would wish for change in Saudi Arabia to come only by evolution, the historical phenomenon of the fall of monarchies in the Middle East offers nothing other than precedents of violence followed by radicalism. Perhaps Saudi Arabia will prove enlightened enough to lead the way in breaking this pernicious precedent in Arab politics.

In the meantime, a conservative Saudi Arabia could also be expected to intervene more actively if serious internal disorders take place in any of the small Gulf states. Iraq will likely contest all Saudi interventionism in the Gulf if it is protective of the status quo, but Iraq will also seek to deny any gains to Iran in the region as well.

If a revolutionary Saudi Arabia were to develop a policy of expansionism, however—particularly with the prize of increased oil holdings at stake—the nature of the three way competition between Iran, Iraq, and Saudi Arabia is hard to calculate. The closest thing to an international consensus that might exist in the Gulf would be the prevention of a resurgent or expansionist Saudi Arabia from gathering even more of the Gulf's oil resources under the monopoly of one state. Saudi Arabia is better positioned to seize regional oil assets than either Iraq or Iran.

The oil market is probably best insulated from violent change if it is reasonably decentralized; de facto Saudi centralization of oil resources through expansion would be in almost nobody else's best interest. In short, the dropping of the "third shoe" of revolution in the Gulf will bring sharp reorderings of relationships hardly foreseen today.

Notes

1. Martin Kramer, "Behind the Riot in Mecca," Research Memorandum, Policy Focus Number Five, Washington Institute for Near East Policy, August 1987, p. 3.

2. R. K. Ramazani, *Revolutionary Iran, Challenge and Response in the Middle East* (Baltimore: Johns Hopkins University Press, 1986), p. 67.

3. See Robert Litwak, *Security in the Persian Gulf 2: Sources of Interstate Conflict* (Aldershot, U.K.: International Institute for Strategic Studies, Gower Publishing Company, 1981), for a full discussion of the range of unresolved Gulf disputes.

4. Charles Wallace, "With Oil Drying Up, Bahrain Finds New Luster in Pearls," *Los Angeles Times*, 9 November 1988.

7

Iran, Lebanon, and the Arab-Israeli Conflict

The Islamic movement met its first saboteur in the Jewish people, who are at the source of all the anti-Islamic libels and intrigues current today.
—*from* **The Sayings of Ayatollah Khomeini**

Islam was dead or dying for nearly fourteen centuries; we have revived it with the blood of our youth. . . . We shall soon liberate Jerusalem and pray there.
—*Ayatollah Khomeini in Qom, 1979*[1]

Iran's involvement in Levantine politics underwent a sea change with the departure of the Pahlavis and the advent of Ayatollah Khomeini. Iranian policy toward the Lebanon-Syria-Israel triangle changed more dramatically than toward any other part of the world, save the United States. Iran adopted the cause of the Lebanese Shi'a and in a brief period helped create a radical political movement that went on to employ terror and guerrilla tactics against the U.S. and Israeli presence in Lebanon more effectively than any Lebanese group had ever done before. For the first time, the Lebanese Shi'a were actively—and perhaps permanently—enlisted into the anti-Israeli struggle.

Israel was the supreme loser: Iran moved from a smooth working relationship with Israel under the shah to a position of extreme hostility, adopting a more radical agenda toward the existence of the Israeli state than the radical Arab states themselves. Iran also developed a strategic relationship with Syria, founded on a common antimoderate agenda—one that has strengthened the capabilities of both parties in the region. Syrian ties with Iran are based on several common regional goals, but extend even more deeply into ideological and even religious affinities that have helped preserve this relationship longer than most observers would have expected.

119

Iran will not readily abandon the Lebanese Shi'ite cause, one of Khomeini's major successes abroad. Ties with Israel are never likely to return to the degree of cordiality under the shah as the legacy of the Islamic Republic fortifies a natural Iranian inclination toward nonalignment—in which Israel is perceived as an oppressor of Muslims and especially the Palestinians and symbol of a Western dominance in the region.

This chapter examines the remarkable evolution of Iranian policy in the Levant from the shah to the ayatollah and assesses the long-range character of Iran's interest in the Arab-Israeli struggle.

Modern Iran is a newcomer to Arab politics of the Eastern Mediterranean. To be sure, the ancient Achaemenid and even the Sassanian empires once periodically embraced large portions of the Levant. The cultural influence of the great Islamic cities such as Cairo and Damascus have touched Persian/Islamic cultural life as well. But in the last few centuries the Iranian state remained aloof from any significant political involvement in the area almost until the last Pahlavi shah, Mohammed Reza.

Political ties are not necessarily the most interesting story, however. In the Middle East, sectarian, religious, or confessional ties are often much closer to the heart of a man's identity than his state. Thus, for at least four centuries, the venerable and sizeable Shi'a community of Lebanon enjoyed some pride of place in the constellation of Shi'a communities around the Middle East. The Safavids, who formally imposed Shi'ism on all of Iran in the sixteenth century, cast their theological nets wide to locate Shi'ite clerics around the Muslim world who might come and help propagate the official new faith throughout the Safavid realm. Many Shi'ite clerics were thus summoned to journey to Iran to assist in the Shi'ification of Iran.

But it was not just the pull of Safavid Iran that affected Lebanese Shi'ite clerics. The Sunni Ottoman Turkish state—overlord of Lebanon and Syria as well—had been locked in religious and territorial wars with Iran from the first appearance of the zealous Safavids. Ottoman officials in the Levant thus viewed the Shi'a of Lebanon as an integral part of that broader Safavid, heretical, anti-Sunni cabal—and persecuted them accordingly. Many Lebanese Shi'a thus migrated to Iran for reasons of safety as well as the ideological call. What was to be a four-hundred-year pattern of cultural intercourse between the two Shi'ite realms had thus been established.[2]

But official state Safavid interest in Lebanon did not last that long. It was the informal, personal and *clerical* ties with Lebanon that survived on into the later centuries of palsied Persian power. Thus it was that in the late 1960s a charismatic Iranian cleric, Imam Musa al-Sadr, was invited by the Mufti of Tyre in Lebanon to serve as spiritual leader of the Lebanese Shi'a community. Al-Sadr purportedly traced his own family background right back to the Shi'ite community of southern Lebanon and in this sense was "coming home." Al-Sadr galvanized the backward, oppressed, and despised Shi'a community of Lebanon and led it to into an unprecedented blossoming of self-awareness, social organization, and political activism. By the late 1970s Musa al-Sadr's Shi'ite movement, *Amal* (Hope), had emerged out of a community of the downtrodden to deliver a political challenge to the frozen status quo of traditional Maronite Sunni-dominated Lebanese politics, thereby altering the face of Lebanese politics to this day.

One searches the annals of Pahlavi power almost in vain for serious indications of political interest in the Shi'a of Lebanon or in any role they might play to further Iranian state interests in the Levant. As always, it was the clergy—an entirely separate and self-sustaining institution in Iran—that seems to have perpetuated and energized the communal ties between Iran and the important Shi'a communities of Iraq and Lebanon. Apart from an unsubstantiated statement by Prime Minister Bakhtiyar (who took over as the shah fled) that the shah had at one time been interested in a "Pan-Shi'ite" union of Iran, Iraq, and Lebanon, there are few other indicators that the shah thought in these sectarian terms.[3] As we have seen in Gulf politics, the shah probably felt that to play the "Shi'ite card" anywhere could only strengthen the hand of his clerical adversaries. It is doubtful, then, that the government of Iran sustained any significant interest in the political use of the Lebanese Shi'a until the Islamic revolution.[4]

If Shi'ite politics were not among his chosen instruments in Middle East policy, the shah nonetheless could not remain aloof from broader Arab politics as a whole. As we noted earlier, it was the Arab nationalist challenge from Nasser's Egypt that rang the first regional warning bell. It was not long, therefore, before the shah was drawn into the eddies of the Arab-Israeli conflict as part of his broader security vision.

Enemy of My Enemy

Few geopolitical relationships have been as mercurial over such a short period of time as the Iranian relationship with Israel. Indeed, classic geopolitical considerations on both sides have been the very marrow of this unconventional relationship.

Iran's early interests in Israel sprang from several factors. The closeness between Israel and the United States suggested to the shah that good ties with Israel would assist his own relationship with Washington and gain the goodwill of the American Jewish community overall—a perception Israel was only too happy to encourage.[5] By the mid-1950s the shah had come to focus sharply on the growing radical Arab nationalist movement that threatened most moderate regimes in the Middle East. In the time-honored tradition that "the enemy of my enemy is my friend," the shah recognized that Israel served as a useful counterpoise to radical Arab power. As the shah began to devote ever greater resources to the development of the Iranian military, Israel became an important source of high-technology arms. Toward the end of the shah's reign, Iran had become the single biggest customer of Israeli foreign arms sales; Israel, furthermore, purchased 75 percent of its oil from Iran.[6]

This evolution in the shah's thinking led to public de facto Iranian recognition of Israel in 1960—immediately impelling Nasser to break diplomatic relations with Iran. Tehran's perception of the regional usefulness of Israel in controlling radicalism came to be shared by Turkey and Pakistan as well.[7]

For Israel, the calculus was slightly different and reflected an even longer range—although not necessarily more accurate—view of regional geopolitics. Israel, too, had long subscribed to the notion that the enemies of Israel's enemies were potential friends and had operated successfully on this basis in the diplomatic arena for some time. Israeli thinking ran deeper, however. The question of "enemies of enemies" was conceptualized into a pattern of concentric circles in the Israeli strategic vision whereby the outer tier of states ringing the confrontation states could possibly be corralled into strategic association with Israel. This was particularly the case when the outer circle comprised non-Arab or non-Muslim states. Hence, Christian elements in Lebanon, Kurds in Iraq, Turks, Persians, Pakistanis, Ethiopians, and others were all potential allies against the Arab radicals.

In Israel's case, the theory was not simply one of cold geopolitical calculation. Indeed, a deeper craving ran through the political psyche of this scarred nation: a hope that Israel's political problems with the region did not involve something as basic as ethnic or religious hostility, but rather a local strategic/military conflict over turf. Good working ties with Turkey and Iran were ipso facto reassuring demonstrations that Israel could in fact comfortably coexist with Muslims. The shah's cordial relationship with Israel showed that opposition to Israel in the region was not universal—and suggested that over time perhaps even Arab views could change.

The Iranian clerics—already deeply hostile to the Pahlavis—had sought to further demonize the shah by claiming him to be abjectly pro-Israel—a considerable distortion of the facts. The shah was always on record as sympathizing with the legitimate rights and national aspirations of the Palestinian people. The shah avoided gratuitously pro-Israeli positions and kept the Israeli diplomatic presence in Iran discreet and unadvertised.[8] Israel also quietly supported the shah's secret support for the Iraqi-Kurdish war against the Iraqi regime from 1973 to 1975. The Israeli secret service, Mossad, played a major role in training SAVAK, the shah's feared and pervasive security service.[9]

Israel Redemonized

The fall of the shah and the advent of Khomeini brought an extraordinarily swift reversal of affairs.

- The Iranian clergy was naturally strongly sympathetic to the Palestinian cause in its struggle against "Zionist usurpers."
- Revelation after the fall of the shah of the close association of Israel with the hated SAVAK only heightened popular Iranian anger with Israel.
- Israel was perceived by most in the Middle East as existing only due to U.S. support—as was the shah himself. In the popular mind the shah was thus locked into the Israeli-U.S.-Iranian strategic triangle—an instrument of U.S. policy.
- The new Islamic Republic was radical and antiforeign in nature; Israel was identified as an alien, essentially Western colonial element in the region and a policeman for the status quo.
- Although few Persians have much love for Arabs, and Jews have generally fared well living in Iran for over a thousand years, there is still a relatively mild, but latent, anti-Semitism among the population that the Islamic Republic brought out; an anti-Israeli policy was not unpopular with the masses.
- Indeed, the Islamic Republic felt it was a quintessential demonstration of its Pan-Islamic and revolutionary credentials that it should firmly embrace an anti-Israeli position.

From the outset the Islamic Republic's position on Israel outdid the Arab world by becoming in fact more radical than almost any radical Arab state. In 1981 Iran rejected even the creation of a Palestinian state on the West Bank as a solution to the Arab-Israeli problem, on the grounds that not all Palestinians in the diaspora could be accommodated there.[10] Iran had thus eclipsed most of the rejectionists in adopting this extreme formulation: All of Palestine must ultimately be returned to its true Islamic owners.

Israel Encounters the New Iran

Israel, of course, was deeply shocked by the intensity of the about-face in its relations with Iran. Impelled by the same geopolitical thinking that had guided their strategy in earlier decades, however, Israeli leaders were instinctively inclined to believe that events in Iran were a temporary aberration, that the natural Israeli-Iranian geopolitical coincidence of anti-Arab interests in the region would eventually prevail. This proposition was to be sorely tested almost immediately in Israel's own back yard, Lebanon.

The 1982 Israeli invasion of Lebanon was the seminal event that swept the Iranian state deeply into Lebanese politics. The Islamic Republic was vividly aware of the great political importance of Musa al-Sadr's work in forging a new Shi'ite political community in Lebanon—dedicated to gaining full political rights commensurate with the Shi'a's demographic position as the largest single confessional grouping in the country. Musa al-Sadr had also opened the door to another transformation in the Shi'ite world view: The Shi'a had traditionally not identified their own interests with the Arab-Israeli struggle or with Palestinian rights; these were, after all, Sunni issues and Sunni causes. Indeed, the Palestinian presence in Lebanon had greatly complicated the life of the Shi'a: Palestinian guerrilla attacks against Israel, operating out of the vicinity of Shi'ite villages in the Lebanese south, exposed the Shi'a population to Israeli acts of retribution. But many of the Shi'a were to undergo a marked shift in political/religious perception: The more religiously oriented elements among the Shi'a began slowly to embrace the Palestinian cause, now seeing it as in fact consonant with the Shi'ite world view of suffering and martyrdom—especially at the hands of non-Muslims. As that perceptive observer of Middle East society, Fouad Ajami, noted:

> Khomeini's revolution brought a change in the relation of the Shi'a to the larger Arab world and its symbols. In times past, when Pan-Arabism was the strident faith of large Arab cities, the "Persian connection" of the Shia of Lebanon and other Arab realms was carried like some embarrassing and insinuating baggage. But the Iranian revolution stood history on its head. A major revolt succeeded in the name of Islam and cultural authenticity. The material for messianic politics and radicalism was there. . . .[11]

Thus significant elements of the Lebanese Shi'ite community were on their way toward a newfound political/religious commitment against Israel. Yet one wonders whether this sea change in the world view of the Shi'ite community was completely inevitable. Was Israel itself perhaps not also at fault through its failure to recognize the sweeping social implications of the Al-Sadr movement and to make some accommodation with its aspirations early on in their invasion? The Shi'a, after all, sought what they firmly believed was a greater political voice in Lebanon based on their demographic preponderance. U.S. policy was similarly short-sighted in missing an opportunity for some kind of sympathetic posture toward the Lebanese Shi'a—a critical omission that inadvertently helped foster the creation of one of the most radical groups among world Shi'ite organizations: the *Hizballah,* or "Party of God."

Iran quickly took advantage of the Israeli invasion of Lebanon to dispatch a large contingent of its own Revolutionary Guards to guide the radical Hizballah movement. They provided it with material and spiritual support, lent ideological direction, and turned it first of all not toward the domestic political goals of the Shi'a in Lebanon but toward the geopolitical and ideological enemies of Iran itself: Israel and the United States.

The radical Shi'a at this point were not working alone. They were able to combine forces with the force of Syrian rejectionism to form one of the most potent anti-Western combinations Lebanon had ever seen. Two short years after the Israeli invasion—a fateful span of time littered with numerous car-bombs, truck-bombs, and suicide missions—both the United States and Israel found the heat greater than they could politically bear and pulled out their bruised militaries. These events have to rank high among Iran's most sensational accomplishments in the export of the Islamic revolution: No other force in the Middle East has been able to expel both the United States and Israel from its soil.

While the Shi'a undoubtedly have their own major political agenda in Lebanon aimed at winning political recognition of their demographic plurality, they will probably now maintain a generally hostile view of Israel. Even though the Lebanese Shi'a are divided into more moderate (Amal) and radical (Hizballah) forces, the trend is toward confrontation rather than accommodation with Israel. Indeed, the more the once-isolated Shi'a are accepted into the mainstream of Lebanese political culture, the more the Shi'a are likely to share much of the basic Sunni outlook toward Israel. If the Shi'a have in fact turned a permanent ideological corner, it represents a signal shift in the tectonic plates of Arab politics.

Iran and Syria: Marriage of Convenience or Ideological Kinship?

Iran's entrance onto the Lebanese stage was only a sideshow compared to the broader significance of its newfound friendship with Syria.

Damascus had long cornered the market on rejectionist skills in the Arab-Israeli conflict, standing athwart virtually all U.S. attempts to find a comprehensive solution. Iran's new role in the region was warmly greeted by Syria; the fruits of the new cooperation were readily apparent to U.S. and Israeli military commanders who acknowledged the devastating fervor of Shi'ism in their decisions to withdraw from Lebanon.

The Iranian-Syrian alliance formed in March of 1982 represented much more than a marriage of convenience. To be sure, large elements of convenience were there: Both Syria and Iran were deeply hostile toward Iraq and naturally cooperated against Baghdad; Syria needed oil, and Tehran was willing to provide it at special discount, especially because Syria was willing to close the Iraqi pipeline through Syria; Syria welcomed the bold, rejuvenated, and successful anti-Israeli, anti-U.S. role that the radical Shi'a of Hizballah were able to provide—despite some of the complications it presented to Syria's dominant role in Lebanon.

But other psychological and ideological elements also drove Iran and Syria that are important in understanding the psychology of political interaction in the region. In the Syrian view, the shah had been a supporter of Israel and a major barrier to the spread of radicalism in the Middle East. Syria had harbored antishah elements in Damascus for years. The fall of the shah was thus greeted warmly by Syrian President Hafiz al-Asad who saw new opportunity for more effective combined action among the regional anti-U.S. forces with Iran's shift into the radical camp. Both countries moved quickly to improve relations as soon as the Islamic Republic was declared.

To Damascus, the 1980 Iraqi invasion of Iran that launched the Iran-Iraq War, was a blunder of the first magnitude. Iraqi President Saddam Husayn had immediately termed his war a "holy struggle" of Arab versus Persian and attempted to draw in all Arab states into an anti-Iranian phalanx. By this one act, Iraq had obliterated Syria's hopes for the signal new role the fledgling Islamic Republic could play in the Middle East radical-conservative struggle: Iraq had cast Iran once again into the role of an anti-Arab state. Damascus still insists that the war was not an Arab-Persian affair at all, but a private Iraqi war that has weakened and divided the unity of radical ranks in the struggle against Israel. Syria therefore has consistently defended its break with Arab ranks in forming its alliance with Iran.

After nearly a decade of close working relations, and despite some serious differences in outlook over Lebanon policy, the Iranian-Syrian alliance is still intact. The longevity of the relationship indeed suggests that this is more than just a quick tactical marriage of convenience against Iraq as many observers have claimed. Only the defeat of Asad's grand strategy for Syrian strategic preeminence in the region will be likely to cause him to abandon the once-fruitful Iranian connection.

'Alawites as Honorary Shi'a?

The Syrian-Iranian nexus runs even deeper than mere shared radical views on regional politics. The ruling Syrian 'Alawite minority senses an immeasurable but nonetheless real psychological link with the Shi'a of Iran, the kind of association that so often creates political bedfellows in the confessional ghettoes of the Middle East. The 12 percent 'Alawite minority of Syria—who politically dominate the 70 percent Sunni majority—has long suffered from a sense of isolation as a disdained heterodox community in a largely Sunni world. Its religious beliefs—a strange blend of deification of the Prophet's son-in-law 'Ali, secret esoteric rituals, lack of formal prayers or use of mosques—have led most Arabs to view them as heretical and outside the realm of Islam entirely.

The 'Alawis' craving for religious orthodoxy and legitimacy in their existence among a largely resentful Sunni society has impelled the 'Alawite political leadership of Syria periodically to attempt to demonstrate 'Alawite affiliation to orthodox Islam—by claiming that 'Alawite belief is in fact part of the Shi'ite faith. The 'Alawis' problem is that senior Shi'a clerics in Iran and Iraq have remained unwilling—to this day—even to sanction the 'Alawite religion as orthodox Shi'ism. The Syrian 'Alawis have in fact garnered a few endorsements from some prominent Shi'ite clerics—most notably from Imam Musa al-Sadr in Lebanon, but then al-Sadr was first and foremost interested in expanding the reach of his Shi'ite community to include as many groups as possible, even the unorthodox 'Alawites. But the judgments rendered by these few clerics have been universally perceived as political rather than theological in character. The 'Alawis—despite formal protestations that they are Muslim and Shi'a—do not even observe basic Shi'ite rituals and principles and do not recognize the authority of the Ruling Jurisprudent in Iran. The longed-for political legitimacy, that only Islamic orthodoxy can help bestow, thus continues to elude the ruling 'Alawis in Syria.[12]

Yet Syria's enduring political association with Iran has suggested to the Islamic world that perhaps the 'Alawis did have a place under the Islamic sun, that the 'Alawi faith was legitimate, even if not mainstream. The Islamic Republic has carefully avoided any pronouncements on the subject—perhaps instinctively feeling that however theologically shaky the 'Alawite claim to Shi'ite status may be, the 'Alawis strengthen Iran's overall political goals in the Arab world.

But all of this smacks of angels on the head of a pin. Ask any Sunni on the street, and he will tell you that 'Alawis are indeed Shi'a—and he doesn't mean it as a compliment. In the popular mind of much of the Sunni Arab world, Syria's association with Iran against Iraq in the Iran-Iraq War came down to a simple confessional struggle of Shi'a versus Sunni. The final Iranian setbacks on the Iran-Iraq War battlefield thus have had immediate psychological and communal implications for the grip of 'Alawite rule in Syria.

The theology may be medieval and abstruse, but on such fragile psychological threads hang many Middle Eastern relationships—where perceived kinships and perceptions of confessional power matter more than the reality. The 'Alawis of Syria, uncertain on their throne, do in fact bear some psychological similarities to the minority, suffering-and-martyrdom syndrome of the Shi'a. The relationship between Iran and Syria thus runs much deeper in its instincts than most political observers have been willing to allow—and hence has survived a long series of tactical crises and differing goals to go on to another day.

These fascinating and complex relationships are immensely instructive about the possible range of Iranian behavior in the Lebanese-Syrian-Israeli context in the future. The Iranian clergy's own intense interest at the time of the shah in the far-flung Shi'ite communities of the region anticipated clerical policies when they came to power after 1980. These relationships thus seem to possess considerable power of continuity and rationale.

Of course, political relationships in the Middle East can be notoriously fickle and transient. Hafiz al-Asad, and probably his 'Alawi successors, will continue to field a complex regional agenda in which Iran, in the end, may not figure as a priority. But as long as the 'Alawis run Syria, and Iran maintains its interest in the politics of Shi'ism, this relationship will persist in one form or another—and if sundered, may again find a natural confluence of interests down the road. Should the 'Alawis lose their political preeminence in Syria, however, their Sunni successors will have no truck for ties with Shi'ism, even if they still share the old geopolitical hostility toward Iraq. A Sunni government will swiftly sever any special Syrian ties with Iran.

Competing Models for Iran and the Future of Israel

Of the two contrasting models we have witnessed in the Iranian-Israeli relationship, which one is more likely to endure, the policies of the shah or Khomeini? Where do the geopolitics of the two countries more basically lie: in a shared pro-Western, anti-Arab bias, or a more anti-Western, anti-Israeli bias? The shah clearly demonstrated his commitment to an antiradical, pro-Western orientation, while the Islamic Republic has done the opposite. In the end, although the future may lie somewhere nearer the middle, the Khomeini pattern is more likely to represent a "normal" postmonarchical, nationalist Iranian policy than is the shah model. Iran will undoubtedly carry a permanent legacy of nonalignment that may permit renewal of correct ties with Israel but hardly a cordial one as in the past.

With its revolution, Iran has now moved toward a much more nationalist phase, marked by the full expression of its latent anti-Western, antiimperialist views. Israel, as a symbol of a "Western outpost" in the Middle East and perceived instrument of U.S. policy, will represent a negative image to most Iranian leaders of the future. Israel is deeply associated with the Iranian *ancien regime*, is perceived as quintessentially anti-Islamic, and an oppressor of Muslim rights. Iran's latent historical anti-Semitism, while not a strong impulse, helps place Jews more easily into the anti-Islamic category; any close Iranian association with Israel is not perceived as a "natural" relationship in the eyes of the public. Iran will probably associate itself closely with broad antiimperialist, "Third World" causes for the foreseeable future. Its nationalism contains deeply xenophobic roots. The character of these roots works against close ties with Israel.

New circumstances can create new needs, and Iran will not likely preserve a militantly anti-Israeli posture if it comes at the cost of other more important policy interests. Israel, after all, does not loom large on the spectrum of gut interests for Tehran. Indeed, the pressures of the Iran-Iraq War led Tehran to do discreet business with Israel in order to acquire critically needed spare parts early on after the revolution.[13] So while de facto contacts, discreet trade, and possibly some deals in the area of high-tech military equipment may well emerge in the future of the Islamic Republic, there almost surely will be no formal diplomatic relations—much less any return to the kind of strategic relationship that existed under the shah. There is a strong likelihood that over the short-to-medium term Iran will remain actively anti-Israeli in policy and will compete with other radical forces in the Middle East for a role in the anti-Israeli struggle. One should not rule out some modest Iranian contribution to possible military support to anti-Israeli forces and to anti-Israeli fundamentalist forces among the Palestinians. None of this implies that the clerical regime might not be simultaneously capable of covert contacts with Israel to obtain key strategic military items that cannot be acquired elsewhere. The Islamic Republic has shown itself remarkably capable of ignoring its most cherished ideological beliefs to meet temporary tactical needs.

If the strongly internationalist Islamic orientation of Iran should over time give way under different leaders to a more nationalist phase, the anti-Israeli impetus may diminish somewhat, but close Israeli ties will still not come easily or naturally to a "neither-East-nor-West" orientation that will mark the spirit, if not the heart, of future Iranian foreign policy. Khomeini has furthermore transformed the traditional lack of interest of the Shi'a communities of the world in the Arab-Israeli struggle. While those communities once looked to Iran (and Iraq Shi'ite shrines) as the cultural and political focus of their interests, they have now been called upon to widen their horizons to perceive the Palestinians as among those Muslims who have undergone oppression, humiliation, and suffering at the hands of the Western world. They will now share with the Sunni world a more active sympathy for the Palestinian struggle for statehood. It is unlikely that over the longer run the Islamic Republic can "out-Arab" the Arab rejectionists themselves on the Arab-Israeli issue, but Tehran will at the same time almost surely oppose any settlement with Israel by the moderate Arabs, including the moderate PLO under Yasser 'Arafat, but cannot go further than Syria or the radical PLO in taking steps to prevent it from happening. Iran will remain a logical source of support for Palestinian radical Islamic groups.

The Israeli debate over whether Iran or Iraq posed the greater threat to Israel went on until Saddam's aggressive rhetoric against Israel in early 1990. Much of Israel, especially the military, had remained fixated on the size, and combat experience, of the Iraqi military machine. Others, especially in the Israeli Foreign Office, had been more impressed by what the rising power of Islamic fundamentalism was able to do in the region, fueled above all by Iran. The debate will likely continue, even with the weakening of the Iraqi military in the Gulf War of 1991. For Israel the most salient fact remains the hostility of both Iraq and Iran toward Israel. In the end there is little firm basis for any assumptions by Israel that somehow Iran will rapidly drift back to a "normal" relationship with Israel.

Stirring the Lebanese Cauldron

Has the end of the Iran-Iraq War and the new focus on domestic reconstruction brought about a major diminution in Iran's overseas commitments in more distant places such as Lebanon? I would argue that Iran's interest in Lebanon will remain—even if at a slightly reduced level:

- The clergy has always had strong interest in Lebanon as one of the major Shi'a communities in the world. Although the dominant hand of the clergy will eventually falter in Iran, I believe that almost any future leaders of Iran will wish to maintain the communal ties as entree into broader Levantine politics. We have discussed this rationale in connection with the Shi'a communities of the Gulf. Iran will, of course, have to balance its communal interests in the Shi'a community against other regional goals.

- To the extent that Iran will fundamentally pursue an anti-Israeli policy, it will wish to support those elements in Lebanon engaged in the struggle against Israel.
- Iran will remain interested in supporting the struggle of the Lebanese Shi'a to attain their own political aspirations within Lebanese politics.
- Lebanon has already been the preeminent success story of Iranian foreign policy, serving as the scene for two major victories against satanic adversaries: Israel and the United States. These victories argue for the power of the revolution. It is a key fiefdom of Iranian radical factions. Objectively viewed, however, Iran has enjoyed unusual entree and freedom in Lebanon mainly due to the collapse of local government authority. Any restitution of Lebanese central governmental authority will inevitably begin to circumscribe Iran's freestyle politicking in Lebanon.
- The Lebanese Shi'a themselves, although unwilling to cede overall political leadership to Tehran, will certainly find it useful to maintain a source of external support, just as do almost all of its other rivals for power in Lebanon. Iran's continued role in Lebanon will also remain dependent upon Syrian acquiescence, suggesting a need for continuation of the strategic cooperation between Iran and Syria.

Several factors could affect Syrian-Iranian cooperation, however, both positively or negatively.

Iraqi-Syrian Hostility

This conflict too, is deeply rooted and is unlikely to be permanently "settled." Iraq was already busy in Lebanon by 1989 attempting to undermine the Syrian position. Iran can be of use to Syria in supporting operations there against the Iraqi presence or against Iraq's Maronite clients of the moment. Nonetheless, a tactical change in Syrian-Iraqi relations will have direct impact on Syrian-Iranian relations.

Resolution of the Struggle Between the
Radical Shi'a Organization Hizballah and
the Moderate Grouping Amal

For a long period Hizballah had been gaining the upper hand in the rivalry for leadership of the Shi'a community, particularly due to the major support Hizballah receives via the Iranian Revolutionary Guard presence in Syria, in turn supported by Iranian radical elements. Shi'a politics in Lebanon are complex in any case. Iran may opt to unify Shi'ite forces rather than allow divisions to weaken the overall Shi'ite cause over the longer run. Syria may also press Iran to lessen inter-Shi'ite strife, especially when Hizballah takes a hostile position toward Syria. Obviously neither the radical nor the moderate Shi'a want to become mere instruments of broader Iranian policies, despite the benefits of accepting aid from Iran.

The Hostage Problem

Syria has operated a complex calculus of interests in tolerating the hostage-taking activities of the Lebanese Shi'ite radicals. Syria shares the general radical goal of weakening Western influences in Lebanon, and the radicals are additionally useful as anti-Israeli assets. Because Syria does not directly control the activities of these radical Shi'a, Syria enjoys the additional benefit of plausible deniability if accused of supporting terrorist activities. When the radical activity reaches a level where it can start seriously damaging Syria's own interests in Lebanon, then Syria has usually pressured Iran to ease off. Syria at the same time also gains the ritual gratitude of Western states for helping extricate Western hostages under certain conditions.

Iran also must balance the benefits that these groups represent in Lebanon as potent anti-Western instruments against the overall price that Iran must pay in incurring American and European anger. Conflict over the utility of foreign hostages in Lebanon could be one serious area of contention between Iran and the Lebanese Shi'a since their immediate tactical interests may diverge at any point, particularly during stages of Iranian moderation. In any case, Syria and Lebanon must negotiate their respective mutual interests in the use and control of the radical Lebanese Shi'a.

Syrian Interest in a Peaceful Settlement to the Arab-Israeli Struggle

Syrian interest in a peaceful settlement runs counter to the essence of the Syrian geopolitical vision of nearly three decades. Syria derives a great deal of its regional clout from its radical and intransigent position. Nonetheless, some constellation of circumstances is conceivable whereby Syria becomes compelled to join the peace contingent: the collapse of the 'Alawite regime, major pressure from the USSR, the defeat of Syria in a war with Israel, and the seeming long-range inevitability of a

Palestinian-Israeli settlement with the PLO, with moderate Arab state blessing. Under these circumstances Syria could find the Iranian presence in Lebanon—once a key asset in blocking moderate forces in the region—a liability.

Iran and the Arab World

Iran will seek to avoid the recrudescence of a common Arab front against itself—such as it created in the Gulf through broad policies of confrontation with nearly everyone simultaneously. As a new, ambitious, intensely nationalist radical state, Iran will almost surely seek a broader role in the politics of the Arab and Islamic world—suggesting the continuation of a relatively radical, antiimperialist orientation. In any continuing struggle with Iraq, Iran will seek to avoid alienating potential anti-Iraqi allies among the Arab states.

Serious deterioration of the Palestinian-Israeli struggle could also bring Iran into a strong and active anti-Israeli posture, but it could not do so alone. If Israel should engage in severe and bloody repressions on the West Bank or in mass expulsions of Palestinians from the West Bank, Iran will seek to make common cause with any Arab states that take the lead in anti-Israeli actions. Iran might be particularly interested in supporting fundamentalist groups in Jordan, especially if Jordan should undergo violence and turmoil in the process of "Palestinianization" in the years ahead and become a natural cockpit for the expression of Syria-Iran-Iraq rivalry for influence in that country. Although the Iraqi invasion of Kuwait galvanized most Palestinian-Jordanians into looking to Saddam Husayn as the potential strongman who might stand up to Israel, this was but a fleeting dream, for the path to the Palestinian state will never lie through Baghdad. Nonetheless, both Iraq and Iran can serve as magnets to this frustrated people to whom almost any radicalism may prove attractive in the face of Israeli obduracy on a land-for-peace settlement.

If Iraq should assume from Syria the long-range mantle of anti-Israeli leadership, Iran will be hard pressed, however, to make common cause with Iraq on this issue. It would take a highly radicalized leadership in Tehran to overlook the geopolitical rivalry with Iraq in favor of the ideological cause. Iran will also not wish to see Iraq gain any further stature in the region and would instinctively not assist Iraq in the cause. Thus Iraqi leadership of the anti-Israeli struggle is more than any single factor likely to weaken Iran's interest in the struggle.

Although the shah possessed an extraordinarily broad vision of Iran's proper role in the world-at-large, Khomeini has probably had more lasting impact in reorienting Iran's policies in the Arab world into line with mainstream Arab radicalism—or whatever is left of that Arab radical impulse. This places a future Iran on a very different strategic footing. A major question mark will be how much old Persian versus Arab feelings will give way over the longer run to the ideological orientation of the new Iran.

Tehran remains confronted with the same classic dilemma that faces it in Gulf policy: whether over the long run to emphasize the sectarian Shi'ite aspects of its interests or pursue a broader universalist-Islamic strategy. As in the Gulf, the presence of Shi'a communities in part force Tehran's hand: It cannot abandon the aspirations of local Shi'a who are Tehran's first and most natural constituents abroad. Yet support for these communities, as in Lebanon, nearly automatically casts Iran into the posture of an anti-Sunni force. This factor is the chief drawback to an Iranian Shi'ite-oriented policy.

In purely geopolitical terms, Iran needs counterweights in the Levant to the power of Iraq and Saudi Arabia. Under the shah, Israel and post-Nasser Egypt fulfilled that role. For the Islamic Republic, Syria under 'Alawite leadership has come closer to fulfilling that function than any other Arab state. In future years Egypt very likely will again become such a long-range partner. Egypt has had interest in the Gulf for well over a century and it will persist. Although relations between Cairo and Tehran are currently hostile due to Egypt's peace settlement with Israel, that will probably change in time if and when Iran comes to focus more upon nationalist geopolitical interests and less upon ideologically driven internationalist policies. Egypt's leadership of the Arab military campaign to get Iraq out of Kuwait in 1990 represents a further major step toward a potential Egyptian-Iranian rapprochement, but Iran will still be averse to Egypt's embrace of the U.S. military role in the process. Once the United States is gone, Egypt and Iran might find more in common.

Israel, too, could play such a long-range support role to Iran in an anti-Iraqi posture, especially with the attractions of its high-tech capabilities; Iran will nonetheless be constrained, as we noted earlier, by the "foreign" character of Israel's presence in the region, especially while Iran is concerned with the symbols of nonalignment. Iran will see Israel as a natural balance to the Arab world only to the extent that Iran's policies are "anti-Arab" in the broader sense. To the extent that Iran pursues a flexible and differentiated policy among various Arab states, Iranian ties with Israel will come less naturally. An Israeli settlement of the Palestinian problem will of course sharply alter the role of Israel in the region and will open the likelihood of much stronger Israeli-Iranian ties.

Notes

1. Amir Taheri, *The Spirit of Allah* (Bethesda: Adler and Adler, 1985), p. 243.
2. Fouad Ajami, *The Vanished Imam, Musa al-Sadr and the Shia of Lebanon* (Ithaca, N.Y.: Cornell University Press, 1986), p. 29.
3. Augustus Richard Norton, *Amal and the Shi'a: Struggle for the Soul of Lebanon* (Austin: University of Texas Press, 1987), p. 41. Norton believes there is reasonable evidence that the shah did supply some initial funding to Musa al-Sadr until a later serious falling out between the two.
4. The shah would generally have been interested in Lebanese politics because Lebanon was one of the key pro-Western Arab countries targeted by Nasser and by Arab nationalists for forcible conversion to a policy of support for the Arab nationalist position. The shah might thus have had some interest in supporting any group that opposed radical Sunni politics in Lebanon—the only rationale I can see for any initial support by the shah to Imam Musa al-Sadr's presence there.
5. See Sohrab Sobhani, *The Pragmatic Entente: Israeli-Iranian Relations, 1948–1988* (New York: Praeger, 1989), p. 6.
6. A former Israeli general officer in a private interview, January 1989. See also *ibid.*, pp. 115–119, 128–133, for further details on this developing arms relationship.
7. Rouhollah K. Ramazani, *Iran's Foreign Policy, 1941–1973* (Charlottesville: University Press of Virginia, 1975), p. 281.
8. R. K. Ramazani, *Revolutionary Iran, Challenge and Response in the Middle East* (Baltimore: Johns Hopkins University Press, 1986), p. 151.
9. See Sobhani, *op. cit.*, pp. 28–29.
10. Ramazani, *op. cit.*, p. 154.
11. Fouad Ajami, "Lebanon and Its Inheritors," *Foreign Affairs*, Spring 1985, p. 786.
12. Much of the data in these few paragraphs is drawn from Martin Kramer's fine essay, "Syria's Alawis and Shiism," in *Shiism, Resistance and Martyrdom*, ed. Martin Kramer (Boulder, Colo.: Westview Press, 1987).
13. See Sobhani, *op. cit.*, pp. 153–157.

8

Iran and Russia: Tsar Versus Shah

As for the Muscovites, they are not Europeans—they are less than the dogs of Europe.

Then come those heretics of Muscovites, a most unclean and accursed generation. Their country is so large, that one extremity is said to be buried in eternal snows, whilst its other is raging with heat. They are truly our enemy; and when we kill them, we cry Mashallah, praise be to God!

—*Hajji Baba of Ispahan*

The Russian landmass represents a stark permanent geopolitical reality for Iran, which lost more territory to Russia than to any other modern state. Indeed, Russia's long expansion southwards seemed to have no finite limits; even today, in the wake of the Soviet invasion of Afghanistan as recently as 1979, no Iranian can state with confidence that Russia's process of territorial expansion southward is over.

Iran was caught in the vice of the British Empire to the south and the Russian Empire to the north. By the first decade of the twentieth century, these two states had almost completely snuffed out any Iranian claim to genuine sovereignty and self-determination. While the Bolshevik Revolution in Russia somewhat changed the character of the instruments of control employed by the tsars against Iran, the Soviet Union continued to employ numerous other instruments as the new Pahlavi dynasty at the end of World War I gradually but successfully sought to reassert national sovereignty.

This chapter reviews the historical process of Russian Tsarist expansion against Iranian territory and the geopolitical dilemma of determining where the "permanent" stopping place of that expansionism is. It examines the instruments of control used by the Russian Empire to dominate Iran's political and economic life up until World War I, with an eye to the possible perpetuation of these instruments in the future. This chapter also examines some of the continuities and changes in Soviet policy after the Bolshevik Revolution and notes the sharply changed dynamic in Iran under the new nationalist Pahlavi dynasty under Reza Shah. This period is of major importance in Iranian history both for the psychological impact of these events on Iran and for the important precedents set by Russia in its relations with Iran—a legacy to be overcome if a "new Russia" is now born under Gorbachev.

The Historical Threat from the North

Russia is the single greatest geopolitical fact of life for Iran. No other power in the region is capable of invading, defeating, occupying, and exercising hegemony over Iran except the Soviet Union. This is Iran's central, immutable foreign policy reality.

The threat to Iran from the north long predates the historical expansion of the Russian people southward. Indeed, the steppes of Central Asia visited upon Iran many of its greatest invasions—in the form of various Turkic-Mongol populations. Both the Mongols, whose invasion and destruction of Iran was utterly devastating, and the various Turkic tribes, who conquered and controlled Iran for several hundred years, were peoples whose historic homeland was Central Asia.

In the end, however, no other state has permanently seized from Iran as much Persian territory—lands that were under long-term historical Persian cultural domination—as has Russia. The Georgian, Armenian, and Azerbaijani states of the southern Caucasus have for long periods of time either been under Persian domination or at least nominally under Persian suzerainty. Much of Central Asia has been a preeminent center of Persian culture and civilization for nearly three millennia, most of the time under some degree of Persian political control. Iran to this day has not forgotten its historical role and maintains special interest in developments in the Caucasus and Central Asia.

Iran gained its first real whiff of Russian power as Peter the Great made plans for extending Russian authority down into the Black Sea and the Caucasus. Russia at the outset was to share an appetite for Persian territory with rival Ottoman Turkey: Both states sought to divide the spoils of their wars against Persia. But Turkish power, as a rival to Russian influence on Persia's borders, was receding by the late eighteenth century. The British were now well on their way to becoming Russia's chief rival for expanding Asian empire. From this point on, the growth of Russian influence in Iran was to follow an ascending curve; by 1900 Russia was the dominant foreign power in Iran.

Russian influence and constant interference in Iranian affairs during Tsarist times is thus sharply etched into the Iranian psyche. Only Great

Britain shares with Russia the distinction of having exercised the greatest colonial control over Iran of any state in modern times. U.S. influence in Iran came only in the last few decades, and not in a traditional colonial context—but perceived no less vividly by the clergy as an enemy. Indeed, it has only been under the Islamic Republic in the 1980s that the USSR has been required to cede first place honors in Iranian eyes to the United States, as Khomeini's demonology relegated the Kremlin to the position of the "Lesser Satan" as against the American "Great Satan."

The Nature of the Challenge

Iran has undergone at least four separate phases of challenge from its confrontation with the Russian/Soviet empire:

- A period of Russian territorial expansion, in which the *physical territory* of Persia was permanently seized;
- A Russian *colonial* period during the late nineteenth and early twentieth centuries when Moscow sought not so much territory as dominant *political and economic* control in Persia;
- The Soviet period involving political, territorial, and a new *ideological* challenge. Communist control of Russia introduced a new technique of *political subversion* through the use of left-wing political/ideological groupings and parties within Iran to gain influence, or even bring about revolution in favor of Soviet interests.
- Periods during which Moscow made efforts to *politically dismember* Iran by attempts to establish autonomous regions or independent republics among the northern Iranian provinces of Gilan, Azerbaijan, and Kurdistan.

The record of Tsarist moves against Iran are important because they establish at least some of the major instruments of Russian control and influence over Iran—and determine the nature of the conflict. Although instruments of control and influence were to change somewhat following the Bolshevik Revolution, many of the same characteristics remained. Indeed, a key task in analysis of the Russian-Iranian relationship is to determine just how permanent—or transient—these Russian instruments of control have been. This chapter treats Russia as the primary actor in the relationship—rather than Iran—because Iran was in fact largely the passive object of Russian policy until the establishment of the Pahlavi dynasty after World War I.

Russian Goals in Iran

Over several centuries the Russians have employed a great variety of instruments in order to attain their goals. Although those goals have shifted from time to time, they can be best summarized as: territorial acquisition where possible; denial of Iranian territory to states hostile to Russian interests; acquisition of dominant influence over Iranian domestic and foreign policies in order to minimize foreign state influence in Iran and to extract maximum Russian economic and political benefits from Iran.

The Problem of Territorial Expansion

Living on the border of a great empire is a precarious proposition for any smaller state. Iran was inevitably to come into conflict with an expanding Russian state in the course of Moscow's four hundred years of expansion. The Persians and the British spent much of the nineteenth century watching this inexorable Russian process with concern. The analytic problem is still with us today: How do we determine when the southward expansion of the Russian state into Iranian territory has reached its limit? When do border states of the USSR no longer need fear physical absorption?

It is important to recognize that Russo-Persian conflict did not represent typical interstate contest over territory historically claimed by the same two peoples. The Russian Empire was clearly on the offensive in moving into areas that had *never* been Slavic or Russian. For long periods these regions had been under either Persian control or powerful Persian cultural influence—despite the fact that most of Central Asia had gradually become Turkic-speaking over the last millennium. Iranians still have a keen sense of having lost extensive territory to the Russians. How can Iran be analytically certain that the process is over—in view of near loss of Iranian Azerbaijan in 1945 and the lessons to be drawn from the 1979 Soviet invasion of Afghanistan, only so recently terminated?

The Analytic Dilemma of Russian Expansionism

What is the character of Russian historical expansionism? What kind of "Manifest Destiny" was involved, and what will delimit it? Was it merely accident that Russia stopped where it did when it did? These questions lie at the heart of understanding the character of the Russian imperial thrust.

There is no convincing evidence that the present borders between Iran and the USSR represent anything more than a *freezing in place* of the "Great Game" between Britain and Russia at a given point in the late eighteenth century. These borders represent no clear-cut ethnic, historic, cultural, or geographic boundaries that would have given the Russians true pause in stopping the physical expansion of empire where they did. Only in linguistic terms can some argument be made that Russia was in fact beginning to approach the borders of the Persian-speaking world in the Caucasus—but there is little ground to believe that this constituted any kind of cultural deterrent in itself. Russia had already begun crossing linguistic borders from its first move against the Kazan Tatars several hundred years earlier. It continued to move into Persian-speaking areas as it moved ever further south into Central Asia. On the contrary, there is good evidence that many Russian statesmen, down through Stalin, viewed the eventual further expansion of Russia into Iran as an inevitability.[1]

The True Restraints:
Political/Military/Opportunity Costs

For the rulers of Iran, contiguous Russian land power was not going to go away—in sharp contrast to the expansion of European power periodically projected across the seas into Asia. But, however threatening the Russian challenge was to Iran, its ambitions met formidable check from the equally powerful thrust of British imperialism into Asia, culminating in the establishment of the British Raj in India. Britain was poised to block the indefinite expansion of Russia southward, intent on maintaining Iran as a buffer zone, blocking Russian moves south to protect Britain's "lifeline" to India. Thus began the Great Game of Anglo-Russian rivalry that was to dominate Asian politics for at least two hundred years. Britain was the only power over several hundred years consistently in a position to credibly deter Russian expansion southwards. The first phase of a *containment policy* toward Russian land power was thus born—one based on imperial dynamics rather than on the ideological framework of struggle more characteristic of the post–World War I period.

The present borders between Iran and the USSR can therefore be best described as a *historical accident*—where the process of southern expansion happened to be stopped. There is no reason to believe that Russia ever reached any kind of conscious decision about how far its expansion would go: Empires never do. The process is organic—as is the process of contraction. Russia up to today has constantly had to weigh the relative costs and benefits of further expansion at any particular time. Imperial Russia probably did intend to continue its physical acquisition of territory south when the circumstances were again propitious. But as global politics evolved in the late nineteenth and early twentienth centuries, Russia found sufficient disincentive not to make further territorial acquisition at Persian expense, when gauged against its other interests. What were its options and how do they apply today?

Russia's Options

Russia was not, of course, simply driven by mindless expansionist impulses. Petersburg faced a variety of options and opportunities as the growing state looked around its periphery. In the late nineteenth century Russian goals were under debate; choices were required among various competing pressures and interests. Several factors weighed in the Russian calculus.

- On the one hand, Russia had constantly to focus on European politics because this was the most likely source of attack against Russian soil and against Russia's various European allies.
- Alternatively, Russia had been expanding eastward at a steady rate without opposition. The navy was interested in dedicating state resources to the Far East, especially in light of the growth of Japanese power.
- Still other statesmen saw the southern Balkans/Black Sea/Bosphorus/Dardanelles as the key goal of Russian strategy, outweighing the strategic interest of Iran. Britain, in addition, had quite unambiguously blocked off any possibility of Russian presence in the Persian Gulf, where Russia was ill-equipped to challenge her.[2]
- Russia could choose to avoid military confrontation with Britain by settling on a strategy of dominant *political* influence in northern Iran as opposed to territorial acquisition. Throughout most of the nineteenth century Russia had in fact enjoyed such a dominant position, permitting it to conserve military resources for other competing interests.

Some elements of Russian geopolitical thinking believed that Iran would eventually and inevitably fall into Russian hands anyway—it was primarily a matter of time and historical evolution. This line of thinking reflected the old Russian search for access to a warmwater port. The Persian Gulf was a natural such target.[3]

The Hitler-Ribbentrop agreements granting the USSR dominance over Iran in a postwar settlement suggest that this "historic inevitability" was still on Soviet minds. The shifting European political kaleidoscope also caused Russia to recalculate her interests and threats: By 1907 both

Britain and Russia perceived the specter of rising German power in Europe and in the Middle East to be a greater threat than either Britain or Russia was to each other. This perception led to an historic 1907 Anglo-Russian agreement to recognize and codify mutual spheres of control in Iran. Interestingly, the respective imperial factions of both countries raised opposition to this Anglo-Russian imperial accomodation. Both of these groups felt that each state had conceded to the other a geopolitical advantage that need not have been granted.

In sum, the present borders between the USSR and Iran represent the freezing of an arbitrary stopping place of the Russian advance in the nineteenth century. There was nothing permanent about it at the time; only force of circumstance and the passage of time has rendered it the "permanent" border between the two countries today. That degree of permanence is still an issue of geostrategic concern in the world today.

Other Instruments of
Russian Influence and Control

Moscow had been increasing its influence in Persia throughout the nineteenth century with great effect. Indeed, well before the Bolshevik Revolution Russian relations with Iran had assumed an extremely negative nature, as Tsarist policy turned to a great variety of economic, political, administrative, and military instruments:

- The intimidating precedents of past seizure of major chunks of the Iranian Empire in the Caucasus and Central Asia;
- Periodic temporary occupation of Persian territory as a means of exerting ad hoc political pressure on Tehran;
- The extortion of concessions involving extraterritorial privileges, especially in the area of customs, finances, and raw materials;
- Opposition to the construction of any railroad line from the Gulf into northern Iran because it would give Iran the alternative of shipping its goods south for export rather than to Russia—otherwise Iran's only option. More importantly, a rail link from the Gulf to the north would have given British manufactured goods market access to northern Iran—in direct competition with Russian goods. By 1889 Nasir al-Din Shah had promised to grant no railroad construction concessions to anyone except Russia.
- Determined opposition to any reform of the tariff system that enabled Russian merchants to export their goods to Iran almost without any tariff.[4]

- Virtual control of all of northern Iran by the end of the nineteenth century;
- Control of Iran's finances through the granting of loans which the shah sought for personal use but could not repay—for which Russia extracted further concessions;
- The demand that any concessions granted to England be also granted to Russia;
- Establishment of a Russian state bank in Iran whose seductive personal loan policies led eventually to a Russian financial grip over most of the elite of the country;
- The use of corruption and bribery to vouchsafe Russian influence in the court, government, and provinces;
- Control of most of Iran's foreign trade;
- Control of Tehran's crack military unit, the Russian-trained Cossack Regiment, to be used against nationalist and democratic movements inhospitable to Russian interests;
- The virtual destruction of Iran's nationalist-reformist-parliamentary movement by granting unstinting support to the shah's efforts to destroy it.

In fact, Iran may owe its survival in one piece to the very rivalry between Britain and Russia. Britain was determined to diminish Russian influence wherever possible in Iran and to maintain the country intact as buffer to further Russian expansion. Although Russia likewise sought to break British influence in Iran, Petersburg had virtually no strategic commitment to the integrity of Iran unlike Britain.

As the nineteenth century progressed, local opposition to the rapacious policies of foreign powers gained ground among the more knowledgeable elite within Iran. Ironically, however, most of Iran's successful opposition tactics were those directed against British rather than against Russian influence, even though Petersburg enjoyed the greater and more dangerous influence. It was indeed an indicator of the power of Russian influence that it could help stir up opposition (including clerical) against British privilege, while largely stifling any such expression against Russia.

At the turn of the century Russia had achieved major control over Persia's financial system through the use of foreign loans. Two major loans to the Persian government amounting to some 4 million sterling in 1900 and 1901 equalled the whole of Iran's revenues for the same period, with no evidence that any of it was used for productive purposes. Much of it was primarily spent on a lavish trip by Muzaffar al-Din Shah to Europe and to cover the costs of a large and corrupt bureaucracy.[5]

Foreign trade with Russia was equally skewed in Russia's favor and imposed upon Tehran. A commercial instrument stemming from 1828 afforded Russian extraterritorial privileges and capitulatory terms, already afforded to Britain. Because Russian goods were even then not competitive with European goods, Russia abolished the free trade route to Europe through the Caucasus, helping ensure a monopoly for itself in Iran. Customs fees were established virtually at Russian fiat. These concessions, strengthened by the conditions of Russia's loans to Persia, conspired to tie Persian trade closely to Russia.[6] Popular protest against these policies was ignored by the shah.

Thus loans, concessions, and a highly skewed foreign trade pattern formed the triad of oppressive instruments that held Iran in a straitjacket in the early years of the twentieth century. However successful Russia may have been in limiting and destroying Iranian sovereignty, Britain's role was only slightly less deleterious in acquiring for itself major privileges and concessions: for a brief period the British gained control of *all* Iranian development, industrial planning, and natural resources, and London rivalled Russia in granting constricting loans to the shah.[7] But because Britain's area of control lay primarily in the south, it never could challenge Russian domination of the central politics of the country from the capital region of the north.

Political Intervention

Russia Stifles Nascent Democracy in Iran

Russian control over so much of Iranian life was extended in an even more damaging direction as Iran moved toward its own constitutional and nationalist revolution from 1905 to 1913. Nationalist sentiment had been growing strongly during the late nineteenth century; it was powerfully fueled by the deep resentment on the part of the Iranian elite and merchant class of the humiliating concessions and controls enjoyed by a multitude of European states in Iran. There was also anger at the fickle, arbitrary, and despotic character of the shah and at the lack of central government control over the country as it increasingly descended into the hands of local aristocracy, brigands, tribes, and foreign consuls.

As the Qajar dynasty lurched toward ever greater impotence, incompetence, and national disaster, forces grew for the creation of a constitutional government that would limit the powers and authority of the shahs. Genuine nationalist and reformist forces began to emerge, in part joined by more liberal clergy, artisans, merchants, and others. *Resentment of foreign interference* was its driving force. Russia naturally saw this constitutional movement as a direct threat to its own interests and ability to manipulate Iranian affairs. It therefore moved to ally itself directly with proshah and anticonstitutionalist forces.

The constitutionalist movement aimed at establishment of a Parliament (Majles) that would take over from the shah control of the budget, finances, and national resources, as well as the power to grant foreign concessions. Britain, which had generally been more sympathetic to reform forces in Iran and objected to deeply established Russian influence, was initially positive toward the constitutionalist movement.

But by 1907 international events were conspiring to seal Iran's fate in the form of Anglo-Russian collusion. Both England and Russia had come to fear the rising force of Germany in Europe and Germany's interest in spreading its influence to the East through Ottoman Turkey. Britain was also concerned with the possible penetration of Russian influence into the Persian Gulf where British interests were complex, widespread, and strategic. London recognized furthermore that Russia had in effect "won" the struggle for influence in Iran. Russia itself was weakened from its loss to Japan in the Russo-Japanese War and was looking to delimit competition. The resulting Anglo-Russian agreement of 1907 explicitly recognizing each other's spheres of influence in Iran granted Russia a virtually free hand in Iranian internal politics. Iran had lost all room to maneuver.

Russia proceeded to combine threats of military intervention, actual military invention, financial pressures, arrests, bribery, and manipulation of the Russian-trained crack Persian "Russian Cossacks" on behalf of Mohammed 'Ali Shah who had now become virtually a Russian instrument. Civil war ensued. By 1912 parliamentary forces were finally able to win the day for a two-year period with the grudging acquiescence of Britain and Russia. But Russia had virtually destroyed the reformist movement against the shah and the county was in chaos and anarchy. Russia occupied much of Iran during World War I along with Britain and Ottoman Turkey, despite Iranian declarations of neutrality. But the situation was to change radically with the advent of revolution in Russia in 1917.

In sum, we have a portrait of a classic imperial relationship with many well-established mechanisms for Russian domination of Iran. Circumstances were to change somewhat once the Bolsheviks came to power, but Russia was to continue to seek new forms and means of domination and influence. What is important to note is _why_ the means of domination had to change slightly and what the natural limits on future Russian influence would then be.

Old Wine in New Bottles—the Bolshevik Period

The clock was running out on the classic age of Imperialism by the end of World War I. The Ottoman Turkish Empire, the Imperial Russian

Empire, as well as the venerable Austro-Hungarian and the more recent German Empires had all collapsed. It was specifically in this antiimperialist environment that the Bolshevik Revolution found fulfillment. On the surface, the differences between the old Tsarist and the new Bolshevik policies toward the East were striking. Lenin immediately moved to denounce the old imperialist-colonialist system and to publicly disavow all of the Tsar's territorial ambitions, treaties, and secret protocols for the annexation of territory in Turkey, Iran and elsewhere after the war was over. To strengthen the propaganda clarion, a massive proclamation to "All the Toiling Muslims of Russia and the East" called for the overthrow of European colonialism everywhere, a process in which the newly born Soviet Union would serve as ally. 1920 saw the first "Congress of the Peoples of the East" in Baku calling for world revolution among the colonial peoples. Iranians made up the second largest foreign delegation there. (The Turks were first.)[8]

The high-flown proclamations of principle did not last long in the face of the needs and ambitions of the new Russian state. Several imperatives were at work.

Security. The fledgling Soviet state feared the overthrow of Bolshevik power through foreign state support to the White Army and other resistance forces inside Russia. Britain was the chief supporter of this movement. It was imperative for the Bolsheviks to lever the British army out of the Caucasus where it was directly assisting anti-Bolshevik forces.

Retention of Territory. The Soviet state was determined to restore the former Tsarist non-Russian possessions in the Caucasus, Central Asia, and elsewhere. Armenia, Azerbaijan, Georgia, and several Turkic regions in Central Asia had taken advantage of the revolution to declare independence and had to be brought back quickly into the fold by force.

Strategic/Ideological Considerations. The Bolsheviks nourished the longer-range goal of fomenting revolution throughout the colonial world as a way of weakening and ultimately bringing about Communist revolution in the advanced states of Europe. Foreign policy became dedicated in part to weakening the European powers by striking at their interests overseas.

Bolshevik Instruments of Influence and Control

Dismemberment Attempts:
Iran's First Communist Republic

If classic aggrandizement of territory was no longer politically appropriate, Moscow was inaugurating a new ideological form of the old puppet state: the establishment abroad of quasi-independent Communist regions or states—mirroring those already being established in the non-Russian areas of empire. Through this device Moscow could still establish politically—and now ideologically—subservient states on the periphery. This technique set major new precedent in Soviet policy—to be employed even more dramatically after World War II in Eastern Europe.

Moscow's first candidate emerged in the northern Iranian province of Gilan where a leftist/nationalist uprising had been under way since 1916. Its leader, Kuchek Khan, had requested Soviet support as early as 1918. It was not until 1920, however, that the Red Army, in the process of restoring Soviet control over the Caucasus, landed troops on the Caspian shores of Iran to support the newly proclaimed Iranian Soviet Socialist Republic in Gilan. Soviet forces then proceeded to displace the nationalist Kuchek Khan from leadership in favor of more orthodox Communist leadership.[9]

A second important precedent then occurred: a voluntary Soviet decision the following year to withdraw support from the new Iranian Soviet Socialist Republic in favor of a deal with the newly emerging nationalist leadership of Iran—promising a genuine buffer state that might keep Moscow's potential adversaries at bay.

The Pahlavi Dynasty Changes the Game

Iran—a supine and paralyzed state after World War I—was probably saved from falling under deep Soviet influence by the emergence of a skilled, energetic, practical, bold, single-minded, and harsh new leader, the likes of which Iran had rarely seen over the past century or more. Iran was unified, strengthened, and thrust into the modern world by the remarkable founder of the new Pahlavi Dynasty, Reza Shah. Reza Khan was born in humble circumstances, but worked his way up in the Iranian military, ultimately becoming commander of the Cossack Regiment. From there he was positioned to assume de facto power in the environment of turmoil and weakness of postwar Iran. He proceeded to make himself prime minister and then to name himself Reza Shah, founder of the new Pahlavi Dynasty.

Reza Shah was the quintessential man on horseback destined to turn Iran around. He was a dedicated nationalist determined to create a strong, united, centralized, and modern state on the European model, relatively free of foreign influence and domination. He worked with considerable effectiveness toward fulfillment of these goals, ruling Iran with an iron hand, in part inspired by the Westernizing model of his contemporary in neighboring Turkey, Mustafa Kemal Ataturk. For the first time in well over a hundred years, Iran was now largely master of its own fate, with an independent foreign policy and national army to enforce the will of the state in the outlying regions long used to enjoying virtual autonomy from Tehran.

Second, Reza Shah was determined to remove the British military presence from Iran. After the collapse of the Tsarist regime and the emergence of Soviet power in Russia, Britain had taken advantage of this event to occupy *all* of Iran and to use it as a base for supporting anti-Soviet forces in the Caucasus and Central Asia in the Russian civil war. The occupation was justified by the British in an Anglo-Iranian treaty of 1919 imposed upon an impotent Iranian government. Reza repudiated this treaty on 26 February 1921; significantly, on that very same day he announced a Treaty of Friendship with the USSR. Under the terms of this treaty, the Soviet Union would withdraw its forces from Iran, including the Soviet Republic of Gilan.

The limited strategic value to Russia of the Soviet Republic in Gilan, as weighed against the major strategic gain of achieving the withdrawal of British forces from the Soviet border—coupled with other internal pressures on the new Soviet regime at home—all helped impel the USSR to abandon the new Soviet Republic of Gilan in favor of the Treaty of Friendship with Iran. The terms of the treaty, however, still provided powerful pretext for Soviet intervention in Iran in the future: The famous Article VI of the treaty explicitly upheld the right of Soviet troops to enter Iran to counter any hostile foreign presence using Iran as a base for hostile activities against the USSR if the Iranian government could not itself eliminate the threat.[10] This virtual carte blanche to intervene has not to this day been renounced by the USSR—despite constant Iranian efforts and later Iranian disavowal of the treaty.

A second and important Non-aggression and Neutrality Treaty was signed between Iran and the USSR in 1927 which, among other things, stipulated that neither party would take part in de facto or de jure political alliances or agreements directed against the security, territorial integrity, independence, or sovereignty of the other country or to join in an economic boycott or attack with third parties against the other party.[11] This treaty, too, would be cited by the USSR later to object to the last shah's security ties with the West.

Soviet Goals During
the Reza Shah Period (1921–1941)

Since the establishment of the Pahlavi dynasty under Reza Shah in the 1920s, the USSR has pursued a differentiated set of goals in its dealings with Iran.

Defensive Security Goals

With the rise of the Bolshevik state and subsequent civil war, the new Soviet state continued to be obsessed with its security from all peripheries. Denial of Iran to its adversaries, or potential adversaries, was the preeminent goal. If the state could not be easily absorbed and integrated into the Soviet Union, then at least maintenance of Iran as an independent and nonaligned state was the next most desirable priority. The USSR, unlike the Tsarist Russia, was rapidly coming to appreciate the value of local nationalism as an instrument against its rivals. Reza Shah for nearly two decades fulfilled this requirement until, in the early 1940s, he committed the fatal mistake of moving too close to Nazi Germany.

The tsars had also been concerned for the security of the country from outside forces, but not quite to the degree of obsessiveness that characterized the Soviet state. For by the very adoption of the philosophically aggressive ideology of communism—a self-fulfilling prophecy—the new Russia guaranteed that it would have enemies. But the main change in the security equation came not from Russia, but from Iran. The Soviet Union could tactically support an independent-minded buffer state because, for the first time in over a century, Iran was now seemingly capable of pursuing a truly independent anti-British nationalist course. The Soviets had not given up ambitions for a more dominant influence in Iran, but there were limits on what Reza Shah would permit; in Moscow's calculations, greater Soviet influence could perhaps come in time. The immediate Soviet security needs were met.

Economic Dependency

Economic policies were still aimed at keeping Iran as tightly bound as possible to the USSR—as was the case under the tsars. Preeminent among the Soviet Union's instrumentalities was its traditional monopoly over the northern Iranian economy–an advantage easily perpetuated for at least another decade. In economic terms it was only northern Iran that mattered anyway—with the important exception of oil in the south—because the north possessed the most fertile agricultural lands and the beginnings of industry. Russian transportation networks to the Iranian border were also well developed, whereas Iran had almost no other commercial and trade outlets from the country. There were no usable road or rail links to Turkey, India, or the Gulf.

The USSR from the outset did not hesitate to exploit Iran's near total dependence upon the Soviet Union as a market for its raw materials and as a source of industrial goods. Iranian efforts to improve trade terms led to Soviet manipulation and pressure through imposition of temporary boycotts of Iranian goods, delays or curtailment of transit rights, manipulation of market prices, and so on. Only slowly was Reza Shah able to improve these trade terms, step by step renegotiating the commercial relationship in various short-term agreements over the years. Soviet trade practices were viewed by the Iranians as exploitative, disadvantageous, and one-way, but the shah felt he could only make gains vis-à-vis Soviet policies on an incremental basis, all the while building a groundwork designed to free Iran from this dangerous dependence upon Russia.[12]

Ideological Subversion

While Tsarist Russia had maintained certain clients and factions in Iran, these groups did not constitute ideological instruments in the fashion that Communist parties do. The use of the Communist party was an ideological innovation of the Bolsheviks in the conduct of foreign policy. Thus the USSR maintained support for the Iranian Communist party—founded in 1920—even though much of it was in exile in Europe or Soviet Azerbaijan throughout this period. Although the Iranian Communist party played a minimal role in bilateral Soviet-Iranian relations under Reza Shah, the same would not be true of its successor organization, the Tudeh party, under the last shah. Reza Shah was mindful of the dangers of Communist and separatist influence—especially centered in Iranian Azerbaijan—and he moved to stifle nationalist sentiments there, including the banning of the Azeri language.[13] Reza Shah was also deeply suspicious of the Communist party as a foreign-dominated group working against Iranian independence; he dealt harshly with it.

Territorial Invasion

Iran's growing ties with Germany in the second half of the 1930s created the greatest alarm on the Soviet side—a view shared by Great Britain. Once again the Soviet Union becomes fearful of enemies infiltrating a border state. Once again the German threat unites Britain with the Soviets in a common anti-German posture at Iran's expense. Reza Shah's efforts to remain neutral during World War II and his refusal to expel the German mission from Tehran was to cost him his throne: The British and the Soviets jointly forced his abdication. The USSR invaded Iran two months after Hitler invaded the USSR and maintained its military occupation of Iran until the end of the war—and beyond. British forces occupied southern Iran. Moscow explicitly invoked Article VI of the 1921 friendship treaty with Iran to justify its intervention, demonstrating the power of this instrument.[14]

Indeed, one of the causes of Reza Shah's close ties with Germany was his interest in pursuing a "Third Power policy" by which to balance off the influence of Britain and Russia in Iran. This has become a standard policy of Iran in its quest to avoid dangerous and binding ties with superpowers.

Thus, despite the radical changes in government in both Russia and Iran following World War I, geopolitical circumstances within two decades had again caused the total flouting of Iranian sovereignty and renewed foreign occupation by the Soviet Union (and Britain). Although Reza Shah's more independent government and Bolshevik Russia's newfound "antiimperialist" policies had helped remove some of the most blatant day-to-day colonialist interventionist facets of Russo-Iranian relations of the pre-Bolshevik era, by the end of Reza's reign Soviet use of *force majeure* seemed not to have changed things very much after all.

Iran's Own Calculations

With the accession of Reza Shah to the throne after World War I, Iran for the first time was able to act—rather than merely react—in establishing the bilateral character of relations with Russia. The change of governments in both Russia and Iran after World War I did, in Reza's view, offer opportunities for reorienting Iran away from dependence upon its powerful northern neighbor. Reza Shah identified several imperatives in his goal of maintaining Iranian national sovereignty: the withdrawal of Soviet forces from Iranian soil, the destruction of the Communist republic in Gilan, and the renewal and reorientation of the critically needed trade between Iran and Russia.[15]

If he could break the pattern of Russian domination, Reza Shah was willing to make some concessions toward good relations with the Soviet Union. The first of these concessions was the signing of the 1921 Friendship Treaty, which promised to put relations on a more correct and legal basis, despite the worrisome intervention clause of Article VI. In short, Reza was seeking to gradually regularize, formalize, and codify his relations with Moscow as the best means to build a more independent relationship with Russia—in sharp distinction to the irregular, unequal, and nonformalized relations characterizing the Tsarist period of intervention in Qajar Iran.[16]

Simultaneously, Reza Shah moved to improve Iran's own infrastructure that would enable him to ease out of the Soviet stranglehold. Reza Shah's landmark decision in the 1930s to build the Trans-Iranian rail line was the first step by Iran in the direction of establishing an alternative trade route—from the Caspian to the Gulf. This project opened up opportunities for the domestic distribution of Iranian agricultural goods; even more important, it enabled the importation of foreign goods via non-Russian channels. Secondly, Reza began to develop his own industries—especially textiles—the lack of which had constituted a chief form of import-dependency upon Russia.

As a result of these measures, the Soviet Union began to face increasing challenge in maintaining its major point of influence in Iran as Iran's premier trading partner; by the mid-1930s Germany began to surpass the USSR in volume of economic relations. By 1938 trade with the Soviet Union had virtually ceased because Iran would no longer accept Soviet-imposed trade terms.[17] This was deeply disturbing to the USSR since it paralleled the growth of German power in Europe and in the Middle East as a whole.

Reza Shah's accomplishments in markedly reorienting the character of Iranian-Soviet relations between 1920 and 1940 was a signal success and a major step toward the greater independence of Iran from dependency and vulnerability to foreign powers. Even then, Reza was ultimately to fall victim to his own worst nightmares, with his deposition by Iran's classic imperialist oppressors—Russia and Britain—in 1941.

Notes

1. Aryeh Y. Yodfat, *The Soviet Union and Revolutionary Iran* (New York: St. Martin's Press, 1984), pp. 2–8, and p. 15 for discussion of historical Tsarist interest in acquiring Persia, and Stalin's agreement with Nazi Germany for uncontested sphere of influence in Iran.

2. *Ibid.*, pp. 2–5.

3. *Ibid.*, p. 7.

4. Rouhollah K. Ramazani, *The Foreign Policy of Iran, 1500–1941* (Charlottesville: University Press of Virginia, 1966), p. 68.

5. *Ibid.*, pp. 72–73.

6. *Ibid.*, pp. 73–75.

7. *Ibid.*, pp. 66–67.

8. George Lenczowski, *Russia and the West in Iran, 1918–1948* (Ithaca: Cornell University Press, 1949), p. 6.

9. David B. Nissman, *The Soviet Union and Iranian Azerbaijan* (Boulder, Colo.: Westview Press, 1987), pp. 19–20.

10. Yodfat, *op. cit.*, p. 13.

11. *Ibid.*, p. 14.

12. Ramazani, *op. cit.*, pp. 194, 217.

13. Nissman, *op. cit.*, p. 28.

14. Alvin Z. Rubenstein, *Soviet Policy Toward Turkey, Iran and Afghanistan* (New York: Praeger, 1982), p. 62.

15. Ramazani, *op. cit.*, p. 212.

16. *Ibid.*, p. 213.

17. Yodfat, *op. cit.*, p. 15.

9

Iran and the USSR After World War II

If Reza Shah established the foundations for Iranian national power, enabling him to begin a relationship of greater independence vis-à-vis the Soviet Union, his son, Mohammed Reza Shah, was able to carry this process significantly further under the circumstances of the extraordinary growth of Iran's economic and military stature. But because of his early fears of Soviet power and intentions, and Moscow's support for regional radicalism, Mohammed Reza Shah violated the basically nonaligned orientation of his father to move further toward alliance with the West. With Iran's many new options, Moscow rapidly concluded that intimidation would be less effective than more positive instruments of influence. These new instruments worked to improve Iranian-Soviet relations considerably, particularly in the economic sphere, even while the shah worked to foil many of Moscow's key strategic interests in the region. Moscow's goals appeared reduced to biding its time and seeking to limit the damage of Iran's Western orientation.

Although the Islamic revolution of 1979 brought hopes of new opportunities for Soviet inroads into Iran, the expulsion of the United States was not matched by an equal gain for Soviet influence in its place. In Moscow's long-range calculations, the Islamic Republic had at least created a political environment that might serve Soviet interests over the longer run. The end of the Iran-Iraq War has enabled Moscow to reorient its relations with Tehran, albeit under the dramatically different ideological and policy goals and instruments of Gorbachev.

This chapter reviews those new conditions that emerged in Iran under the last shah and the rapidly evolving new rationale behind the process of improvement of relations between Moscow and Tehran that could presage a sharp departure from the traditional character of Russian-Iranian relations.

154

Mohammed Reza Shah Steps on the Stage

Reza Shah's son, Mohammed Reza Shah, began the early years of his reign in 1941 inauspiciously with two unforgettable reminders of Soviet intentions and capabilities toward Iran: the invasion and occupation of the country by the Soviet Union and Great Britain in 1941, forcing the abdication of his father; and Soviet support in 1945 for two separatist Communist republics, the Autonomous Soviet Government of Azerbaijan and the Kurdish Soviet Republic of Mahabad.

Mohammed Reza was to be reminded only a decade later that the power of external intervention was still not a monopoly of the Russian north alone: He himself had to be restored to power by the combined covert intervention of Britain and the United States in 1953—when long-term nationalist disorders stemming from the oil nationalization policies of Prime Minister Mossadegh drove the shah from the country.

Indeed, no Iranian ruler could ever afford to forget the potential of great power action against him: The shah remained deeply mindful of those factors he believed important to preserving his throne in the face of superpower competition. His perception of the intensity of the Soviet danger impelled him to seek a deep U.S. commitment—bordering on dependence—to help preserve Iran's independence from Soviet threat. But his rationale was based on his belief in the theoretical capability of the United States in any case to remove him at will from power—so he felt he had little to lose by such an alignment. The shah also seemed to cling to the belief that if he was not actively opposed by the United States and the USSR, his throne was secure, that is, no significant domestic threats could exist as long as a shah is secure in the support of foreign powers. This rationale—a legacy of the long tradition of imperialist intervention up until 1953—obviously played a key role in the political and dynastic mentality of the country. Indeed, in the end, after the dying shah was compelled to leave Iran by the disorders of the rising Islamic revolution at the end of 1978, he never overcame the suspicion that the United States had perhaps engineered his fall by encouraging domestic disorder and pulling the string on him—just as his father had been forced to abdicate.

The shah was by no means trapped in craven fear of external power, however. Indeed, as the shah worked to establish his own hold over the country and achieve security arrangements with external powers, he grew more confident. The USSR, too, began to apply more carrots in its approach to Iran, ultimately leading to a sharp reduction of the salience of the Soviet factor in Iranian thinking and to the establishment of greater equality in the Iranian-Soviet bilateral relationship than had ever before existed.

Characteristics of the
New Soviet-Iranian Relationship

Changes on the Iranian Side

This period, in fact, marked a profound shift in the Soviet-Iranian relationship—much of the change stemming from the new strength of the Iranian state as established by Reza Shah. This new strength, affecting Soviet calculations, was evident in several areas. First was the Iranian move toward alignment starting in the mid-1950s. The West, and especially the United States, was extremely vigilant toward possible Soviet penetration of Iran following the pattern of Soviet expansion into Eastern Europe at the end of World War II. These concerns were heightened by the Soviets' delay in withdrawing its occupational forces from Iran after the war and Soviet establishment of two new Communist governments in Iranian Azerbaijan and Iranian Kurdistan. These republics were only abandoned by the USSR under considerable Western pressure and adroit Iranian diplomatic maneuver. As a result, both the United States and Great Britain worked for the inclusion of Iran into Western defense arrangements, either multilateral or bilateral. The shah maintained this posture of close alignment until he felt more secure.

Iran's increasing wealth played a major role in the shah's new clout. Iran's growing oil industry and, in the early 1970s, the tremendous increase in the price of oil, brought untold new wealth into Iranian coffers enabling it to rapidly develop its economy. With its newfound wealth, supported by defensive ties with the West, Iran was now able to arm itself and to become the preeminent military power in the region. Soviet armed power obviously remained overwhelming, but Iran's military position had to become a consideration in the psychological relationship with the Soviet Union for the first time—at least in the Iranian mind.

Lastly, the shah demonstrated increasing skill in playing off the United States against the USSR, stimulating each superpower's interest in retaining optimum relations with Iran.

Changes on the Soviet Side

On the Soviet side, several changes had occurred that influenced its policies toward Iran. Most important was a broad shift in strategy after the death of Stalin in which the USSR sought to improve its ties with the Third World as a whole. (Real change in tone toward the shah, however, came only in 1962, well after Iran had moved away from an initial postwar nonalignment into security ties with the West.) Moscow's time-honored goal—to deny Iran as a base for anti-Soviet operations—remained intact. But Moscow had perceived that bluster in the end served only to push the shah closer to the West. Nonetheless, despite quite good relations between the Soviets and Iran by the 1970s, the shah never abandoned his deep concern for long-range Soviet intentions toward Iran and his regime.

Finally, Soviet economic instruments of influence largely began to move away from the crude attempts of previous years to gain special privilege. Economic and technical assistance, designed to meet the clear interests of Iran, were used as blandishments in order to influence Iran's policies more positively.

Ironically from the Soviet point of view, by 1975 the shah had in fact developed what was by any measure an extraordinary ability to act against Soviet interests in the region.

- The shah was able to overcome a serious internal challenge from the 1952–1953 Tudeh (Communist)-supported disorders that drove him temporarily from the throne: He returned and succeeded in crushing the Tudeh party and denying it any legal status within Iran.
- He broke away from a position of neutrality to align Iran with the West in a military pact directed against the Soviet Union.
- He armed the Iranian state heavily with U.S. weaponry and permitted the establishment of sophisticated U.S. electronic listening posts on the northern Iranian borders with the USSR.
- He challenged Soviet influence in pre-Communist Afghanistan through financial blandishments designed to try to draw Kabul away from close ties to Moscow.
- He moved to make Iran the most powerful regional force in the Gulf in an explicitly antileftist, anti-Soviet context.
- He directly challenged and destabilized a major Soviet client state, Iraq, and forced it to diplomatic agreement from a position of weakness.

- He helped crush a Communist uprising in Oman's Dhofar province that was directly supported by the only Marxist-Leninist state in the Arab world, the People's Democratic Republic of Yemen.

While pursuing all these regional policies, the shah was also able to impose much stiffer natural gas prices on the USSR through tough bargaining. He went on to gain important Soviet aid and technical assistance for over 100 industrial projects in Iran. And through it all he managed to maintain sufficient Soviet tolerance that the USSR still sought to compete for favors in selling weapons to Iran.

Indeed, it was the shah's ability to play off East against West that, more than any other factor, helped grant him greater leverage with the Soviet Union. Iran had never before been able to deal with the Soviet Union from such a position of strength and ability to direct its own national affairs. All the while, the shah seemed to have a good intuitive grasp of just how far he could go before crossing the Soviets' ultimate security "red line" that might unleash a truly dangerous Soviet response. The shah's willingness to enter the Baghdad Pact, CENTO, and sign a bilateral security pact with the United States met with vehement, even vituperous, opposition from the Soviet Union. The shah was careful not to permit, however, any U.S. or NATO forces to be established on Iranian soil and hastened to ensure the Soviets in 1962 that he would not permit Western missiles to be established in Iran.[1]

What caused the shah to draw the line where he did, rather than commit himself even more deeply to a Western security role? The shah would probably have joined NATO if he could have, for he was constantly searching for ever greater security commitment from the United States. Could Iran have actually provided bases to the United States, for example, following the example of Turkey? Much is made of the fact that the shah began to cool toward the United States as his sole source of security in the 1960s. Several factors are usually cited to explain the shah's cooling attitudes toward the United States: President Kennedy's increasing unwillingness to provide economic and military aid to an oil-rich country; the shah's concern about U.S. reliability as an ally, due to its failure to intervene in Iraq, a Baghdad Pact country, after radical leftists overthrew the Iraqi monarchy in 1958, and the absence of U.S. support to another ally, Pakistan, in the 1965 Indo-Pakistani War; increasing U.S. pressure on Iran on human rights issues; the diminishing importance of Iran to the Unites States as a base for missiles in view of technological advances in missilery.

In the end, the shah's natural instincts, bolstered by a long historical record, were to distrust any one power and to move toward a greater state of equilibrium in his relations between the superpowers. This would likely have been the case regardless of U.S. inaction in Pakistan or other U.S. policies. The assurances to the Soviet Union that U.S. missiles would never be stationed in Iran came years before the Indo-Pakistani War in any case.

The Soviet Strategy

Moscow's chief imperative was that Iran not serve as a security threat to the Soviet Union; once reassured that the shah would not permit U.S. bases in Iran, Moscow was able to deal with the shah more generously—in an effort to encourage the shah not to move any closer to the United States. But what of the broad range of other Iranian policies that ran counter to Soviet interests in the region? Why were they apparently tolerated by the USSR?

Two complementary features seem to characterize Soviet strategy and behavior in dealing with its neighbors. On the one hand, Russia's patterns of expansionist behavior are a matter of clear historical record. This national pattern is intensified by the *inherently expansionist implications* of Marxist-Leninist historical determinism that proclaims the ultimate inevitability of worldwide communism—with Russia as its primary vehicle of implementation. On the other hand, Kremlin strategists have also seemed to believe that history is not in any rush—that the USSR should be prudent in pursuing opportunities in order to avoid conflict, while remaining confident in the belief that sooner or later events will move in the right direction and opportunities will present themselves for the further advance of communism. Two corollary principles have also characterized Soviet expansionist behavior: (1) when a major opportunity for a relatively cost-free gain abroad presents itself, take it; (2) the benefits of moving to establish new gains abroad must be balanced against all the other international interests of the USSR at the same time. Although most states might operate along similar lines of prudence and calculated interest, the unique feature of Soviet Marxist-Leninist behavior is the impulse to foster permanent expansion of the Communist order derived from a comprehensive historically ("scientifically determined") ideological vision. Indeed, one of the ideological debates among Soviet scholars of the Third World has been over the degree to which Moscow should "hasten history along" with support for coups by left-wing movements in states where the objective Marxist conditions for a successful socialist revolution seem to be lacking.[2] Lenin often gains the upper hand over Marx in suggesting that, on occasion, objective conditions be damned—Communist parties should seize the opportunity for taking power when an opening appears, regardless of whether a country has passed through a capitalist phase or not. Certainly both the Soviet October Revolution (Coup) itself and the Afghan coup of 1978 are but two of many such examples.

Whatever the finer points of ideological debate might be, this approach has enabled the USSR to take a longer range view of potential geopolitical gains around the world, including in Iran. As long as Iran respected Moscow's ultimate security concerns, Moscow could play for the long run and bank on the hope that political, economic, and social forces in Iran eventually would bring about a regime more sympathetic in Soviet ideological terms. This kind of rationale seems to have enabled the Soviet Union to adopt surprising tolerance toward the shah's main regional policies—that in most ways ran counter to immediate Soviet interests.

Soviet Instruments

Moscow therefore employed a variety of devices to exert influence in Iran during the reign of Mohammed Reza Shah.

Territorial Threats. During the Soviet military occupation of Iran in World War II, the Soviets laid the political and military groundwork for the establishment of two breakaway Communist governments in Azerbaijan and Kurdistan. Soviet troops refused to pull out of the country at the end of the war until the Iranian government granted a major oil concession in northern Iran to the USSR and promised they would not interfere against the two new Communist governments. The Iranian prime minister cleverly agreed—thus securing the Soviet troop withdrawal—then sent in the Iranian army to dislodge the two Communist republics, and finally allowed the Iranian Majles to overwhelmingly refuse the Soviet oil concession. The Soviets had been outsmarted by a series of wily Iranian ploys, but they had also been under heavy pressure from the West to withdraw their forces. Moscow probably would not have even bargained away the Azerbaijani and Kurdish breakaway governments if it had not come under such external pressure. Stalin probably also figured he had bigger fish to fry in establishing solid footholds in Eastern Europe.

Economic Demands. As noted above, Soviet demands immediately after the war for oil concessions in northern Iran represented a bid for dominant influence in the Iranian north and established the high-water mark of the Soviet search for special economic privilege early on under the new shah. No comparable demands for direct privilege have since been levied on Iran, although there was some hard bargaining over the price of natural gas exported to the USSR in 1974–1975—in which the

Soviets actually capitulated in the end to Iranian insistence on a higher price.

Economic Blandishments. After Stalin's death and Iranian assurances to Moscow that Iran would not allow the United States to establish any missile bases in the country, Soviet economic policies toward Iran sharply changed character and became very positively oriented: Major industrial and aid projects, technical assistance, and increased trade were all employed to dispose Iran toward greater balance in its policies between East and West.[3] These economic policies remained essentially positive for the last two decades of the shah's rule and represented the most benign and positive Soviet economic policies toward Iran in centuries. In part the legacy of Reza Shah had succeeded: Iran now possessed alternatives to economic dependence upon the USSR, requiring the USSR to change tactics if it wished to engage successfully with Iran.

Subversion. The USSR nonetheless continued support for Iran's Tudeh party throughout the shah's reign, which consistently pursued a slavishly pro-Moscow line. The Tudeh was powerfully arrayed against the shah in 1952 and was capable of marshalling considerable underground assets. But for hesitation on the part of Moscow and Tudeh, the party might have been able to come to power during the intense turmoil of the Mossadegh oil nationalization crisis—when the shah was forced to flee from Iran.

Propaganda was a regular instrument of Soviet influence as well in seeking to weaken the shah domestically. After deep Soviet anger at the shah's signing of a bilateral defense treaty with the United States in 1959 Moscow inaugurated a clandestine radio station, "The National Voice of Iran"; inflammatory broadcasts purportedly in the name of the Iranian people (actually based on Soviet soil) virulently criticized the shah's policies and called for the shah's overthrow.

Intimidation. In view of the negative history of Soviet intentions toward Iran, the shah's near fall from power in 1953 under the nationalist movement of Mossadegh, and the near seizure of power then by the Tudeh party, Iran was ready in 1955 to join the Baghdad Pact—over Soviet objections and warnings. The Soviets cited both the 1921 and 1927 treaties with the USSR—brandishing the infamous Article VI again—as prohibiting any alliances directed against the Soviet Union, but the shah insisted the alliance was purely defensive. The shah took an even bolder step toward "alignment" with his signature on a bilateral mutual defense treaty with the United States in 1959 and a unilateral rejection of Articles V and VI of the 1921 treaty. This brought down upon him immense Soviet vituperation for a three-year period. As threatening to Moscow's interests as these defensive moves by Iran were, Moscow seems to have considered that it could not afford to move against Iran militarily in view of Western support for the shah. But it employed as many other means as possible in this period, seeking drastic change either in Iran's government or in its policies.

Regional Radical States as Threats to Iran. In a new Soviet tactic, for the first time the shah found himself threatened by Soviet support for radical elements in the Middle East who were profoundly opposed to the shah. Although Moscow neither created these radical states nor needed to direct them against Iran, both Egypt and Iraq maintained a distinctly threatening line against the shah's position. Both radical states were of course heavily armed and supported by the Soviet Union.

Thus Moscow's policies maintained their classic two-tiered elements: on the one hand, starting in the early 1960s, state-to-state relations were very correct, diplomatic ties warmed considerably, and Moscow became highly tolerant of much of the shah's policies despite his closeness to the United States. On the other hand, Moscow was also playing its own form of hard ball as we have noted above, hoping to array domestic and foreign forces in such a way as to hasten the development of more "progressive" elements in Iranian policy. The shah was well aware of the distinction between Moscow's short-term and long-term approach toward the Iranian monarchy and maintained constant vigilance toward Moscow up until his forced departure from the throne in 1978. But ironically, by 1978 the shah was more willing to entertain the notion that it was perhaps the United States, and not the USSR, that was forcing him from the throne.

Communist Russia Encounters a Radical Islamic Iran

The fall of the shah came as no less a surprise to the Soviet Union than it did to Washington. Indeed, Moscow seemed to believe that the United States would intervene to protect its ally at an early stage. Moscow saw any U.S. intervention in Iran as a major threat to its interests; Brezhnev accordingly issued a warning to the United States about the need to keep hands off.[4] The Soviets in the end must have been astonished that the United States was in fact unable to protect its position in Iran. For Soviet policy, the shah's collapse seemed to be a Godsend—a term the clerics, if not Brezhnev, would have invoked.

Once the shah had fled and Khomeini had returned to Iran to propagate his viscerally anti-U.S. vision, Moscow recognized that the Soviets' preeminent security concern in Iran seemed to be moving toward quite favorable resolution: The new regime in Tehran was determined not to establish security ties with the United States or to allow the United

States a privileged position in Iran. Once clerical power was complete, it was clear Tehran wanted no U.S. presence whatsoever in Iran. At one fell swoop the first half of Moscow's ambitions had been realized: the elimination of the U.S. presence in Iran. But the USSR then sought to fulfill the second half of its goals: to achieve a privileged position for itself within Iran and edge the country toward the Soviet orbit.

The instruments of Moscow's policies in this period were designed (1) to prevent any U.S.-Iranian rapprochement, however unlikely, (2) to curry favor with Khomeini's regime and keep it well disposed toward Moscow, and (3) to encourage developments inside Iran that would ultimately move the country in directions ideologically favorable to communism.

Propaganda and Ideology. Moscow immediately hailed the revolution as "objectively progressive"—an old Soviet euphemism for a development that, regardless of its apparent character, actually serves Soviet interests. The Soviet Union suddenly discovered something new in Islam; Soviet scholars began to write about the progressive character of Shi'a Islam and its revolutionary potential.[5]

The Use of the Tudeh Party. The long-time head of the Tudeh party was removed and replaced by a figure who was willing to cooperate with Khomeini and who proceeded to enunciate the astonishing declaration that the ayatollah's goals were the same as the Tudeh's.[6] Thousands of old-time Tudeh sympathizers who had long been in exile in the USSR were permitted to cross the border back into Iran to infiltrate the new regime (only to be subsequently purged.) In Moscow's eyes, however, Tudeh was probably more valuable as a means of maintaining an anti-U.S. atmosphere than it was as a potential claimant to power in the near term.[7]

Moscow viewed clerical influence as almost surely transitional and felt encouraged to believe that progressive forces in the country would soon be able to come to the fore and eventually take power in Iran in the chaos of the collapsed Pahlavi regime and the flight or elimination of most pro-Western elements. Few in Moscow, or the West, could foresee that the clergy would be capable of taking power, holding on to it, ruthlessly eliminating its enemies, and institutionalizing its own mechanisms of rule.

Soviet Disillusionment

If the good news for Moscow was the ayatollah's deep fear and hatred of the U.S. role in Iranian affairs, the bad news was that the ayatollah and the clergy had vivid historical memories—not only of the centuries-long Tsarist role in Iranian history but also of the atheistic character of

Soviet ideology and Moscow's consistent designs upon even modern Iran. The USSR could draw little comfort from its relegation to the secondary role of "Lesser Satan." Bilateral relations began to deteriorate as the Soviets saw that the clergy was not responding positively toward the new Soviet initiatives.[8]

Moscow's chief instruments of influence in the Khomeini period remained remarkably similar to those of the Pahlavi period, although Moscow hoped that the environment of these relations would be warmer than it in fact was.

Tudeh. The revolution's elimination of vast portions of the Western-educated and -oriented middle and upper class was a profound blow to any longer range orientation of Iran toward the United States. But despite the Tudeh's support for Khomeini, it supported early on a policy of greater autonomy for Iran's ethnic minorities—flagrantly contrary to Khomeini's policies.[9] Tudeh's fate was virtually sealed when, based on the information provided by a Tehran-based KGB officer who defected to the West, the Iranian Republic undertook a roundup of Tudeh members and sympathizers, many of whom had secretly infiltrated high positions in the government. Subsequent investigations and confessions led to the banning of the party outright in May 1983.[10] Nonetheless, the Islamic Republic had been less concerned about the Tudeh than it was about other leftist elements in Iran who possessed a paramilitary capability—which the Tudeh never did.[11]

Arms Sales. Moscow's initial hopes for the Islamic Republic led it to turn more strongly toward one of its historic instruments of influence and leverage in the Middle East: use of arms sales as a source of important political entree—an instrument also employed with the shah. Despite the existence of a Treaty of Friendship with Iraq, early on in the Iran-Iraq War Moscow seems to have halted arms shipments to Iraq in order to keep their options open, and, according to the Iranian prime minister, to have offered arms to Iran, which were refused. Soviet arms very probably did reach Iran via Syria, North Korea, Libya, and Eastern Europe.[12] At a time when a U.S.-sponsored arms embargo was placed upon Iran by many Western countries, it was clearly in the Soviet interest to leave open this door to future influence in Iran by allowing some East Bloc arms to trickle in indirectly.

Potential Threat of Intervention. Despite repudiation by both the shah and the Khomeini regime, the USSR still saw fit to reaffirm in February 1979 the chilling terms of Article VI of the 1921 treaty between Iran and the USSR, explicitly upholding Moscow's right to intervention in Iran.[13] This carte blanche proviso still remains a disquieting feature of Soviet relations with Iran.

The Lessons of Afghanistan. The Soviet invasion of Afghanistan obviously had immense geopolitical implications for Iran. The Islamic Republic, far from cringing or seeking to reach quick accomodation with the Soviet military presence, quickly moved to denounce it and to provide overt assistance to the anti-Soviet mujahidin, without seeking any allies outside to protect them from possible Soviet threat.

Khomeini's reaction is interesting, because the reaction of the shah almost certainly would have been different: The shah would probably have moved immediately to strengthen his bilateral security ties with the United States in the face of the modern-day Soviet invasion next door—a move that strongly suggested Soviet expansionism was still alive and well in Moscow even in the early 1980s. The Islamic Republic was probably driven by two considerations: First, the zeal of the revolution lent Tehran a new elan and confidence, a sense that they were ready to take on the world—a reaction perhaps less likely from a more mature regime. Secondly, the Islamic Republic had likely considered that U.S. warnings to Moscow to keep hands off Iran would probably serve to deter further Soviet adventurism without any request for such help from Tehran.

Economic Assistance. Soviet economic policies toward the Islamic Republic were still predicated primarily on the political relationship between the two countries: to make Iran as dependent as possible upon the USSR in trade and economic matters and to keep Iran isolated from the West. In most cases the USSR was willing to overlook economic differences where political gains could be realized.

Transit Rights. The USSR took the opportunity of the U.S. hostage crisis with Iran to offer enhanced rail transit rights through the Soviet Union to help skirt the U.S. embargo. Indeed, such transit rights for Iranian imports and exports from the USSR, Europe, and the Far East have proven particularly important when Iran had been constrained in its use of the Gulf during the Iran-Iraq War. Moscow played a much tougher game, however, in using transit rights as an instrument to gain concessions on Iran's natural gas prices to the USSR. Nearly 100 years later, Iran's traditional rail links with the USSR thus still wield important impact on bilateral relations.

Expanded Rail Ties. The USSR sought to assist the Khomeini regime in improving and expanding the capacity of its rail ties with the Caucasus. In 1987 approximately one-fifth of Iranian imports entered via this route. For the USSR the magnitude is considerable: In recent years as much as 53 percent of container traffic on the Trans-Siberian railway has been destined for Iran. Those figures are likely to go up as Moscow's ties with Iran improve. Moscow has additionally proposed the extension of new rail lines between Turkmenistan and Iran, which would help deepen the economic reliance of Iran on the USSR. Such a Turkmenistan line might go directly to Iran's Indian Ocean port of Chah Bahar, acquiring major strategic importance for the USSR as well by giving it important commercial access to the Indian Ocean that it has hitherto lacked.[14] The importance of such access would of course create some considerable dependency by Moscow upon good ties with Iran as well.

Dependence has not been entirely a one-way street in the area of resources either. The Islamic Republic insisted early on on quintupling the price of its natural gas to the USSR—up to world market prices—and cut off those gas deliveries to the Caucasus when Moscow failed to meet Iran's terms; this action imposed some shortages on the USSR over the winter of 1978–1979.[15] Economic and technical assistance to the Islamic Republic had been offered off and on, depending upon the political climate, and involved some 153 projects by 1984.

Soviet-Iranian relations have therefore undergone considerable change since the end of World War II, the death of Stalin, the consolidation of the late shah's reign, his eventual fall, and the emergence of an unprecedented Islamic Republic in Iran. The key changes were Iran's achievement of sufficient military and economic power, independence of policy, and security ties to the West that the USSR found itself required to woo rather than intimidate Iran in pursuit of its own goals. In judging Soviet behavior in this period, despite considerable tactical change of approach, the Soviet Union's approach does not seem to have startlingly changed in strategic outlook and goals. That kind of change had to await the Gorbachev era, which was to set these relations on the road to potentially profound transformation.

In the next chapter we shall see how these further changes in Iran, the USSR, and in the world may make for a markedly different pattern of relationship between the Soviet Union and Iran—without entirely nullifying some of the ineluctable geopolitical realities that surround it.

Notes

1. Aryeh Yodfat, *The Soviet Union and Revolutionary Iran* (New York: St. Martin's Press, 1984), p. 28.

2. See, for example, Jerry Hough's interesting analysis of this material in Chapter Six, "Political Development and Revolutionary Strategy," in *The Struggle for the Third World: Soviet Debates and American Options* (Washington, D.C.: Brookings Institution, 1986).

3. According to Alvin Rubenstein: "The intensive economic interactions of the early 1970s were the most tangible payoff from the political rapprochement of the 1960s. Total trade quadrupled, expanding from more than $250 million in 1970 to in excess of $1 billion by 1978. In 1976 Moscow undertook a threefold

expansion of the Isfahan steel complex . . . and development of additional sources of iron ore and coal. Soviet participation in Iran's development program accounted for 90 percent of Iran's coal, iron ore, and cast iron production, and for 70 percent of its steel capacity. By 1978, 78 of the 134 projects in which Soviet assistance was involved had been completed. In addition to being the largest Third World purchaser of Soviet machinery and equipment, Iran negotiated contracts worth several billion dollars. . . . " See Alvin Z. Rubenstein, *Soviet Policy Toward Turkey, Iran, and Afghanistan* (New York: Preager, 1982), p. 77.

4. Yodfat, *op. cit.*, p. 48; Rubenstein, *op. cit.*, pp. 93–94.

5. Muriel Atkin, "Soviet Attitudes Toward Shi'ism and Social Protest," in *Shi'ism and Social Protest*, ed. N. Keddie and J. Cole (New Haven: Yale University Press, 1988).

6. Yodfat, *op. cit.*, pp. 55–56.

7. Rubenstein, *op. cit.*, p. 114.

8. Yodfat, *op. cit.*, p. 59.

9. Rubenstein, *op. cit.*, p. 114.

10. Yodfat, *op. cit.*, p. 132.

11. Rubenstein, *op. cit.*, p. 115.

12. *Ibid.*, pp. 110–111.

13. *Ibid.*, p. 104.

14. Milan Hauner and John Roberts, "Moscow's Iran Gambit: Railroading a Friendship," *Washington Post*, Outlook Section, 16 August 1987.

15. Rubenstein, *op. cit.*, pp. 111–112.

10

Iran and the USSR:
The Shape of Future Relations

The principal problem with your country is neither ownership, economics, nor freedom; rather your problem is non-belief in God. . . . I hope that you will achieve the true glory of eradicating the last rotten layers of seventy years of deviousness of world communism from the face of history and from your own country.
—*Ayatollah Khomeini, letter to Gorbachev, January 1989*

History reveals a number of geopolitical issues that will continue to lie at the core of Iranian relations with the USSR. Chief among these are the overlapping nationalities on both sides of the Soviet-Iranian border and Iran's particular interest in Islam in the Muslim regions of the USSR that once lay under Iranian cultural domination. These two issues, once minor or almost nonexistent in bilateral relations, may now become dominant themes in the relations between the two countries. Traditional trade issues, and especially transit and railroad access from Russia to the Arabian Sea, will likewise remain central to the interests of both states.

As the world has evolved over the past century, the grossly unequal character of Russian-Iranian relations has gradually grown more favorable to Tehran, as Iran has grown in strength and independence, its borders and sovereignty more secure and respected in a changing world order.

Sweeping change in Soviet ideology, policies, and tactics under Gorbachev, if enduring, show signs of already profoundly changing the nature of Russian-Iranian relations. The Russians have shown a fine understanding of Iran's deep desire for a paramount role in regional affairs, and Iran's leaders have been flattered that the Soviet Union has so far found it useful to acknowledge that role. This change has brought Soviet and Iranian interests into a more parallel course on such issues as the settlement of the Iran-Iraq War, the settlement of the Afghan conflict, and even some mutual interests in the resolution of Soviet Muslim minority questions.

Russia is likely to continue to view Iran as the power to be reckoned with in the Gulf and the Northern Tier. The Russians likewise may have concluded that force and intimidation are increasingly less effective means for the attainment of Russian goals in Iran than ever before.

This chapter examines those geopolitical issues that have been constants in Iranian-Russian relations throughout history and how these issues have evolved in the present day. Areas of potential conflict for the future are discussed and viewed against the backdrop of major changes in the world order and the Soviet system over time.

As Iranian relations with the Soviet Union move into the future, dramatic new issues are emerging that will likely profoundly reshape the character of relations between the two states. On the Soviet side, these new factors involve the emergence of Mikhail Gorbachev in the USSR, his revolutionary policies of *perestroika*, the unleashing of new democratic forces within the USSR, the explosion of nationality problems within the country, the reemergence of Russia as a distinct entity, and the impact of a potential collapse of the Soviet Empire. On the Iranian side, new factors include Iran's increased freedom of diplomatic maneuver with the ending of the Iran-Iraq War, new Iranian determination to play a key regional role—in ways that affect Soviet interests—and the power of Islamic populism as an Iranian instrument of influence among newly emerging Soviet Muslims. Iran itself will likewise face new vulnerabilities to problems among its own minority groups if it is not attentive to potential contagion from dramatic change among Soviet minorities themselves—especially in this new era of increasing world democracy and emphasis on human rights. These new factors are in the process of decisively reordering many of the traditional relationships between Iran and Russia.

Geopolitics

Iran must continuously devote more concern to the Soviet state than to any other factor—simply because of its overwhelming *potential* impact on the Iranian state. Of the states in the region, only Russia is capable of totally dominating Iran. However, on the day-to-day level, the Russia's status as a great power suggests that it will be less mercurial and tactical in the perception of its interests and guided more broadly by an overall balance of its interests on the world scene as a whole. Smaller regional states, conversely, can be much more volatile and can more quickly embroil the interests of the Iranian state in crisis.

Although the revolutionary domestic and foreign policy changes in the Soviet Union under Gorbachev indicate the possibility of a far more benign Russian-Iranian relationship in the future, Russian policy has a deep and long-standing historic legacy to overcome before the Iranians will—if ever—lose their anxiety over Russian territorial and political intentions. The Soviet invasion of neighboring Afghanistan is far too fresh in Iranian minds to enable Tehran to assume an enduring change in Russian geopolitical conduct has taken place. And yet it possibly has. But sweeping and enduring change in the USSR only increases, rather than decreases, Iran's own nationality challenge.

Nationality Problems—Iran's Permanent Dilemma

Iran's large number of ethnic and religious minorities have historically identified the country as vulnerable to nationality problems. Arabs, Turkic-speaking Azeris, Turkmen and Qashqai, Kurds, Baluch, Armenians, and others all make up the ethnic map of Iran—in which native Persian speakers may number less than 50 percent. We have seen how the Gilan Republic after World War I and the Azeri and Kurdish regions after World War II were used by the Soviet Union to establish breakaway governments and to serve as centers of Communist movements.

Soviet ideology, because of the multinational character of the USSR itself, had developed a considerable body of theory on nationality questions that it has tended to apply to countries outside the Soviet Union as well. The concept of regional, ethnically based republics and autonomous regions has historically been a common Soviet recipe for solving nationality conflict in many places in the world—Moscow proposed it even for the United States—but this approach has obviously been of limited appeal to the leadership of most countries, including Iran. Indeed, the manipulation of nationalist frustrations abroad, including the concept of establishing autonomous regions for disgruntled minorities, has also served as a Soviet instrument by which to threaten the integrity of states hostile to the USSR. Thus Moscow has long evinced particular—and not always welcome—interest in Iranian nationality questions. Not surprisingly, the Tudeh party has invariably reflected this Soviet thinking, and as recently as the mid-1980s was still advocating greater autonomy for Iran's minorities—an idea fiercely rejected by Khomeini.

Iran's nationalities remain a potential target to any nation intent upon destabilizing Iran—especially a neighboring one. (The British were themselves able to use the breakaway propensities of the Khuzestan Arabs in the early part of the century as Britain sought to gain maximum control over oil exploitation in Iranian Khuzestan.) The USSR made it abundantly clear to Iran ever since the fall of the shah, in both clandestine broadcasts and in the Soviet press, that it had special interest in Iran's nationality problems. Moscow furthermore was able to maintain contacts with most of the ethnic movements inside Iran—and possessed a known ability to exacerbate them if Iran did not adopt a positive attitude toward Soviet policies.[1] Russia in principle will always remain capable of providing funds and arms to potential revolutionary or breakaway movements as an instrument of pressure against Iran. So can newly emerging border republics such as Azerbaijan or Turkmenistan. No Iranian government can remain insensitive to this potential—or actual—threat.

Of all its nationality questions only three are strategically threatening to Iran: the Baluch, the Kurds, and the Azeris. Baluchi separatist aspirations are exploitable, especially in conjunction with Afghanistan and Pakistani politics. (This will be discussed in Chapter 13.) Iranian Baluchistan is not, however, contiguous to the Soviet Union and does not naturally fall into the area of a bilateral problem.

The Kurds present a problem because of their own long history of separatist movements and parties, historic Soviet contact with the Kurdish movement, and the international character of the Kurdish problem due to the presence of large Kurdish minorities in Iraq and Turkey, and the existence of a Kurdish minority in the USSR. (The Kurds are discussed in greater detail in Chapters 2 and 11.) Of all three potential nationality problems, Russia has historically been most capable of affecting Azerbaijan. For Iran, the Azeris matter most of all because of their numbers—approximately one-third of Iran's population, their historic prominence in Iranian society and government, their history of separatist movements, and their common border with Soviet Azeris. Azeris in Soviet Azerbaijan number approximately 6 million, as opposed to approximately 9 million in Iran.

Nationality Problems as a Two-Edged Sword

Seventy years of Soviet power have familiarized us with Soviet abilities to exploit nationality problems around its periphery—perhaps even leading us to overlook the degree to which nationality problems had in fact constituted a serious internal problem for the Tsarist empire itself. These same problems had indeed also plagued the early days of Soviet power, until Moscow was finally able to apply brute force to quell such nationalist manifestations. But nationality problems across both sides of the Soviet border have now become a two-way street—in which the Soviet Union itself is now increasingly vulnerable, even to manipulation by Iran.

While the iron grip of Stalinism and the tight controls of the Soviet system had kept internal Soviet nationality issues relatively quiescent for nearly seven decades, in fact the internal tensions, pressures, and "contradictions" continued to grow during that period. Gorbachev's policies of *glasnost* have finally brought out into the open what could not in any case have been suppressed indefinitely. Unfortunately for Moscow, the gradual reemergence of nationality problems in the USSR has coincided with the emergence of Islamic policies under Iran's clerical rule that call for strong backing for all oppressed Islamic peoples of the world. Iran obviously feels particular interest for the Muslim minorities in the Soviet Union, especially because most of them at one time have been part of the Persian Empire.

Azerbaijan

The two-edged sword of nationalism is nowhere more vividly manifested than in Azerbaijan. The USSR has historically exploited the interest of Iran's Azerbaijan population for greater cultural and political autonomy and has periodically posed pregnant questions about the "unity of the Azeri peoples" as an instrument of pressure against Iran. As of 1990, however, the USSR itself faces a greater threat of Azerbaijani separatism from the Soviet Union than does Iran.

- Informal relations between the two regions of Azerbaijan were quite close during the first two decades of the twentieth century, with each side playing a role in the social and political movements of the other.
- The very creation of Soviet Azerbaijan as a Soviet republic with its own distinctive alphabet, language, and culture greatly strengthened the concept of separate Azerbaijani national consciousness that scarcely existed at the turn of the twentieth century.[2] The Soviets, in any case, have never needed to *create* nationalist feelings among the Soviet Azeris in order to exploit them against Iran. It has been more a question of *permitting* their expression, unleashing for certain periods of time the Azeris' own aspirations for closer ties with Iranian Azerbaijan.
- Soviet encouragement of Soviet Azeri interest over the years in their brothers in Iran—primarily intended to intimidate and weaken Tehran's control in the north—has undoubtedly whetted interest in Baku for closer ties with their kinsmen in Iran.
- The increasingly violent expression beginning in 1988 of historical tensions between Armenians and Azerbaijanis in the Caucasus has stimulated intense nationalist feelings among the Soviet Azeris.

The (dubious) Azeri perception that Moscow has been "pro-Armenian" in the Armenian-Azeri conflict over the autonomous regions of Mountainous Karabagh (*Nagorno-Karabakh* in Russian, *Arsakh* in Armenian) and Nakhichevan has kindled great anger against Moscow; the use of Soviet troops to occupy Baku in January 1990, leading to large numbers of casualties among the Azeris has stimulated intense dissatisfaction with Communist rule and led to the virtual destruction of the Azerbaijan Communist party and to the de facto control of the republic by the informal National Front Organization (Milli Cephe).

Soviet Azeri nationalists are powerfully attracted to the concept of union of northern and southern Azerbaijan because of the power a "Greater Azerbaijan" could wield. A union of the two regions would more than double the overall Azeri population,bringing it to an overall level of at least 15 million people.[3] That power would first and foremost be directed at meeting the irredentist challenge from Soviet Armenia— a struggle frozen in place by the Red Army in the early 1920s but now taking on major dimensions under the thaw of *glasnost* and *perestroika*. Any predisposition by Moscow to placate Armenian nationalist demands will further anger the Azeris and create additional appeal for a united Azeri movement to confront all regional opponents. The rest of the Muslim population of the USSR nourishes sympathies with Azeri grievances against Armenia and could lend weight to support them—especially if the problem increasingly comes to be perceived as a righting of historical territorial and cultural wrongs against Soviet Muslims as a whole.

Baku, as the capital of Soviet Azerbaijan, clearly dominates its sister capital city Tabriz in Iranian Azerbaijan as the center of Azeri intellectual and nationalist activity. Baku has long been much more developed than Tabriz and enjoys—even if much circumscribed by Soviet reality—an active culture expressed in its own native language. Azeri, as a written language in Iran, except for brief periods, has generally been banned. Just as Baku in the early twentieth century served as a major international petroleum-producing center and a magnet for nascent socialist movements in Iranian Azerbaijan, so today Baku is a potential center for Iranian Azeris should they undertake greater nationalist activity themselves.

Conversely, Iran enjoys vastly greater freedom of religion; its active Shi'ite culture is already having some impact in Soviet Azerbaijan where the predominantly Shi'ite population had been largely forbidden to practice religion for nearly seventy years. Greater freedom of Islam in Soviet Azerbaijan under the new Soviet policies of religious freedom will only serve to increase the ties between northern and southern Azerbaijan, as a complement to, not a distraction from, nationalist sentiment.

In the end, however, the ultimate calculus of the historical "longings for unity" (a Soviet Azeri term) of the Azeri peoples is highly uncertain. At whose cost would unity be established? Historically, Iranian Azerbaijan has nourished largely negative views toward union with Soviet Azerbaijan, precisely because the north has been Russian-dominated and Communist. With overwhelming change in the Soviet Union, the Communist factor will now have largely disappeared, leaving Baku freed of ideological baggage and far more attractive than it was previously.

For Tehran, any kind of unity scheme is potentially destabilizing. It would obviously be far preferable that the smaller population of Soviet Azerbaijan join Iranian Azerbaijan *within* an Iranian state. Even if Tehran came out as the "gaining party"—with Soviet Azerbaijan joining Iran—it would sharply upset the demographic balance within Iran, making the Azeri Turks the dominant political and economic force within the Iranian state. Indeed, Iranian officials today seem to be militantly self-confident that Iran is by far the greater cultural magnet for Soviet Azerbaijan, dangerously underestimating the sense of Turkicness that is nearly pervasive in the national self-identity of the Soviet Azerbaijanis. Such a sense of Turkicness in Baku does, in fact, contrast with the far more ambivalent sense of national identity among Iranian Azeris. Although all Iranian Azeris recognize, and value, the fact that they speak a Turkic language in their homes, they are uncertain as to whether they are actually ethnically Turkic, or simply Iranians who, through historical circumstance of Turkic invasion, happen to speak a Turkic language. Their Shi'ite faith helped distinguish them from the Sunni Ottoman Turks and to this day, even among Iranian Azeris, the term *Tork* (Turk) usually carries a slightly pejorative connotation of a culture less sophisticated than Persian. Such ambivalence distinguishes Iranian Azeris from the vast majority of other Turkic-speaking peoples who fully and wholeheartedly identify themselves with all other Turkic peoples of the world.

Richard Cottam's study of nationalism in Iran cogently argues that the history of twentieth century Iran reveals that there is no real powerful separatist sentiment at work in Iranian Azerbaijan: grievances and desire for greater autonomy, yes, but little clear-cut desire to secede.[4] He also concedes that should the lower classes, who are less Persianized, come to play a greater role in future politics, they are likely to be more susceptible to arguments about their Turkicness than the old elites. The question still remains open and must be tended to with great care by Tehran.

In any case, Iranian Azeris will not automatically identify with the Turkic cause and will view with ambivalence the benefits of union with Azeris to the north. Nonetheless, Iranian Azeris feel a sense of pride for their language and region and could even eventually move toward union if the policies of Tehran continue to forbid the use of their language and otherwise discriminate against the region. Iranian Azerbaijanis were restive under the policies of the shah. They have already grown dissatisfied with Tehran under clerical rule—an attitude expressed in their strong support for the senior Azeri cleric Ayatollah Shariat-Madari, who, until his death, was a major ideological opponent of Khomeini's concept of clerical rule.

Expression of ethnic Azeri feelings today are also the vehicle for anticlerical views as a whole. Indeed, even the very emergence of separatist feelings in Soviet Azerbaijan today greatly strengthens the bargaining power of Tabriz vis-à-vis Tehran. Tehran therefore would not seem to have a lot to gain from the resurgence of any Azerbaijani nationalism or separatism and very likely will gravitate toward a common position with Moscow in seeking to avoid independence or union of the two Azerbaijans. Tehran probably also underestimates the potential drawing power of Turkey to Soviet Azeris.

The Iranian regime itself has shown ambivalence about the Azerbaijani issue. However, President Rafsanjani has demonstrated caution in attacking Moscow's nationality policies; even Moscow's military occupation of Baku in January 1990 only evoked from the Foreign Ministry a call for the Soviets "to halt violent encounters with the people of Azerbaijan and resolve the issue by employing peaceful means."[5] In taking this position Rafsanjani has been balancing his interests in the Azerbaijan issue against his overall interests in cooperation with Moscow on a broader variety of regional issues (to be discussed later) as well giving tacit expression to the natural ambivalence Tehran feels on an issue that now may have negative consequences for Iran itself.

Radicals within the Iranian government, however, have emphasized the Islamic—rather than nationalist—character of the disorders in Baku and have suggested that the problem is part of an overall Muslim awakening. Iranian spiritual leader Ayatollah Khamene'i stated that "it is a great blunder to think that ethnic and national motives are behind this. The sentiments are Islamic and have their attractions for 1 billion Muslims worldwide."[6] Tehran's press went further in stating that "what the [Soviet] empire is facing now is basically due to its nature by which it was created, namely annexations. . . . Large parts of Iran in the north were separated into the Soviet empire."[7]

Indeed, many key radicals among the clerics today are of Azeri origin or else have close ties with the region, including the Ayatollah Meshkini, Chief Prosecutor Khoiniha, Ayatollah Musavi-Ardebili, and former Prime Minister Musavi—although none of these would ever countenance Iranian Azerbaijani separatism; on the contrary, they are at the forefront in supporting Soviet Azerbaijani opposition to Soviet rule as an expression of Islamic resurgence in the USSR.

Radical clerics have also made much of the fact that the West, and the United States in particular, is quite willing to countenance Soviet use of force against Soviet Muslims, where they would never tolerate it against Christian nationalities in the USSR. Most of the Iranian press has also attacked the Western press for talking about Azeri "nationalism" in order to conceal the Islamic character of the Soviet Azeri movement. In effect, Iranian policy toward the Azerbaijan issue remains split between a more pragmatic view as opposed to an ideological, Islamic one.

But unionist sentiments go beyond both these positions. They threaten both Iran and the USSR, and they are likely to grow, not diminish, over time in this age of rekindled regionalism and local nationalism. Disorders in Soviet Azerbaijan are already starting to bring a stream of Azeri nationalists into northern Iran that is destined to promote nationalist-separatist impulses there. As the Soviet Union opens up further to the outside world and contact between Baku and Tabriz grows—as it is already doing—the issue will seriously complicate relations between Iran and the USSR. It could bring them into conflict—or communality of interests to suppress it—as the issue evolves. Iran does not win either way. (Chapter 11 examines the further complexity of the Azerbaijani issue when Turkey is introduced as a factor.)

Ideology's New Twist: The Islamic Factor

The Soviet Union has wielded the ideological sword over Iran for nearly seventy years: communism was the Soviets' homegrown threat to the Iranian nation state. Now a new wrinkle has emerged. With the accession of the Ayatollah Khomeini to power, ideology for the first time became a political instrument on the Iranian side—not only disturbing its Islamic neighbors, but creating considerable anxiety to the Soviet Union itself with its 50 million Muslim population. Indeed, the clerics should derive some satisfaction that Islam has now demonstrated its power over the dying corpus of Marxist-Leninist thought. As Ayatollah Khamene'i recently expressed it,

The Iranian nation demonstrated that a superpower cannot make it fall to its knees; and this is thanks to the blessings of this revolution, this doctrine, this Faith, the blessings of Islam. . . . These [East European and Soviet events] are stunning and incredible events, all in the direction of what you believe in—toward the power of spiritual values. . . . What has been proved is that what has collapsed is not merely a government or a state in a particular place in the world, it is a superpower that has collapsed.[8]

Thus, beyond the special nature of the Azerbaijani question in Iran, Tehran will also continue to follow the course of Islamic resurgence in Soviet Central Asia with immense interest; Iran has after all been the patron and wellspring of much of that culture for nearly thirteen centuries. The Islamic Republic has already propagated its Islamic vision over the airwaves in local Soviet Muslim languages for several years. Moscow has increasingly shared in the international anxiety for resurgent Islam—its seemingly inexplicable and alien character inflaming the fears of the atheist Marxist imagination even more than it does the secular-minded Westerner. Iran may now need to tread more lightly in even figuratively brandishing the sword of the Faith on Marxist territory in the future. When Tehran first began its religious appeals to Soviet Muslims, the challenge was largely a theoretical one, and no one could have foreseen that within a decade the very collapse of the Soviet Empire was becoming a realistic possibility. Now that Iran has gotten its wish, so to speak, it may need to be far more circumspect in exploiting its unexpected opportunities. If the Islamic threat assumes greater salience in Moscow's thinking, it may yet turn on Iran to eliminate this source of instability. Iran will have to gauge its overall commitment to the export of the Islamic revolution against its other equities: an awareness that the West is not likely to react terribly sympathetically to calls for security assistance against a Soviet Union consumed with concern for propagation of a virulent and xenophobic Islamic message.

Even here, Iran is unable to view the Soviet-Azerbaijani question free of suspicions of a much deeper Western anti-Muslim agenda:

the West is pursuing Tehran-Moscow ties with concern and is trying to persuade Moscow to commit more genocide and perform more negative acts to mar these relations. . . . The West through its propaganda is leading the Kremlin leadership towards more massacre and revival of the past suppressive conditions in the Muslim-dwelling republics of the Soviet Union.[9]

Washington has implicitly recognized what it calls the right of Moscow to suppress the Muslims. . . . The name of the game is to bait and incite, and this mad rush of Western news agencies to portray the Azeri Muslims as thugs and villains has been joined by the Zionist news agency, which is trying to tease and taunt Moscow over the Caucasus affairs.[10]

Central Asia

Indeed, the future of the Soviet Muslim Republics, especially in Central Asia, is going to prove increasingly difficult for Moscow to cope with in the decades ahead. As those republics call for greater autonomy and freedom in the future, and—in part—look south for mutual expression of their cultural identity, they will inevitably become more involved in relations with Iran, their old cultural center. To some extent Moscow and Tehran—and Turkey—will represent alternative cultural magnets for the orientation of the Central Asian republics.

As in Azerbaijan, Iran may find that getting its wish in Central Asia may be as destabilizing for Iran as for the USSR. While the Islamic clarion into Communist Central Asia was a theoretical Holy War for the liberation of Islam from an alien and atheistic ideology, the actuality of nationalist movements and Turkic irredentism or Turkic solidarity may come to threaten Iran's position in other ways. The geopolitical emergence of Central Asia into the Middle East will thus bring unforeseen consequences to Iran and the region. But as in the Persian Gulf, Iran will have major difficulty in overcoming a perception of the *Shi'ite* character of its Islamic message, despite all its protestations of the Islamic universalism of its call. Apart from Soviet Azerbaijan, most Soviet Muslims are Sunni. They will not view Iran as the sole focus of their resurgent *religious* interest, except as a symbol of how to deal with a superpower. But Iran's neo-Islamic ideology, with its emphasis on political action, can still have impact in Central Asia as well, depending on how skillfully Iran represents it.

As communication and travel between Central Asia and the Islamic world opens up, Iran will surely seek to bid for the religious/political role of mentor to over 50 million Russian Muslims. What other center can readily rival Iran in this capacity and from such proximity? Only Turkey and Afghanistan—and Turkey lacks the immediate proximity.

Moscow well understands Iran's potentially powerful negative influence upon the stability of the Soviet Muslim population. Instead of issuing threats and warnings to Iran in this regard, Moscow has attempted to co-opt Iran by improving its relations with Iran after the Ayatollah Khomeini's death. It has played up to Iran's own view of itself as the power to be reckoned with in the region, particularly in Islamic affairs. President-to-be Ali Akbar Rafsanjani, during his historic and precedent-setting visit to Moscow in June 1989, was afforded an opportunity to preach to Azerbaijanis from a mosque in Baku—surely a first for any Iranian leader. As a result of this, and broader recognition of Moscow's changing policies on freedom of religion and freedom of national development among Soviet Muslims, Iran has publicly acknowledged these changes in the Soviet Union and seemingly is sympathetic to Soviet efforts at reform. A radical publication in Tehran spelled out this relationship arrogantly and without mincing words:

> The Russians' urgent need for the cooperation of the Islamic Republic of Iran and of the Islamic revolution in general in various fields was of great significance to them. The Russians have well understood that by confronting the Islamic revolution, which is considered the hearth of pure Mohammadan Islam, not only will nothing be achieved, but the very existence of the socialist system in the Soviet Union will be threatened because the ideological influence of the Islamic revolution on Soviet Muslims is not something that the Kremlin can ignore. Thus, in order to be able to manage its Muslim-inhabited republics, the Soviet Union had to have friendly relations with the point around which the Islamic revolution of the world pivots—the Islamic Republic of Iran.[11]

Iranian satisfaction with new Soviet religious freedoms and general restraint in criticizing Moscow's nationality and religious policies to date (up until the occupation of Baku by the Red Army in January 1990) is a major step forward for Moscow in co-opting Iran's leadership for support. If the Soviets, in effect, can ask Iran for help in dealing with its Muslim problem, the USSR will have gone a long way toward insuring against Muslim world exploitation of Moscow's Muslim problems. How this issue will play out over the decades ahead is hard to say. The Iranian clergy will continue to be divided into pragmatists and radicals, but both groups recognize the dilemma for Iran in rapidly burgeoning separatist movements in the USSR. However Iran plays it, Tehran is clearly a key force to be reckoned with in the evolution of the Soviet nationality problem.

The Future Role of Ideological Parties

The Soviet Union has a history of using left-wing ideological parties and movements in Iran ever since the Bolshevik Revolution. The Tudeh ("The Masses") is the closest thing to a formal pro-Moscow Communist party and has been slavishly loyal to the Moscow line since its inception. The Soviets in the past have also been interested in other leftist movements such as the *Mojahedin-e-Khalq* (The People's Holy Warriors) but had almost no success in establishing any influence over it because of that group's own suspicions of Moscow and its at least nominal commitment to Islam. Other splinter left-wing groups have likewise not been responsive to Moscow because of a belief that the Moscow line was too conservative—such as in Moscow's general lack of support for armed struggle against the shah.

As has been the fate of most other Communist parties in the world, Tudeh's degree of support from Moscow has been regularly hostage to the vagaries of Moscow's state-to-state relations with Iran. Tudeh has been readily sacrificed whenever Moscow saw greater advantage in emphasizing formal state ties with Tehran. But the party has always been present as an instrument of pressure for Moscow to use whenever the need arose. Its future today, however, remains very cloudy, for Moscow is unlikely to view it any longer as an appropriate instrument of Russian influence in Iran.

First, Moscow cannot hold out great hope for Tudeh's prospects in the near to middle term. Second, after its experience in Afghanistan, the Soviet Union is probably extremely wary of intervening on behalf of any such Communist party that comes to power by military coup. Such parties have proven generally unstable and involve the USSR in deep and unprofitable commitments at considerable political expense to Soviet interests elsewhere. As a dramatic formulation of how far Moscow has reoriented its politics, I contend that Gorbachev's USSR today would probably react negatively to news of a Tudeh coup in Tehran; it would potentially damage the entire agenda of *perestroika* that Moscow has been trying to pursue in its global policies. Moscow may feel compelled to maintain at least pro-forma ties with the Tudeh party for the foreseeable future, even while abandoning it as a meaningful instrument of influence. Whatever degree of influence Moscow will seek to retain in Tehran, it will find that overt—or covert—support for Tudeh will only raise the anxiety level in Tehran and impel it to suppress the party and distrust the Russians further. Moscow will need to develop entirely new, more effective instruments of influence in Iran in the future, perhaps more closely associated with traditional diplomatic, political, and economic instruments. The Tudeh will probably attempt to maintain some political position on the Iranian political spectrum, but lack of meaningful Soviet support is likely to prove highly demoralizing to it. Moscow may well no longer play any significant role in providing support to foreign Communist or radical/revolutionary parties anywhere in the world. If the Tudeh party is to play any role on the Iranian left in the future, it must do so in the capacity of a truly nationalist left-wing party that is not tied ideologically or logistically to Moscow in any way. The Tudeh has not been able to manage this role in the past. It may need to look to left-wing elements in Baku for significant support in the future.

Reorientation of
Moscow's Priorities and Interests

If Moscow indeed is recasting the orientation of its entire foreign policy toward integration into the West and the abandonment of any ideological competition, then its priorities vis-à-vis Iran also shift sharply. The keystones of Moscow's earlier policies fade away under the "new thinking." As we have noted earlier, central to the Soviet's geopolitical strategy was protection of the Soviet Union against potential international forces hostile to Moscow operating out of Iran and to deny the West major influence in Iran in what was a clear zero-sum game with the West.

Today, with the end of the class struggle as an instrument of Soviet policy and the renunciation of ideological competition between East and West, the elimination of the classic elements of "capitalist encirclement" is under way—elements that Moscow had itself provoked into being by its ideological declaration of war against the world. Russia need no longer have major fears of hostile great powers using Iran as a base against it. Simultaneously, the need for Soviet right of intervention into Iran under Article VI of the 1921 treaty and the need for denying the West influence in Iran has also been all but eliminated. A key test of the new directions of Russian policy in Iran will be the abrogation of Article VI and abandonment of the Tudeh. Russian-Iranian relations will most likely come to rest upon more traditional elements of interstate relations. This is not to say that there may well not be conflict of interest between the two states, but those relations are unlikely to be exacerbated any longer by the earlier ideological shadowboxing of the East-West struggle.

An End to the Imperative of Empire?

Indeed, this transformation of relations, if Soviet reform and democratization continues, suggests that the old imperatives of empire that marked five centuries of Russian-Iranian relations will largely vanish. Russia's first expansionist period under the Tsars was typical of the expansion of most nineteenth-century great powers, including the United States, France, England, Germany, and other European powers—except that it involved contiguous expansion. That dynamic of nineteenth-century expansionism and imperial rivalry concluded with the end of most world empires after World War I and in the interwar period.

Russia's second expansionist period came under the expansionist ideology of Marxism-Leninism, this time equally fueled by the endless quest for security against the genuine international hostility that Moscow itself had engendered. Soviet imperial expansion was also facilitated by the legacy of Tsarist empire, and the need to stop anti-Bolshevik invading forces from operating from many of the nationality regions: the Baltics, the Caucasus, and Central Asia.

Today, perhaps these imperatives of traditional Russian expansionism are now fading. If Russia is now to retreat to borders of a great Slavic power, the classic question of traditional buffer zones is now itself transformed. Perhaps the old non-Russian states around Russia's periphery, no longer swallowed up in some kind of ideological Russian Empire, can themselves now play the traditional role of buffer states as they should. Russia's "soft underbelly," if still a valid geopolitical concept, will be protected in part by the relations Russia maintains with these southern flank states such as Azerbaijan, and the Muslim states of Central Asia. For Russia will want and need the goodwill of those regions as an important part of its own strategic depth in the political, military, and economic sense. (We will examine the concept of a Soviet southern flank, or "Northern Tier" states, in Chapter 12.)

The Transformation of Other Traditional Interests

Balance of Powers

Because of the immense power of the Russian colossus looming to the north, Iran will always need to keep decent ties with other potentially balancing powers to ensure that it is not entirely at the mercy of the whims of a future Russian polity—as yet unforeseen. Historically Iran has always sought to balance off those powers active in the region. But what can be said of the virtues of a policy of balance? Balance—even of two hostile forces such as Great Britain and Russia—perhaps prevented Russia from absorbing much, or all, of Iran in its day, but did little by way of ensuring Iran's independence or safety from domination by either state. On the contrary, those two powers on at least two occasions colluded to eliminate Iranian sovereignty. Historically then, Iran also sought ties with some "Third Force" to provide alternative options: France (under Napoleon), Germany, the United States, and even Japan and China have functioned in this capacity in some ways in more recent periods.

For Iran—as for many countries—the lesson of history is that no one else can be trusted to vouchsafe Iranian interests. Naturally, all states have their own agendas and Iran can seek to utilize those agendas as long as interests coincide. The shah very clearly relied heavily upon the United States but equally clearly was determined that Iran develop its own independent capability to defend the national interests wherever possible. Future Iranian leaders will undoubtedly emulate the shah's calculated circumspection—especially given the Iranians' immense predilection for belief in conspiracy theory and an unceasing need to search out and uncover the ulterior motives of all political actors.

As a result of traditional Persian statecraft that placed a premium on a complex, multilayered, and suspicious political outlook, and Persians' traditional attribution of labyrinthine motivations to all political actors, Iran will continue to excel at playing one force off against another. Iranian politicians are expert at whispering in the ear of one foreign party in order to heighten the suspicions of the other. The Islamic Republic quite pointedly suggested to both the United States and the USSR on various occasions in the last few years of the Iran-Iraq War that the other country was about to gain special unilateral advantage in Iran unless the first power took steps to avoid it.

To the extent that world politics is moving away from its earlier bipolar character, and the zero-sum relationship in U.S.-Soviet relations diminishes, Iran will need concern itself less with the state of U.S.-Soviet relations and will gain greater freedom to play upon the international scene. Other major players will also step upon the Iranian political stage as well: China, Japan, Western Europe, Turkey, Pakistan, and India—apart from the Arab players. The old concept of balance of power is likely to become far more fluid and tactical than ever before.

Trade and Transit Rights

As symbol of the "new thinking," Moscow commentators have noted quite openly that the West will likely and naturally play the predominant role in the reconstruction of the Iranian economy now that the Iran-Iraq War is over.[12] One commentator made this observation rather matter-of-factly, only stating that if some parts of the Iranian government were worried about too strong a dependency upon the West, the improvement of trade ties with Moscow would help bring some balance.[13] The Soviet Union is well aware that it cannot outbid the West in areas of technical and economic assistance. Yet, even if the USSR no longer need fear the use of Iran by hostile Western states to subvert the USSR, Moscow will always retain a fundamental interest in not allowing Iran to slip completely out of Moscow's orbit as a trading and transit partner of importance.

Competition between Russia and other major world powers is likely to persist, even if it no longer carries the more momentous overtones of East-West struggle. Moscow's best means of balancing the impact of strong Western economic ties with Iran lie through economic offers that Iran can credibly and profitably accept without fear of longer-term reversal of those terms. Over the longer run Moscow is likely to be more interested in Iranian oil as an alternative to its own increasingly costly oil production costs. And Soviet arms are a logical barter commodity. The 1989 Rafsanjani visit to Moscow heralded Soviet announcement of new commercial and economic relations between the two countries that are likely to grow in the future, as are the important future rail lines from Central Asia to the Arabian Sea, as discussed in the last chapter.

Arms and Military Assistance

In the years following the crushing costs of the Iran-Iraq War, Iran will devote major efforts to strengthening its military position—both as a deterrent to Iraq and as a means of exercising authority in the Gulf and beyond. Russia will almost surely seek to meet Iran's needs as soon as Tehran expresses the interest. Moscow must, of course, be cautious to avoid being perceived as heavily arming Iran at any time when Arab Gulf nervousness over Iran's intentions is high. But Moscow will probably want to have a major role in Iran's longer-term process of arms acquisition. First, Moscow will be unwilling to grant monopoly of arms sales to any other power—particularly the United States—given Iran's political and economic importance. Second, arms sales and their concomitant demand for training are a natural entree for Russia into a key area of Iranian aspirations. Precisely because Iran wishes to avoid excessive political and military reliance upon Russia—and the United States—it will surely seek to diversify its arms supplies. Nonetheless, Russia will have major opportunities here. And as in trade relations, political abuse of the potential leverage Moscow gains from arms sales will only lead to the ultimate weakening or elimination of that very instrument—especially so if Tehran can command many other global resources of arms supply. This trend has already begun with an initial arms agreement signed during Rafsanjani's trip to Moscow in June 1989 in the wake of the Ayatollah Khomeini's death—in which both states took their first major step to placing bilateral relations on a sound footing. On that occasion, Moscow announced that it had "agreed to cooperate with the Iranian side with regard to strengthening its defense capability."[14]

Iran's Regional Policies—
and Moscow's Interests

Longer-term Russian relations with Iran will partially reflect the extent to which Moscow perceives coincidence of interest between itself and

Iran in the region. The 1989 Rafsanjani visit seemingly produced remarkable concurrence of views on regional and world affairs—at least
on the surface. At a Kremlin dinner Rafsanjani was quoted as saying
that the Soviet Union and Iran "share a common viewpoint on the
overwhelming majority of international and regional problems and questions of bilateral relations. . . . To be frank, we did not think such a
course of development possible in view of the internal problems within
socialist countries."[15] What coincidence of regional interests might exist
here?

The Northern Tier States

From the point of view of Realpolitik, Moscow is unlikely to favor
the development of close working ties among Turkey, Iran, Afghanistan,
and Pakistan. These states have always shared a geopolitical concern
for Soviet policies; Moscow would prefer the advantages of dealing with
them singly rather than as a strengthened and more coordinated grouping.
As friction fades between Moscow and the West, however, this aspect
will feature less critically in Russian thinking. In this sense, the Islamic
Republic will suit Moscow's goals just fine: an assurance of strong
neutrality, lack of warm working ties with its immediate neighbors, and
an antipathy for the West and to any security ties with it. (This issue
will be discussed in greater depth Chapter 12 on the Northern Tier.)

Afghanistan

The Soviet withdrawal from Afghanistan removed a major impediment
in Soviet-Iranian relations. Not only did Tehran strongly object to the
Soviet invasion of Afghanistan and provide military support to (mainly
Shi'ite) elements of the Afghan mujahidin there, but Tehran perceived
that the implications of the invasion were highly ominous for Iran itself.
Soviet withdrawal eliminated the immediate friction of the Soviet presence
in Afghanistan but certainly not the disturbing precedent of the invasion.
Moscow will naturally not abandon an interest in maintaining continuing
influence in Afghanistan; by so doing it remains a natural geopolitical
rival with Iran for influence in Afghanistan. Iran's interest at a minimum
calls for a nonaligned Afghanistan and preferably one also responsive
to Iranian political interests. Since the cease-fire in the Iran-Iraq War,
Iran has shown heightened interest in the role of the USSR in helping
reduce Iran's isolation, and Moscow has equally skillfully played to Iran's
prejudices to induce it in policy directions very favorable to Moscow's
interests in Afghanistan. Tehran has all along suggested to Moscow that
Iran is the power to be reckoned with in the region, and holds the keys
to a settlement in Afghanistan, especially one that excludes U.S. influence.

Moscow flattered Tehran's leadership by accepting that suggestion and got Iran to agree in 1989 to the necessity for a political settlement to the Afghan struggle between the People's Democratic Party of Afghanistan (PDPA) and the Afghan mujahidin—as opposed to a military victory by the mujahidin. Iran was particularly disposed to accept this approach because the mujahidin refused to include the eight Iranian-supported Afghan Shi'ite parties in their interim government. By calling for a political solution and the inclusion of the Shi'ites, Tehran in practice weakened the unity and legitimacy of the Afghan interim government, complicated U.S. and Pakistani efforts to unite and legitimate that interim government, and has directly served Moscow's interest in bringing about a political, rather than military, solution—thereby vindicating Moscow's overall campaign for political solutions of "national reconciliation" to regional conflict everywhere. Rafsanjani's opportunity to address Azerbaijanis in a Baku mosque was Russian icing on the cake to woo Iran. To date, therefore, Soviet handling of relations with Iran has demonstrated great diplomatic skill and perceptive understanding of Iran's mentality and world view.

The Gulf

Russia under any leadership will look to expand its influence in the Gulf—political, military, and economic—regardless of relations with the West. The region is simply too close to Russian territory and too important to ignore. Russia and Iran are natural allies in seeking to weaken an existing monopoly of U.S. influence in the Gulf; Russia will be adamantly opposed to unilateral U.S. power projection in the region, even if it no longer views the U.S. presence in the Gulf in zero-sum terms. Here Moscow is likely to encourage the idea that regional security should be up to the regional powers themselves, and not to external powers. Only at such time as Moscow itself should come to feel its own interests highly constrained by security arrangements among the Gulf regional powers will it seek to weaken those regional ties in its own favor.

For the foreseeable future the West will be in a better position to exercise military power in the Gulf—both on grounds of historical precedent as well as superior power projection capability. Cooperation between the United States and Russia on the handling of regional conflict will probably increase in the Gulf—especially as *perestroika* and "new thinking" in foreign policy establish a track record. Moscow's denunciation of the Iraqi invasion of Kuwait and its support for the international anti-Iraqi war coalition are powerful signs of the new order. Although there has been some unhappiness and criticism of Gorbachev's cooperation with the United States in the Gulf among hardliners in the Communist party and the Soviet military, a return to the old days of U.S.-Soviet zero-sum competition are gone—even if Moscow is uncomfortable with the full range of U.S. military policies against the old Soviet ally Baghdad.

Russia will have to view Iran as the single most important power in the Gulf to deal with for the attainment of its own broader goals, Iraq notwithstanding. In this sense Russia will inevitably pay greater diplomatic attention to Iran—although support to rival Iraq will remain a primary means of countering Iranian influence if such is called for.

Moscow's role in a more unstable Gulf in the future—in the event of drastic changes in regimes and especially of a major change in Saudi Arabia—will introduce new complexities as to how Moscow might then play emerging triangular relationships among Iran, Iraq, and Saudi Arabia. Moscow could find itself in conflict with Iran over issues of instability or change, especially if Iran were to try to take advantage of the situation in ways that affected Soviet broader interests. As long as Iranian policies are not foolishly aggressive and belligerent, however, Moscow will definitely view Iran as the preeminent force in the Gulf to be reckoned with. This sheer act of recognition alone will go a long way toward reassuring Iran about the Russian role—as long as a direct clash of interests does not emerge.

Clandestine Propaganda

Ever since the late 1950s Moscow has supported clandestine radio stations broadcasting into Iran in Persian, allegedly representing "the people," but in fact representing the Tudeh: first the Iran Courier, and in 1959, the National Voice of Iran.[16] Although the Soviet press itself has found it useful to pursue a more balanced portrayal of Iranian affairs in its coverage of Iran in the past several decades, these radio stations' virulent line has reflected much more accurately the ideological side of Moscow's vision of Iranian developments. Up until the period of "new thinking" in Soviet foreign policy the clandestine radio broadcasts variously threatened Iran, condemned its policies, and called for revolution against the shah; they had also moved toward harsh condemnation of the ayatollah.

With Gorbachev's new policies, Moscow radio and press have taken a sharply different line in which Radio Moscow has directly addressed the Iranian leadership on policy issues of concern to Moscow, such as the need for Iran to downplay its heavyhanded Islamic ideological line in looking at Azerbaijan, and on issues of Iranian support for unconstructive and radical forces in Lebanon and elsewhere in the Middle East. The tone of Moscow's broadcasts are now balanced, constructive, and thoughtful, completely abandoning the stridency of earlier periods.

Clandestine radio out of Baku in the name of the Tudeh are now an instrument of the past, closed down coinciding with Rafsanjani's 1989 Moscow visit.

Contemporary Constraints on Moscow

Although the Soviet-Iranian borders of today reflect only an arbitrary freeze of Russian expansionism at a given historical point, they have since come to take on a "permanent" quality, reflecting changes and values in the international system since World War II. Seventy years of a containment policy in operation against the Soviet Union have served to reinforce the legitimacy of Iran's borders. Iran was protected by the Sa'dabad and Baghdad Pacts, later by CENTO and by bilateral U.S.-Iranian agreements. Despite Iran's withdrawal from CENTO after the Iranian Revolution, Soviet intervention in Iran was expressly ruled out by the Carter Doctrine.

Apart from these more formal guarantees which have served to deter possible Soviet expansionism into Iran, the contemporary political order makes Soviet territorial aggrandizement at Iranian expense much more "unacceptable" in the international order. Land grab is no longer a recognized part of the international political process, regardless of the political device used to disguise it. Nonetheless, the Soviet invasion of Afghanistan is too soberingly fresh in memory to utterly dismiss the prospect of further Russian expansionism out of hand.

The decades of the 1970s and 1980s have furthermore demonstrated the changing calculus of the small state pitted against the larger state. Although great power muscle in nineteenth and early twentieth centuries was able to work against small states with impunity, changes in the international environment, the growing sanctification of the present world state system through bodies like the UN, and the increasing constrictions upon the freedom of maneuver of the great powers have all moved the equation of relative influence in bilateral relations far along in favor of the smaller powers. The Vietnam War, Afghanistan, and the dealings of both the United States and the Soviet Union with their respective client states have demonstrated the dwindling clout that great power bestows in these circumstances. Iran is one of the chief trumpeters of this message internationally.

Thus Russian-Iranian relations have undergone marked shift in character over the past century, in part due to the increasing multipolarity of the world over the last few decades and now the sharp diminution of U.S.-Soviet rivalry in the Third World. A state like Iran will unquestionably encounter some kinds of friction in its dealings with Russia, but on a far less virulent level and with lower stakes than during the Cold War.

The revolution in the Soviet Union under Gorbachev has probably undercut any last possibility of Communist-style Soviet invasion or absorption of Iran. Moscow's priorities have simply shifted too far to accommodate this kind of old activity.

Iran will nonetheless always have to live with the historical record of Russian policy toward Iran. And however benign Moscow's territorial policies toward Iran may be in the future, geopolitics dictate that Moscow will always have reason to seek a regime in Tehran that is sensitive to broader Russian international interests. The future of Russian-Iranian relations is now likely to turn on the much more complex regional relationships that will be emerging with newly autonomous or even independent Soviet Muslim states. These states will develop their own clear-cut interests and diplomatic alliances in which Iran will inevitably play an integral role. It will be in that environment that Russia will need to exercise its new diplomacy in a new geopolitical game on the southern flank of Russia, far removed from the "Great Game" of the nineteenth century.

Notes

1. Aryeh Yodfat, *The Soviet Union and Revolutionary Iran* (New York: St. Martin's Press, 1984), pp. 86, 120, 144.

2. Tadeusz Swietochowski, *Russian Azerbaijan, 1905–1920* (Cambridge: Cambridge University Press, 1985), p. 191.

3. Statistics on ethnic breakdown in Iran are scarce, but a Western study places the number of Iranian Azeris at 9 million. See Patricia Higgins, "Minority-State Relations in Contemporary Iran," in *The State, Religion, and Ethnic Politics: Afghanistan, Iran and Pakistan*, eds. Ali Banuazizi and Myron Weiner (Syracuse: Syracuse University Press, 1986), p. 178. The overall number of Azerbaijanis in the USSR is estimated at 6 million in 1979; see Alexandre Bennigsen and S. Enders Wimbush, *Muslims of the Soviet Empire* (Bloomington: Indiana University Press, 1986), p.133. By 1990 both the Iranian and Soviet figures are undoubtedly low.

4. See Richard Cottam, *Nationalism in Iran* (Pittsburgh: University of Pittsburgh Press, 1979), pp. 118–133.

5. Nick B. Williams, "Soviet Enclave Declares Independence," *Los Angeles Times*, 21 January 1990.

6. Nick B. Williams, "Iran Warns Against 'Harsh' Soviet Moves in Azerbaijan," *Los Angeles Times*, 9 February 1990.

7. Nick B. Williams, "Iran Steps Up Its Criticism of Soviet Actions in Azerbaijan," *Los Angeles Times*, 25 January 1990.

8. Khamene'i Speech to Air Force, Tehran Domestic Service, 8 February 90, in FBIS-NES-90-028, 9 February 1990.

9. See Moscow Radio Peace and Progress in Persian to Iran, 8 February 1989, FBIS-SOV-89-027, 10 February 1989.

10. Persian daily *Jomhuri-e-Islami*, 21 January 1990, quoted in Tehran IRNA in English, FBIS-NES-90-014, 22 January 1990.

11. *Pasdar-e-Islam*, 23 July 1989, in FBIS-NES-89-154.

12. Tehran IRNA in English, 19 January 1990, as quoted in FBIS-NES-90-014, 22 January 1990.

13. See Moscow Radio in Persian to Iran, 12 October 1988, in FBIS NES-88-201.

14. See Moscow TASS International Service in Russian, 22 June 1989, in FBIS-SOV-89-119.

15. See Moscow PRAVDA in Russian, 22 June 1989, FBIS-SOV-89-119.

16. Yodfat, *op. cit.*, p. 44.

11

Iran and Turkey: Rivals for Central Asian Leadership

Those Turks, those heavy buffaloes of Turks. . . .[1]

Nothing, I found, was so easy as to deceive the Turks by outward appearance. Their taciturnity, the dignity and composure of their manner and deportment, their slow walk, their set phrases, were all so easy to acquire, that in the course of a very short time I managed to imitate them so well that I could at pleasure make myself one of the dullest and most solemn of their species.[2]

—Hajji Baba of Ispahan

You must know, that although the Curds do not allow that they are subject to any power, yet our ancestors grazed their flocks and pitched their tents in that part of the Curdistan mountains belonging to Turkey which are situated in the government of the pasha of Bagdad. . . . Such is the experience I have of Turkish governors, that, when once they have a pretext in hand for oppression, they never fail to make use of it.[3]

—A Kurd speaks of Turks in **Hajji Baba of Ispahan**

Kırk Arabın aklı bir incir çekirdeği doldurmaz.

The brains of forty Arabs will not fill the seed of a fig.

—Old Turkish proverb

We turn now to examine the often rocky course of relations between Iran and Turkey—two countries with intimate historical familiarity with one another. Turkey is important to Iran because it is the gateway to Europe, both geographically and intellectually. The future evolution of relations between these two major powers will have great impact on the future geopolitical shape of the Middle East as a whole.

191

The 1920s brought remarkable transition from centuries of antagonistic Persian-Turkish relations to a fresh modus vivendi; this shift was primarily due to the new nationalist leadership that came to power in both countries, wiping away the intense ideological confrontation between the centers of world Shi'ite and world Sunni power.

While neither state possesses irredentist views toward the other, several geopolitical issues of potential friction will abide between the two countries: Kurdish problems, the future of Azerbaijan and Central Asia, Iraqi policy, and oil pipeline security. Despite long-term disavowal by the Turkish state of any Pan-Turkist ambitions (which would directly affect Iranian Azerbaijan), the new uncertainties and fluidities of ethnic problems in the USSR open up possibilities of future Turkish involvement in the fate of these Turkic peoples that would directly affect Iran. Despite historical antagonisms, Turkey is likely to share with Iran many common regional interests that lessen the likelihood of major conflict between them. Turkey, nonetheless, is destined to play an increasingly important and active role in the Middle East—from which it has almost unnaturally excluded itself for nearly seven decades. Under circumstances of more geographically extensive Turkish activism, Turkey could reemerge as a geopolitical rival to Iran once again in ways that could affect the balance of power in the Gulf.

This chapter examines the factors that have changed the Turkish-Iranian geopolitical relationship in the past and those that might upset the cordiality of ties once again in the future under changing circumstances.

Ideological Struggle

The sixteenth century was witness to the greatest ideological confrontation between Shi'ite and Sunni states of all time. The relatively harmonious ties between Turkey and Iran today conceal a long history of religious struggle for the soul of Islam waged between these two states for nearly 150 years. For with the adoption of Shi'ism by the new Safavid dynasty in 1500, the new Persia poised itself for confrontation with the capital of the Sunni world over ideological influence and regional power.

We have seen that the official embrace of Shi'ism by Persia in 1500 had major—and from some points of view, disastrous—consequences for the country's development. Persia with this one act had set itself apart from the rest of the Muslim/Sunni world—quite possibly by design as a deliberate expression of Persian separatism and distinctiveness. Apart from more than a century of war, the Turkish-Persian conflict inflicted even greater long-term damage on Iran in cutting it off from the influences of Europe, and even isolating it from the rest of the

Muslim and Arab world, then centered foursquare in the Sublime Porte of Istanbul.

Ottoman Turkey was fearful of the Shi'ite contagion even before Shi'ism was adopted as the Persian national cause. Shi'ite sects in Turkey had already nourished subversive goals toward the Ottoman state even before gaining the support of the Persian Safavids. With encouragement from Persia, Ottoman Turkey now saw distinct threat from the newly emerging Persian state and moved to crush it. Exchanges between the two states were couched in Islamic ideological invective. As the Ottoman Sultan Selim I wrote to the Persian Emperor Shah Isma'il in 1514:

> The Ulema and our teachers of the law have pronounced death upon thee [Shah Isma'il], perjurer and blasphemer as thou art, and have laid upon every good Mussulman the sacred duty of taking arms for the defence of religion and for the destruction of heresy and impiety in thy person and the persons of those who follow thee.[4]

Ottoman Turkey was champion of the Sunni world; its conquests deep into Persia were equally applauded by the Arab world as a blow for the orthodox Sunni Faith against "heathen Persian."

The future of the Islamic world was irrevocably determined by the outcome of this Persian-Turkish confrontation. For the Safavids nourished the ultimate ideal of expanding Shi'ism throughout the Muslim world. For Turkey, the possibility existed of overturning Safavid rule and restoring Iran to the Sunni world—a development that would have had immense consequences for the modern Middle East had it occurred. In the event, Turkey stopped short of destroying the Safavids. The shock of a series of crushing defeats eventually led Iran 139 years later to back away formally from its messianic mission.

In what was a historic development in the Middle East—comparable to European agreements to end religious wars in Europe—Turkey and Persia agreed to recognize for the first time the legitimacy of each state's faith within its own borders.[5] These historic events echo down through Islamic history and are etched in the minds of the Iranians—especially the clergy—even today. The ideological struggle between Sunni and Shi'ite states was seemingly resolved several centuries ago, but the overtones are still deeply embedded in Khomeini's vision for the Islamic Republic today.

Iran and Turan

But Turk and Persian were intimately known one to the other long before the establishment of the Ottoman Empire. The Persians had lived alongside of various Turkic tribes for nearly one thousand years before the Safavid state became pitted against the Ottoman. A series of Turkish clans and tribes had variously infiltrated, transited, conquered, and governed parts or all of Iran over long historical periods in the great odyssey of Turkic peoples across Central Asia to Anatolia. The Seljuk Turks had ruled Iran for some two hundred years starting in 1037— playing a major role in the reinvigoration and spread of Islam westward into Byzantine Christian Anatolia. The forerunners of what were to become the Ottoman Turks had also passed through Persia in this period. In starker cultural terms the Persians perceived the Turks (or Turanians) as the classic barbaric aliens outside the gates of Persian culture. Indeed the dichotomy between the civilized world of Persia (Iran) from that of the Turks (Turan) lies deep in the Persian tradition. The long presence of Turan inside Iran is one of the many features that have helped fracture Persian society along its manifold fault lines for over one millennium.

The first two hundred years of the Safavid existence were thus threatened from two fronts—Ottoman Turkey, and increasingly, Russia. At some points Turkey and Russia cooperated in fulfilling their respective territorial designs against Iran; at other times Russia opposed the spread of Turkish influence—when Turkey seemed to covet the same turf as Russia itself sought. Azerbaijan was just such a place that both Russia and Turkey each hoped to possess—the Turks because they perceived the Turkish-speaking Azerbaijanis as kinsmen, the Russians because it lay in the path of Russia's expansion beyond the Caucasus.

Conquests and Borders

Safavid ambition was therefore sharply repelled by Turkey in a series of stunning defeats in which Persia lost most of its western territories to the Turks—first in the sixteenth century and then in the eighteenth century. After each occasion Persia somehow managed to produce a skilled ruler capable of restoring most of Persia's losses and keeping the western territories of the Persian empire largely intact. Border uncertainties and problems naturally figured as a constant theme in relations between the two states. Much of that disputed territory lay in fact in modern-day Iraq, and early on involved demarcation of the Shatt al-'Arab waterway—an issue that has yet to be definitively "resolved" in the course of the last three hundred years. The settlement of borders between Turkey and Iran proper would have to await the twentieth century.

Kurds

But the issue of borders involved more than just land, it concerned people as well. The question of nationalities on each side of the border had always played a role in the claims of both states, but the Kurds presented a special interstate problem at least as early as 1821 when they precipitated one of the many Persian-Turkish wars. The Kurds, still tribal, tended to wander back and forth over the borders at will, often seeking refuge with one or the other of the regional authorities when in trouble.

Despite the sharp improvement of relations after World War I—when a new Turkish national state emerged under Mustafa Kemal Ataturk to parallel the new nationalist Pahlavi dynasty in Iran—the Kurdish issue still proved to be the single most disturbing and provocative issue between the two states. Kurdish insurrections in Turkey in 1925 and 1929–1930, put down by the Turkish army, caused many Kurdish tribes to cross the borders over into Iran, creating claims and counterclaims between Ankara and Tehran.[6]

Only the 1932 Frontier Treaty between the two states was at last able to definitively settle the border question; both Tehran and Ankara were by then keenly interested in the resolution of outstanding bilateral issues. The border settlement helped improve adjudication of the Kurdish issue, but only in part. Today the Kurdish problem still represents a serious and unresolved point of friction between Iran and Turkey—not to mention Iraq—due not so much to unresolved borders as to the potentially destabilizing character of the problem for all involved. (This issue is considered in more detail in Chapter 2 on Iraq.)

Both Iran and Turkey (and Iraq) are mutually influenced by each other's policies toward the Kurds. If the Kurdish issue should achieve greater salience as an international cause—as it almost surely will—Iran and Turkey may come into greater conflict over this problem. Very large areas on both sides of the border between the two countries are inhabited by Kurds—a permanent explosive factor.

The Kurdish problem between Turkey and Iran is of a substantially different character than it is between Iraq and Iran. Ever since World War I, Turkey and Iran have enjoyed basically good relations and neither side has been intent on destabilizing the other. This is not the case between Iraq and Iran; since at least the fall of the Iraqi monarchy in 1958 Kurds have been a natural instrument of exploitation by which both Iran and Iraq could attempt to destabilize the other. As we have seen, the Iranians have tended to exploit the problem with greater impunity than has Iraq.

As long as Turkish-Iranian relations remain on sound footing, neither state is likely to wish to exploit the Kurdish issue against the other. There is apparently little indication that the Iranians—even under the most zealous days of the early Islamic Republic—sought to incite the Turkish Kurds, regardless of Khomeini's basic antipathy to Turkish secularism.

But Turkish-Iranian relations are rendered partially hostage to deteriorating Iran-Iraq relations on the Kurdish issue. Both in the early 1970s, and again in the course of the Iran-Iraq War the Islamic Republic actively assisted the Iraqi Kurds, both in their insurrection against the Baghdad authorities and as instruments of irregular warfare to help Iranian troops against Iraq along the Iran-Iraq border. On both occasions Turkey has shown considerable sensitivity to this Iranian incitement of the Kurds out of concern that it would spill over and infect the large population of Kurds in Eastern Turkey. Indeed the threat is very real for Turkey. The Kurdish issue therefore figures prominently in Iran's relations with Turkey even though Turkish Kurds have not themselves been target of Iranian incitement. Given the long-range prognosis for hostile Iran-Iraq relations, and a growing Kurdish national movement, the Kurdish issue will surely loom up again in its periodic cycles of crisis in the region—affecting Turkish ties with Tehran.

It is conceivable that both Iran and Turkey could come to collaborate in putting down any Kurdish national stirrings in either country. But even here their vision of the problem differs. A Turkish Kurd can attain high position in Turkey as long as he turns his back on his Kurdish nationality and becomes a "Turk." Autonomy in the Kurdish regions of Turkey has been unthinkable in Turkish policies toward the Kurds since the establishment of the Turkish Republic. In Iran (as in Iraq), autonomy is a distinct possibility as a longer range solution for Kurdish aspirations. Thus cooperation between Iran and Turkey on this issue would emerge largely in the face of massive threat to the territorial integrity of both states. Short of that, serious political troubles with the Kurds in one state are bound to affect the other, not least of all through possible border crossings of refugees.

As theoretical as much of this discussion has been about possible Turkish military intervention in the region to subdue potential chaos or destabilizing circumstances, the Iran-Iraq War provided some indication that elements of Turkey's own bolder geopolitical thinking are not absent: Kurdish guerrilla forces in northern Iraq in the 1980s, profiting from the preoccupation of Iraqi forces along the Iranian border, looked like they could establish an independent Kurdish state in the event of an Iraqi collapse. The mere prospect of such an eventuality sparked Turkey into discussing quite openly the prospect that it might need to consider invading a crumbling Iraq to seize the northern oilfields from the Kurds and contain any possibility of Kurdish separatism. In the end, Turkey was never required to take this step, but the historical fact of former Ottoman possession of the Iraqi Mosul oil region was high on Turkish minds. Drastic challenge can evoke drastic geopolitical response deeply rooted in the past.

The Watershed: New Nationalist States in Turkey and Iran

In view of the millennium of rival, and often hostile, dealings between Persian and Turk, it is important to examine how such an extraordinary change could come about, almost overnight, in the relations between the two countries—only a few years on the heels of combat in World War I. The question is of interest not only to the history of the Turkish and Iranian peoples but also to the annals of state conflict in general.

The most obvious reason for the massive change in relations was the revolutionary course of events in Turkish politics. World War I uncorked a series of disasters for the Ottoman Empire that led to its utter collapse and partition among the Allied Powers. It was only the emergence of the extraordinary figure of Mustafa Kemal Ataturk that rescued Turkey from humiliating long-term occupation and devastating loss of national sovereignty. Ataturk at once understood that Turkey could only survive as a new nation state based on Turkish ethnic nationalism rather than Islamic/Ottoman imperial internationalism, or even Pan-Turkism. The new Turkish national state transformed the very basis of its existence, from the floundering, helpless position of "Sick Man of Europe," to assume the borders of a new state based on largely ethnic Turkish borders—although still including large parts of the former empire that is primarily Kurdish in character.

Ataturk was determined to Westernize and modernize Turkey—terms nearly synonymous at the time. Sweeping reforms were undertaken in virtually all walks of life to emulate European models of state. A new Turkish-based ethnic nationalism was fostered. The caliphate, the religious leadership of world Sunni Islam, was entirely abolished and Turkey was transformed into a secular state—the first Muslim state ever to do so.

Turkey's goals moved inward—to focus upon the creation of the new nation state. Ottoman history had taught Ataturk that transnational ideology, such as Pan-Islam and Pan-Turkism, could only lead to disastrous adventures abroad in conflict with other regional nationalisms—a process that would not serve Turkey's interests. Good relations with all Turkey's neighbors became a priority goal of Ankara, Turkey's symbolic new capital.

Such radical change in Turkey's character and policies had immediate effect upon the nature of Turkey's relations with Iran. But the regional transformation was not yet complete, for Reza Shah was also in the process of achieving power in Iran and establishing the new nationalist-oriented Pahlavi dynasty. Reza Shah sought out Ataturk as a conscious model for Iranian development, despite the very different nature of the two states' national evolutions. Reza Shah also wished to focus on building national unity and strength after the humiliations and impotence of the nineteenth and early twentieth centuries.

What could have been more natural, therefore, than for the leaders of both these countries to set their relations on an entirely new footing, largely eliminating in several bold moves the weighty history of ethnic rivalry and conflict of over one thousand years? The special historical characteristics and contemporary needs of each country seem, therefore, to have brought about the emergence of this new regional relationship. The geopolitical character of contiguous warring nationalities seems to have been subsumed into new and different national interests. Yet, is there no broader principle involved here in such a rapid transformation of historical relations? The following factors seem to bear some relevance:

- Abandonment by Turkey of transnational and imperial ambitions— which inevitably foster conflict beyond the borders of the state;
- Abandonment by the Safavid dynasty several centuries earlier of its own ideological/religious Shi'ite mission, thus serving to deflate the charged *religious* atmosphere of the conflict and to reduce it to "merely" a struggle of competing empires for territory; the dei-deologization of the conflict was a critical first step in diminishing the intensity of the conflict.
- Sublimation of the new nationalist impulses into internal reform, modernization, and the strengthening of the nation state; external conflict is now perceived as a distraction of energies and waste of resources.
- Recognition that far more powerful enemies could still threaten the sovereignty of both states.

For Turkey, the most recent threat had come from the wartime anti-German entente of Britain, France, Italy, and Greece—all of whom had been partners to the postwar temporary partition of Turkey. For Iran, the occupying powers had been Great Britain and Russia. (Iran and Turkey had, of course, faced periodic *common* threats in the nineteenth century from Britain and Russia. But both Iran and Turkey had been so firmly locked into their own traditional regional rivalries that they had not even conceived of making common cause against European threats until the end of World War I.) Perhaps only these new nationalist statesmen were able to envisage their countries as now integral parts of a broader international state system that required new principles, rules, and priorities to succeed.

Iran, indeed, did not worry about regional threats—except for the USSR—from the 1920s until the 1950s. It was only the emergence of radical ideological states in the region—especially Egypt and Iraq—that once again threatened conflict on ideological grounds not witnessed in the region for a long time.

Finally, neither Iran nor Turkey had nationalist irredentist claims against each other. There were no significant Persian speakers living in Turkey.

The Reemerging Azerbaijan Issue

The converse is not fully true, however: There are Turkic speakers in Iran, as we have noted earlier. The Azerbaijanis, or Azeris, represent a *potential* long-term interest for Turkey. But any pursuit of this goal implies Turkish involvement in territory lying within both Iranian and Soviet territory, rendering the political consequences of doing so very high, and directly in contradiction to Ataturk's principles of eschewing Pan-Turkism abroad. Nonetheless—significantly—Turkey quite carefully sought a small corridor of land from Iran in the Turko-Iranian border negotiations of 1932 to ensure a narrow but common border of land linking it with Azeri-controlled Nakhichevan Autonomous Region— making it the only direct Turkish access to Soviet Azerbaijan. Indeed, the Azeri population of Nakhichevan, which otherwise lies surrounded by Armenia, tore down the Soviet border installations separating it from Turkey in January 1990 and asked for assistance from Turkey as well as from Iran. The implications and fruits of this Turkish link to the Soviet Azerbaijani population have yet to be realized, but Soviet Azerbaijan is only now entering the throes of its own ethnic claims in the region.

Turkey is still far from ready to move toward any kind of activist policy reversal yet, but a surge in Azerbaijani nationalism or even separatism over time is bound to evoke strong Turkish interest—possibly forcing Turkey to reverse its historic policy of noninvolvement in Pan-Turkic questions. The consequences are unforeseeable, given the extraordinary development of new nationalist factors emerging worldwide.

Indeed, there are other historical precedents as well for close Turkish-Azerbaijani interrelationships. Pan-Turkist elements of the collapsing

Ottoman army occupied both Persian and Russian Azerbaijan for a period in 1918, but were insensitive to the aspirations of the Azeris in both areas, leaving a negative legacy for the character of Turkish interventionism and serving to convince both Azeri groups that union with Turkey, at least in prerepublican Turkey, was not desirable.[7]

Despite disavowals of any irredentist aims, the new Turkish Republican leadership has never altogether abandoned interest in the fate of Turkic peoples, especially those outside the more dangerous arena of the USSR. Turkey has expressed regular concern over the Turks on Cyprus (and even invaded to safeguard their rights), in Greece, Bulgaria, Yugoslavia, and even, modestly, in Iranian Azerbaijan. Richard Robinson quoted a spokesman for the Turkish General Staff as far back as 1952 who said privately that Turkey and the Western allies should take a greater interest in the aspirations of the Middle Eastern peoples. "Take Azerbaijan, for instance. The people there are Turks. Aid to the Iranian Government helps them not at all. They want to be separate from Iran. We could help them achieve that independence." Robinson, in 1963, concluded prophetically:

> This thread of Pan-Turanian feeling still pervades the thinking of Turkish leaders, though under present circumstances they almost never make public reference to it. . . . But one wonders what the Turkish position would be vis-à-vis these "overseas Turks" if for one reason or another Soviet power were to weaken appreciably relative to the West, or if Soviet power were to collapse altogether in Central Asia. Would we see another Turkish drive for empire?[8]

As noted in the previous chapter on Iran and the USSR, it is presently the Soviet Azeris who are most likely to seek some kind of independence, as compared to the far more ambivalent Iranian Azeris. But Turkey enjoys only a tiny common border with Soviet Azerbaijan, in contrast to the long border with Iranian Azerbaijan. If a radical or strongly nationalist regime should come to power in Turkey in the future, it could well decide to pursue a policy of support for an independent Azerbaijan in the USSR and even Iran. In such a case the Turko-Iranian border question would be opened up anew and Turkey might provide significant support for an Azerbaijani independence movement—or even make some kind of claim on ethnic grounds to parts of Iranian Azerbaijan.

Turkish support for the "liberation" of Iranian Azerbaijan would immediately invoke powerful Soviet reaction in support of Iran in order to deter any possible Turkish provocation in Soviet Azerbaijan. Soviet support for Iran in the face of Ottoman Turkish designs upon Iranian Azerbaijan provide historical precedent from several hundred years ago as well as from 1918. In the event of an independent Azerbaijan, the Soviet Union most likely would still not favor its union with Turkey because it would only serve to strengthen Turkey as the center of a Pan-Turkist movement that is basically not in the Soviet interest.

While this issue seemed only of academic interest in early 1988, by late 1989 it had become less far-fetched in light of the turmoil and growth of a non-Communist Popular Front in Baku. The rebirth and expression of national consciousness in the USSR is restimulating impulses frozen since the Stalinist ice ages. Given the retarded historical development of nationalist feelings there, they can now evolve in directions as yet unforeseen. Any movement toward independence of the Azerbaijanis in either Iran or the USSR, or unification, will unquestionably invoke interest on the part of some unforeseen Turkish regime of the future.

The Ataturkist legacy of eschewing Pan-Turkist goals has been a healthy force for the region. But there are no guarantees that it will remain a timeless legacy. Its abandonment could have serious consequences for the region, not least of all for Iran. We are concerned here with the possible recrudescence of historical geopolitical interests—which rarely disappear permanently. And as a serious geopolitical observer of the Middle East has pointed out, "the most plausible candidate, in geopolitical terms . . . [to make] a regional effort to organize the Middle East . . . would be Turkey."[9]

Other Significant Bilateral Iranian-Turkish Issues

Cross-Border Access for Iran

Border problems between Ottoman Turkey and Iran were of course more intense up to World War I when modern-day Iraq was part of the Ottoman Empire. Indeed, most of the Ottoman-Persian border problems related to the *Iraqi*-Persian area more than it did to the Turkey-Persian area. (These problems are discussed in Chapter 2.) Although the first treaty of friendship between Turkey and Iran was signed in 1926, the border problem was not successfully negotiated until 1932— after several periods of border tensions.[10] Uppermost in Reza Shah's mind was the longer range option of using Turkish ports and transportation routes so as to minimize dependence on the USSR for the passage of goods.

Turkish transportation routes continue to matter very much to Iran. The roads were of singular importance to Iran during the Iran-Iraq War. This geopolitically determined factor will always be an essential ingredient in Iranian foreign policy calculations toward Turkey, given its lack of any other road links to Europe, except through the USSR.

Oil

Oil affects Iran's relations with Turkey due to Turkish interest in Iran as a source of oil supply, Iranian ability to disrupt Turkey's very important oil supplies from Iraq, and Turkish ability to interrupt Iraqi (and perhaps in the future Iranian) pipelines through Turkey. Turkey has long been concerned with the protection of its lines of communication and supply with the outside world. Possible communication links with the Persian Gulf have always been a geopolitical consideration, including its land lines with Iran. Turkey has discussed the possibility of extending a pipeline from the oilfields of Qom to Turkey ever since the signing of the Baghdad Pact in 1955.[11] Given Iran's own long-range concerns for diversifying its capabilities for exporting oil—dramatized by Iraqi strikes upon Iranian oil shipping during the Iran-Iraq War—Iran will surely have interest in considering such a pipeline through Turkey to the Mediterranean. And Turkey, for diversification of its own oil supplies, would probably also welcome such an arrangement; an Iranian pipeline would parallel its very important Iraqi pipeline arrangements for which Turkey receives both royalties as well as a source of oil.

During the Iran-Iraq War, Iran threatened on several occasions to sabotage Iraq's pipeline through Turkey as a means of denying Iraq revenue. This gambit was particularly attractive because Iran could strike at the pipeline in Iraqi Kurdish territory where Iran could effectively manipulate dissident Kurdish elements. Turkey remains profoundly sensitive to such a maneuver by Iran, both because such a move would have as direct impact on Turkey's finances and oil supply and because it involved inciting Kurds against targets that also bear directly upon Turkish security. For all of these reasons, after several attempts, Iran abandoned any concerted effort at destroying these pipelines to Turkey.

Both of these oil issues are likely to reemerge in the future. Iran, under most normal circumstances, should value the importance of Turkey as a strategic overland link to the West—enough to refrain from provocative action—but oil remains a potential instrument of conflict or cooperation between the two countries.

The Rebirth of Religious Ideology
Under the Ayatollah

Although the first cycle of Iranian Shi'ite state zealousness in the sixteenth century had begun to give way to a more secularized Iranian monarchy by the start of the seventeenth century, religious strife between Turkey and Iran did not completely die away at any time.

Ataturk's radical act of abolishing the Islamic Caliphate in 1924 stunned the entire Muslim world, leaving the Sunni world essentially without religious leadership—to this day. Although Iran was unmistakably Shi'ite, the Iranian clergy still got the message. They were deeply concerned as they watched Ataturk secularize the Turkish state and reduce the Sunni clergy to docile employees in the service of the state. They were determined that this should not happen to them, especially given the long history of the clergy's struggle against the power of the shah over the centuries. Indeed, Reza Khan, before assuming the title of Pahlavi Emperor, was able to exploit clerical prejudice against the secular implications of a republic to facilitate his own decision to establish a new dynasty in Iran—rather than ruling as a republican leader. Ataturkism has remained the epitome of demonic force in the minds of nearly all fundamentalist clerics in the Islamic world, scarcely distinguishable from atheistic communism; indeed, Ataturkism was worse than communism, for it was imposed by a nominal Muslim on his own Islamic state—a state that had gloriously led the Islamic world for centuries.

Ataturk continued to be a hated symbol for the Iranian clergy as Reza Shah continued his own sweeping reforms—most of them at the expense of clerical authority and power—in emulation of the Ataturkist experience. Thus when the Ayatollah Khomeini astonishingly attained ultimate power in Iran in 1979, Ataturk and the modern Turkish experience were hardly unknown elements to the new clerical rulers of Iran. Iranian clerical state visitors to Ankara have pointedly rejected the ritual visit to Ataturk's tomb—an incendiary, calculated political insult to the Ataturkist Turkish elite that has won Iran very few friends in Turkey.

Today the Islamic Republic maintains feelings of considerable ambivalence toward Turkey. On the one hand, for Iran much about Turkey is still negative. Turkey is secular—a symbol of everything that the Islamic Republic thinks is wrong with the Muslim world. It is closely allied with the United States through its NATO membership. And it strives to live up to a European model and join the European community, largely rejecting its former Islamic heritage.

On the other hand, Turkey has been enormously important to Iran in the course of the Iran-Iraq War. With the Gulf passage vulnerable to Iraqi bombing, the road overland through Turkey has been essential to the passage of goods to and from Europe. Turkish products have likewise been of major importance to the Iranian economy. Despite its distaste for Iran, the Turkish government made a point of scrupulous neutrality in the war—a precious commodity to Iran, which could not afford to alienate Turkey, even while alienating most of the Arab Gulf states.

Over 1 million Iranian refugees are in Turkey, mostly in Istanbul. Most of them are anti-Khomeini and hence not themselves sources of fundamentalist rabble-rousing. The average Turk has an unmentionable opinion of Iranians, however, perceiving them—though not their historical culture—as effete, hypocritical, and dishonest.

Iran has made some formal efforts to propagate its Islamic political beliefs through its cultural centers in Turkey. Some Turks have been attracted to the power of the Islamic movement in Iran, more admiring its *political success* in achieving power than as a model for emulation. Sunni Turks in any case would have little desire to adopt what they perceive as the Shi'ite character of the Islamic Republic.

Iran has likewise commented caustically on Turkish aspirations to be a European nation and to enter the European Community.

> Entering the EEC has become the major desire of some Turkish officials. They are aware that as long as the roots of Islam appear to hold strong in their country, the Europeans will consider their presence among them as unsuitable and will prevent their entry into the EEC.
>
> Apparently, until before the Salman Rushdie problem and the worldwide opposition of the Muslims to this Western plot, the Turks were taking effective and, at the same time, quiet steps toward ridding Turkey of Islam. However, the opposition that spread among the Muslims of Turkey to Rushdie and the "Satanic Verses" by the religious leaders of that country actually neutralized the propaganda of the secular regime; and it appears that the attempt to ban Islamic garb in the universities is actually a measure designed to gain the favors of the EEC, Salman Rushdie's main mentor.[12]

A Tehran radio commentary levelled further warnings to Turkey about preservation of its Islamic roots: "In any case, Turkey today is the remnant of a great empire and is in its present condition because it has lost all its possessions. However, the framework specified by the FRG chancellor [for EEC membership] will definitely culminate in the country being absorbed in the culture of Europe."[13]

In the event of serious pro-Islamic disturbances in Turkey in the future, the Islamic Republic would strongly support a Turkish move away from secularism in the direction of a more Islamic policy. Iran regularly publicly inveighs against Turkey's "anti-religious" positions. It is doubtful, however, that Iran can have major impact on Turkey on its own, although it could help fund Islamic orders in Turkey—some of which already receive funding or assistance from other Islamic countries such as Saudi Arabia. There are no significant ethnic Iranian elements in Turkey who could serve as instruments of Iranian political action, apart from recent refugees from Khomeini's policies.

Turkey does possess its own small Shi'ite population, however, that off and on over the centuries has been used by Iran as a potential fifth column; this population may number as much as 15 percent, but not all of whom by any means belong to the same Shi'ite sect as Iran.[14] The presence of the Shi'a cut ethnically across both Turkish and Kurdish lines. Because the Shi'a are themselves divided, however, they are not in a position to have broad influence over the course of Turkish religious movements. As in the Gulf, Iran's most powerful card is likely to be the demonstration effect of what an Islamic movement was able to do in dethroning the shah and defending itself against Iraq. The Turkish government would, in any case, react harshly against clear-cut evidence of Iranian support for clandestine or subversive Islamic activity in Turkey. It is a point of extreme sensitivity; Turkey would not shrink from taking a hard line with Tehran. Support for separatism in Iranian Azerbaijan could be a key Turkish instrument of response.

A future nationalist regime in Tehran would obviously find few grounds for friction with Turkey on any religious issues, although other geopolitical grounds for dispute still potentially exist as we have noted elsewhere in this chapter. Assuming that Iran almost surely will be a long-range mainstay of nonaligned, Third World policies in the region, even a nonreligious regime will almost surely favor any Turkish move toward greater political neutrality and a more regionally oriented policy.

Turkey and Iranian Stability

Turkey has always remained highly concerned about Iranian stability in the past, especially when the disorders of the revolution could have led to potential Soviet invasion or takeover by the Tudeh party. But chaotic events in Iran during the Islamic revolution never came close to evoking a suggestion of Turkish interventionist action. Today, the decline of Soviet power and the end of the Cold War and the ideological struggle may now reduce all Middle Eastern nations' concern for the dangers of *superpower conflict* on their turf, but regionally fired instability may take a new lease on life. Acts by one state against another will no longer have the profound East-West implications that they once did. In effect, regional restraint and concerns for stability worldwide will probably be less now than at any time since World War II. Indeed, several regional states may be tempted to act more boldly in the absence of the enforced caution of the Cold War days. Iraq's invasion of Kuwait is a case in point. (Turkish-Iranian relations in the context of regional security relationships will be discussed in Chapter 12.)

Turkey is destined to play a considerably greater regional role in the decades ahead; it possesses the territorial, intellectual, demographic, institutional, economic, and historical wherewithal to do so. If the Soviet Union should continue to move in a less-threatening long-term posture to the region under Gorbachev and his successors, Turkey's particular security focus on the USSR is likely to give way to increased attention to regional affairs. Turkey is already showing indications of greater interest in Middle Eastern affairs—previously shunned under the more Ataturkist leadership of the past, which saw Turkey's only appropriate focus as being toward the West rather than the ruder former colonial areas to the east and south.

Iraq's invasion of Kuwait moved Turkey a major step further in the direction of playing a major regional role. Turkey quickly moved to cut off Iraq's oil pipeline through Turkey and to ready troops for any trouble along the Turkish-Iraqi border. Unofficial groups have reiterated Turkey's interest in the oil-rich region of Mosul and Kirkuk where a large Turkish population exists and which remained part of Turkey even into the early days of the Turkish Republic. Turkey has demonstrated unusual interest in joining with the international community in containing Iraq, including the provision of its bases for air strikes against Iraq in the Gulf War. Ankara will now be a key player in any future security arrangements in the region.

If Turkish activism in the Middle East—already given some impetus during the Iran-Iraq War and the Iraq-Kuwait crisis—continues to develop, Turkey is more likely to find itself drawn into potential friction with some other regional players—depending on the character of political events. Turkey could emerge again as a geopolitical rival to Iran in a way it had not been ever since the 1920s. Iranian-Turkish relations will certainly involve more complex geopolitical equations than before. The geopolitical background of relations between the two states offers some— although not comprehensive—indicators of what issues might yet arise between them.

Notes

1. James Morier, *The Adventures of Hajji Baba of Ispahan* (New York: Modern Library, Random House, 1954), p. 423.

2. *Ibid.*, p. 394.

3. *Ibid.*, pp. 129, 136.

4. Quoted in Rouhollah K. Ramazani, *The Foreign Policy of Iran, 1500–1941* (Charlottesville: University Press of Virginia, 1966), p. 17.

5. Majid Khadduri, *The Gulf War: The Origins and Implications of the Iraq-Iran Conflict* (New York: Oxford University Press, 1988), pp. 12–13.

6. Ramazani, *op. cit.*, p. 270.

7. Tadeusz Swietochowski, *Russian Azerbaijan, 1905–1920* (Cambridge: Cambridge University Press, 1985), pp. 131–132.

8. See Richard Robinson, *The First Turkish Republic* (Cambridge: Harvard University Press, 1963), pp. 188–189.

9. L. Carl Brown, *International Politics and the Middle East* (Princeton: Princeton University Press, 1984), p. 176.

10. Ramazani, *op. cit.*, pp. 270–271.

11. Robinson, *op. cit.*, p. 186.

12. Tehran *Jomhuri-e Islami*, 12 March 1989, in FBIS-NES-89-051.

13. Tehran Domestic Service in Persian, 21 December 1989, in FBIS-NES-89-245, 22 December 1989.

14. See Moojan Momen, *An Introduction to Shi'i Islam* (New Haven: Yale University Press, 1985), pp. 269–272.

12

Iran and the Northern Tier Concept

[Reza Shah's] adoption of the good-neighbor policy was a complete reversal of [Iran's] traditional policy.

—*Rouhollah K. Ramazani*[1]

The "Northern Tier" concept suggests a relationship among several states that is deeply grounded in geopolitics—the reality of the USSR as the key defining geopolitical factor for those countries whose northern borders lie along the Soviet Union. Yet strangely, despite Russia's long threat of expansion south, the Northern Tier concept did not really come into being until after World War I with the establishment of independent, ethnically based national states in Iran and Turkey. Iraq only fleetingly became a member of the grouping—although not directly bordering on the USSR. Afghanistan, with at least as much reason for defensive concerns, has only been a sometime participant in Northern Tier regional associations; Pakistan—also not on the Soviet border—became a firm member on becoming a state in 1947. Although nearly all of them had been locked in conflict and war among themselves for many centuries, for the first time in history these Northern Tier states now had more to fear from a state other than themselves.

The logic of the Northern Tier associations is based on much more than a Soviet threat; it is founded on a common recognition of a shared Muslim heritage as well. Beyond that, most of these states have found common allies in each other in the absence of other natural ethnic or cultural allies with whom to share key economic, political, and defense concerns; these alliances helped create a counterweight, as it were, to the USSR, the West, the Arab world, and the Indian subcontinent. Iran's continued interest in adherence to the Northern Tier concept—even after the Islamic revolution and despite the alignment of two of its key members with the United States—suggests the psychological importance the concept still holds in Iranian geopolitical thinking.

Although the four key members of the various Northern Tier associations had maintained frequently hostile relations with each other until after World War I, it is striking that none of them have seriously sensed genuine threats from the other members since that time, including from revolutionary Iran.

As the Soviet threat recedes sharply and a new geostrategic character of international politics emerges, the concept of the old Northern Tier may well die too. It might fall apart into rivalries, each state seeking new alliances with the newly emerging Muslim states of the Soviet Union. Conversely, these new Soviet Muslim states might gravitate into close relations with the traditional Northern Tier states, creating perhaps a new "super Northern Tier," defined in part by association in history with a Persian cultural sphere. Such a new alignment could sharply rival the Arab bloc for influence in Muslim world politics and Iran would seek to lead it.

This chapter analyzes the origins of the Northern Tier movement, its sharp geopolitical break with the past, the key bonds of the relationship and its prospects for the future in Iranian foreign policy. •

Russia is the key geopolitical reality behind the concept of the "Northern Tier" states, looming over the northern borders of Turkey, Iran, and Afghanistan—with Iraq and Pakistan often included in the grouping. Without the existence of a Russia, there would not really be a Northern Tier grouping, with its suggestion of shared defense concerns. Yet, as basic a geopolitical fact as Russian power would seem to be, the concept of a Northern Tier came remarkably late to those states involved. If the threat of Russian expansionism was a fact of life in the region for over two hundred years—why was it only after World War I that these regional states finally felt a desire to group together in common cause? A major reason is the earlier fixation of most of the Northern Tier states primarily upon each other as immediate threats, at least as much as they were upon Russia.

- Turkey remained hostile to Iran right up into World War I, when it invaded Iran yet again.
- Afghanistan, a former vassal state of Iran, declared its own independence from Iran in 1747—a major loss of historic Iranian territory; Afghan independence was deeply resented by Iran and barely accepted by Iran until Reza Shah in the 1920s.
- Pakistan had not yet come into existence, but its territory was ruled by Britain, making it an object of Afghan hostility.
- Iraq was under Ottoman Turkish control and hence represented basically hostile territory to rival Persia.

In short, it was not until Reza Shah's arrival in the early 1920s, his sharp shift of priorities over to the Iranian domestic scene, and the emergence of a new Turkish state, that brought about an Iranian change of attitude toward its eastern and western neighbors. Iran only then could focus more single-mindedly on coping with Russia to the north, and on the elimination of remaining British influence in the region.

A second key reason for the emergence of the Northern Tier defensive concept only after World War I was the transformation in that same period of the traditionally expansionist Russian Empire into an even more dangerous Bolshevik state, now ideologically threatening as well. Iran was henceforth to view the geopolitics of the region very differently than before the war.

A third reason for the new relationships among the Northern Tier states was reflected in the fact of their own newly found determination to maintain national sovereignty and independence from external powers, especially from Western powers. The new relationships among them provided them with regional allies for the first time—of potential assistance in their common economic, political, and defense interests.

The Evolution of Northern Tier Pact Relationships

The key stages in the transformation of formal political ties among the various Northern Tier states emerged in an evolving sequence of treaty relationships.

The 1937 Sa'dabad Pact

The concept of a Northern Tier alliance first comes to life with the signing of the Sa'dabad Pact in 1937 among Iran, Turkey, Iraq, and Afghanistan. By this point Reza Shah had signed some ten different treaties with his neighbors designed to regularize borders and normalize relations. The signing of the Sa'dabad Pact was in a sense, therefore, a capstone, an overarching agreement to formalize the broader structure of Iran's new relations with its neighbors.[2] The pact expressed the joint agreement of all the signatory states to noninterference, nonaggression, consultation on security affairs, and arbitration of problems.

Because the pact made no provisions for the use of any unilateral or joint military power, it was able to accomplish little in itself to deter outside aggressors. Interpretations abound as to specifically what security goals this pioneering regional instrument was actually intended to achieve. At the time, the four countries stated that they were "actuated by the common purpose of ensuring peace and security in the Near East by means of additional guarantees within the framework of the . . . League of Nations."[3] Some observers attribute the main initiative to Iran, others to Turkey[4] because of Turkey's rising concern for Italian expansionism east toward Greece. Yet others attribute an anti-Soviet impetus to the Pact[5] or even an anti-British orientation. It is likely that the USSR was on the minds of most of the players—given their historical experiences with Russian power—but there seems to have been no obvious motivation at that specific time for an explicitly anti-Soviet grouping, and there is no suggestion that the USSR was the immediate target. The USSR, which had welcomed a three-way Iran-Turkish-Afghan Friendship Treaty in 1926 as strengthening regional states against Western imperialist enemies,[6] by 1937 had come to view the Sa'dabad Pact with suspicion and as a British anti-Soviet ploy.[7]

In fact, it is most likely that both Iran and Turkey were attracted above all to the idea of expressing regional solidarity in general terms against an outside world. Turkey and Iran, along with Iraq, had been "born again" as states and almost certainly found in the signing of the pact important psychological and political expression of their existences as newly independent sovereign states with radically new visions of themselves, their domestic goals, and their foreign relations. Such a pact could not actually deter a potential aggressor, but it did place greater international encumbrances on any would-be aggressor: These states were now on record as formalizing their intentions to act in more sovereign and equal fashion than history had ever permitted most of them to do before.

Lastly, of course, the Sa'dabad Pact set an important precedent for future regional cooperation arrangements among the Northern Tier countries, perpetuated in the later Baghdad Pact, the Central Treaty Organization (CENTO), and the Regional Cooperation for Development (RCD) organizations.

The Baghdad Pact and CENTO:
The Move Toward Alignment

As many observers of Iranian politics have pointed out, from 1941 to approximately 1952, during the early days of Mohammed Reza Shah's rule, Iran actually pursued a policy of neutrality and avoidance of alignment. The grounds were there. The Soviet wartime occupation and later Soviet support for breakaway Communist republics in northern Iran, coupled with Britain's dominance in Iranian oil affairs, all tended to impel Iran toward a policy of "negative equilibrium," opposed to, and balancing between, both Britain and the Soviet Union, both of whom had proven so damaging to Iranian sovereignty during World War II.[8] This tendency was strengthened by the shah's relative weakness and a fairly strong, if mercurial, Majlis-dominated government. This was the "parliamentary period" of the last shah's rule.

Indeed, the natural populist instincts of Iranian politics would seem to be instinctively antiforeign, suspicious of outside forces, and reluctant to align itself with anyone. Iranian Prime Minister Mossadegh, who took on the British by sparking the oil nationalization crisis of the early 1950s, was the quintessential figure of this approach. It may be that in the absence of overwhelming imminent peril to the state, Iran's natural instincts for neutrality—in a negative sense—can only be overcome by powerful executive strength. And the shah only began to develop that strength after the fall of Mossadegh and his restoration to the throne with both domestic and foreign support. Even the shah, from 1962 to his fall twenty-five years later, had engaged in a gradual process of reversion to a slightly more balanced, if not neutralist, position on foreign affairs.[9]

The shah thus once again became the most powerful determinant of Iranian foreign policy following his return to power in 1953. He was driven by a desire to strengthen his personal rule and the power of Iran as a whole. The military was the premier instrument for the attainment of both of these goals, accompanied by major reform efforts. The shah perceived that foreign assistance was the most efficacious route to that end.

If the Sa'dabad Pact was a broad statement aimed at codifying the striking new relationships among the independent and modernizing states of the Northern Tier, the Baghdad Pact of 1955 and its CENTO successor were much more clearly directed against the specific threat of the USSR. But by 1952, in fact, Stalin was dead and the USSR was groping toward a newer, mildly less ideologically truculent, and more flexible approach to the Third World, recognizing that powerful anti-Western impulses there could be usefully exploited to Soviet benefit against the West.

Turkey was the primary regional impulse for the pact, emboldening Iran to adopt the anti-Soviet posture implicit in the security arrangement. In the case of both Turkey and Iran, the desire to gain U.S. commitment to their security was paramount. By 1955 the pact was a reality, composed of Britain, Turkey, Iran, Iraq, Pakistan, and Afghanistan. Iran's constant anxiety was that the nonmembership of the United States in the pact—later CENTO—implied less than full U.S. commitment; Iran's goal was to greatly extend the U.S. security umbrella to cover Iran, a goal shared by most of the member states of CENTO, as the Baghdad Pact soon came to be called.

It is important to recognize that most of the impetus for seeking extended U.S. commitment came from the member states themselves, nearly all of whom shared deep concerns for Soviet intentions and capabilities. But visions of the Red Army invading across the southern borders of the USSR were not what concerned them most. Changes in Soviet policy had led to a dropping of Stalin's postwar territorial demands, and the Soviets were focused far more on exploiting the potential of the new radical states in the Middle East, of which Nasser's Egypt was paramount. The subversive potential from this kind of *regional* radicalism was much more immediate and threatening–not only to the Baghdad Pact members themselves, but to their own moderate allies and friends in the region who were coming under assault. And the member states were uncomfortable, precisely because arrangements like CENTO were vague about the Western commitment to *non*-Soviet, regional radical threats. This discomfort was heightened by the wrath from both the USSR and the regional radicals directed against CENTO members for being in league with "imperialist forces."

These concerns for regional threats were probably the healthiest features of the CENTO group, for they demonstrated an accurate grasp of the major threats of the period, and as such represented a *regional initiative* to cope with problems that extended beyond the willingness or even ability of the United States and Britain to meet. In other words, the regional CENTO members were not simply an instrument of U.S. anti-Soviet policy in the region. To be sure, the existence of CENTO also made it abundantly clear to the USSR that any territorial invasion of the member states would draw swift results. But that threat was distinctly secondary to those of regional instability. The bloody coup in Baghdad in 1958 that included the overthrow of the Hashemite monarchy, the execution of its key government figures, and the establishment of a bloody-minded Arab nationalist regime under 'Abd-al-Karim Qasim was precisely the kind of incident that had all along motivated the fears of CENTO's member states. Internal subversion, not external attack, had struck down a key member of the original pact—and the only Arab member at that. And indeed, not only had the pact not been designed to meet this kind of threat, but neither the United States, nor Britain, nor any other member state took any action to counter this strategic triumph for the radical forces of the region. The fall of Baghdad was to spark further search for regional cooperation—and further support from the United States on bilateral bases.

The First Purely Regional Pact: The RCD

Failure of the United States to assist Turkey in its struggle with Greece over Cyprus and to assist Pakistan in its struggle with India over Kashmir, and CENTO nonintervention in the 1958 Iraqi coup against the monarchy, all helped stimulate awareness of CENTO's limitations. Mounting member state dissatisfaction soon led to the establishment of a new organization: the Regional Cooperation for Development (RCD) in 1964, composed of only Iran, Turkey, and Pakistan. (Afghanistan had dropped out of Northern Tier security arrangements out of pique that the West favored Pakistan over Afghanistan—discussed in the Chapter 13.) Interestingly, the USSR itself initially found positive elements in the establishment of the RCD. Moscow viewed it as an implicit criticism of CENTO and even tried to portray it as an anti-CENTO instrument. The strongly regional nature of the agreement was encouraging to Moscow as a potential step away from Western-spawned alliances that were directly anti-Soviet in nature.[10] The extremely narrow nature of the U.S. defensive commitment impelled the RCD to meet member state needs by proposing mutual military and diplomatic support during any crisis. Nonetheless, the RCD's capabilities as a security pact were clearly limited, as even the name implies. But beyond that, it was a statement of *regional interest and concern* by three different states, each of whom had different reasons for a conservative stance toward regional developments, but who shared (1) common perceptions about radicalism, (2) concern for the links between the USSR and the regional radicals, (3) varying degrees of ambivalence toward the Arab world, and (4) a shared, reasonably comfortable relationship with the West (at least at the official level), especially in security affairs.

Despite the flurry of encouraging new aspects of regional cooperation, in the end only separate bilateral arrangements between the United States and the member states could serve their security needs most closely, providing important security assistance—even where U.S. commitments to the defense of those countries could not be ironclad.

Iranian cooperation and closeness of ties with Turkey and Pakistan continued right down to the Khomeini revolution. All three now shared a concern for Gulf stability in the light of British withdrawal and for the threatening character of Iraqi activity that targeted the interests of all three countries during much of the 1970s.

The Character of Northern Tier Interests

The fall of the shah ruptured the linkage of the three key Northern Tier states. But how valid is the concept of the Northern Tier over the long run, particularly in the Iranian world view?

We have seen how much of a novelty the concept of Northern Tier solidarity was in the 1920s, involving a radical reorientation of interests and perceptions on the part of states that in many ways had been fundamentally mutually antagonistic for centuries. But what are the characteristics of the Northern Tier states—especially the hard-core members of Turkey, Iran, and Pakistan—that make a perpetuation of the Northern Tier concept viable? This question is of major geopolitical importance because these states are among the most important of Iran's neighbors. Are there any important common features that suggest that these countries will tend to have special and amicable relationships and shared interests among themselves into the future?

Anti-Russianism. The Northern Tier was primarily defined by its character of proximity to the USSR. But we noted that commonality of interest did *not* exist among many of those states in earlier centuries when the Russian threat was no less. Was it only the Bolshevik Revolution that further heightened the anxieties of these new countries? Clearly the Soviet threat was a major, but not the sole, factor.

Source of Western Assistance. Most of these states also found it useful to use the reality of the Soviet threat to garner security assistance from the West. In a sense, they had a vested interest in the Cold War.

Extraregional Stability Concerns. Interestingly, few of the member states seemed to feel real anxiety about any increase in the armed strength of its other member states while they were allied. Each state expressed concern for possible instability or revolution in the neighboring countries, but seemed to have confidence that continued nonradical leadership in the other member states would not pose meaningful threat to themselves. Even the radical character of the Islamic Republic did not raise great fears that the new Iranian state posed a critical threat to most of its Northern Tier neighbors of a kind that would require special external assistance.

Non-Arabness. All of the states are non-Arab—with the exception of Iraq's brief, and aberrant, membership, terminated early in 1958. (Iraq's membership, even in the Sa'dabad Pact in the 1930s, was questioned by many Iraqis as running counter to the spirit of Arab solidarity—presaging the problems of any Arab state joining a non-Arab security grouping, especially the Baghdad Pact.)[11] This is not to say that the Northern Tier concept is an anti-Arab one, but its members are vividly aware of themselves as *non-Arabs*—a meaningful distinction in Middle East politics, although not in Islamic theology.

An "Alternative Ally" System. Because of their non-Arab character and distinct political, linguistic, and cultural differences even among themselves, no Northern Tier state has any "natural ally" among its neighbors in any ethnic sense. The Arab states represent a permanent—albeit swirling—pool of alternative allies within the kaleidoscopic Arab-world geopolitical game. But each of the Northern Tier states is alone and on its own, its allies emerging more from international circumstance than common culture. Does this suggest that the concept of Northern Tier solidarity embodies enduring *geopolitical*, rather than ethnic and cultural, roots? Or is it perhaps more subject to the whims of international circumstance?

Mutual Tolerance? The Khomeini revolution is instructive because it radicalized Iran overnight and promised to destroy most of the bases of Iran's traditional ties with its neighbors. Yet, as this chapter on Iran's Northern Tier neighbors demonstrates, even rampant Shi'ite radicalism—utterly repellent as a doctrine to each of its Sunni neighbors—taxed but did not fundamentally reorient Iran's ties with those neighbors. Despite sharp Iranian ideological differences with its neighbors—especially on issues of security orientation toward the United States, Iran chose to downplay those differences in the interests of maintaining broader ties. Self-interest? Indeed. But Iran's ideological salvos were in fact still directed primarily at the Arab world, regardless of self-interest.

Was this because Iran was attacked by Arab Iraq? An examination of events suggests that Iran was essentially seeking to politically challenge Iraq in any case, on grounds discussed in earlier chapters—Iran's close ties with the Iraqi Shi'a being paramount. If Iraq had not attacked, would Iran perhaps have turned its initial ideological blockbusters against the pro-U.S. states of Pakistan and secular Turkey? Perhaps. If Iran had not faced a powerful challenge to its own revolution, Turkey and Pakistan might have fared much less well in the vision of the Iranian Revolutionary clerics.

Our discussion of a general framework for the Northern Tier states is partially flawed by the omission of a key country: Afghanistan. We will discuss Afghanistan in greater detail in Chapter 13 on Iran's geopolitical interests to the east. I only note here that Afghanistan's geopolitical behavior has differed somewhat from the other Northern Tier states, primarily because it is smaller and more at the mercy of the larger Northern Tier states themselves that surround it: Iran and Pakistan. Thus Afghanistan has been at least as concerned with threats to its security from those quarters as from the USSR—a mistake, as hindsight now affords the insight. Whereas each of the other Northern Tier countries by the post–World War I era (Pakistan did not yet exist) had come to feel that its fellow members no longer constituted serious threat to its own security, Afghanistan did not share that feeling. Its move toward greater nonalignment has thus been at odds with the character of the larger states around it.

In sum, the very term "Northern Tier" is geopolitical by definition. But how does a more benign, nonideological Soviet landmass to the north affect the Northern Tier as a defensive concept? Might it diminish one of the unifying factors among this bloc of states?

First, while the Soviet state will never go away, a diminished Soviet threat will indeed affect the outlook of these states. The unifying concepts of an earlier period may seem less vital in a new international environment. Although there are other unifying ideas as well among the Northern Tier states, they may now be challenged by possible developing rivalries among these states themselves. The single biggest new element capable of sparking new rivalries is the remarkable reemergence of the Muslim states of the Soviet Union.

As we have discussed in other chapters, the newly autonomous or ultimately even independent states of Central Asia and the Caucasus in one way or another have reason for special ties with Turkey, Iran, and Afghanistan. Their emergence also means that the Northern Tier states will be less isolated, and may well find for the first time "natural" ethnic allies to some extent to the north. Those states will come to constitute a new buffer zone between Russia and the Northern Tier states, diminishing the meaning of the traditional "buffer zone" of the earlier Northern Tier pacts. Rivalries among the Northern Tier states for ties and alliances with the Soviet Muslim states will create potential new frictions and power arrangements whose character is as yet unpredictable. In short, just as the many new features of the post–World War I world helped create the concept of the Northern Tier, that concept may now come to be sharply challenged and altered in the new post-Gorbachev era.

As always, a major threat from the north can again revivify the geopolitical sense of solidarity among the Northern Tier states. These states will continue to share important interests along their East-West axis, but the force of that axis will now be diluted by new North-South interests as well.

Interestingly enough, Iran itself has shown definite continued support for the concept of a Northern Tier grouping over the longer run, even under Khomeini. The establishment of an Economic Cooperation Organization[12] in 1988, made up of Turkey, Iran, and Pakistan, with Afghanistan perhaps to join, suggests just how alive the concept still is, especially when shorn of security ties with the West. More important, Iran sees it as an instrument that will increase Iran's own role in the region and perhaps strengthen its hand vis-à-vis the Arab world and the Gulf states.

Iran may be the one central state in all this grouping to find the ideas of the Northern Tier as a potential instrument of immense value to its own ambitions. In Iranian terms the region could come to represent a whole new counterweight to the Arab Bloc. Indeed, the people of the Northern Tier states have all been deeply immersed at one time or another in traditional Persian culture and statecraft. If there is a "Persian-influenced region," it would certainly include the states of Iran, Azerbaijan, Central Asia, Afghanistan, and even Turkey to a lesser extent. While few of these peoples are likely to feel any special debt to Iran, and will not accede to Iran any role of leadership, they may feel that this region can yet become a new "super Northern Tier" with more distinctive character and raison d'etre that can rival the weight of the Arab world in international Islamic politics. Iran may find this idea especially attractive and will be assuredly bidding for the role of leadership. If the old Northern Tier is dead, the new one may be arising.

Notes

1. Rouhollah K. Ramazani, *The Foreign Policy of Iran 1500–1941: A Developing Nation in World Affairs* (Charlottesville: University Press of Virginia, 1966), p. 275.

2. *Ibid.*, pp. 273–274.

3. *Ibid.*, p. 272.

4. Majid Khadduri, *The Gulf War: The Origins and Implications of the Iran-Iraq Conflict* (New York: Oxford University Press, 1988), p. 39.

5. George Lenczowski, *Russia and the West in Iran* (Ithaca: Cornell University Press, 1949).

6. See George Lenczowski, *The Middle East in World Affairs* (Ithaca: Cornell University Press, 1956), p. 171.

7. See Ivar Spector, *The Soviet Union and the Muslim World 1917–1956* (Seattle: University of Washington Press, 1956), p. 108.

8. Shahram Chubin and Sepehr Zabih, *The Foreign Relations of Iran* (Berkeley: University of California Press, 1974), pp. 2–4.

9. Ramazani draws careful distinction between "neutrality" and "neutralism," the former connoting a stance apart from conflicting parties, the latter an entire "philosophy of nonalignment" that has its own particular leanings and biases. Ramazani, *op. cit.*, p. 274.

10. Rouhollah K. Ramazani, *Iran's Foreign Policy, 1941–1973: A Study of Foreign Policy in Modernizing Nations* (Charlottesville: University Press of Virgina, 1975), p. 341.

11. See Majid Khadduri, *Independent Iraq: A Study in Iraqi Politics from 1932 to 1958* (London: Oxford University Press, 1960), pp. 346–348.

12. See Mushahid Hussain, "Iran Forges New Links," in *Middle East International*, No. 344, 17 February 1989, p. 17.

13

❧

Iran Faces East:
Afghanistan, Pakistan, India,
and East Asia

Brave, independent, but of a turbulent vindictive character, [the Afghans'] very
existence seemed to depend upon a constant succession of internal feuds. . . .
They knew no happiness in anything but strife. It was their delight to live in a state
of chronic warfare. Among such a people civil war has a natural tendency to
perpetuate itself . . . but side by side with other Asiatic nations, their truthfulness
and honesty were conspicuous.

—*Sir John William Kaye, 1851*[1]

*Iran's relations with Afghanistan have undergone several basic metamorphoses
over time that make for uncertainty in gauging their long-term relationship into
the future. Despite a number of cultural similarities with Iran, Afghanistan, like
Turkey, was another geopolitical rival to the historic Iranian state. Iran's relations
with Afghanistan underwent sharp change for the better only with the establishment
of the nationalist Pahlavi dynasty and its "Good Neighbor Policies." Both states
in the post–World War I era enjoyed a common regional outlook as part of the
Northern Tier concept.*

*But whatever natural geopolitical defense interests Afghanistan might have
shared with Iran, they were torn asunder by a smoldering legacy of British rule
in India: the fateful British bisecting of the Pashtun people—the historically
dominant nationality in Afghanistan—between Afghanistan and the newly founded
state of Pakistan in 1947.*

*The subsequent "Pashtunistan question" has served to poison Pakistani-Afghan
relations to the point where, in the end, it drove Afghanistan to eschew the
security ties of the Baghdad Pact and CENTO precisely because of Pakistan's
central role in those organizations and Western reluctance to arm Afghanistan.*

Fatefully, Afghanistan determined instead to develop much closer ties with the Soviet Union in an effort to protect itself from potential Soviet threats—paving the way for the ultimate Soviet invasion of Afghanistan.

The Islamic Republic of Iran was no less ardent than the West in its determination to eliminate the Soviet presence from Afghanistan. To that end, Tehran provided support—of only limited value—to the Shi'ite mujahidin. With the Soviet withdrawal from Afghanistan, however, Iran has begun to work with the USSR in attempting to establish itself as the key regional determinant of Afghan political orientation, and to keep U.S. and Saudi influence at bay as well.

Iranian relations with Afghanistan may well continue to exhibit some sense of rivalry—especially if Islamic fundamentalists should come to power in Afghanistan where they might pursue their own regional Sunni fundamentalist vision. Iranian relations with Afghanistan will always be strongly affected by the Pakistan factor, much the more important country in Iran's eyes. Both Iran and Pakistan are vulnerable to Afghan manipulation of any breakaway tendencies among their respective Baluch populations. Iran, for similar reasons, has conspicuously failed to support Afghan claims against Pakistan on the Pashtunistan issue over the years. Iran is likely to remain closer to Pakistan than to Afghanistan in the future, especially in the absence of any ostensible Soviet threat to the region.

Iran's geopolitical interests lie in keeping any foreign state influence out of Afghanistan that could rival Iran's own interests there. Pakistan is, of course, such a potential rival, but ever since the foundation of Pakistan, Iran has enjoyed almost universally good relations with that state, under both the shah as well as clerical rule. Afghanistan is likely to remain odd man out in this triangular relationship.

Iran's expanding ties to the outside world have also moved to engage India, China, and Japan. Trade interests and nonalignment are key features of these ties. Iran and India could develop closer working ties in support of a demilitarized Indian Ocean, but elements of rivalry are also present in seeking future control of the "northwest quadrant" of the Indian Ocean, especially as India strengthens its interests in the Gulf to match the already large presence of Indian workers and merchants there.

Although Western attention has focused almost exclusively on Iran's policies and actions directed toward the West, the Persian Gulf, and the Arab world, the lands east of Iran make up an equally important component of the Iranian world view. Iran's attention to the East has assumed even greater salience in the last few decades as Iran has grown more global in outlook. Afghanistan, in particular, is unique to Iran since it is the only other country that intimately shares broad elements of Persian language and culture. This natural cultural affinity between the two countries, however, has in no way precluded sharp political rivalry and frictions: There have been few periods in history when Iran and Afghanistan have viewed each other as allies.

Afghanistan also shares with Iran the unhappy distinction of broad exposure to the nineteenth-century "Great Game" of intrigue between Britain and Russia in Central Asia. But Iran's role as buffer state between Russia and the British lifeline to India could not be performed as easily by Afghanistan: Unlike Iran, Afghanistan was also territorially contiguous to British India and thus ineluctably drawn into British subcontinental policies. British policies, not surprisingly, therefore heavily influenced Iran's dealings with Afghanistan in the nineteenth century.

Iran's formal embrace of Shi'ism in the sixteenth century exerted immense cultural impact upon its eastern neighbors. With the emergence of the Safavid dynasty, all the Sunni countries to Iran's east were at once physically cut off from the western world of Islam and the roots of the Sunni culture they had shared. Afghanistan, whose Persian-based culture had nonetheless not followed the Safavids into Shi'ism, thus found itself increasingly oriented toward the Islamic centers of India for its spiritual sustenance—and has remained so to this day. Most of the Afghan leaders of the anti-Soviet Islamic jihad were schooled in India.

The Cultural Links

Far from being a Central Asian backwater, Afghanistan has been home to a long series of civilizations within its borders going back at least to the Gandharan culture of several centuries B.C.—a fusion of Hellenistic and Buddhist cultures with a rich artistic tradition. Indeed, because of its strategic location on the Central Asian route connecting India and Western Asia, Afghanistan became known as the "Highway of Conquest" because of the multitude of conquerors that have swept across it.

The Afghan Durrani Empire during the second half of the nineteenth century was in its time actually the second biggest empire in the Middle East after the Ottomans—its rule stretching over almost all of present-day Afghanistan and Pakistan.

Like other countries in the region, large parts of Afghanistan had for many periods been part of a broader Iranian empire, starting with the Achaemenids and including the Safavids. Afghanistan's assertion of its independence in 1747, thus represented a major blow to Iranian imperial aspirations, and recovery of Afghanistan became one of the natural targets of Iran's frustrated irredentist efforts in the eighteenth and nineteenth centuries. Much of Iran's cultural heritage sprang from artists, poets, and thinkers who participated in mainstream Persian culture from cities that today lie within present-day Afghanistan such as Balkh and Herat. These solid links of culture and history lend complexity to the Iranian view of Afghanistan. If Afghanistan itself had been all Persian-speaking, the relationships might have been easier. But the dominant Afghan *political* culture, over the past three centuries at least, emerges from the *Pashto*-speaking population. Pashto (or Pakhto) is related to Persian linguistically but is not mutually comprehensible. And Pashtuns are fiercely tribal and clannish, not given to the kind of centralized instruments of rule favored by Persia's empire builders.

Adding further psychological complexity to the portrait, it was not any of Iran's historic great enemies to the north or west, but Afghan tribal forces that had the distinction of bringing down the Shi'ite Safavid dynasty in Iran, with the Afghan attack and occupation of the Safavid capital of Isfahan in 1722. The Safavid collapse in turn opened the gates to Turkish and Russian invasions of Iran as well—both empires eager to feast on the Safavid territorial corpse. It was only eight years later that a vigorous new Persian leader, Nadir Shah, was able to recover most of Iran's lands from the three foreign invaders and expel the Afghans.

Afghanistan is therefore of considerable importance to Iran because of Afghanistan's unique three-way orientation:

- Toward Western Asia, to share in both historical Iranian culture and traditional Sunni western Islamic culture in the Middle East;
- To the north, sharing both the Persian-oriented culture of Central Asia and the cultures of many of the populations that straddle the Soviet-Afghan border;
- To the east, because of Afghanistan's religious ties to Indian Islam and at least two major conquests of northern India that originated from Kabul. This orientation of Afghanistan toward the Indian subcontinent is one of the magnets drawing Iran into political and religious issues among Afghanistan, Pakistan, and India.

Lastly, Afghanistan importantly shares with Iran and Pakistan in the three-way division of Baluchistan, the ethnic homeland of the Baluch people—linguistically related to Persians and Pashtun—who live athwart the triangular intersection of the borders of Iran, Afghanistan, and Pakistan. The volatility of Baluchi ethnic discontent in both Iran and Pakistan, and its implications for the territorial integrity of all three countries, is a permanent geopolitical feature of potential regional conflict even today.

Irredentism—Historical and Cultural

Both Afghanistan and Iran have vivid historical memories of periods of domination of each other's territory. Iran has been the dominant force of the two, however. In ethnic terms the population of western Afghanistan, centered in Herat, has identified closely with Iran, speaking a dialect of Persian almost identical to that of Iran—but is mostly Sunni rather than Shi'a in faith.

British colonial authorities approached the question of Afghanistan with some ambivalence. The primary goal was to preserve Afghanistan as a buffer to Russian expansion southward into India. But ironically, the very first alliance Iran ever formed with a western state was with Britain in 1801—when the British sought Iranian help in an offensive alliance to forestall an Afghan invasion of India.[2] Iran was happy to oblige because it had been hoping to regain the border city of Herat from Afghanistan for many years. In the end, the alliance was never actually implemented.

Yet, when Iran in fact tried to reassert a claim to Herat thirty-five years later in 1836, this ambition was now directly opposed by the British, who reasoned that Iran's ambitions for Herat would weaken Afghanistan and thus facilitate Russian penetration. In any case, the Afghans repelled Iran, which promptly blamed the loss on British pressure. Britain again intervened more directly, applying military force directly from the Gulf, to stop Iran from occupying Herat in 1856. Iran was thus compelled to take the painful historic step, in the 1857 Treaty of Paris, to formally renounce territorial claims on Afghanistan and to at last grant de facto recognition to Afghan independence that had been established 110 years earlier.[3]

The only portion of Afghanistan contested by Iran in modern times, however, is the region of Sistan (Nimroz and Helmand Provinces today) in the southwestern corner of Afghanistan, including the agriculturally important waters of the Helmand River that flow through Sistan. As they had done with Herat earlier, many British strategists invested Sistan with special geostrategic qualities as a pivotal point of influence, lying as it did at the convergence of Iran, Afghanistan, and British India. The British thus sought to arbitrate conflicting Afghan and Iranian claims in 1872.

Although the Iran-Afghan territorial issue was thus largely settled in 1872, the critical issues of water use and damming rights were not. The Helmand waters issue has been arbitrated repeatedly since then, several times reaching the point of ratification by the Iranian Majles, but never by the Afghan parliamentary body. The issue managed to elude final settlement for over 100 years under a great variety of politically changing circumstances—generally foundering on strong Afghan nationalist reluctance to compromise, even when Iran seemed content with arbitration. Only in 1973 was agreement reached and a treaty regulating the use of the waters finally ratified in both countries. Significantly, Communist members of the Afghan government, five years before a Communist takeover of Afghanistan, opposed ratification of the settlement, preferring instead the perpetuation of this conflict with the shah's pro-Western Iran.[4] One wonders today whether a leftist or nationalist regime in Afghanistan would seek accomodation on this issue with a clerical Iran either.

One other small territorial dispute at the border at Islam-Qala was jointly negotiated by both countries starting in 1975, but final agreement had not been reached when the 1978 Communist coup took place. It still awaits resolution. Given the small size of the territory in question, it is unlikely that this area would serve in itself as an issue of major conflict between the two countries in the future. But to what extent has territorial conflict been "permanently" resolved between the two countries? If either Iran or Afghanistan should seek pretext for armed conflict, there are more logical issues to exploit than the small unresolved Islam-Qala salient. Indeed, the Helmand waters, although officially resolved between the shah and Afghanistan, still could reemerge as a point of conflict if the water needs of the countries change, if water usage patterns are abused, or simply because one or the other state seeks a *casus belli*. The issue has always held emotional content for both sides.

Good Neighbor Relations

Afghanistan fell very much into the pattern we observed earlier in relations between Iran and Turkey: After World War I both countries turned their focus upon modernization, nationalist policies, and emphasis upon internal development. Good relations with their immediate neighbors—where possible—became the new priority. Reza Shah immediately sought to improve Iran's historically troubled relations with Afghanistan, reaching a basic treaty of friendship as early as 1921, while leaving the more contentious issues for solution at a later juncture. Afghanistan was amenable to such an approach and found its dealings with Pahlavi Iran to be generally quite correct, and even moving toward considerable improvement in the mid-1970s—despite a long-term conviction on the part of Afghans that the Iranians are overbearing and inclined to look down on the Afghans as a lesser breed. Afghans will always nurture some suspicion about the nature of Iranian intentions toward their country and believe that Iran cannot resist interference in the internal affairs of the country.

Nonetheless, throughout most of the 1970s the shah was careful to remain somewhat aware of Afghan sensitivities—especially because he viewed Afghanistan as strategically important to Iran and vulnerable to Soviet threat. Indeed, the shah probably was one of the few statesmen in the world to remain deeply concerned about Soviet and Communist activities in Afghanistan during the 1970s.

Iran and Afghanistan were now both to undergo cataclysmic change—within one year of each other—with the Communist coup in Kabul of April 1978 followed eight months later by the fall of the shah. The Islamic Republic, in a geopolitical response that would have made the shah proud, immediately expressed strong hostility to the Communist takeover and quickly moved to support anti-Communist, anti-Soviet resistance forces in Afghanistan. Khomeini, of course, justified his action on the basis of Islam. He further focused his support upon the Shi'ite elements of the Afghan population. Neither the Islamic Republic nor Communist Afghanistan demonstrated any public sign of irredentism toward each other. Such absence of territorial ambitions to date does not at all necessarily exclude them in the future, however, or eliminate possible serious military clashes. While the USSR occupied Afghanistan, a distinct possibility existed that Iran's support for the Afghan mujahidin could have served as grounds for Afghanistan to menace Iran. At the time, however, both parties were intensely preoccupied with more critical issues: Iran in the war against Iraq and the Afghan regime in a basic struggle against internal resistance.

But Iran's relationships to the East were never that simple. Iran did not deal with Afghanistan in isolation: Kabul was only part of a broader strategic triangle of relationships that included Pakistan—which also shares borders with Iran. The complexity of this triangular relationship had already created a major anomaly among the Northern Tier states: an Afghan drift toward neutrality starting in the 1950s. Afghanistan's nonaligned posture and increasingly close relations with the USSR—viewed by Iran with great concern—sprang directly out of Afghan problems with Pakistan.

Afghanistan, after all, had joined the Northern Tier Sa'dabad Pact of 1937, along with Iran, Turkey, and Iraq. But the situation after World War II was now quite different. Afghanistan had its own deep-seated irredentist claims that had locked it into conflict with the British over the Northwest Frontier (NWF) area of British India—today part of Pakistan. The population of the NWF is almost entirely Pashtun, ethnically virtually indistinguishable from the Pashtuns of Afghanistan who make up the dominant ethnic political element of that country. The NWF

Pashtuns, furthermore, were denied full choice about their future when the British left India, being allowed to choose only between joining modern India or modern Pakistan, but no option of joining Afghanistan as most of them wished. And in 1949 with the support of the Afghan government, the Pashtuns inside Pakistan declared an independent state of Pashtunistan, but were never permitted by Pakistan to implement the idea.[5]

Afghanistan, furthermore, had never accepted the Durand Line—the border between Afghanistan and British India that had been forcibly imposed by the British upon the Afghan ruler in 1893—precisely because it sundered the Pashtun people in two. To this day Afghanistan has not accepted the legality of the Durand Line, and the concept of a united Pashtunistan or Greater Pashtunistan remains vividly alive in the Afghan mind. The Pashtunistan concept, of course, poses a direct and critical threat to Pakistan's own territorial integrity. And Pakistan's national psyche was not engaging in mere fanciful paranoia: It had already undergone the agony of the breakaway of Eastern Pakistan in 1971, when that area, with Indian help, declared itself the independent state of Bangladesh. As early as the 1970s Pakistan had begun to support radical Islamic rebels inside Afghanistan as a means of striking back at Kabul's Pashtunistan policies; this was to be a forerunner for later Pakistani support for Afghan fundamentalist mujahidin.

India Complicates the Equation

When the British prepared to "quit India" in 1947, the Afghans were quite concerned about what the successor regime in India might bring. The Afghans had long been fierce opponents of the Hindu rulers of India: A united, independent Hindu India would have been a recipe for border trouble with Afghanistan that so long had seen itself as protector of Islam in the Indian subcontinent. Afghanistan had, after all, been one of the few independent Islamic countries in the world for several centuries while colonialism held sway in most of the Middle East, Africa, and Asia. Yet, as the British prepared to pull out of India, there was talk of partitioning India between Hindus and Muslims in ways that could only further complicate the new geopolitical picture in South Asia. And however much the Afghans had fought the British, they recognized that a British presence in India had played a significant role in preserving a balance against Soviet encroachments from the north. The newly emerging powers in the subcontintent therefore posed a critical question mark for Afghanistan's relations with them.

In the end, although Afghanistan welcomed the establishment of a non-Hindu, Muslim state on its eastern border with the creation of

Pakistan, it was now Pakistan that inherited the troubled border issue with Afghanistan. Afghanistan was no more ready to accept the perpetuation of the Durand Line with the new Muslim state than it had been with Britain and rapidly came into conflict with Pakistan on the issue. If Pakistan's internal politics had been relatively quiet, the issue might have loomed less prominently; but in fact ethnic conflict in Pakistan was becoming a dominant and corrosive issue—only whetting Afghan interest in the political struggles of their kinfolk over the border. Indeed, the Pashtunistan issue basically became the tragic root of conflict between Afghanistan and Pakistan, preventing what might otherwise have been a natural strategic relationship between the two countries. One analyst in fact argues persuasively that it was this conflict that led to the alienation of Afghanistan from CENTO and thus inevitably to the Soviet Union's position of dominance in Afghanistan that permitted the Communist revolution of April 1987 to come about.[6]

Indeed, because Pakistan had moved quickly into a strategic relationship with the United States as a key player in the Baghdad Pact of 1955, Afghanistan encountered reluctance from the United States to supply the Afghans with significant arms as long as they remained locked in conflict with Pakistan over the Pashtunistan issue. Not only did Afghanistan not join the Baghdad Pact, but as a demonstration of its nonalignment—and feelings of vulnerability to the USSR—turned to sharply improve relations with Moscow, in both the military and economic spheres. Kabul felt that only a cordial policy toward the USSR, balancing Pakistan's tilt to the West, could safeguard it from any threat from the USSR. Whatever the geopolitical rationale may have been, Afghanistan's strategic decision eventually proved a tragic miscalculation.

Disquiet in Tehran

The shah's concerns for Soviet and Communist activity in Afghanistan was quite specific. He was well aware that the USSR had trained a high proportion of Afghan army officers in the Soviet Union and was the major source of arms to the Afghan military, giving Moscow particular leverage over an important segment of the government and society. Those fears were heightened when, in 1973, Afghan Prime Minister Muhammad Daoud led a coup to overthrow the Afghan monarchy, with the close participation of many Afghan Communists, both civilian and military. In the end, of course, it was precisely those Communist elements of the Soviet-trained officer corps that spearheaded the coup that overthrew Daoud in April 1978, bringing communism to power.

The shah was not simply a bystander watching the turmoil of Pakistan's relations with its several ethnic groups unfold. As we noted earlier, the

Baluch, who make up the Pakistani province of Baluchistan, spill over demographically into both Iran's own province of Baluchistan, and southern Afghanistan. The prospects for separatism in Baluchistan were quite realistic: Years of rebellion, especially in the 1970s, saw Islamabad unable to maintain security in the province. Afghanistan made no secret of its support for the concept of an independent Baluchistan as well,[7] and at the very least provided assistance to Baluch refugees and permitted safe havens to Baluch fighters crossing into Afghanistan. Many prominent rebel Pakistani Baluch leaders also resided in Afghanistan and Iraq. Willing fishers in these troubled waters were not hard to find: In 1973 Pakistani authorities seized a large cache of weapons actually sent by the Iraqis through their diplomatic facilities into Pakistan, destined for Baluchistan, and most probably for the Iranian Baluch.[8] This event helped crystallize the shah's belief that the Baluchistan issue contained profound separatist dangers for Iran itself and was actually being exploited by Iran's enemies.

For this reason Iran was highly concerned about Afghanistan's support for the Baluch movement in Pakistan, just as it was to Afghanistan's more vigorous pursuit of the Pashtunistan issue over the years. The shah sought repeatedly to negotiate the Pashtunistan problem but without success. A senior Afghan official nonetheless has stated that the shah acted correctly during this period and did not openly take sides in the conflict.[9]

The shah himself was on the horns of a dilemma. Unquestionably his sympathies lay more with Pakistan. It was a larger and more important country than Afghanistan. It shared fully in the shah's strategic view of the region, opposed the USSR, was an ally in CENTO, and enjoyed an overall affection in the Muslim world as the only country ever created purely on the basis of Islam. However, the security of Afghanistan was critical to the shah if he wished to avoid encirclement by hostile states. Sensitive to Afghans' own strong nationalist feelings, the shah recognized he could not afford to further alienate Afghanistan and push it into a tighter relationship with the Soviet Union. His approach worked fairly effectively in that Afghanistan's ties with Iran had actually begun to improve considerably in the mid-1970s, right up to the 1978 Communist coup.

Communist Afghanistan

A Communist coup in Afghanistan, followed within less than a year by the Khomeini revolution in Iran, radically reshuffled the geostrategic deck. The eventuality most feared by the shah in both countries had actually come to pass. The geostrategic challenge was to grow yet worse with the actual invasion of Afghanistan by the Red Army in late 1979. A new Communist Afghanistan now faced a new radical Islamic regime in Tehran—and the two moved into clear positions of hostility toward each other.

Iran's geopolitical situation was now vastly more serious in view of the options it provided the USSR. For Iran's de facto border with the Soviet Union had now expanded to face the presence of yet more Red Army troops, this time along the Afghan-Iranian border—providing the Soviets a variety of opportunities for hot pursuit into Iran in the struggle against Afghan insurgents. An Iranian decision to assist selected elements of the Afghan insurgents increased the likelihood of direct conflict.

In the end, Iran's policies toward Soviet-occupied Afghanistan were rather shortsighted, for they entailed aid primarily to the Shi'ite minority, the Hazaras, who represented only 20 percent of the population and were not in any case central to the military or political struggle in Afghanistan. Indeed, Iranian assistance had the effect of setting one Shi'ite group against another, rendering the overall struggle against the Soviets even less effective. Iran at one point offered to assist other non-Shi'ite resistance groups, but only conditioned upon support for Iran's overall foreign policy, including adoption of sweeping anti-American positions. Concrete Iranian aid was in any case rather modest.[10] Despite the highly vituperative rhetoric employed against the USSR, Iran was rather careful not to allow its aid to the Afghan mujahidin to become too provocative against the USSR and sought to channel it all through Pakistan. Iran did not need additional complications in the course of its war with Iraq.

Iran undoubtedly views the Soviet withdrawal from Afghanistan as a major victory for Islam, as indeed it was in many senses. Iran will have constantly to balance its interests in Afghanistan against the relative importance of its bilateral contacts with the USSR. As we noted in an earlier chapter, these relations have markedly improved since the end of the Iran-Iraq War, the Soviet withdrawal from Afghanistan, the death of Ayatollah Khomeini, and the broad changes in the Soviet Union under Gorbachev.

Has the Afghan war of resistance changed Iranian perception of the geostrategic Soviet danger in Afghanistan? If the shah were still in power, he would undoubtedly have felt that the Soviet invasion and withdrawal was a strategic turning point in Soviet conduct. His worst case scenario had actually come into being with the Soviet invasion; even more unforeseeably, the withdrawal had set a stunning historical precedent, involving actual Soviet withdrawal from a contiguous country that would lead to the neutralization and eventual disappearance of a

Communist regime in Afghanistan. Although the geostrategic threat from the Soviet Union in principle remained, the withdrawal from Afghanistan and Soviet statements on the new rationale of their foreign policy have rendered that threat vastly less than before.

Prospects for Afghanistan in the Iranian View

The future of Afghanistan is, of course, highly uncertain with, in 1991, the struggle between the mujahidin and the Peoples Democratic Party of Afghanistan still unresolved. Iran will remain directly concerned for its future and will seek to increase its influence there. Iran sees itself as the key regional player in resolving the Afghan question and to this end it has, surprisingly, found common interest with the USSR in limiting the role of both Saudi Arabia and the United States in a future Afghan government and in enhancing the role of the Afghan Shi'a in an eventual settlement. If Tehran's policies are to be effective, however, it will have to work within a broader political spectrum than the Shi'ite Hazara community as a vehicle for influence. Iran, in fact, commands only modest resources to help postwar reconstruction in Afghanistan, but will almost surely wish to associate itself with that effort. Iran will also strongly support a nonaligned Afghanistan and will not wish to see either superpower enjoy much influence there.

The dissolution of the Soviet empire, however, also raises potential questions of instability and rivalry between Afghanistan and Iran. The proximate destabilizing factor here is most likely to be Soviet Tajikistan. The population of Tajikistan in 1979 was 3.8 million, in which the Tajiks made up some 56 percent of the population, followed by Uzbeks at 22.9 percent and Russians 10.4 percent.[11] Yet the number of Tajiks in Afghanistan is nearly twice that of Tajikistan—some 3.5 million in the late 1970s.[12] In effect, the demographic attraction of Afghanistan to Tajikistan is greater than the reverse. Although analysts during the 1970s worried about the possibility that the USSR might opt to abandon the struggle against the Pashtuns of Afghanistan and to take over all of Afghanistan north of the Hindu Kush—an area primarily populated by Tajiks and Uzbeks—the threat is now from the other direction. The Afghan Uzbeks and Tajiks might themselves opt for independence from the politically dominant Pashtuns in the south and to form their own state, possibly in conjunction with the Soviet Republics of Uzbekistan and Tajikistan—never before a possibility since Russian domination of Central Asia in the mid-nineteenth century. A time of instability might therefore lie ahead in this region if neonationalisms flourish. As we have noted earlier, Iran itself will be intensely interested in the fate of the

Soviet Muslims, and especially in Persian-speaking Tajikistan. Iran and Afghanistan will be natural rivals for influence in Tajikistan.

Historic conflict will probably prevent Iran-Afghan relations from ever being truly cordial. Much of course will depend on the character of the regime that ultimately comes into being in Afghanistan. If there is a long civil war and struggle for power in post-Communist Afghanistan, Iran will opt for the most nonaligned and possibly for the most Islamic of the elements, rather than for some of the more moderate, Western-oriented religious groups. A strongly fundamentalist regime in Kabul, however, could itself move into conflict with Iran if it has its own independent, Sunni, Islamic agenda for the region.

Nor will Iran be alone in competing for influence there. The Sunni fundamentalist elements among the resistance vastly outweigh the Shi'ite groups. Many of the Sunni fundamentalist groups—and none of the Shi'a—have been heavily supported by Saudi Arabia, for example, which will not cut its ties in the postwar struggle for influence. Under such terms a *Sunni* fundamentalist leadership—not necessarily radical in character—will almost surely perceive its interests more in line with other Sunni Arab religious movements than with Iran—whose intentions toward Afghanistan have been historically ambiguous in any case. If Iran continues its rivalry with the Gulf Arab states, as it almost surely will, then Afghanistan may become recipient of support from many of Iran's rivals.

In short, Afghanistan's position as odd man out among the Northern Tier states may persist, tending to move it into a position of conflict with Iran rather than ally. The less the threat from the Soviet Union, the greater the likelihood of Iranian-Afghan antipathy in any case.

Pakistan: With or Against Iran?

Iranian-Afghan relations are directly affected by the presence of Pakistan in the equation: Afghan-Pakistani tensions in the past have presented Iran with a dilemma in which it has been more sympathetic to the Pakistani position. But to what extent has the joint Pakistani-Afghan struggle against the Soviet occupation made historic inroads against past mutual hostilities? All Afghans appreciate the central role that Pakistan has played in providing a safe haven, serving as a weapon conduit, and providing refuge to nearly 4 million Afghan refugees in Pakistan. Many Afghans realize that it was the Pashtunistan issue in the past that helped isolate Afghanistan from a common Northern Tier approach to security, unleashing the chain of events that led to ultimate Soviet invasion. But has the legacy of warm cooperation during the anti-

Soviet jihad fundamentally changed Afghan views on the Pashtun question?

Although any moderate regime in Kabul will seek to avoid provocation of problems on the Pashtun question, this built-in geopolitical and ethnic fact of life can never go away. Afghanistan almost surely will continue to periodically clash with Pakistan on the question of Pashtunistan—a "permanent" irredentist cause at the disposal of radical leadership in both countries. Even if there is a "settlement," the issue is a permanent latent source of conflict: Pashtun dissatisfaction will always exist to one degree or another with rule by the dominant Punjabis in Pakistan. Kabul, almost certainly dominated by Pashtun leaders over the longer run, will be drawn to periodic support of their fellow Pashtuns for a variety of reasons. In short, conflict between Pakistan and Afghanistan cannot readily be eliminated from the geopolitics of the region. Iran will be obliged to adopt some sort of position on the issue, especially because irredentism on the Pashtun issue has indirect implications for Baluch irredentism as well, affecting Iranian territorial integrity directly.

Fundamentalist Islamic politics can create strange bedfellows, however. One reason Pakistani President Zia ul-Haq strongly supported fundamentalist leadership among the Afghan mujahidin was that group's religious antipathy to the concept of states founded on an *ethnic* basis as opposed to an Islamic basis. Fundamentalist groups are the least likely to support separatist ethnic movements, either inside Pakistan or in Afghanistan. For them, Islam is the sole legitimate unifying factor that transcends ethnicity in importance. Such leadership is not likely to support a greater Pashtunistan from Kabul, a critical factor in Islamabad's thinking—unless the government in Pakistan is viewed by a ruling fundamentalist regime in Kabul as "un-Islamic"—in which case Kabul might even have recourse to the Pashtunistan lever as a political, more than ideological, instrument. That ideological view, coupled with Pakistan's long-time support for several of the Afghan fundamentalist leaders such as Gulbuddin Hikmetyar—even preceding the Communist coup in Kabul—suggests that Pakistan would enjoy more cordial relations with an Islamic regime in Kabul.

Presumably Iran would be pleased with such a religiously based Sunni regime in Kabul because it would be both neutralist and Islamic in character. Tehran would have to face the reality, however, that such a regime would also enjoy close ties with the Gulf Arab states, especially Saudi Arabia. (Indeed, we have no historical precedent for understanding how Iran would get along with a radical Sunni fundamentalist regime in the world. Rivalry might be at least as likely an outcome as cooperation.) Finally, Iran probably has no foreseeable interest in conflict per se between Afghanistan and Pakistan, unless one or the other were to adopt a hostile position toward Iran.

Pakistan historically feels a sense of isolation from the Islamic world and paranoia about its precarious existence on the edge of a Hindu sea. Pakistan is likely to continue its exceptional efforts to get along well with any Iranian regime, unless Tehran were to adopt policies directly and seriously hostile to Pakistan's interests—highly unlikely. Indeed, despite Pakistan's close alliance with the United States over the years, and especially during the Afghan resistance, Iran has not seriously sought to destabilize Pakistan. To be sure, incidents did take place in which Iranian diplomatic officials were observed to be supporting agitation and demonstrations among Pakistan's Shi'ite minority. But such policies seemed more to reflect the actions of certain radical factions within the Iranian government and were not in keeping with the broader tenor of Iran-Pakistani relations.

A Radical Regime in Pakistan? Pakistan is therefore the more important relationship for Iran to maintain—if there is any choosing to be done between Afghanistan and Pakistan. But all of this calculus is founded on Pakistan's continuation of a moderate foreign policy. A radical regime in Islamabad could again change the calculus. The future of Baluchistan province in Pakistan bears directly on Iran's own territorial integrity and will be a permanent joint interest. Potentially, a radical regime in Islamabad could even use the Baluchistan issue as an instrument against Iran—as well as against Afghanistan, but the scenario seems less likely given the trade-offs involved in Pakistan's own interests. Afghanistan—perhaps because it has never been truly integrated as a nation state—seems to have less to lose from threatened separatism at this stage of its history than do either of its two neighbors.

Afghanistan promises to retain the ambivalent position in Iranian calculations that it always has—a strong but secondary interest relative to Pakistan. A long-time geopolitical ambition of Afghanistan—to break out of its landlocked position and to establish some sort of corridor to the sea—would almost surely evoke unhappiness on the part of Iran: It would involve some greater linkage between the Baluch portions of Afghanistan and those of Pakistan, thereby strengthening the Baluch as an ethnic element—a contingency certainly not favored by Iran.

Indeed, the Soviet occupation of Afghanistan provided a geopolitical field day to analysts of the Northern Tier region. Such a drastic shift in regional power promised to test the validity of a number of speculations about possible Soviet efforts to exploit latent geopolitical opportunities involving:

- A definable interest on Moscow's part to meddle in Baluchistan in order to weaken Pakistani support for the Afghan mujahidin;
- Soviet desire for access to a southern warm-water port;
- Soviet opportunity to invoke Indian pressure against Pakistan; Indian Prime Minister Indira Gandhi in 1984 could well have launched a preemptive strike against Pakistan's nuclear facilities, toppled the Pakistani government, and brought in a new government in Islamabad more sensitive to the Soviet dilemma in Afghanistan and less overtly aligned with the United States.
- Soviet opportunity to place pressure upon Iran from Baluchistan as well.

Most of these events did not actually take place, although they were unquestionably considered and represented real options for Moscow if circumstances had moved in different directions in the USSR, in India, and elsewhere.

In assessing the geopolitics of the coming decades in this region, analysts must consider these same factors as still latent; major violence in particular can unleash one or more of them. Pakistan's long-range stability ranks high among the question marks.

Iran and the Indian Ocean

Iran will envisage its eastern borders in terms of not only land-based politics but also the sea. The shah's own grand vision for Iran involved the extension of Iranian sea power well out into the Indian Ocean. (This "global vision" of the shah will be discussed in greater detail in the Chapter 14.) Part of the shah's rationale was a lack of confidence in the willingness and ability of other states to defend Iran's vital interests, such as the sea lines of communication critical to oil and trade links with Japan and East Asia. Baluchistan immediately figures prominently here: Hostile control of the Indian Ocean coast near Iran's major Indian Ocean port, Chah Bahar, would affect the security of approaches to Iran and the Gulf from the east.

The Indian Factor

India is the dominant geopolitical reality of South Asia. Any state interested in the security of Pakistan must focus on India's role above all else. Concern for Pakistan's security is not an abstract concept: Pakistan and India have gone to war three times since Pakistan became independent. With both states in virtual possession of a nuclear capability, will the "balance of terror" establish a new relationship between them, or will the prospects for further conflict be heightened? India is likely to want a Pakistan that is strong enough not to align itself heavily with outside powers such as the United States but not so powerful as to be unresponsive to Indian security interests in the region. In short, India would like a Pakistan that is well aware of India's strategic superiority but secure enough in its own resources to avoid excessive outside dependence.

The shah clearly recognized India as the important determining factor for Pakistan's security and sought correct relations with it. Indira Gandhi paid a state visit to Iran and the shah provided India with economic aid as well as concessionary oil terms after the skyrocketing of oil prices after 1973.[13]

Iran and India in some senses represent the major potential powers of the northwest Indian Ocean. Elements of competition and even conflict exist here in the future, as well as possibilities for cooperation. At best, Iran's interests and capabilities in this area will always have to be modest relative to India's, but the precedent is there.

If the encouraging shifts in Soviet foreign policy away from challenges to the West in the Third World persist, *regional superpowers* are going to loom far more prominently on the global scene. Iran and India represent two obvious candidates for this role and have already established some credentials in the area. As we have noted elsewhere in this book, in the absence of a major regional threat from the USSR, Iran is likely to strongly prefer a Gulf and northwest Indian Ocean that is free of superpower presence. Iran will be readily attracted to concepts such as a neutralized Indian Ocean and will find common cause with India here. The USSR, that under almost any circumstances is permanently interested in limiting the power projection capabilities of the United States near Soviet shores, will likely join both India and Iran in this quest. Moscow will eventually wish to continue developing its own Indian Ocean capabilities—but will try to avoid invoking the ire or even anxiety of those states about its own regional intentions.

India and the Gulf

Given India's own major resource base for the long term, New Delhi will evince a deepening interest in the Gulf itself. After all, British policy toward much of the Middle East, the Gulf, and Iran emanated more from the British Raj in India than it did from Whitehall. It was the colonial government of Delhi that executed daily responsibilities for the defense of the Gulf. The probability is high that the sovereign government of India today will continue to see the world in much the same geopolitical terms.

The drift of Indian population westward into the Gulf over the decades creates another ingredient of New Delhi's interest. Merchants from the subcontinent have long been an integral part of the Gulf mercantile scene, thereby making English often a more useful language for bazaar haggling than even Arabic. But it was the oil boom of the early 1970s that flung open the manpower floodgates from the subcontintent into the countries of the Gulf. In 1979 there were at least 300,000 Indians in the Middle East, mostly in the Gulf.[14] Six years later another researcher reported a total Indian population in the Gulf as slightly less than 2 million.[15] India thus cannot fail to have an interest in Gulf affairs, and it is not far-fetched that this population, coupled with an equally large Pakistani population in the smaller Gulf shaykhdoms, could even end up altering their pattern of quiescence to become a source of some agitation or disorder in the future, further involving Indian interests.

The rivalry and conflict between Pakistan and India has also extended westward into the Gulf and the Middle East. Pakistan obviously enjoys a favored position among Muslim states—an advantage it will always retain. Nonetheless, India has also done fairly well in conducting its own diplomacy among the Arab states—particularly in appealing to the nonaligned preferences of the Arab world. Although Pakistan has been committed to alignment and military pacts with the West, India has not. It has been India that played a crucial role in the heyday of the nonaligned movement and was highly regarded by leaders such as Nasser on this basis. Consequently India has been influential in its ties among many Arab states, including the provision of military expertise.

Iran will therefore continue to find some common ground with India in the future, particularly if Iran persists in a strongly nonaligned outlook—by far the strongest probability. Tehran's ties with Pakistan, as a contiguous state with shared security interests, will always rank high. But so will the Indian factor: another regional superpower (potentially, but not automatically, a rival) and a leader in nonaligned affairs sharing with Tehran a focus on the exclusion of external powers from the region. Conversely, although Pakistan will always have reservations about the reliability of its external security ties—such as with the United States—it will permanently fear the strategic dominance of India and will not readily be able to break away into a truly nonaligned position— in distinction to Tehran's preferences.

Islam will also be a constant factor in the Tehran–New Delhi equation. One of India's obsessions is the problem of the indigestibility of its own Muslims into the Indian secular state system. India reacts viscerally to Pan-Islamic calls and has responded quite negatively to Iranian-supported

Islamic agitation in India among the Muslim population. The powerful impulse of Muslim separatism in Kashmir is especially worrisome to India and, as the intensity of the struggle grows, increasing sympathy and interest from the Muslim world will result. The Islamic Republic of Iran is likely to strongly support the cause of Kashmiri independence, which will negatively affect Iranian-Indian ties and bring Iran and Pakistan closer together. If Tehran is determined to pursue a strongly Islamic agenda, India will distance itself from Iran and could even seek to weaken Iran if India perceives Iran's role in supporting an independent Kashmir as considerable. In the final analysis, Iran probably has more important priorities with India than simply agitation of India's Muslim community, but a strong Islamic agenda in Iran will always represent a cooling factor between the two states. Should Iran revert to a more secular nationalist set of policies then its strategic interests with India might overlap considerably. Under any circumstances India's policies toward Pakistan at any given time will be a considerable determining factor in Iran's relations with India.

Emulation of South Asian Nuclear Developments?

In nuclear terms, Iran will surely seek to emulate the experience of Pakistan and India in developing its own nuclear capability. Iran, with its obsession for independence and nondependency upon the great powers, will feel compelled to develop an independent defense capability and remain beholden to no one. Pakistan is not likely to view such an eventuality with high concern because Iranian-Pakistani relations from the very creation of Pakistan have not shown signs of natural geopolitical conflict. Those regional states most likely to attempt to prevent the development of an Iranian nuclear capability would be the USSR and Iraq—and possibly Israel. In any case, over the longer run, Iran is one of the more natural candidates for the development of a nuclear capability. Even after the end of the Iran-Iraq War, Iranian leaders have spoken of the imperative nature of "fully equipping itself in the offensive and defensive use of chemical, bacteriological and radiological weapons."[16]

China: The Silk Road Connection

Iran's ties during the last shah's reign came to include East Asia, both as a function of Iran's widening ties and interests and the increasing activity of China and Japan in the Middle East as well. China and Iran have been intimately linked in cultural contacts across the Silk Road for nearly three millennia. The art and music of the two countries share many common roots. China has been long been affected by Iran as a world culture.

China came only late onto the Iranian world scene in modern times. Driven for several decades by Mao's own uncompromising vision of the world order, China saw Iran as simply a cats-paw of Western imperialism, a monarchy dedicated to a reactionary anti-Communist policy. During this period China lent support to many regional liberation movements, including the Popular Front for the Liberation of the Occupied Arab Gulf (PFLOAG), which conducted subversive activities the length and breadth of the Gulf—and was totally hostile to Iran.[17] Iraq, too, was one of many strong patrons of that movement.

It was China's own shifting geopolitical requirements after the break with Moscow in the late 1960s that impelled Peking toward policies of normalization of relations with all states, regardless of political philosophy. Iran responded in kind, recognizing that China could be of use to Iran in strengthening its coalition of support against possible threat from the Soviet Union. Thus both China and Iran essentially developed initial ties as a function of negative policy toward the Soviet Union. China, a staunch supporter of Pakistan in China's own geopolitical struggle with Soviet-backed India, came to understand that good ties with Iran flowed naturally from China's own close relations with Islamabad and Iran's own importance in the Gulf.

China has continued to maintain good ties with Iran right on into the Islamic Republic, although it undoubtedly does not look with favor upon Tehran's outspoken policies on Islamic liberation, given China's own large Muslim population in western China.

China is yet another regional superpower that will, over the long run, seek to discourage extraregional powers from exercising great influence in the region. Both China and Iran support an Indian Ocean zone of peace. They share a strong common concern for Pakistan's integrity as well as a mutual concern for Soviet expansionism. China and Iran are likely to have growing ties in the future—stronger than at any time in the past—particularly based on a common nonaligned view of the world. This interest in a nonalignment will transcend improvement of both China's and Iran's ties with the Soviet Union.

Trade will undoubtedly figure prominently in the Sino-Iranian equation, especially in the arms field. China's military sales to Iran led to considerable notoriety during the latter stages of the Iran-Iraq War when China provided Iran with some 30–35 Silkworm missiles that were actively used against a variety of targets,[18] much to Washington's dismay. Although ostensibly neutral in the war, China showed much greater attentiveness to its relations with Iran.

Japan: Oil Links

Japan has emerged onto the Middle East scene only recently as it struggles to find a political approach consonant with its ever-expanding economic interests. Japan has been particularly concerned about the Persian Gulf, from where it derives the overwhelming part of its oil imports. The Iran-Iraq War was extremely disturbing to Japan with its implications of a possible cut-off of oil supplies—an eventuality that fortunately never came to pass. Japan made meticulous and successful efforts to remain neutral between Iran and Iraq and even offered to play a role as mediator.

Japan has already supported major economic projects in Iran— especially the huge $2 billion Mitsui petrochemical plant—Japan's largest private overseas investment[19]—where construction was closed down during the war. Japan is currently very interested in postwar construction projects in Iran. Economic relations should expand considerably in the years ahead.

For Iran, Japan is more than a customer for oil or a source of high-tech imports. Japan is living proof of the viability of the aspiration to successfully pursue a policy of "neither East nor West." Japan was an Asian power that vaulted itself into the forefront of major industrial nations in a do-it-yourself style that seemingly has not compromised its traditional culture, values, or religion. Japan thus enjoys extreme respect in Iran where it is regarded as something of a model. Although the parallels in the development of the two states cannot be pushed too far, Japan in fact strikes many aspiring nationalist Middle Eastern states as a potential model. Indeed, Japan has attracted developing nations as far back as 1905 with its impressive victory over Tsarist Russia in the Russo-Japanese War. Japan is also a source of technology free of compromising political ties. The future of Japanese-Iranian ties is therefore rather promising as well.

Conclusion

In sum, Iran's view East is a complex one, involving many different patterns of interests. Unless Iran comes under direct and intense regional challenge itself, however, its preference for nonalignment and a distancing of the superpowers from the Gulf area will probably be the first and most reliable touchstone of Tehran's policy preferences among the complex equation of South Asian and East Asian power politics.

Notes

1. See Sir John William Kaye, *History of the War in Afghanistan*, quoted in "The Great Game Replayed: On the Russians and Afghanistan," by Michael Charlton, *Encounter*, April 1989, p. 20.

2. Rouhollah K. Ramazani, *The Foreign Policy of Iran, 1500-1941* (Charlottesville: University Press of Virgina, 1966), p. 39.

3. *Ibid.*, p. 48.

4. Abdul Samad Ghaus, *The Fall of Afghanistan* (London: Pergamon-Brassey, 1988), p. 99.

5. See Sultana Afroz, "Afghanistan in U.S.-Pakistani Relations, 1947-1960," *Central Asia Survey*, Vol. 8, No. 2, 1989, pp. 135-137.

6. *Ibid.*, p. 131.

7. *Ibid.*, p. 137.

8. Rouhollah K. Ramazani, *Iran's Foreign Policy, 1941-1973* (Charlottesville: University Press of Virginia, 1975), p. 434.

9. Ghaus, *op. cit.*, p. 149. Ghaus was himself deputy foreign minister of Afghanistan under the Daoud regime.

10. J. Bruce Amstutz, *Afghanistan, the First Five Years of Occupation* (Washington, D.C.: National Defense University, 1986), pp. 358-361.

11. See Alexandre Bennigsen and S. Enders Wimbush, *Muslims of the Soviet Empire* (Bloomington: Indiana University Press, 1986). Figures on the overall number of Tajiks is obviously higher today.

12. See Robert L. Canfield, "Ethnic, Regional and Sectarian Alignments in Afghanistan," in *The State, Religion, and Ethnic Politics: Afghanistan, Iran, and Pakistan*, eds. Ali Banuazizi and Myron Weiner (Syracuse: Syracuse University Press, 1986), p. 78.

13. Alvin Cottrell, "The Foreign Policy of the Shah," *Strategic Review*, Fall 1975, p. 39.

14. Allen G. Hill, "Population, Migration, and Development in the Gulf States," in *Security in the Gulf*, eds. Shahram Chubin, Robert Litwak, Avi Plascov (Aldershot, U.K.: Gower, for the International Institute for Strategic Studies, Gower, 1982), p. 77.

15. W. Howard Wriggins, "South Asia and the Gulf: Linkages, Gains, and Limitations," *Middle East Review*, Winter 1985/86, p. 30.

16. FBIS, 7 October 1988, Tehran Domestic Service quoting speaker of Parliament Hashemi-Rafsanjani on 6 October 1988.

17. Lillian Craig Harris, *China's Foreign Policy Toward the Third World*, Washington Paper Number 112, (Washington, D.C.: Praeger/Center for Strategic International Studies, 1985), p. 54.

18. See Molly Moore and David B. Ottoway, "U.S. Reacts to China's Silkworm Sale," *The Washington Post*, 23 October 1987.

19. Michael M. Yoshitsu, *Caught in the Middle East* (Lexington, Mass.: Lexington Books, D.C. Heath and Company, 1986), p. 41.

14

Iran and the Global Vision

Iran's acknowledgment of its losses and its acceptance of its diminished frontiers did not necessarily mean recognition of its position as a weak state. The Shahs were still Shahinshah, King of Kings, and Iran continued as an "Empire." The empire had died, but the myth survived, the ever-present past with its real as well as its mythological glories lived on. The lure of this past was a powerful influence in Iran's foreign policy. . . .

—*R. K. Ramazani on nineteenth-century Iran*[1]

After the collapse of traditional Iranian empires over several millennia, the history of twentieth-century Iran has demonstrated anew Iran's constant urge in the direction of a global foreign policy vision. This vision was facilitated by Iran's participation in the global character of the Cold War, Iran's oil revenues that made pursuit of the global vision more practical, and the universal vision of Iran's Islamic ideology under the clergy. Although over time the ideological vehicle for Iran's ambitions may change, the grand vision remains an inseparable part of the Iranian national character.

Quest for World Status

The legacy of Iran's ancient past, as the center of several "world empires" of its day, has been unambiguously retained in Iran's view of itself and its surroundings to this day. Iran is not content with just "being Iran." Or, to put it another way, to "be Iran" is to operate within a special geopolitical sphere where—without necessarily furthering any new territorial claims—Iran believes it has the historical, cultural, even moral weight to powerfully shape the region where classic Persian empires have at one time held sway. Persian ambitions strain to reach beyond present cultural-linguistic frontiers that only serve as frustrating

241

reminders that Iran has been much more in its day. This kind of vision is not unique to Iran; indeed, it is known in much of the world where great political empires of the past have been compelled to confront unpleasant contemporary realities of vastly reduced size, relative weakness, and even subordination to the more recent power of the Western world. (Indeed, the United States itself has a long-standing sense of "mission" and an appropriate global role that is now tangling with numerous jarring post–Cold War realities.) But nineteenth-century Persian impotence—Iran as the plaything of European imperial ambitions—has only thrown the gap between Persian aspirations and political reality into greater relief. The presumptuous vision of the imperial shah as "The Center of the Universe," always aspiring to assertion of Iranian sway over parts of Arab and Turkish lands, could not easily acquiesce to the raw power of imperial Britain and Russia. In today's Tehran a sense of frustration of national ambition still lies just under the surface of the Iranian political psyche.

The legacy of a glorious past in fact lies heavily on most of the major peoples of the Middle East—and perhaps elsewhere in the world as well. Both Arabs and Turks can hark back to centuries of triumph and extraordinary accomplishment on the world scene as rulers of "universal empires" at one point or another. Arabs are haunted by the fact that present-day reality falls short of the dream of a united Arab world; indeed, Arab unity remains an elusive target that the Arab political system still aspires to recreate in a modern era. But Arabs tend to curse *themselves* for their failure to reestablish the ideal of Arab unity even more than they blame imperialist machinations that frustrate the accomplishment of that goal. Quest for that goal nonetheless still hinders the normal development of the Arab nation states today.

Turkey, too, after World War I came to clear recognition of the fact that the modern nation state is, in fact, the most effective vehicle for the long-term well-being of the modern Turkish people. Abandonment of the pretenses of Ottoman power has been a willing and conscious selection by the overwhelming majority of the Turkish intellectual and political elite. Those external enemies who would have truncated the borders even of modern Turkey after the Ottoman collapse in 1918— to force it to live within much harsher and more confining borders— were successfully repelled by Ataturk, enabling Turkish honor to remain intact.

Persian honor is not intact, however. And Iranian leadership has perhaps thought in less practical terms than Turks. Whereas Turkey as a nation by and large still feels comfortable with its status and relative weight in the world, the sense of victimization runs far deeper in the Iranian collective mind. The perceived ability of external forces to manipulate Iran has created an even more powerful urge to break the back of these forces.

The founding of the Shi'ite Safavid dynasty in 1499 spawned one of the last gasp efforts to restore the former imperial boundaries of ancient Iran. For a while, until the state's reach far outran its practical capabilities to fulfill its ambitions, the Safavids made a powerful mark upon the region with its challenge to the Sunni world of Ottoman Turkey and reassertive moves into the old Iranian turf of Afghanistan and Central Asia. With only one or two exceptional reflarings of imperial strength, the remaining centuries brought only a slew of humiliating reminders that Iran was indeed no longer master of its own fate.

Despite the end of the "imperial age" for much of the world in the ashes of World War I, the two remarkable and ambitious shahs of the Pahlavi dynasty set out once again—slowly, deliberately, and more realistically within the terms of twentieth-century politics—to redefine Persian power. Reza Shah began building the essential infrastructure of state—the sine qua non of any extension of Persian power to the outside world. Based on the foundation of the nation state structure created by his father, Mohammed Reza Shah proceeded to expand those institutions and establish a political vision that proclaimed the shah's serious pretenses to become the fifth most powerful state in the world. By hindsight, such goals were hopelessly pretentious and unattainable. Furthermore, that aspiration collided cruelly with the serious imbalances of a badly skewed developmental policy, a pace of social development spinning out of control, and even the return of the foreigner to a (limited) place of some technical dominance and cultural pressure on Iranian society. Harsh internal security practices, perhaps not dissimilar to some other authoritarian Third World regimes or the Communist world—and mitigated only partially under U.S. pressure—helped fuel the ultimate collapse of the Pahlavis' dream. But the last shah, for all his well-documented shortcomings, developed a comprehensive vision of neo-Iranian world power that, coupled with massive oil income, might have held out some prospect of at least partial fulfillment.

It is easy to sneer at the ambitions of the shah. Armed with the vision of hindsight, we now see why the shah had in fact overreached his grasp—particularly in remaining blind to the critical political, social, and economic imbalances developing at home and the immense resentments among the population spawned by development at a severely dislocating pace. If just the shah alone had been blind to these negative developments, the indictment might be more severe. In the event, there were hosts of foreign advisors, experts, and observers of all nationalities who failed to grasp the depth of the developing social dislocations.[2] Although a handful of observers felt presciently uncomfortable at the nature of Iran's lopsided development, few described the shah's policies as fatally flawed until near the end of the four decades of the shah's rule.

Whatever the shortcomings of the shah's developmental program, it is the dimensions of his foreign policy vision that prompt attention here. As he matured in power, gained self-confidence, and his financial base multiplied, the shah increasingly reverted to a *global vision* of Iran's influence and interests.

Oil and the Imperial Vision

We do not have to turn solely to the annals of Iranian imperial history to find justification for the shah's tendency to think in more global terms. The blessings of large oil reserves also work powerfully upon the perspectives of most major oil-producing states: The very nature of this commodity immediately links the producer to the global economy, to an obligatory familiarity with the economic needs and vulnerabilities of the world's biggest economies, international industrial needs, and the actions of a multitude of other producers around the globe. The shah's belief at that time that Iran's oil reserves would probably carry Iran no more than about forty years into the future strongly affected the shah's sense of the use of this commodity and the urgency of building an economy that would sustain Iran long past the exhaustion of this precious resource. And last but not least, oil revenues do wonders for providing the wherewithal to pursue a foreign policy of broader range. Oil therefore served as the springboard for the gradual expansion of Iran's overseas interests toward ever more distant areas.

The increasing discovery of offshore oil deposits in the waters of the Gulf heightened the importance of Iran's relations with the other Gulf states; the stakes over conflicting territorial claims were now far higher. Developing offshore drilling and production technology also hastened Iran's interest in Gulf oil politics. The dependence of Iran on the Strait of Hormuz for the export of oil rendered Oman—lying athwart the choke point—of major importance to Iran. Whatever historical interest Iran had in Oman, Iran's dependence upon Oman's maritime and defense posture transformed its importance to the shah. The development of a preeminent naval force in the Gulf became an early imperative in the shah's mind—an interest already initiated by his father.

But the shah's maritime strategic interest was now expanding well beyond the mere confines of the Gulf itself. The very approaches to the Gulf began to take on a significance for the security of oil and commercial shipping routes to Iran. The imperial navy envisaged the development of the new Arabian Sea port of Chah Bahar—beyond the reach of any hostile stranglehold on the straits—as a critical point for Iranian longer range defense.

The shah's growing awareness of the implications of the departure of British power, and the unreliability of the United States—or any foreign power—to permanently defend Iranian interests in the region, further impelled him to project Iranian naval force out into the Indian Ocean. He foresaw a role by which Iran would ultimately adopt responsibility for the "northwest quadrant" of the Indian Ocean, in conjunction with power sharing with India, Australia, Indonesia, South Africa, and others. Iran, while supporting U.S. development of facilities at Diego Garcia as a temporary expedient, went ahead to acquire port facilities at Mauritius as an independent long-range Indian Ocean capability.[3]

Regardless of his security ties to the United States, however, over the longer run the shah gravitated toward the concept of an Indian Ocean free of superpower involvement, based on the collective security measures of Indian Ocean powers. To this end the shah visited Australia and Singapore to promote the idea. Indeed, the shah extended economic agreements as far afield as Muslim Senegal for the building of a refinery and petrochemical plant.[4]

The Red Sea and its approaches equally concerned the shah as part of his critical "lifeline" to Europe—both for the transport of oil and for commercial shipping. Interest in the Red Sea littoral countries sprung from this concern, including the Horn of Africa where the USSR was intent upon developing influence in Somalia and Ethiopia.

Indeed, it was this very propensity to think in global geostrategic terms that helped the shah impress a series of U.S. presidents to develop ever closer strategic ties with the United States—especially in the Kissingerian 1970s.[5] The United States, more than any other single power, bears responsibility for pushing the shah in the direction in which he was in any case powerfully impelled to go: major partnership in the global U.S. effort to block Soviet expansion. The global vision of Iran continued to encompass ever greater horizons.

Self-Reliance

However closely the shah sought to identify with the U.S. geopolitical vision, he was even more profoundly driven by a sense of the need for Iranian self-dependency and self-reliance. Superpower interests and support inevitably entailed conditions and strings that could on occasion compromise Iran's vital interests and even infringe upon Iran's very sovereignty. This exact sentiment is precisely echoed by the current leadership of the Islamic Republic: strong emphasis on self-reliance—but this time permitting no superpower even to serve as vehicle for Iranian ambition.

The shah's ambitious vision of Iran in the world may indeed have reflected the instincts of an overweening leader reaching well beyond the capabilities of a country still at a limited state of development. But for all his failings, the shah charted a certain course of approach to the surrounding world that any subsequent leaders of ambition in Iran will inevitably have to reckon with in the decades ahead—whether they admire the shah or not. Khomeini was to pursue the same global vision—cloaked this time in Islamic garb.

The Islamic Republic and the World

As we have noted in earlier chapters, Khomeini's vision of a universal Islamic ideology helped thrust Iran into the forefront of world Islamic politics. Iranian emissaries fanned out over the entire Muslim world after the revolution, propounding the Imam's message of universal justice, and the struggle against imperialism, "global arrogance," and oppression. Iran organized a whole series of regional and international conferences designed to analyze the predicament of the Islamic world from the Philippines to Africa and even to the Muslims in Latin America in order to develop a common ideology and strategy. Indeed, the clerics in their initial zeal felt a sense of identification with nearly all revolutionary movements, including even the Nicaraguan Sandinistas and other Marxist parties in the world, engaged in antiimperialist solidarity. At times Islam even seemed to take a backseat to the imperatives of antiimperialist action.

Although the ardor of the radical clergy has either cooled or been displaced by more practical considerations, the same universalist ambitions have remained. Iran still sees its role in a global sense. The crucial decision lying ahead is whether Tehran will envisage its calling in primarily religious/Islamic terms, or secular/nationalist/antiimperialist terms. Although the vehicle may over time shift, the ambitions will not. The implications of these choices will be discussed in the final chapter.

Notes

1. Rouhollah K. Ramazani, *The Foreign Policy of Iran, 1500–1941* (Charlottesville: University Press of Virginia, 1966), p. 62.

2. James A. Bill's *The Eagle and the Lion* (New Haven: Yalé University Press, 1988), superbly documents this process of ambition spiralling into folly with the full support of many echelons of the U.S. government, academia, and corporate world.

3. Alvin J. Cottrell, "The Foreign Policy of the Shah," *Strategic Review*, Fall 1975, p. 37.

4. *Ibid.*, p. 42.

5. James Bill, *op. cit.*, p. 232.

15

Iran and the United States

America cannot do a damned thing.

—*Ayatollah Khomeini*

The focus of this book is on Iran's geopolitical relationships with its neighbors; the United States is not, of course, a neighbor. Indeed, the United States does not really have a geopolitical relationship with Iran as such except as a distant and sometimes countervailing power—one that has had occasion to intervene increasingly sharply in different ways in Iranian affairs over the last century.

Iran's relationship with the United States was intimate under the shah but would not have been so had the monarchy not existed, for the shah used the ited States in part to bolster his own domestic and foreign position.

Iran is inclined to view the United States as the chief source of "imperialist oppression" over the past many decades, supplanting the British, and even the Russians in this capacity. Such a vision of the United States currently reflects the radical ideology of the clergy, who see American culture as the single greatest threat to Islamic government and way of life. But deep-seated hostility to the United States is also shared equally by the left in Iran as well.

The United States may well remain the chief challenger to Iranian power in the region in any case, particularly if other smaller Gulf states have recourse to the United States in a defensive capacity. The United States is also the most likely power to intervene in the event of a threat to the flow of oil from the region—as has already occurred in the Iran-Iraq War and in the U.S. war with Iraq following the Iraqi invasion of Kuwait. The United States, in this sense, remains the most probable external source of military intervention to rival Iran in the foreseeable future.

Iran and the Great Powers

It is a basic thesis of this book that Iran will always coexist uncomfortably with the great powers. Iran perceives itself as the preeminent regional power. Any great foreign power in Iran's eyes thus represents a permanent potential threat to Iran's independence, national sovereignty, and territorial integrity, a permanent rival for regional influence, and—only under circumstances of extreme duress to Iran—a potentially indispensable but undesirable ally.

U.S. involvement in Iran did not become part of U.S. global strategy until after World War II, when Iran became one of the many cockpits of the East-West struggle. In fact, however, Iran's behavior in the nineteenth-century rivalry between Russia and Great Britain demonstrates a great many of the traditional characteristics of Iranian behavior toward major powers in general.

- Russia and Britain were rivals to be played off against each other.
- Russia constituted the greatest immediate (and long-term) menace because of its geographical proximity to Iran. Britain helped obstruct Russian territorial threats to Iran's integrity—but only when such Russian acquisition of territory and influence in Iran threatened Britain's own interests.
- Because even the two great rival powers could collude to the detriment of Iran's interests, as in 1907, Iran was always interested in identifying some "third power" that could delimit the influence of the other two. At various times, starting in the nineteenth century, France, Germany, the United States, and later, China or Japan were partially able to serve in this third power capacity.
- Impotence vis-à-vis the outside world was the key determining attitude toward the great powers. This determinant only began to change as Iran gradually acquired the wherewithal to stand on its own and acquire instruments of power and influence that could be used for bargaining, or that could actually limit the ability of the external world to act against Iran's interests.

The United States and Iran

The U.S. relationship with Iran was originally perceived as another third power relationship, designed to buffer British and Russian influences, starting in the constitutional period of the early 1900s. By the end of World War II, however, the United States was coming gradually to replace

Britain as the chief foreign state of recourse to protect Iran internationally and to strengthen the shah's own position domestically. In the eyes of Iranian liberals and nationalists it was also the United States, together with Britain, that helped put an end to the last great era of liberal parliamentary government in Iran—with the overthrow of Premier Mossadegh in the 1950s when the shah was restored to the throne. This joint British-American covert operation may well have been a critical turning point in modern Iranian history that doomed the development of any kind of liberal democratic experiment for at least half a century. And it was the intensity of Iran's relationship with the United States that was ultimately one of the important factors leading to the shah's downfall in 1978.

Was the Shah a Unique Phenomenon?

The unusual closeness of relations between the United States and the last shah was a particular product of the shah's own insecurity, his ambitions for Iran, and the bipolarization of world affairs following World War II, placing severe strains upon Iran's normal proclivity to keep its distance from the great powers and to view them all with suspicion. Was the shah's move toward alignment with the United States an excessive reaction to the Soviet and radical threat? Some argue that it was. However, it is important to note that both Turkey and Pakistan— two nations that also cherished an independent world view—felt the same necessity of entering similar defensive alignments with the West in NATO and CENTO, each for their own reasons.

But even when the Soviet threat receded in the early 1960s, the shah in no way diminished his drive for closer security relations with the United States. In fact, a good case can be made that the shah in part exploited U.S. concerns over rivalry with the USSR in the Third World as grounds for strengthening his regional military position, regardless of the degree of Soviet threat.[1] And such U.S. support likewise directly strengthened his domestic position, until it went too far and became a negative rather than a positive factor in his own survival.

If one argues that the post–World War II period of intense bipolarization constitutes a unique period in modern history, then the characteristics of the last shah's reign in this era cannot be taken as representing any kind of norm for judging the long-range future characteristics of Iran's foreign policy. It is significant to note that it was precisely during the period of the shah's greatest weakness—in the late 1940s and early 1950s when Parliament and public opinion played the greatest role— that the interlude of nonalignment emerged so strongly in Iran's foreign policy, scarcely less than a decade after Soviet occupation and Russian support for breakaway Communist republics in Iranian Azerbaijan and Kurdistan. This interlude lends further weight to the argument that alignment does not seem to represent a strong or dominant trend in Iranian foreign policy.

This inclination is yet further reflected in the lack of widespread support within Iran for Iran's entrance into the Baghdad Pact in 1955. A strong feeling existed among the public that the pact affected Iran's national independence and could complicate its relations with the USSR.[2] The shah was primarily responsible for affirming Iran's commitment to the pact.

Iran will seek to diversify its relations with major foreign powers as much as possible to meet its more routine security needs in the future. Indeed, it is hard to imagine what those overwhelming security needs will be if Russia is seen no longer to constitute a major threat. The United States is left as the only major external power that has, and might yet again, use force to block Iran's ambitions in the region. In the absence of great powers in future regional power struggles, Iran most naturally will make common cause with other regional states against the threatening regional state to form a balance of power. Thus, should Iraq threaten the status quo, the Gulf states, Syria, Turkey, and even Saudi Arabia could all become natural allies of circumstance. That Iran did not take this leading role during the Iraqi invasion of Kuwait is primarily attributable to its great military weakness in the aftermath of its war with Iraq and the instant readiness of the United States to intervene to challenge Iraqi power. Without external intervention, it is interesting to speculate how and when, if ever, the regional forces would have acted to deny Kuwait to Iraq.

The anti-American virulence of the Islamic Republic must thus be seen in part as a legacy of the shah's abnormally close ties with the United States. Yet Iran's special venom for America is not only the product of U.S. involvement and influence in Iran over a thirty-year period: after all, the U.S. role in Iran was only mildly intrusive compared to the crude armed interventionism of Britain and Russia for more than a century. But times had changed, public opinion was far more aware, and Iranian tolerance for foreign influence was now vastly less; indeed, the United States was partly reaping the bitter fruit of both Iran's experience with the British and the Russians and other national frustrations deeply rooted in Iranian history. There was a great deal more going on than the mere anger of the clergy toward strong U.S. support for the shah.

The U.S. Is the Great Satan

In fact, the United States had also come to bear the brunt of an increasing clash between Western and Islamic culture. The West in the past had usually come to Iran in the form of conqueror, proconsul, or debt collector. But the West was obviously a revolutionary force—in positive as well as negative ways—in introducing concepts of the modern rational bureaucratic state, political pluralism, social equality, popular electoral franchise, and other political and social values. Nearly all states in the Middle East were profoundly affected by these Western influences— introduced primarily through Western colonialism, Western education, and the travel of Middle Easterners to the West. Unfortunately, these same values did not necessarily guide Western behavior in dealings with Iran.

In the post–World War II world, the challenge of the West to Iran grew increasingly intense, invading the sphere of daily cultural life at the popular level, and bringing about major social and economic upheavals associated with Westernization—and all at the very citadel of Shi'ite Islam. In the end it was the crushing dominance of sheer American cultural weight internationally that constituted the spearhead of this cultural assault. Modern media, Western education and technology, and an army of expatriate Americans and others were powerful vehicles for bringing non-Islamic ideas to the heart of the country. If raw force and military coercion were now sharply diminished instruments in the West's approach to the Middle East, the newer forms of seductive cultural intrusion were far more threatening. The clergy was the most intense in its reaction.

Indeed, the radical Islamic clergy had come to view the United States itself as a greater danger to Islam than any other external power had ever been—and certainly more than the Soviet Union could ever be. Moscow, after all, could influence Iran only by force of arms and through a small revolutionary grouping of pro-Moscow Tudeh party Communists. There was no *cultural threat* at all from Moscow through which Soviet life was an enticement to Iranians as a whole. The United States, on the other hand, did represent a major cultural threat to Islam: American popular culture, secularist attitudes, emphasis on individualism over society, pursuit of self-gratification, lax and permissive sexual mores, and consumerist-oriented life-style, and the internationally pervasive character of the American media—all insinuated itself into Iran where it was often accepted as an eagerly sought commodity. Iranian students and Westernized elite were being seduced away from Islamic cultural and traditional values through attraction to American-style life. As the Ayatollah Khomeini stated in his will read after his death:

One of the conspiracies that has had a great influence in various countries including our own dear country—and whose effects to a large extent still remain—is the alienation of colonized countries from their own identity, so that they turn toward West or East; so that they see no value in their own culture and their own strengths, while they regard the two powerful blocs as a superior race with a superior culture; so that they regard these two powers as the point the whole world should turn toward. . . .

A more tragic fact is [the two blocs] have kept the oppressed and dominated countries behind in every way and have turned them into consumer countries. They have so overawed us with their progress and their Satanic tricks that we do not dare to take any initiative. We have surrendered everything we have to them, and we have entrusted our fates and the fates of our countries into their hands. . . .

[Our leaders] should prevent the import of wasteful and home-destroying commodities. . . . I ask all the young people . . . to preserve their independence, freedom and human values, even through hardship and toil, and not to respond to the call of the tyrants of arrogance and their decadence and obscene ceremonies, who invade you as if you are nationless.[3]

Worse, from the point of view of the clergy, this kind of life-style was achieving a degree of acceptance among upper classes in the Islamic world as a whole, and even making inroads into fundamentalist countries such as Saudi Arabia. Khomeini has repeatedly referred to this kind of Muslim accommodation to U.S. culture as characteristic of what he calls "American Islam":

Yes, a religion that places the material and spiritual resources of Islamic and non-Islamic countries at the disposal of superpowers, that exhorts the people to believe that religion is separate from politics—*that* religion is the opium of the masses. However, such a religion is no longer the true religion, but is a religion which our people call American-style Islam.[4]

In effect, then, the Islamic clergy does indeed have more to fear from the United States than from almost any other country as the beacon of an antithetical culture supremely threatening to Islam. This reality will, furthermore, not change—at least in the eyes of radical Islamic clergy— anywhere in the Islamic world.

The clergy will not always dominate in Iran, however, and secular processes are already under way in Iran that weaken the concept of *Velayat-e-Faqih* or direct clerical rule. Large elements among the population oppose the narrowness of the clerics' religious outlook. But tensions will always exist between those concerned for the preservation of Iranian/ Islamic values—on the left and the right—and those who are attracted to Western life-styles. Indeed, a class clash between Westernized elites on the one hand, and a lower middle class and the have-nots on the other, is also implicit in this cultural struggle. Here again, many Iranians may find that closer political and economic ties with Western countries other than the United States are less inherently overwhelming.

Abiding Fear of Foreign Intervention

Running like a leitmotif through nearly all of the pronouncements of the Islamic Republic is the now fully articulate sense of Iran's permanent vulnerability to foreign interests and foreign intervention. As the deputy foreign minister pointed out in a major foreign policy address in August 1989:

> Our region is a region of controls. Its geography is very simple. Some of the countries are under the control of Britain, some are under U.S. control, and Iraq has been under Soviet control. This is the local geography. First of all these [powers] want to keep their influence, and second they want to expand their influence. From this geography we grasp the dynamics of control in the region. This means we can read accurately the changes in the region, because the intentions are quite clear. . . .
>
> Our ties with other countries have to be useful to us in [various different ways]. . . . As long as there is no talk of [foreign] control, [anything] can be dealt with. As soon as you bring up the issue of control, the entire project collapses. The dialectic of our relations with the world is very clear. We cannot overlook the possibility of someone wanting to gain control over us. . . . The United States is one of those countries which has always meant to control, each time it has tried to contact us. . . . So we have told them a big "no" and they have left after losing their dignity. . . . The British have been the same. . . . There should only be mutual respect . . . but the British could not control themselves. The Salman Rushdie affair directly contradicted their [supposed desire for mutual respect].[5]

Iranian mention of the Salman Rushdie affair, and British publication of his *Satanic Verses* cuts very deep into the heart of Iran's psychology. This was not simply a novel by a Muslim (and naturalized British subject) that treated the Prophet in terms blasphemous to Islam. To the clergy it was seen as a deliberate assault against Iran and the Muslim world as a whole, designed to demean, mock, and weaken Islamic culture—a theme touched upon repeatedly in the Iranian press.

> A considerable softening of attitude has occurred among the promoters of "The Satanic Verses" in their [belated] admission that the book is insulting to things considered holy by Muslims. This [softening] is seen

as a major victory for the Muslims. . . . The West's aim undoubtedly was to destroy a culture whose growth endangered all its colonialist goals. Western animosity toward Islam has been the main cause of this culture's growth. . . .[6]

As the Iranian deputy foreign minister put it,

The best position is the one we took during the Rushdie affair [in placing a price on Rushdie's head]. I think that the Rushdie affair was planned by the United States and by Zionism to deliver a blow against Iran. The United States and Zionism have the biggest fear of our position in the Islamic world. The position taken by the late Imam [Khomeini] in the Rushdie affair, which was a political masterpiece, exactly reversed the plot hatched by the American and the Zionist. . . . This affair had no effect other than to raise our standing in the Islamic world.[7]

Iran's suspicion of the outside world, and focus on itself as victim and coveted object of desire by the great powers, has thus led to an intensely inward-looking and egocentric sense of Iran as the focal point of world calculations. International issues regularly have a way of being portrayed as consciously directed against Iran—or Islam. The Salman Rushdie incident was of course a key event in what Tehran sees as a neverending series of assaults against the crusade of Iran for justice and independence for the Islamic world.

This fixation on the role of the great powers—deeply rooted in history as we have seen—is dramatically demonstrated in the American hostage crisis in 1979 and also in the Iran-Contra affair of 1987. In both cases it was not only the desire to manipulate the hated United States, but to belittle the superpower opponent as well, and to demonstrate, as Khomeini said during the hostage crisis, that "America cannot do a damned thing." The object in part is the humiliation of the opponent as a key instrument in the struggle against a vastly unequal adversary.

This attitude carried over automatically from President Reagan to President Bush; witness the Ayatollah Khamene'i, the spiritual successor to Khomeini, in a Friday prayer speech in early 1989:

Now the new U.S. President has stated that he is ready to resume relations with Iran, subject to this and that. He is setting conditions! We do not accept your conditions! You have nothing to say to us. We object, we do not agree to a relationship with you! We are not prepared to establish relations with powerful world devourers like you! The Iranian nation has no need of the United States, nor is the Iranian nation afraid of the United States. . . . We are the ones who have conditions and do not accept your

behavior, your oppression and intervention in various parts of the world.
. . .[8]

Not only do the great powers prey upon the smaller countries of the
world in Iranian eyes, but they are engaged in a dog-eat-dog relationship
among themselves. The Iranian press is filled with international analyses
indicating the struggles of competing powers, especially between the
United States and the USSR. A calculating and conspiratorial view is
projected onto other powers as well, especially as relates to their
relationship with Iran.

It is also true that both the United States and Zionism are determined
that Iran should not become prosperous or powerful. . . . They are scared
of our having ties with Western Europe. Why? . . . Western Europe is no
longer the United States' primary trade partner. This means that U.S.
foreign trade has moved toward the Pacific. . . . This is why Europe is
trying to find a market in the Soviet Union, independent of the United
States. They are after markets in the Middle East, including the Persian
Gulf. So it is in the interest of Western Europe to have peace in the
Persian Gulf, so that they can have good relations with everyone. This
is exactly against U.S. interests, and this is why the Americans stir things
up once in a while. . . .[9]

The Iran-Contra affair, of course, also fulfilled Tehran's image of the
struggle between the United States and the Soviet Union over control
and influence in Iran. And indeed, Washington's motives in attempting
to establish secret contact with Iran in the mid-1980s—Gorbachev had
only recently come to power—were in part driven by concern that the
total absence of U.S. contact and dialogue with Iran could play directly
into the hands of the USSR, which, unlike the United States, had a
presence in Tehran, a potential ability to sell strategic arms, a military
presence in neighboring Afghanistan, and a major opportunity for
strategic inroads into Iran as Tehran grew increasingly desperate in its
isolation in the middle of a devastating war.[10] The elaborate means of
secret contact played out by National Security Council official Oliver
North, further convinced Iran of its centrality and the unceasing quest
for dominant U.S. influence. This same deep sense of Iran's centrality
is also evident in earlier chapters on Iranian-Russian relations where,
too, Iran perceives itself as pivotal to current Soviet needs to gain
influence in the Middle East, to solve the Afghan morass, and to help
manage the Soviet Union's own Muslims. The ending of the Cold War
will only partly erode Iran's ready image of superpowers at each other's
throats for the "strategic prize" of Iran; political interrelationships of
the region remain complicated enough that Iranian leaders can still

envisage themselves as at the center of the regional geopolitical spider web.

Doing Business with a More Pluralistic Iran

Authoritarian regimes simplify diplomatic intercourse. Power is centrally located, decisions can be made easily, and complicating domestic factors within a country's polity can be largely ignored. Foreign countries can tailor their policies for the autocrat in question. The United States' intimate relationship with the shah in part fell into this convenient category. Even while official U.S. policy encouraged greater freedom and political pluralism in Iran, the shah was still the center of the Iranian universe, the indispensable node through which all transactions passed.

With the passing of the monarchy, and the emergence of a far less centralized form of government in Iran, dealings with that country are automatically far more complicated now for the United States—ideological hostility aside. (Indeed, the decentralized character of the U.S. government tends to make it, too, one of the most difficult and complex governments in the world for foreigners to conduct relations with—for different reasons than Iran.) Competing centers of power now exist in Iran that complicate the policy process within the Iranian government. Greater room for the role of individuals and factions emerge than ever before. To be sure, the United States, even during the shah, tended to be confounded by the complexities of dealings with various factional elements even within the relatively circumscribed character of the monarchy. "American diplomats never felt comfortable with the other major actors of the Iranian political scene. Shrewd, experienced statesmen such as Musaddiq and Qavam seemed terribly unpredictable and in many ways anachronistic."[11] Indeed, the shah seemed supremely "Western" in his style to those Americans at all levels who dealt with him, in contrast to the more traditional, but no less sophisticated, skills of more traditional politicians. It is a thesis of this book that these more characteristically Iranian features of doing business will, from now on, be the dominant forces in future Iranian governments—pushing Americans into similar patterns of discomfort as before, in a political culture sharply different from the American. As we noted in the first chapter, such long-established Iranian skills as indirection, the use of the irregular personal relationship, the mixing of personal, partisan, and national agendas in the same individual, coupled with the deepest suspicion and paranoia toward the outside world—qualities that so frustrated American players in the Iran-Contra negotiations—will now be a more regular feature of doing business with Iran. Traditionally, Americans who tend to be bound to their own cultural models find this kind of interaction difficult; they will run the risk of being bested at it.

But Iran's ties with great powers should not be understood solely in a political and security context. Economic and technological ties will represent an equally important magnet of attraction for relations with the great powers. And economic projects, joint ventures, acquisition of technology and purchase of advanced military equipment need not be the exclusive monopoly of the great powers in any case. Iran will almost surely be attracted to dealing with other powers if they can provide much of the same needs: Japan, China, Western Europe, North and South Korea, Brazil, India, and so on.

Economic independence from the great powers will thus be a major policy goal of Iran. Iran cannot, of course, determine its degree of independence on its own; its freedom of maneuver will depend in part upon the relationship between the great powers themselves. While East-West tensions and rivalries almost certainly will continue to diminish as the realignment of Soviet foreign policy continues, some more normal elements of competition are bound to remain—and indeed would be normal, just as it exists between the United States and its European and Japanese allies in a search for markets in the Middle East. Under these circumstances Iran will continue to try to use its historically acquired skills in playing off one great power against the other for its own advantage. Iran is unshakably confident of its position as the geopolitical "prize" of the region and will assume that other great powers are all eager for close ties with it.

U.S.-Iranian relations are therefore not likely to be cordial in the decades ahead—which does not mean they cannot be correct and mutually beneficial. But the bilateral relationship now carries a great deal of negative baggage from the past. Iranians will remain suspicious of U.S. intentions, and maintain a propensity to believe that the United States is able to manipulate events in Iran as well as in the region. Iranians will continue to maintain strong convictions that the CIA is deeply knowledgeable of all that takes place inside Iran. This presents the United States with a double dilemma. On the one hand, the United States will be suspected as the ultimate author behind domestic Iranian events and international developments in the region. On the other hand, the possibility of U.S. mistakes, miscalculations based on ignorance, or simply indifference, will be seen by many Iranians as inconceivable, given an omniscient CIA: All such mistakes or even nonaction will be interpreted as representing deliberate, even cunning, policy. Iranians are powerfully inclined to read immense amounts of subtle information into the simplest and most casual acts of U.S. policy. It is one of the highest expressions of Iranian egoism to consider that the United States is consumed day and night with its relations with Iran and that so many of its acts are directed against Iran. The Shi'ite sense of victimization is merely the other side of the Iranian coin of self-importance: the conviction that Iran lies at the center of everyone else's calculations. And indeed, it has been only militant Shi'ite Islam that has sometimes caused Washington officials to privately muse in the past that Islam is more hostile to America even than communism. Expression of these sentiments only further convinces Iran that it is the focal point, the supreme threat to U.S. interests and ultimate counterfoil to U.S. imperialism.

It may be that with the end of the Cold War and diminution of East-West tensions U.S.-Iranian relations can fall into a more "normal" pattern. In one sense, Iran already "matters less" to the United States as the East-West factor loses salience. Iran has furthermore largely been a marginal player in the Iraq-Kuwait crisis, although the destruction of Iraq's military capabilities by the United States has hastened the return of Iran to a strategic role in the region.

This diminished role in Washington's eyes may ironically give Iran greater freedom of action in the region for the foreseeable future, now that Iraq has temporarily supplanted Iran as the fixation of Western security attention. But Iran will of course always matter very much as the preeminent Gulf power over the long run. It will be Iran, restored to a more normal state of military capability, that will serve as the "organic" counterweight to Iraq in the region. U.S. participation in the destruction of Iranian power at the end of the Iran-Iraq War to a large measure gave birth to the phenomenon of unbridled Iraqi power in 1990. Perhaps the reduced prominence of Iran and America in the other's lives will serve better than anything else to allow U.S.-Iranian relations to move toward some degree of normalcy in the future and overcome what has been one of the most intensely emotional and visceral confrontations between the United States and any other country in the world in recent times.

Notes

1. Richard Cottam goes so far as to argue that the shah did not really see his policies at all as a battle against international communism or a perceived Soviet threat. This argument goes too far in ignoring the waves of radicalism that were sweeping through the Gulf and the region in the period of the 1950s and 1960s—about which the shah had reason to be concerned. Nonetheless, Cottam certainly has a case that the shah had considerations and aspirations in mind other than pure anticommunism or anti-Sovietism. See Richard W. Cottam, *Nationalism in Iran* (Berkely: University of California Press, 1979), pp. 339, 341.

2. James A. Bill, *The Eagle and the Lion* (New Haven: Yale University Press, 1988), p. 117.

3. From Khomeini's will, Tehran Domestic Service, 6 June 1989, FBIS-NES-89-108, 7 June 89.

4. Khomeini letter to Gorbachev quoted in "Iran Warms to Soviets—But Not to America," by Charles P. Wallace, *Los Angeles Times*, 1 February 1989.

5. Larijani Interview, in *Refalat*, Tehran, 7 August 89, FBIS-NES-89-164.

6. *Keyhan*, Tehran, 11 March 89, FBIS-NES-89-054.

7. Larijani Interview, *op. cit.*, FBIS.

8. Khamene'i Friday prayer sermon, Tehran Domestic service, 7 January 1989, FBIS-NES-89-018, 30 January 89.

9. Larijani Interview, *op. cit*, FBIS.

10. Bill, *op. cit.*, p. 310.

11. *Ibid.*, p. 117.

16

Conclusion: The Anatomy of Iran's Future Foreign Policy

The idea of achieving economic independence in today's Iran—a country that has attracted the attention of the entire world like a diamond in a ring, a country whose strategic position and political and economic status makes it coveted by the world's greedy vultures who have always thought of dominating it, a country in which every colonialist has always sought a foothold for himself; to achieve economic independence in a country like Iran which for hundreds of years has been crushed under the boot of the world's dastardly elements—is no doubt difficult.
> —*Iranian President Ali Akbar Hashemi-Rafsanjani,*
> *Inaugural Address, August 1989*[1]

Historically, as we have seen, the person of the Iranian monarch was virtually the sole determinant of foreign policy. In the modern era, public opinion and a more diverse, informed, and pluralist society have gradually been exerting increased influence over the foreign policy of Iran—particularly when the shah was weak— starting first at the turn of the century and gaining strength again during the late 1940s and early 1950s when nationalist power in government ran strong. The last shah was finally able to regain primary control of foreign policy starting in the mid-1950s.

But the foreign policies of the last shah must not be taken as the norm for Iranian foreign policy views; indeed, it can be argued that the foreign policies of the Islamic Republic lie closer to the "norm" of the Iranian outlook than did the shah's. The Iranian public, exerting greater influence over policy today than during the shah's reign, seems basically comfortable with the general thrust of clerical foreign policy—as long as adventurism does not inflict genuine hardships upon the people, such as the prolongation of the Iran-Iraq War and isolation of the country demonstrably has done.

The overall policy options of the Islamic Republic were highly circumscribed by the war launched against it by Iraq at the outset of the clergy's accession to

*power. The war dominated a decade of decisionmaking. The gradual cooling of
revolutionary Islamic ardor, and the greater freedom of maneuver with the end
of the war, presents Iran with far greater options than it had during the 1980s.*

*The next ten years—hopefully free of military conflict—are therefore likely to
be even more instructive about the "basic character" of postmonarchy Iran than
the last ten years have been. But a general xenophobia, deep distrust of the West
and the great powers, a drive for regional superiority and hegemony, and a
powerful sense of nonalignment and commitment to Third World causes are likely
to be the hallmark of Iranian policy—tempered with a sense of self-preservation
and pragmatic self-interest that will help avoid the worst ideological excesses of
the first decade. The oil wealth of the Gulf virtually guarantees that the Gulf will
be the most natural point of potential foreign intervention in the world—thereby
serving only to whet further Iran's natural resentment of this phenomenon.*

Imperial Monopoly of Foreign Policy?

As Iran moves into the future, its governance will require an increasingly broad spectrum of both national expertise and public support
for policies—domestic and foreign. How much more participatory is
Tehran's policymaking likely to be?

The shah has been the focus of a great deal of this study, as the
central figure and determinant of Iranian foreign policy. Yet the situation
is now markedly different. Even with Khomeini's central role in the first
decade of the Islamic Republic, we are still witnessing a much broader
and more complex foreign policy culture, far less dependent on the
personality of one man than in most earlier eras. Only the relatively
democratic period of the Mossadegh era in the early 1950s shows
comparable public participation.

The Historical Emergence of Domestic Politics
as a Factor in Foreign Policy

This book has tried to identify a number of geopolitical constants in
Iran's behavior toward each of its neighbors. The elements of geopolitics—
the permanency of geographic, ethnographic, demographic, and even
historically engendered cultural factors—have all left their mark on Iran's
approach to the region. But no country is purely hostage to these
determinants; the role of personal leadership and the national will
obviously help mold the geopolitical raw materials that characterize the
country.

Critical political decisions by Iranian monarchs have been able to sharply alter or even reverse some major trends in Iran's conduct of foreign policy. The advent of the Pahlavi dynasty, for example, probably produced the single greatest change in centuries to Iran's attitudes and style of approach to its regional neighbors.

Leadership, of course, does not reside solely in the hands of the monarch, even in a system so long dominated by a powerful, central, absolute monarchy. Yet throughout this analysis we have devoted very little attention to the role of domestic Iranian politics in the conduct of foreign policy. As we noted in the introduction, a key reason for this omission is simply that for so many centuries it has been difficult to speak of centers of foreign policy influences apart from the monarch. To be sure, important political personalities in Iran's court have regularly played major roles of influence vis-à-vis the shah, but these actors have exerted an ad hoc influence, as personalities rather than representatives of institutional interests that play a persistent, systematic, predictable role in policy formulation. Regional lords and tribal powers have also obviously been able to influence the shah's options, particularly in terms of war with neighbors and a willingness to help fund the central treasury. But these idiosyncratic influences, too, cannot be spoken of as systemic influences in the foreign policy process.

The first dramatic introduction of domestic elements into the Iranian foreign policy process came with the emergence of the Constitutionalist Movement in 1905, whose disorders and demonstrations led to the establishment of a first Parliament, or Majles, in 1906. A review of the various parliamentary factional interests are a study in themselves, but an examination of conflict between shahs and Parliament indicates that the Parliaments have consistently stood for a more nationalist, more antiforeign position than the ruler himself. In the early twentieth century the Parliament stood foursquare against concessions to the foreigner and attempted to stop the shah from bargaining away national power. Seizure of the budget, the foreign concessionary mechanism, and the right of treaty-making were the key aspirations of the Parliament in order to deprive the shah from further ruinous, fickle concessions to foreign powers. As a contemporary British observer captured the environment surrounding the creation of a parliamentary opposition:

The mere tyranny of an autocrat would hardly have driven the patient and tractable people of Persia into revolt had tyranny at home been combined with any maintenance of prestige abroad or only moderately effective guardianship of Persian independence. It was the combination of inefficiency, extravagance, and lack of patriotic feeling with tyranny which proved insupportable; and a constitutional form of government was sought not so much for its own sake as for the urgent necessity of creating more honest, efficient, and patriotic government than the existing one.[2]

Indeed, such foreign policy interests as existed apart from the shah stemmed largely from three sources: (1) an emerging bourgeoisie of merchants and artisans whose commercial opportunities had been damaged by foreign dominance of the Iranian economy; (2) the clergy who resented the power of the foreign Western presence and sought to limit the power of the shah under any circumstances; and (3) intellectuals and educated elites who were able to perceive the degrading effect of the monarchy upon the Iranian national interest at the time. This informal coalition above all sought to limit the shah's power—in foreign and domestic affairs. As noted in earlier chapters, the movement toward more parliamentarian democracy was largely subverted by Britain and especially Russia in the years before World War I—but not before the groundwork for a new, more nationalist policy had been laid. A few outstanding statesmen emerged in this period, most notably Mushir al-Dawla, who played the key role in the delicate operation of extricating Gilan Province out from under Soviet occupation in 1921. Indeed, Reza Shah was to adopt much of the nationalist agenda of many of these Persian statesmen in the transitional period from the Constitutionalist Period up until his accession to power in the early 1920s.[3]

Major Pahlavi innovations in foreign policy were also in keeping with other momentous changes in the world order after World War I, such as the collapse of empires, newly emerging states assuming greater independence, and a nascent concept of regional solidarity and even "Third World solidarity" stepping onto the scene. These trends were hardly unique to Iran: They were accompanied by the gradual worldwide emergence of newer, better-educated Third World elites who demanded increasing voice in the determination of their nation-state's affairs, thereby creating a new role for public opinion. Many of these states for the first time began to grant tentative recognition to democratic principles that were to strengthen the foundations for a more pluralistic society.

Reza Shah and Mohammed Reza Shah were at the helm of Iranian policy at this period of general worldwide transition. They both introduced change in foreign policy, while simultaneously reflecting changing values within the country as well. To be sure, the Pahlavis were still influenced by the permanence of many of those geopolitical factors we observed earlier. But for the first time it is possible to talk more meaningfully about domestic components of Iranian foreign policy.

Reza Shah, despite his dedication to a new nationalist course of action at home and abroad, did not permit the existence of a meaningful domestic opposition during his rule. The Parliament thus played little independent role in the formulation of Iranian foreign policy during his reign. Public opinion, a limited commodity in any case, did tend to exert some influence in the general sympathy Iranians felt for the growing power of Germany—seen to be ethnically akin to the Aryan Persians, representative of a modern, successful power, and as a rival to the dominating presence of Britain and Russia, states that were always a butt of popular resentment.

But a precedent had been set. Following the foreign overthrow of Reza Shah in 1941, and with the establishment of a much stronger Parliament after World War II, the nationalist-oriented Parliament sought to move Iran toward a more neutralist position in the East-West conflict than Mohammed Reza Shah wanted and was strongly nationalist on issues of oil concessions to either the Soviet Union or Britain. The Parliament was also less hostile, as we have seen, to the emerging, implicitly anti-Western Arab nationalist movement, but would of course concede nothing to the Arab states in Iran's territorial claims in the Gulf in the 1960s and 1970s. While parliamentary opposition by this time included an increasingly broad spectrum of Iranian opinion—monarchists, nationalists, socialists, Communists, and Pan-Iranianists—the nationalist strain was uppermost. And, as always, a key feature of the Parliament's agenda has consistently been to whittle down the powers of the shah relative to the Parliament. The Parliament was invariably out ahead of the shah in supporting nationalist causes. And public opinion during the reign of the last shah was now swollen with the impact of a rapidly increasing educated, informed class with broad exposure to foreign education. Resentment against the shah's toadying to the West was on the rise.

Public Opinion in the Islamic Republic

The evolution of domestic factors in foreign policy is further illuminated by the experience of the Islamic Republic, offering additional insight into what a theoretical Iranian foreign policy "norm" might be. Under neither the shah nor Khomeini were elections truly free, of course; elections to the Majles under the Islamic Republic are designed to exclude most parties that are not basically sympathetic to the principles of the ruling clerics; thus no avowed Communist, secularist, or monarchist would find a place. Nonetheless, there has been some considerable spectrum of debate, placing Iran's Majles among the most outspokenly free parliamentary bodies in all the Middle East today. Of course, the Majles is largely "Islamic" in outlook, but debate now revolves more around the trade-offs involved in pursuing either a more, or less, revolutionary and adventurist foreign policy. A radical stance in foreign policy often parallels radical views on domestic policies as well. Hence, the more conservative members of the Majles have opposed radical foreign interventionism when there is fear that it would redound negatively upon the power of conservatives in domestic politics, upon the welfare of the general public, and the stability of the Islamic Republic itself.

We are left with a critical analytic question: Would unfettered public participation in the Majles' formulation of foreign policy significantly modify present policies? It can be argued that, under the last shah, increased public participation would have undoubtedly pushed the shah to the left: toward a more neutralist policy on East-West issues, greater solidarity with many Third World movements, and less tolerance for a role of major Western and American influence in the country. But is the converse true? Would greater freedom of expression under the Islamic Republic lead to moderation of its radical foreign policy?

Iranian public opinion will always be infused with nationalist, xenophobic impulses—tempered by self-interest. If foreign policy adventurism leads to greater public hardship—as the prolongation of the Iran-Iraq War demonstrably did—public opinion would probably have ended the war much earlier. Public opinion is also less likely to support the strongly ideological approach to most of Iran's neighbors that created a virtually solid phalanx of enemies around Iran for nearly a decade. In short, public opinion and democratic participation can partially serve as a moderating influence when the cost of radicalism to the public is immediate and palpable.

Conversely, those same nationalist and xenophobic influences will probably continue to support a general policy of coolness toward the Arab world, sympathy for Shi'a communities in the world, and deep suspicion, if not hostility, to the Western powers. To be sure, these policies emerge more readily in the present social structure of Iran that has exiled an elite of tens of thousands of Western-educated, upper class, and more liberal elements that have fled the country. Yet it would also be a mistake to assume that the sizeable Westernized, pro-Western class under the shah represented an entirely typical Iranian approach either: The shah had encouraged the emergence of this class, a great segment of which was to develop powerful vested interests in military-security ties with the West and in the immense wealth that these contracts and purchases brought in. Although many members of these upper classes may at some point return to Iran, a social revolution has already taken place in which the old Westernized classes will never regain their former position. Deep-seated Iranian instincts against the dangers of close alignment with great powers will prevail, leading to support for a moderated nationalist policy, including even some elements of a moderated "Islamic" (radical internationalist) policy, that the new leadership under President Rafsanjani is likely to espouse.

Clearly, with the passage of time and evolving national development, the role of domestic factors will further increase in the formulation of Iran's foreign policy. Such a pattern is in keeping with movements worldwide in which democratic, moderating, pluralistic trends eventually emerge as societies grow more complex, manifold, educated, and skilled.

Continuity and the Islamic Republic

Indeed, even as the Ayatollah Khomeini excoriated the shah, he himself prepared to set in place a series of geopolitical relations that differed remarkably little from the course set by the shah. Relations with the United States, Egypt, Saudi Arabia, and Israel were the primary casualties, mainly due to the shah's special ties with those states. Few other state relationships significantly deteriorated. Basically, national interests, and *raisons d'etat*, prevailed in determining correct relations with other states, regardless of their ties with the United States: Turkey, Pakistan, and Oman are all notable examples of military allies of the United States.

If the ayatollah had inherited much of the shah's global vision for Iran, it was intensified through the new prism of Islam. Indeed, the universal character of Islam lends greater potency to Iran's global ambitions; it was the broader sweep of Iran's ideological vision that outflanked even radical states such as Iraq.

It is therefore difficult to foresee how any successor regime to the Islamic Republic will be able to entirely abandon the combined visions— the Iranian national past and the Islamic mission—that characterized the long reign of Mohammed Reza Shah on the one hand and Khomeini on the other. A critical determinant of Iran's success will reside in its selection of tactics. An Iran that presents itself as a regional firebrand, a flaming ideological threat exporting terrorism and subversion to all of its neighbors simultaneously, will only create powerful defenses against it, even leading to the introduction of foreign protective powers, as during the Iran-Iraq War.

Alternatively, an ambitious Iranian national vision does not necessarily have to invoke revolution, terror, and war. Indeed, the primary task of Khomeini's successors will be how to maintain Iran's broad regional and global agenda while maintaining at least correct relations with most of the world. It can be argued that if Iran cannot combine a sweeping vision with reasonably normal ties with its neighbors, then its policies are doomed to failure. "Iran-against-the-world" can command a great deal of attention, but it cannot be indefinitely sustained as a viable policy designed to meet long-range national interests.

Nor must Iran's Islam be militant to be effective. Iran's second challenge is to build an Islamic Republic that may gain it some regional support as a model for government. This is a tall order, for the whole Muslim world continues to grapple with the dilemma of undertaking modernization of society while maintaining a meaningful Islamic framework. To date, no Islamic state has yet produced an Islamic model of government deemed worthy of emulation by the rest of the Muslim world.

What Is the Iranian Foreign Policy "Norm"?

The thesis of this book, therefore, is that Iranian foreign policy under the Islamic Republic does not represent quite the sharp aberration in Iranian foreign policy behavior that it is usually assumed to be. Even less accurately can the policies of Mohammed Reza Shah be in any way interpreted as an Iranian "norm." If anything, the foreign policy of the Islamic Republic is closer to the "norm" of Iranian character than the foreign policy of the shah. To be sure, Tehran's rhetoric is indeed more excessive, and some of the tactical recklessness—alienating nearly all potential allies simultaneously—has been counterproductive. But the general goals, world view, and neutralist, Third World outlook of the Islamic Republic strike chords with the broad Iranian public on both the right and the left.

The alternative to the Islamic Republic is not a return to Pahlavi-style policies, but rather to a synthesis of the two foreign policies. Otherwise, style and tactics, rather than substance, mark a great deal of the transition to the policies of the Islamic Republic. Iran's assertion of regional leadership, support for the Shi'a communities in the Middle East, and the expulsion of U.S. and Western power from the region are not fundamentally unpopular as long as they do not lead to deeply negative consequences for the country. Future Iranian policies are likely to remain highly nationalist, anti-Western in instinct, nonaligned by preference, and in support of Iranian regional hegemony. The excesses of the Islamic radicals have not necessarily permanently denigrated the concept of an ambitious, challenging, Iran-first foreign policy that stands up to all foreign powers and especially the great powers.

Not all features of an Islamic Republic of Iran in power are clearly revealed yet either, for the clerics' first decade evolved under the extraordinary constraints of war—much as befell the early Bolshevik party in Russia. The Iran-Iraq War had been the one dominant constant of policymaking for nearly a decade. Only with the Iran-Iraq War cease-fire has the regime begun to have a chance to show its "true" policy colors through selection of policy options far broader than those afforded by war. Indeed, the Republic is still sharply divided between relatively radical and relatively moderate factions within the clergy; the struggle between these two groups is reflective of sharply differing attitudes at the national level that extend well beyond the clergy. One or another faction may gain the upper hand for a period, but such diverse ideological viewpoints cannot basically be ever "resolved," for they are part of the dynamic of Iranian politics.

If the Iran-Iraq War dominated the first decade of Iranian foreign policy thinking, what will be the dominant characteristic of Iranian policy in the 1990s? The initial phase of the Iraq-Kuwait crisis has found Iran strangely passive, lacking a clear-cut vision of the geopolitical dilemma before it. Several factors have contributed to this unusual ambivalence and indecision.

- On the one hand, deep geopolitical opposition to any possibility that Iraq might permanently strengthen its position in the Gulf through the acquisition of Kuwaiti territory and oil;
- On the other, profound anguish at the renewed appearance of U.S. military intervention in the Gulf, this time bidding for perhaps a long-term military presence in Saudi Arabia;
- Iranian military weakness stemming from the end of the Iran-Iraq War, making military intervention by Iran nearly impossible at this point;
- A desire to make common cause with regional states to roll back the Iraqi bid for power, balanced by an ideological contempt for those very Gulf monarchies that have run to the United States for protection;
- A desire to see the downfall of the non-Islamic Gulf monarchies that cling to the United States for security support, offset by a desire to take advantage of Iraq's aggression to strengthen Iran's own ties with those same states.

How Iran will square these conflicting goals has not yet been resolved. There is still no consensus in Tehran on foreign policy priorities. This absence of consensus on such a major geopolitical event as the Iraq-Kuwait crisis, and current Iranian military weakness, will paralyze Iran's role in the region. It must be resolved quickly if Iran is to return to a leading role in the Gulf.

It is at just such a time that the United States and the West must decide how much it is in their own interests to help restore Iran to the position of countervailing weight in the Gulf. That decision lies not only in Western hands: Iran too must decide what its relationship with Western powers will be if the West is to assist significantly in the restoration of Iran to a "normal," key Gulf role. From the U.S. point of view, that decision rests in part on the U.S. vision of its own role in the region. If the United States believes it must itself maintain the role of preeminent unilateral actor in the region, then Washington is less likely to be interested in restoring the "organic" character of strategic countervailing forces in the Gulf. If the U.S. vision is toward a more multilateral security order in the world, then the restoration of Iran, for all its drawbacks, will assume greater prominence in American thinking.

What Are Iran's Foreign Policy Alternatives?

In the end, what are the philosophical alternatives for Iran's foreign policy? This question is intimately linked with Iran's own vision of itself and its role in the world. Iran in principle has several choices, some of which have already been reviewed in previous chapters of this book. Is Iran basically Persian in character? Or Shi'ite? Or Muslim? Or even Western in its orientation, as the shah aspired? These distinctions are not necessarily mutually exclusive. If the shah saw Iran as Persian and Western in outlook, Khomeini saw Iran as Shi'ite and Muslim in its orientation. Obviously Iran is all of these things in one sense, but any leadership must choose where to place the emphasis. To pose the question in different terms, Is the country's heritage nationalist or religious? This question will remain under debate. Emphasis on one facet will contain its own internal pluses and minuses in policy terms.

Although the clergy's policies are distinctively Islamic in domestic terms, its policies might not differ all that sharply from what a strong nationalist/populist government might pursue: deep suspicion of great powers, a powerful role in the Gulf, geopolitical concern for the Soviet Union and Iraq, hostility toward Saudi Arabia as a rival, an unwillingness to abandon options for playing the "Shi'ite card" in Arab politics, and a dedication to the preeminence of Iran in the region.

An alternative regime to the clergy will naturally be highly critical of Iran's policy blunders leading to total isolation in the Iran-Iraq War, but one does not need to be a nationalist to make this criticism; indeed, moderates among the clergy were able to make the same arguments. Almost no Iranian regime will be able to embrace the West as the shah did, given the legacy of the country.

The national interest of the country will eventually, of course, push any Iranian regime to benefit from close economic ties with the West. But the national political heritage will likely prevent any government from identifying itself too closely with the West, and especially the United States, in the way that the shah did.

Export of the Revolution: Newer Forms

Iran will require some kind of broader ideology if it is going to successfully pursue a policy of leadership and hegemony in the region. The shah had not hit on the right combination of themes. His chief ideological vision for Iran's activist role was the defense of the region from Soviet and radical threat, and a form of Iranian Manifest Destiny in quest of greatness. The shah's role as regional policeman, strongly supported by the United States, basically represented support for the regional status quo—a policy of limited appeal to the broader Iranian public. Likewise, the theme of Iranian national greatness, possibly striking some chords at home, was hardly a productive theme abroad.

For the Islamic Republic, some variation on the Islamic theme is the most likely ideological principle for its foreign policy—a theme that is of course not unique to Iran. As we have seen, Saudi Arabia and, to a lesser extent, Pakistan have also pursued the theme of an Islamic foreign policy. Iran has taken the position, however, that its own version of an Islamic policy is the only true version—not because it is Shi'ite, but because it represents "true Islam," and is directed at liberation of the Muslim world from the thrall of Western power, in distinction to the Saudi regime's "American-style Islam." As Khomeini pointed out, "Our revolution is not tied to Iran. The Iranian people's revolution was the starting point for the great revolution of the Islamic world."[4]

But what might this ideology represent, if it is not a threat to the regional status quo? In fact it inevitably must be a threat to the status quo, for the strength of the ideology lies precisely in the idea of liberation, of Islamically inspired universal justice, of social revolution, of empowerment of the downtrodden, of self-assertion, and change. This ideology must basically remain threatening to the conservative leadership of the region. Iran could likewise seek to be a leader of the "South" against the "North," to the extent that the fault lines of international friction will lie here. To fulfill this role—broadly "leftist" in character—Iran will not necessarily have to export a revolution replete with violence, subversion, or terrorism. It can simply articulate its principles, hopeful that in the end the ideology will elicit forces for social change in the Islamic world. Iran would thus hope to be the guide, the beacon of Islam in politics that would attract all Islamic political activists. Cultural programs, Islamic literature, education, and training in Iran—all would represent the stuff of Iran's export of the revolution, including strong diplomatic support for the protection of Islamic countries from pressure or "exploitation" from the larger countries of the world. It would support politically oriented Islamic conferences in Iran designed to shape the Islamic agenda in the Muslim world—in a more radical and activist fashion than Saudi Arabia currently does today. As Deputy Foreign Minister Larijani (a definite pragmatist) articulated in August 1989,

> The first [source of our national strategy] is our position within the Islamic world. This means Iran must not be limited by its geographic boundaries. This does not mean that we want to capture other countries, but rather that our situation is defined within the framework of the [whole] Islamic world, as opposed to one bounded [simply] by geographic boundaries. . . . Iran is not just one among many Islamic countries. Today we face a division of the world into geographic states that has no justice and that has a very bitter past. Now, should we accept these frontiers or not? . . . We do [in fact] accept the world's geographic boundaries—in order to avoid trouble. [But] our Islamic responsibility does not [just] go away. This responsibility crosses borders. . . . We have to plan our policies and our diplomacy in such a way that they match our position in the Islamic world. We have a huge position in the Islamic world. No country other than Iran can lead the Islamic world; this is a historical position.[5]

The Role of Shi'ism

Pursuit of an activist Islamic foreign policy would require Tehran to come to terms with the old dilemma of support for Shi'ite communities, which has often tended to compromise the "purity" of Iran's Islamic vision in areas where Shi'a represent a major portion of the population. If Iran is unable to shake the image of a "Shi'ite power," it will never succeed in pursuing a worldwide Islamic agenda in a basically Sunni world.

Islam Reformed by Shi'ism?

But Shi'ism offers Iran one very interesting special advantage: Only Shi'ism has a promising theoretical basis for dealing with the problem of "up-dating" Islam. The greatest source of reform and change in Islam springs from the concept of *ijtihad*, the concept of reaching new, independent judgment on Islamic law through "interpretation" of the basic Islamic canon. In Sunni Islam the so-called "gates of ijtihad" (*bab al-ijtihad*) were closed several centuries after the establishment of Islam, essentially rendering it very difficult for new interpretations of Islam to be reached by Muslim jurisprudents thenceforth. In Shi'ism the gates of ijtihad have never been closed; indeed, it is the prerogative of the current Ruling Jurisprudent (*Vali-e-Faqih*) to establish the current interpretation and practice of the law. This device is of central importance in any effort to "modernize" or "up-date" Islam in terms of contemporary life.

A creative, forward-looking approach to the interpretation of Islam in contemporary Iran could ultimately have considerable impact on the Sunni world. One only wonders, however, whether the Shi'ite clergy in Iran can in fact rise to the occasion to introduce meaningful reform and contemporary interpretation into traditional Islam. Although Shi'ite thinkers have achieved notable success in transforming traditional Islam into a radical, activist, contemporary, politicized doctrine of revolutionary action, they have not yet been especially distinguished in establishing other innovative interpretations of Islamic practice in government or society. Yet success in this area could have major impact on the overall revivification of Islam and on the establishment of contemporary Islamic practice in closer conformity with the realities of modern life worldwide.

Islamic Democracy?

Yet another ideology lies fraught with meaning for reform of the political face of the Islamic world: democracy. Democracy has demonstrably not fared terribly well in the Muslim world; the bane of authoritarianism and dictatorship bears substantial blame for the paucity of political and social progress in country after country in the region. But democracy is likely to have increasing impact on the region in the decade ahead, especially with the fall of the Communist world and the discrediting of authoritarian socialism everywhere. Indeed, the fate of East European dictatorship has not been lost on Arab or Iranian observers.

The Islamic Republic has not yet been a model here either; it has had more than its share of violation of human rights in the first decade, has dealt ruthlessly with much of the opposition, and tens of thousands of people have been executed. At the same time, however, as we noted above, Iran has held regular elections to the Majles, with electoral lists, albeit limited to a certain range of candidates who are not considered hostile to the regime. Elections are nonetheless competitive and genuine, and are deemed important by everyone for the range of political coloration that they can lend to the Majles and its deliberations. Once elected, debates among delegates have been vocal and spontaneous, sparing no one in the regime save Khomeini himself. It is possible that Iran, given its early, spasmodic experience with periodic parliamentary power over the last century (until crushed by Russia) may be better qualified than most other states in the Middle East to inaugurate what could become fairly genuine democracy—no longer crushed by the power of the shah, or even dominated by the Ruling Jurisprudent. Indeed, Rafsanjani, a world-class politician in his ability to maneuver through the treacherous shoals of Islamic Republic politics from the very outset of the revolution, has resembled Gorbachev in his ability to survive and preside over the stormy periods of change—all the while claiming that he is not betraying the ruling party's heritage. It is not impossible that Rafsanjani may be also inspired by the Gorbachev model to bring about his own politics of Islamic *perestroika*—a policy designed to change the face of Iranian politics in the name of clerical rule, and possibly to restore hope for constitutional rule that has been the aspiration of so many Iranian reformers and liberals over the century.

If Rafsanjani, or any other more moderate or liberal leaders in Iran, can establish some kind of effective and working democratic state under Islamic principles, Iran will have indeed gained special clout in Islamic politics that could be appropriate for "export." The Islamic revolution, admired in the Muslim world primarily for the negative power of overthrowing a powerful ruler and expelling deeply rooted American influence, could then take on the positive attraction of a working model of democratic procedure, melded with some form of contemporary, reformed Islam. While there is scarcely any promise that this rosy ideal will be able to emerge from the present economic and political chaos of the Islamic Republic, the roots of such a metamorphosis are not absent; Iran's historical experience and relative political and social advancement could finally bear fruit.

Iran, Democracy, and the Nationalities Question

Democracy and the emergence of greater national self-expression and self-determination is far from an unmitigated blessing, however, especially for Iran. We have noted in earlier chapters some of the classic vulnerabilities of Iran with its Kurdish, Azerbaijani, and Baluch minorities, among others. Although the course of world history over the past many decades may have served to stress the finality of most national boundaries in the world, the collapse of the Soviet empire may prove profoundly threatening to the national integrity of Iran in ways not foreseen in the 1980s. If the question of Azerbaijani unity is reopened by independence in Soviet Azerbaijan, the Kurdish question, too, then becomes much more salient. So does the Baluch issue. Iran will need to be very careful in maintaining effective, cooperative, and fruitful ties with all these minority areas if it does not itself wish to find its own national territorial integrity threatened. Fundamental unrest and seething ethnic and regional discontent among Iranian national groupings would indeed serve to undermine any boldness in Iran's foreign policy approach and leave the country beset with crippling domestic problems.

As democratic/separatist forces emerge more strongly in this region in the next decade, Iran will be a key player in any new Islamic order emerging in this region—which will surely include the Soviet Muslim republics. If differences among these states can be minimized, Iran has already set down its marker as leader of the Islamic bloc in the greater Central Asian region. Thus, apart from its major Gulf role, Iran will have an "Eastern policy" playing at least as important a role. If Iran can organize its own internal affairs, it will be poised for an activist role in both regions in the next decade, hopefully one in which it will allow instincts of self-confidence, and the lessons of the first decade of the Islamic Republic, to set the character of its policies. Iran is a nation of gifted people and a superb cultural heritage, capable of great potential contribution to the region. The question is whether it can move with new maturity into the future, recognizing that the relations of nearly all states, great and small, may now be undergoing a decisive period of change in the post–Cold War, postnuclear age. What role will Iran adopt for itself in this extraordinary new era?

Notes

1. Rafsanjani Inaugural Speech, 17 August 1989, Tehran Domestic Service, FBIS-NES-89-163.

2. E. G. Browne, "The Persian Constitutionalist Movement," in *Proceedings of the British Academy, London 1917–18*, pp. 323–324, as quoted in Rouhollah K. Ramazani, *The Foreign Policy of Iran, 1500–1941* (Charlottesville: University Press of Virginia, 1966), p. 83.

3. Ramazani, *op. cit.*, p. 186.

4. Khomeini Message to War Refugees, Tehran Domestic Service, 22 March 1989, FBIS-NES-89-055.

5. Larijani Interview in Tehran, *Resalat*, 7 August 89, FBIS-NES-89-164.

Bibliography

Ajami, Fouad. *The Vanished Imam, Musa al Sadr and the Shia of Lebanon.* Ithaca: Cornell University Press, 1986.

Amirsadeghi, Hossein, ed. *The Security of the Persian Gulf.* New York: St. Martin's Press, 1981.

Amstutz, J. Bruce. *Afghanistan, the First Five Years of Soviet Occupation.* Washington, D.C.: National Defense University, 1986.

Bakhash, Shaul. *The Reign of the Ayatollahs: Iran and the Islamic Revolution.* New York: Basic Books, Inc., 1984.

Banuazizi, Ali, and Weiner, Myron, eds. *The State, Religion, and Ethnic Politics: Afghanistan, Iran and Pakistan.* Syracuse, N.Y.: Syracuse University Press, 1986.

Beeman, William O. *Language, Status, and Power in Iran.* Bloomington: Indiana University Press, 1986.

Behnam, M. Reza. *Cultural Foundations of Iranian Politics.* Salt Lake City: University of Utah Press, 1986.

Belgrave, Sir Charles. *The Pirate Coast.* London: G. Bell and Sons, Ltd., 1966.

Benard, Cheryl, and Khalilzad, Zalmay. *"The Government of God": Iran's Islamic Republic.* New York: Columbia University Press, 1984.

Bennigsen, Alexandre, and Wimbush, S. Enders. *Muslims of the Soviet Empire.* Bloomington: Indiana University Press, 1986.

Bill, James A. *The Eagle and the Lion.* New Haven: Yale University Press, 1988.

Binder, Leonard. *Iran: Political Development in a Changing Society.* Berkeley: University of California Press, 1962.

Binnendijk, Hans, ed. *National Negotiating Styles.* Washington, D.C.: Foreign Service Institute, Center for the Study of Foreign Affairs, 1987.

Brown, L. Carl. *International Politics and the Middle East: Old Rules, Dangerous Game.* Princeton: Princeton University Press, 1984.

Chubin, Shahram; Litwak, Robert; Plascov, Avi, eds. *Security in the Gulf.* Aldershot, England: Gower, for the International Institute of Strategic Studies, Adelphi Library 7, 1982.

Chubin, Shahram, and Zebih, Sepehr. *The Foreign Relations of Iran.* Berkeley: University of California Press, 1974.

Cottam, Richard W. *Nationalism in Iran*. Pittsburgh: University of Pittsburgh Press, 1979.

Dupree, Louis. *Afghanistan*. Princeton: Princeton University Press, 1973.

Fletcher, Arnold. *Afghanistan, Highway of Conquest*. Ithaca: Cornell University Press, 1965.

Forbis, William H. *The Fall of the Peacock Throne*. New York: McGraw-Hill, 1981.

Ghaus, Abdul Samad. *The Fall of Afghanistan: An Insider's Account*. Washington, D.C.: Pergamon-Brassey's, 1988.

Gregorian, Vartan. *The Emergence of Modern Afghanistan: Politics of Reform and Modernization 1880–1946*. Stanford: Stanford University Press, 1969.

Harris, Lillian Craig. *China's Policy Toward the Third World*. Washington, D.C.: Praeger/The Washington Papers/112, Center for Strategic International Studies, 1985.

Helms, Christine Moss. *Iraq: Eastern Flank of the Arab World*. Washington, D.C.: Brookings Institution, 1984.

Hough, Jerry F. *The Struggle for the Third World: Soviet Debates and American Options*. Washington, D.C.: Brookings Institution, 1986.

Hunter, Shireen T., ed. *The Politics of Islamic Revivalism: Diversity and Unity*. Bloomington: University of Indiana Press, 1988.

Jamalzadeh, Sayyed Mohammad Ali. *Isfahan Is Half the World, Memories of a Persian Boyhood*, translated by W. L. Heston. Princeton: Princeton University Press, 1983.

Kamshad, Hassan. *Modern Persian Prose Literature*. Cambridge, England: Cambridge University Press, 1966.

Kapuscinski, Ryszard. *The Shah of Shahs*. New York: Harcourt Brace Jovanovich, 1982.

Keddie, Nikki R. *Roots of Revolution: An Interpretive History of Modern Iran*. New Haven: Yale University Press, 1981.

Keddie, N., and Cole, J., eds. *Shi'ism and Social Protest*. New Haven: Yale University Press, 1988.

Kelly, J. B. *Arabia and the Gulf and the West: A Critical View of the Arabs and Their Oil Policy*. New York: Basic Books, Inc., 1980.

Khadduri, Majid. *Independent Iraq: A Study in Iraqi Politics from 1932 to 1958*. London: Oxford University Press, 1960.

_____ . *The Gulf War: The Origins and Implications of the Iran-Iraq Conflict*. New York: Oxford University Press, 1988.

Kramer, Martin, ed. *Shi'ism, Resistance and Revolution*. Boulder, Colo.: Westview Press, 1987.

Lenczowski, George. *Russia and the West in Iran, 1918–1948*. Ithaca, N.Y.: Cornell University Press, 1949.

_____ . *The Middle East in World Affairs*. Ithaca: Cornell University Press, 1956.

Lewis, Bernard. *The Emergence of Modern Turkey*. London: Oxford University Press, 1961.

Litwak, Robert. *Security in the Persian Gulf 2: Sources of Interstate Conflict*. Aldershot, England: International Institute for Strategic Studies, Gower Publishing Company, 1981.

McNaugher, Thomas L. *Arms and Oil: U.S. Military Strategy and the Persian Gulf.* Washington, D.C.: Brookings Institution, 1985.

Miklos, Jack C. *The Iranian Revolution and Modernization.* Washington, D.C.: National Defense University, National Security Essay Series 83-2, 1983.

Millspaugh, Arthur. *The American Task in Persia.* New York: Century, 1925.

Momen, Moojan. *An Introduction to Shi'i Islam.* New Haven: Yale University Press, 1985.

Morier, James. *The Adventures of Hajji Baba of Ispahan.* New York: Modern Library, 1954.

Mottahedeh, Roy P. *The Mantle of the Prophet.* New York: Pantheon, 1986.

Nissman, David B. *The Soviet Union and Iranian Azerbaijan.* Boulder, Colo.: Westview Press, 1987.

Norton, Augustus Richard. *Amal and the Shi'a: Struggle for the Soul of Lebanon.* Austin: University of Texas Press, 1987.

O'Donnel, Terrence. *Garden of the Brave in War: Recollections of Iran.* New York: Ticknor and Fields, 1980.

Pahlavi, Mohammed Reza. *Mission for My Country.* New York: McGraw-Hill, 1961.

Ramazani, R. K. *Revolutionary Iran, Challenge and Response in the Middle East.* Baltimore: Johns Hopkins University Press, 1986.

Ramazani, Rouhollah K. *The Foreign Policy of Iran, 1500–1941: A Developing Nation in World Affairs.* Charlottesville: University Press of Virginia, 1966.

———. *The Persian Gulf: Iran's Role.* Charlottesville: University Press of Virginia, 1972.

———. *Iran's Foreign Policy, 1941–1973: A Study of Foreign Policy in Modernizing Nations.* Charlottesville: University Press of Virginia, 1975.

Robinson, Richard D. *The First Turkish Republic, A Case Study in National Development.* Cambridge, Mass.: Harvard University Press, 1963.

Roy, Olivier. *Islam and Resistance in Afghanistan.* Cambridge, England: Cambridge University Press, 1986.

Rubenstein, Alvin Z. *Soviet Policy Toward Turkey, Iran, and Afghanistan: The Dynamics of Influence.* New York: Praeger, 1982.

Rubin, Barry. *Paved with Good Intentions: The American Experience and Iran.* New York: Oxford University Press, 1980.

Safran, Nadav. *Saudi Arabia, The Ceaseless Quest for Security.* Cambridge, Mass.: Belknap Press of Harvard University, 1985.

Shakeri, Khosrow. *Victims of Faith: Iranian Communists and the Soviet Union, 1905–1985.* N.p., forthcoming.

Shawcross, William. *The Shah's Last Ride: The Fate of an Ally.* New York: Simon and Schuster, 1988.

Sick, Gary. *All Fall Down: America's Tragic Encounter with Iran.* New York: Random House, 1985.

Simpson, John. *Inside Iran: Life Under Khomeini's Regime.* New York: St. Martin's Press, 1988.

Sobhani, Sohrab. *The Pragmatic Entente: Israeli-Iranian Relations, 1948–1988.* New York: Praeger, 1989.

Southgate, Minoo, ed. *Modern Persian Short Stories*. Washington, D.C.: Three Continents Press, 1980.

Spector, Ivar. *The Soviet Union and the Muslim World 1917–1956*. Seattle: University of Washington Press, 1956.

Swietochowski, Tadeusz. *Russian Azerbaijan, 1905–1920*. Cambridge: Cambridge University Press, 1985.

Sykes, Sir Percy. *A History of Persia, Vol. I and Vol. II*. London: MacMillan and Co., 1963.

Taheri, Amir. *The Spirit of Allah: Khomeini and the Islamic Revolution*. Baltimore: Adler and Adler, 1985.

Upton, Joseph M. *The History of Modern Iran: An Interpretation*. Cambridge, Mass.: Harvard University Press, 1961.

Wiarda, Howard J. *Ethnocentrism in Foreign Policy: Can We Understand the Third World?* Washington, D.C.: American Enterprise Institute, Studies on Foreign Policy, 1985.

Wimbush, S. Enders, ed. *Soviet Nationalities in Strategic Perspective*. London: Croom Helm, 1985.

Winder, R. Bayly. *Saudi Arabia in the Nineteenth Century*. New York: St. Martin's Press, 1965.

Yodfat, Aryeh Y. *The Soviet Union and Revolutionary Iran*. New York: St. Martin's Press, 1984.

Yoshitsu, Michael M. *Caught in the Middle East*. Lexington, Mass.: D.C. Heath and Company, 1986.

Zonis, Marvin. *The Political Elite of Iran*. Princeton, N.J.: Princeton University Press, 1971.

Zonis, Marvin, and Brumberg, Daniel. *Khomeini, the Islamic Republic of Iran, and the Arab World*. Cambridge, Mass.: Harvard Middle East Papers, Harvard Center for Middle Eastern Studies, 1987.

Articles

Afroz, Sultana. "Afghanistan in U.S.-Pakistani Relations, 1947–1960." *Central Asian Survey*, Vol. 8, No. 2, 1989.

Ajami, Fouad. "Lebanon and Its Inheritors." *Foreign Affairs*, (Spring 1985).

Entessar, Nader. "Egypt and the Persian Gulf." *Conflict*, Vol. 9, 1989, pp. 120–121.

Hussain, Mushahid. "Iran Forges New Links." *Middle East International*, No. 344, 17 February 1989.

Khalaf, Samir. "Ideologies of Enmity in Lebanon." *Middle East Insight*, Summer 1988.

About the Book and Author

In this original and provocative book, Graham E. Fuller examines Iran and the character of its relations with each of its regional neighbors in the Middle East, Central Asia, the Soviet Union, and around the Indian Ocean. Fuller's geopolitical analysis takes into account the impact of historical events, regional demography, the nature of past conflicts, and the psychological attitudes and political rationale of neighboring nations. Reviewing Iran's geopolitical environment over the course of history, he identifies aspects of Iran's foreign relations that are likely to persist and influence future policies—regardless of the particular regime in power.

The book opens with a controversial discussion of those characteristics of Iranian society that the author argues have persistently affected Iran's view of the surrounding world (such as ethnocentricity, an exaggerated perception of enemies' power and malice, and a tendency to seek the "hidden agenda" behind apparently straightforward events). The subsequent chapters individually analyze Iranian relations in bilateral perspective but collectively work to convey a clear overall picture of regional dynamics and recurring trends in this volatile part of the world. The book includes an analysis of the broad implications of the 1990 Iraqi invasion of Kuwait.

Graham E. Fuller is the former top-ranking Middle East analyst for the Central Intelligence Agency. He is currently senior political scientist at The RAND Corporation.

Selected List of RAND Books

Alexiev, Alexander R., and S. Enders Wimbush (eds.). *Ethnic Minorities in the Red Army: Asset or Liability?* Boulder, Colo.: Westview Press, 1988.

Builder, Carl H. *The Masks of War: American Military Styles in Strategy and Analysis.* Baltimore, MD.: The John Hopkins University Press, 1989.

Dorfman, Robert, Paul A. Samuelson, and Robert M. Solow. *Linear Programming and Economic Analysis.* New York: McGraw-Hill Book Company, 1958. Reprinted New York: Dover Publications, 1987.

Fainsod, Merle. *Smolensk under Soviet Rule.* Cambridge, Mass.: Harvard University Press, 1958. Reprinted Boston, Mass.: Unwin Hyman, 1989.

Gustafson, Thane. *Crisis Amid Plenty: The Politics of Oil and Gas and the Evolution of Energy Policy in the Soviet Union Since 1917.* Princeton, N.J.: Princeton University Press, 1989.

Horelick, Arnold L. (ed.). *U.S.-Soviet Relations: The Next Phase.* Ithaca, N.Y.: Cornell University Press, 1986.

Hosmer, Stephen T. *Constraints on U.S. Strategy in Third World Conflicts.* New York: Taylor & Francis, 1987.

Klahr, Philip, and Donald A. Waterman (eds.). *Expert Systems: Techniques, Tools, and Applications.* Reading, Mass.: Addison-Westley Publishing Company, 1986.

Korbonski, Andrzej, and Francis Fukuyama (eds.). *The Soviet Union and the Third World: The Last Three Decades.* Ithaca, N.Y.: Cornell University Press, 1987.

Levine, Robert A. *Still the Arms Debate.* Brookfield, Vt., and Oldershot, England: Gower Publishing Co., Ltd., 1989.

Morrison, Peter A. (ed.). *A Taste of the Country: A Collection of Calvin Beal's Writings.* University Park, Pa.: The Pennslyvania State University Press, 1990.

Nerlich, Uwe, and James A. Thomson (eds.). *Conventional Arms Control and the Security of Europe.* Boulder, Colo.: Westview Press, 1988.

Nerlich, Uwe, and James A. Thomson (eds.). *The Soviet Problem in American-German Relations.* New York: Crane, Russak & Company, 1985.

Quade, Edward S., revised by Grace M. Carter. *Analysis for Public Decisions* (Third Edition). New York: Elsevier Science Publishing Company, 1989.

Ross, Randy L. *Government and the Private Sector: Who Should Do What?* New York: Taylor & Francis, 1988.

Williams, J. D. *The Compleat Strategyst: Being a Primer on the Theory of Games of Strategy*. New York: McGraw-Hill Book Company, 1954. Revised 1966 edition reprinted. New York: Dover Publications, 1986.

Wolf, Charles, Jr. *Markets or Governments: Choosing Between Imperfect Alternatives*. Cambridge, Mass.: The MIT Press, 1988.

Wolf, Charles, Jr., and Katherine Watkins Webb (eds.). *Developing Cooperative Forces in the Third World*. Lexington, Mass.: Lexington Books, 1987.

Index